# Socialism, Economic Calculation and Entrepreneurship

# NEW THINKING IN POLITICAL ECONOMY

**Series Editor:** Peter J. Boettke, *George Mason University, USA*

New Thinking in Political Economy aims to encourage scholarship in the intersection of the disciplines of politics, philosophy and economics. It has the ambitious purpose of reinvigorating political economy as a progressive force for understanding social and economic change.

The series is an important forum for the publication of new work analysing the social world from a multidisciplinary perspective. With increased specialization (and professionalization) within universities, interdisciplinary work has become increasingly uncommon. Indeed, during the 20th century, the process of disciplinary specialization reduced the intersection between economics, philosophy and politics and impoverished our understanding of society. Modern economics in particular has become increasingly mathematical and largely ignores the role of institutions and the contribution of moral philosophy and politics.

New Thinking in Political Economy will stimulate new work that combines technical knowledge provided by the 'dismal science' and the wisdom gleaned from the serious study of the 'worldly philosophy'. The series will reinvigorate our understanding of the social world by encouraging a multidisciplinary approach to the challenges confronting society in the new century.

Recent titles in the series include:

Institutional Competition
*Edited by Andreas Bergh and Rolf Höijer*

Political Failure by Agreement
Learning Liberalism and the Welfare State
*Gerhard Wegner*

The Neoliberal Revolution in Eastern Europe
Economic Ideas in the Transition from Communism
*Paul Dragos Aligica and Anthony J. Evans*

Employees and Entrepreneurship
Co-ordination and Spontaneity in Non-hierarchical Business Organizations
*Ivan Pongracic, Jr*

Media, Development, and Institutional Change
*Christopher J. Coyne and Peter T. Leeson*

The Economics of Ignorance and Coordination
Subjectivism and the Austrian School of Economics
*Thierry Aimar*

Socialism, Economic Calculation and Entrepreneurship
*Jesús Huerta de Soto*

The Political Economy of Hurricane Katrina and Community Rebound
*Edited by Emily Chamlee-Wright and Virgil Henry Storr*

# Socialism, Economic Calculation and Entrepreneurship

Jesús Huerta de Soto

*Professor of Political Economy, Universidad Rey Juan Carlos, Spain*

NEW THINKING IN POLITICAL ECONOMY

In Association with the Institute of Economic Affairs

**Edward Elgar**
Cheltenham, UK • Northampton, MA, USA

© Jesús Huerta de Soto 2010

First published in Spanish as *Socialismo, Cálculo Económico y Función Empresarial* in 1992 by Unión Editorial (second edition 2001, third edition 2005), translated by Melinda Stroup.

All rights reserved. No part of this publication may be reproduced, stored in a retrieval system or transmitted in any form or by any means, electronic, mechanical or photocopying, recording, or otherwise without the prior permission of the publisher.

Published by
Edward Elgar Publishing Limited
The Lypiatts
15 Lansdown Road
Cheltenham
Glos GL50 2JA
UK

Edward Elgar Publishing, Inc.
William Pratt House
9 Dewey Court
Northampton,
Massachusetts 01060
USA

A catalogue record for this book
is available from the British Library

Library of Congress Control Number: 2009940751

ISBN 978 1 84980 064 8 (cased)
ISBN 978 1 84980 065 5 (paperback)

Printed and bound by MPG Books Group, UK

# Contents

| | |
|---|---|
| *Foreword by Peter J. Boettke* | vii |
| *Preface to the third edition* | ix |

1  Introduction — 1
  1  Socialism and economic analysis — 1
  2  The debate on the impossibility of socialist economic calculation — 5
  3  Other possible lines of research — 8
  4  Conclusion — 13

2  Entrepreneurship — 15
  1  The definition of entrepreneurship — 15
  2  Characteristics of entrepreneurship — 19
  3  Entrepreneurship and the concept of socialism — 35

3  Socialism — 49
  1  The definition of socialism — 49
  2  Socialism as an intellectual error — 52
  3  The impossibility of socialism from the standpoint of society — 54
  4  The impossibility of socialism from the perspective of the governing body — 56
  5  Why the development of computers makes the impossibility of socialism even more certain — 58
  6  Other theoretical consequences of socialism — 62
  7  Different types of socialism — 77
  8  Criticism of the alternative concepts of socialism — 83

4  Ludwig von Mises and the start of the debate on economic calculation — 99
  1  Background — 99
  2  The essential contribution of Ludwig von Mises — 103
  3  The functioning of socialism, according to Marx — 108
  4  Additional considerations on Mises's contribution — 112

|   |   | 5 | The first socialist proposals of a solution to the problem of economic calculation | 119 |
|---|---|---|---|---|

5 The unjustified shift in the debate toward statics: the arguments of formal similarity and the so-called "mathematical solution" — 134
   1 The arguments of formal similarity — 134
   2 Analysis of the mathematical solution — 139
   3 The mathematical solution and its adverse consequences for the debate — 143
   4 The "trial and error" method — 146
   5 The theoretical impossibility of planometrics — 152

6 Oskar Lange and the "competitive solution" — 173
   1 Introductory considerations — 173
   2 Historical precedents for the competitive solution — 175
   3 The contribution of Oskar Lange: introductory considerations — 184
   4 Oskar Lange and his classic model of "market socialism" — 186
   5 Critical analysis of Lange's classic model — 197
   6 The third and fourth stages in Lange's scientific life — 214

7 Final considerations — 233
   1 Other market socialism theorists — 233
   2 Market socialism: the impossible squaring of the circle — 247
   3 Maurice H. Dobb and the complete suppression of individual freedom — 250
   4 In what sense is socialism impossible? — 254
   5 Final conclusion — 259

*Bibliography* — 274
*Index* — 301

# Foreword

## Peter J. Boettke

Jesús Huerta de Soto is one of the great contemporary champions of the Austrian School of Economics. He has been a tireless advocate for the methodological, analytical, and ideological importance of the writings of Mises, Hayek, Rothbard, and Kirzner in his capacity as a book publisher (and translator), professor, and researcher. I think it is safe to say that in the Spanish speaking world, Professor de Soto is the leading representative of the Austrian school today. But we should be quick to add that due to his heroic efforts, a new generation of economists in Spain is emerging that tackles important issues in economic theory and public policy from an Austrian school perspective. It is all very exciting to watch from afar how a man of intellectual and moral conviction can make such a difference armed only with ideas and an educational and research vision.

Professor de Soto's *Socialismo, cálculo económico y función empresarial* has gone through three editions, this is the first edition in the English language. As Professor de Soto reports, the book has been enthusiastically read by undergraduate and graduate students throughout the Spanish speaking economics community. And rightfully so, as the issue of economic calculation is fundamental both to understanding why the market economy works to realize the gains from trade and captures the gains from innovation, while socialism fails to realize its aims, suffers from endemic waste, and delivers the people living under it to a life of economic deprivation and political tyranny.

Simply put, the entrepreneurial market process based on private property can engage in economic calculation while socialist planning run by bureaucratic rules cannot.

As Professor Kirzner has pointed out in discussing economic processes, we must distinguish between the underlying variables of given tastes, technology and resource availability, and the market induced variables of prices and profit/loss statements. It is the entrepreneurial market process that reveals a systemic tendency within the market economy for the induced variables to reflect the underlying variables. Of course, in the real day-to-day market underlying conditions are constantly changing so that the induced variables at any one point in time never perfectly reflect the underlying variable, but any deviation represents opportunities for pure profit that will alert economic participants to the necessary adjustments. Markets work through continuous adjustments guided by relative prices and the lure of pure profit and the penalty of loss. Markets are self-correcting. This point is all the more important to understand and emphasize given the current policy debates world-wide over the Great Recession of 2008.

Government ownership and government planning, on the other hand, is unable to mimic the entrepreneurial market process. Without private property in the means of production, Mises pointed out, there would be no market for the means of production. Without a market for the means of production, there would be no exchange ratios established on the market. Without the exchange ratios of the market, there are no relative prices reflecting relative scarcities. And without the market prices reflecting relative scarcities, economic planners will not be able to engage in rational economic calculation. That is, they will not be able to determine whether it is more economically rational to engage in project A versus project B.

Economic calculation is essential to an economic system because it assures that scarce resources will systematically tend toward being employed in the least cost methods of production with the purpose of satisfying the greatest consumer demand. The economic problem any economic system faces is not just to allocate scarce resources among competing ends. In other words, the economic problem doesn't stop when a choice has been made to pursue A rather than B, but actually just begins. The economic system must find some way to sort out among the numerous technologically feasible ways to pursue A, the most economical way to pursue A. Rational economic calculation is the means by which this sorting takes place. Eliminate the ability to engage in rational economic calculation, and you eliminate the ability to solve the fundamental economic problem of how, what and for whom.

Absent an economic answer to these questions, socialism (both in its comprehensive and piecemeal forms) tends to try to answer these questions with politics. Political criteria substitute for economic, with the result being economic deprivation and political tyranny. To use Hayekian language, the knowledge problems of socialist planning produce the power problems of socialist governance. The Road to Serfdom is thus explained.

Jesús Huerta de Soto's *Socialism, Economic Calculation and Entrepreneurship* is a welcomed addition to the literature in Austrian economics. Capitalism, with its reliance on entrepreneurial appraisement and the discipline of profit and loss provided by a private property market economy, achieves what socialism cannot.

# Preface to the third edition

It gives me great pleasure to present this third edition of my book, *Socialismo, cálculo económico y función empresarial*, to Spanish-speaking readers and students. Four years ago, I made several observations in the preface to the second edition, and today these continue to apply and thus should be taken into account.

Also, in the interim between editions, two important milestones have passed. First, the English version of the book, entitled *Socialism, Economic Calculation and Entrepreneurship*, has been completed, and soon it will be published in England and the United States. Second, an ever-increasing number of researchers, students and professors, in both Spain and the rest of the world, have begun to show an interest in delving into the dynamic conception of competition and market processes, and in applying it to the theory of the impossibility of socialism and economic interventionism. This growing interest has necessitated the establishment of a scientific journal which, under the title, *Market Processes: European Journal of Political Economy*,\* draws together and provides a medium for the publication of research, especially that of the new generations of scholars who form part of what is today viewed on an international scale as the booming and highly productive Austrian school of economics. These scholars are developing a paradigm capable of replacing the one which has prevailed thus far, and which has already entered into a phase of severe crisis, decline and disintegration.

I must acknowledge the great enthusiasm and university spirit shown, year after year, by the students who use this work as a textbook in my undergraduate classes. Together with my doctoral students and assistants as Chair of Political Economy, which I teach at the Universidad Rey Juan Carlos in Madrid, they provide the greatest incentive and support for me to continue advancing in Spain the research program of the Austrian school of economics. Finally, I dedicate this book to Israel M. Kirzner.

Jesús Huerta de Soto<br>Formentor, August 22, 2005

---

\* *Procesos de Mercado: Revista Europea de Economía Política.* Interested readers can request the different published numbers of the journal at ommcamp@teleline.es; see also www.jesushuertadesoto.com.

# 1. Introduction

This introductory chapter will be devoted to an outline of the main features and new insights which distinguish the analysis of socialism contained in this book. We shall briefly summarize and assess the content, structure and conclusions of the work and end the chapter by suggesting some possible lines of research which, if pursued with the proposed analysis as a basis, should be of interest and importance and thus inspire scholars to develop them.

## 1  SOCIALISM AND ECONOMIC ANALYSIS

### The Historic Failure of Socialism

The fall of socialism in the countries of Eastern Europe was a historic event of the first magnitude, and there is no doubt that it caught most economics experts off guard. The issue is not only that economic science failed to rise to the occasion in the face of momentous historical circumstances which economists were unable to predict, but also, and this is even more serious, that it failed to provide humankind with the analytical tools necessary to prevent the grave errors committed.[1] In fact, economists have often done quite the opposite: they have used their scientific aura and prestige to justify and promote economic policies and social systems which have been patently unsuccessful and involved a disproportionate cost in human suffering.

When confronted with this situation, western economists have not appeared uneasy or disconcerted; instead, they have carried on with their science as if nothing had happened.[2] On those few occasions when a prominent economist has raised the uncomfortable question of why most professional theorists have been unable to adequately evaluate and predict the course of events in a timely manner, the answers have been naive and superficial, and thus unsatisfactory. For example, economists have referred to an "error" in the interpretation of statistical data from the systems of the former Eastern bloc, data which may have been accepted in the profession without sufficient "critical" thought. They have also mentioned the inadequacy of the scientific consideration given to the role of "incentives" in the economy.³ The most distinguished members of the economics profession, and the profession in general, have made little further effort to admit responsibility. No one, or rather almost no one, has explored the possibility that the very root of the problem may lie in the methods which prevailed in economics during the twentieth-century period that saw the persistence of socialist systems. Furthermore, we can count on the fingers of one hand the economists who have undertaken the unavoidable, crucial task of bringing to light and reevaluating the content of the debate surrounding the economic impossibility of socialism. Ludwig von Mises started the debate in 1920, and it continued in the decades that followed.⁴ Aside from these isolated and honorable exceptions, it seems as if most economists have preferred to direct their research from this point on with a conscious disregard for all that has been written about socialism up to now, both by them and by their predecessors.

Nevertheless, we cannot advance beyond socialism's chapter in history as if the failure of this system were to exert no influence on human scientific knowledge. In fact, the history of economic thought would suffer considerably if theorists again attempted to focus their concentration on the most urgent specific problems at all times, while forgetting the fundamental need to thoroughly and critically reevaluate and study the analyses of socialism carried out thus far, and particularly the need to produce a definitive, theoretical refutation of this social system. In any case, we must face the fact that economic science has again betrayed the high hopes that humankind is entitled to pin on it. In reality, as an abstract system of thought which is firmly rooted in the innate, rationalist arrogance or conceit of human beings,⁵ socialism will be destined to surface again and again if action is not taken to prevent it. To avert its reappearance, we must seize the unique, and perhaps unrepeatable, historic opportunity now before us to make a thorough examination of the theoretical conscience, to specify the errors committed, to entirely reevaluate the analytical tools used, and to ensure that no historical period is considered closed until we have first arrived at the necessary theoretical conclusions, which should be as definitive as possible.

**The Subjective Perspective in the Economic Analysis of Socialism**

Throughout this book, we propound and develop the basic thesis that socialism can and should be analyzed from the standpoint of a deep and clear understanding of human action and of the dynamic processes of social interaction it sets in motion. For the most part, the economic analysis of socialism carried out so far has failed to satisfactorily incorporate the methodological individualism and the subjectivist viewpoint that Friedrich A. Hayek considers essential to the advancement of our science. In fact, he states: "It is probably no exaggeration to say that every important advance in economic theory during the last hundred years was a further step in the consistent application of subjectivism".[6] Indeed, we have attempted precisely this in our socialism study; namely, to base it on a radical and consistent application of "subjectivism", to build it upon the most intimate and essential characteristic of man: his ability to act in an entrepreneurial, creative manner.

In this light, we have made a sustained effort to free our work, without exception and in all contexts, from the remains of that "objectivism" which still, on either an overt or a covert, subconscious level, pervades many areas of our science and thus cripples its productiveness and severely hampers its future development. Although we can never be absolutely certain that the vain objectivism which floods our science has not furtively crept into our analysis (especially after the long years of academic misguidance all economics students endure while completing their university studies), we have done all within our power to break with the oppressive, prevailing paradigm. Hence, we have taken special care to resist the erroneous view that economic phenomena have a factual, "objective" existence outside of the subjective interpretation and knowledge of them which humans generate when they act. Therefore, we have come to conceive economics as a science which deals with "spiritual" facts, that is, with the subjective information or knowledge that people create in the processes of social interaction.

**Our Definition of Socialism**

Our expressed desire to apply subjectivism with the greatest possible rigor and consistency to the analysis of socialism manifests itself, above all, in our definition of this social system. Indeed, we have already stated our view that the core, or most characteristic feature, of human nature is the ability of all people to act freely and creatively. From this standpoint, we consider that socialism is any system of institutional aggression on the free exercise of human action or entrepreneurship. Later, in Chapter 3, we shall have the opportunity to explore in detail all elements and implications of our definition, and we shall examine its decided, productive comparative advantages over the other definitions used until now. At the moment it is sufficient for us to stress that our conception of socialism as the systematic and aggressive *thwarting of action*, institutional *coercion* in other words, inevitably and necessarily gives our analysis of socialism a wide relevance and makes it an entire *economic theory on institutional coercion*. Moreover, it becomes clear that to examine the theoretical ramifications of the systematic attack on human action and interaction, one must first acquire a deep enough knowledge and understanding of the basic theoretical analysis of unfettered human action. In Chapter 2, which has been given the general title of "Entrepreneurship", we focus entirely on providing this groundwork.

**Entrepreneurship and Socialism**

Our conception of entrepreneurship is both broad and precise. In a general sense, entrepreneurship and human action are considered to be synonymous. In a stricter sense, entrepreneurship consists of the typically human capacity to recognize the opportunities for profit which exist in one's environment. Action is a typically entrepreneurial phenomenon, and we shall study in depth its main components and characteristics in Chapter 2. Among its features, the most outstanding is the creative and coordinating power of entrepreneurship. In fact, each entrepreneurial act generates new information of an unspoken, dispersed, practical and subjective nature and prompts the actors involved to modify their behavior or discipline themselves in terms of the needs and circumstances of others: it is in this spontaneous, unconscious manner that the bonds which make life in society possible are formed. Also, only entrepreneurship can produce the information necessary for *economic calculation* – understood as any estimation of the value in terms of market prices of the outcome of the different courses of action. If we correctly identify and clearly understand the essence of this remarkable process of social coordination and economic calculation, a process only entrepreneurship can initiate, we can comprehend, by comparison and contrast, the severe social discoordination and lack of economic calculation which necessarily follow any institutional coercion against entrepreneurial freedom. In other words, only through a correct understanding of the nature of market processes and society can we fully comprehend all the primary and secondary implications of the socialist system. In Chapter 3, we shall examine them from this viewpoint and consider the connections between them.

**Socialism as an Intellectual Error**

If socialism has been defended in scientific, political, and philosophical circles, it is because it was thought that the systematic use of coercion could make the process of social coordination much more effective. The entire first half of Chapter 3 is devoted to a theoretical refutation of this idea, and our argument is developed from two points of view, the "static"[7] and the "dynamic", which are distinct but complementary. We conclude that in this light, socialism is simply an intellectual error, since according to theory, it is impossible to coordinate society by systematically imposing coercive measures.

The second half of Chapter 3 deals in part with the secondary implications of our basic argument and does so from an interconnected, multidisciplinary perspective. It also includes an explanation and defense of our definition of socialism as opposed to the alternative conceptions which have prevailed in the past. An anatomy of the different historical varieties or types of socialism closes the chapter. Although different in motivation, degrees of intervention, and other particular characteristics, all varieties of socialism share a common denominator: they all rely, to a greater or a lesser extent, on the systematic use of aggression against the free exercise of entrepreneurship.

## 2  THE DEBATE ON THE IMPOSSIBILITY OF SOCIALIST ECONOMIC CALCULATION

The analysis of socialism mentioned above reveals the need for a reevaluation of the debate which took place in the 1920s and 1930s between Mises and Hayek, on one side, and different socialist theorists, on the other, concerning the impossibility of socialist economic calculation. First, let us remember, as we argued earlier, that the historic fall of socialism in the countries of Eastern Europe obliges all serious, reputable researchers to review and reassess the theoretical observations on socialism which had already been offered by those who most diligently and minutely studied the problems involved. Second, our conception of entrepreneurship and socialism is the culmination of a theoretical synthesis which emerged in embryonic form at the start of the debate and gradually evolved and approached completion in the course of it. Hence, it is essential to analyze and reevaluate the controversy in order to clearly and fully grasp all of the implications of the socialism analysis that are put forward here. Finally, by studying the debate, one becomes aware that the mainstream paradigm, which rests on the analysis of equilibrium, has failed to explain the theoretical problems inherent in socialism. Indeed, as this paradigm is based on Newtonian mechanicism and the idea of equilibrium, "repetitive inaction" in other words, it becomes impossible even to distinguish the inescapable theoretical problem that institutional coercion poses. Furthermore, the fact that most authors of secondary sources on the debate and most experts who commented on these writings received their training within the above paradigm shows why they were unable to comprehend the nature of Mises and Hayek's challenge; it also explains why the "myth" that the socialist side had won survived for so many years.

**Ludwig von Mises and the Start of the Socialism Debate**

It was no coincidence that the controversy arose in the wake of Mises's contributions shortly following the First World War. Indeed, only someone who, like Mises, had acquired a profound knowledge of the nature and implications of market processes driven by human action was able to intuit and comprehend the unavoidable economic-calculation problems that socialism involves. Chapter 4 is devoted to an examination of Mises's seminal contribution and the background to it. Special care is taken to place Mises in the historical context in which he made his momentous contribution and in which a typically Marxist conception of socialism predominated. A concerted effort is also make to show that Mises's socialism analysis is one of dynamic theory in the strictest Austrian tradition and therefore bears no relation to static equilibrium analysis or to the "pure logic of choice", which was developed based on it. The chapter ends with a detailed critical study of socialist theorists' first proposed "solutions" to the problem of economic calculation. These included calculation in kind, in labor hours, and in so-called "units of utility", and none remedied the inevitable theoretical problems that Mises raised.

**The Unjustified Shift in the Debate toward Statics**

The idea that only the economic analysis of equilibrium, which underlies and pervades the mainstream paradigm, constitutes "theory" inevitably steered the debate toward the problems of statics. As we shall see in Chapter 5, economists either failed to comprehend Mises's challenge, or they realized that his analysis was not of equilibrium and so considered it practical rather than "theoretical", or, as happened with most, they interpreted the Misesian challenge in the narrow terms of equilibrium and of the strict "pure logic of choice". In the last case, they neglected to recognize that Mises himself, from the very beginning, had very clearly established that socialism posed no problem whatsoever in a static sense, and that thus his theoretical argument against socialism was fundamentally dynamic and rested on his theory of the processes of human interaction which work in the market. The shift in the debate toward statics was *irrelevant*, since statics had nothing to do with the original theoretical challenge, as well as *unjustified*, since the deflection rendered the theoretical controversy entirely fruitless. (The static viewpoint prevented economists from discovering where the problem lay and from grasping its essential, insoluble nature.) In Chapter 5 we also review socialist economists' different attempts at a "mathematical solution", beginning with the arguments of a "formal similarity" in static terms between the market and socialism, and ending with the more serious contributions of Taylor and Dickinson. Finally, we take a detailed look at the "trial-and-error method", which was conceived as a practical strategy for solving the corresponding system of equations. Chapter 5 concludes with a critical analysis of "planometric" models based on the socialist theorists' contributions covered in the chapter, models which economists have remained stubbornly bent on developing up to the present day.

**Oskar Lange and the "Competitive Solution"**

The notion that in terms of theory, Oskar Lange managed to refute Mises's argument against socialism is possibly one of the greatest myths in the history of economic thought. In fact, the leading manuals and textbooks, as well as nearly all secondary sources on the debate, categorically offer this mythical and superficial version. In its turn, this illusion has been passed down, without any justification or critical analysis, to two entire generations of economists. For this reason, it is imperative to do a meticulous critical study of the "competitive solution" proposed by Lange. This study appears in Chapter 6, and its content, length and depth make it perhaps one of the most original and illustrative elements of our effort to apply subjectivist methodology to the economic analysis of socialism. Indeed, it will be sufficient if this study, along with other recent, related writings which will be cited when appropriate, at least helps to dispel once and for all the myth that Lange refuted Mises's argument.

**"Market Socialism" as the Impossible Squaring of the Circle**

The seventh and last chapter completes our analysis of the competitive solution with a look at the contributions Dickinson, Durbin and Lerner made in this area at a time after Oskar Lange presented his ideas. In this chapter, we arrive at the conclusion that competition and socialism, like creative action and coercion, are radically and fundamentally contradictory concepts. Curiously, as we shall see, a whole school of socialist theorists led by Dobb has maintained this same position and has invariably labeled as hypocrites and visionaries those of their colleagues in favor of market socialism. Following a few reflections on the true meaning of the impossibility of socialism, we close the chapter with a brief summary of our most important conclusions.

## 3   OTHER POSSIBLE LINES OF RESEARCH

Logically, the theoretical analysis of socialism that is carried out here leaves plenty of room for future research. In fact, this study is the first step on a path toward a number of research possibilities which could lead to highly promising results if explored or reexamined from the methodological perspective established here. Among these areas of future research, the following appear particularly significant.[8]

**The Analysis of So-called "Self-management Socialism"**

Discredited as "self-management" or "syndicalist" socialism, especially following the economic, social and political collapse of the Yugoslavian model, a study of this brand of socialism using our approach would be of great theoretical interest. This is particularly true in light of the specific coordination problems this model poses at all levels, as well as the fact that it has often been defended as a middle way capable of overcoming the obstacles associated with the traditional conceptions of both capitalism and socialism.

**"Indicative Planning"**

Although likewise practically forgotten nowadays, we feel that indicative planning should be studied for several reasons. First, this model had a large group of defenders, particularly in the 1960s, who attempted to justify their positions with a series of theoretical arguments which in essence closely resembled those underlying the "market socialism" model, and which went virtually unanswered at the time. Therefore, even though indicative planning has fallen into disuse, it is necessary to properly analyze it afresh before closing the theoretical file on it for good. Second, as a result of the curious phenomenon described above (the abandonment or forgetting of a number of theoretical positions without the prior, necessary scientific study and ruling on them), various Eastern European economists have sought to revive indicative planning as a panacea for their economies. Third and finally, we must point out that our socialism analysis is perfectly applicable to the theory of indicative planning, since the theoretical arguments which explain the impossibility of socialism, and which will be examined in this book, are precisely the ones that prevent indicative planning from achieving the intended objectives. The same is true of a whole set of techniques which, like input–output tables, many scientific economists doggedly persist in attempting to use to make planning (indicative or otherwise) feasible.[9]

## The Healthy Acknowledgment of "Scientific Accountability"

The establishment and persistent propagation (for almost 50 years) of the myth that socialist theorists had "won" the debate on the impossibility of socialist economic calculation, and thus that socialism as a model posed no theoretical problem whatsoever, constitutes one of the most curious aspects of the controversy. Particularly responsible for the creation of this myth are the scholars who produced the secondary sources on the debate, as well as an entire legion of economists who, all these years, have either accepted the most popular version without bothering to do any in-depth study on their own, or simply disregarded the whole debate because they considered it obvious that socialism presented no theoretical problem. Although we can confidently assert that, with respect to the difficulty socialism poses, most social scientists have not lived up to the expectations that humankind had a right to place on them and have at least failed to fulfill their crucial scientific duty of informing and warning citizens of the grave dangers inherent in the socialist ideal, a substantial difference exists with respect to the bad faith, negligence, or mere ignorance attributable to each individual theorist. Hence, it becomes essential that we perform the very healthy, instructive exercise of acknowledging the responsibility of different scientists. With respect to ordinary citizens and the future of economic thought, such an exercise should portray each theorist, without regard to name or to current or transient reputation or popularity, in an appropriate light.[10]

## Consequences of the Debate with Respect to the Future Development of Economics

Perhaps the most daring contention expressed in this book is that the fall of socialism will necessarily exert a major impact on the prevailing paradigm and on the future of economic science. It seems clear that a critical element in economics has failed when economists, barring extremely rare exceptions, have been unable to foresee such a momentous event. Luckily, at the present time, the heavy blow received has put us in a position to correctly evaluate the nature and degree of the theoretical short-sightedness that affects the mainstream paradigm, which until now has precluded economists from assessing and interpreting with sufficient clarity the most significant events of the social realm. Moreover, we shall not need to start from scratch, since many of the new analytical tools have been undergoing a process of development and refinement triggered by the efforts of *Austrian* theorists to explain, defend, and fine-tune their positions throughout the debate on the impossibility of socialist economic calculation.[11]

Although it is not possible to list here all of the areas of our discipline which are affected, much less meticulously revise their content, we can offer a few examples. Perhaps we should begin with the *method* appropriate to our science. The factors which make socialism impossible (that is, the subjective, creative, dispersed and tacit qualities of the entrepreneurial information society uses) are exactly the same ones which render unattainable the ideals of empirical verification and precise measuring which until now economists have defended with equal degrees of eagerness and naivety. And not even mentioned are the adverse effects which mathematical formalism and the pernicious obsession with analyses based on complete information and on equilibrium have exerted on the development of our science. It is also necessary to abandon the functional theory of price determination in favor of a *price theory* that explains how prices are dynamically established through a sequential, evolving process driven by the force of entrepreneurship, in other words, by the human actions of the actors involved, rather than by the intersection of mysterious curves or functions which lack any real existence, since the information necessary to devise them does not exist even in the minds of the actors involved. In addition, we must abandon and reconstruct the flimsy, static theory of *"perfect" competition and monopoly* and replace it with a theory of competition understood as a dynamic and purely entrepreneurial process of rivalry, a theory which does away with monopoly issues in their traditional sense by rendering them irrelevant and focuses on institutional restrictions on the free exercise of entrepreneurship in any sphere of the market.

The *theory of capital and interest* is likewise profoundly affected by the subjectivist conception, which depicts as a capital good each and every intermediate stage, subjectively considered as such by the actor, within the context of the specific action in which he is immersed. The actor's experience of culmination gives rise to the subjective idea of the passage of time. Capital appears as a mental category in the actor's economic calculation or subjective estimation of the value of each stage in monetary market prices. This conception explains the leading role time preference plays in determining the interest rate; it also explains the absence of any causal relationship between the interest rate and capital productivity. The belief in such a relationship derives from three distinct but closely linked errors: the analysis of only a perfectly adjusted state of equilibrium, the idea of production as an instantaneous "process" that does not take time, and the notion of capital as an actual "fund" which is independent of the human mind and replicates itself.

The *theory of money*, credit and financial markets represents perhaps the greatest theoretical challenge our science faces in the twenty-first century. In fact, we would go so far as to assert that now that the "theoretical gap" created by the absence of an adequate analysis of socialism has been filled, the least-known field, and the most important, is that of money, where systematic coercion, methodological errors and theoretical ignorance prevail in all areas. For the social relationships which involve money are by far the most abstract and difficult to understand,[12] and therefore the knowledge they produce and incorporate is the most vast, complex and obscure, which makes systematic coercion in this area decidedly the most detrimental. The *theory of interventionism*, in general, and of *economic cycles*, in particular, fit in perfectly with the socialism definition and analysis that is proposed here, which clearly explain the disturbing effects systematic coercion exerts on market intra- and intertemporal coordination in all areas, especially in the monetary and fiscal spheres.

Economists have built the *theory of growth and economic development* upon macroeconomic aggregates and the concept of equilibrium and have overlooked the one, true protagonist of the process: humans and their alertness and creative, entrepreneurial ability. Thus it is necessary to reconstruct the entire theory of growth and underdevelopment and to eliminate all elements which justify the institutional coercion that until now has rendered the theory destructive and fruitless. We must refocus the theory on the theoretical study of the discovery processes which reveal development opportunities that have not yet been exploited, due to a lack of the essential entrepreneurial component. A similar observation could be made about all of so-called "welfare economics", which rests upon the chimerical Paretian notion of efficiency and becomes irrelevant and useless, since its operative management requires a static environment of complete information, and such an environment never exists in the real world. Hence, more than on Paretian criteria, efficiency depends on and should be defined in terms of the capacity of entrepreneurship to spontaneously coordinate the maladjustments which arise in situations of disequilibrium.[13] The *theory of "public" goods* has always been constructed in strictly static terms and based on equilibrium, and theorists have presumed the circumstances which give rise to "joint supply" and "nonrivalry in consumption" to be given and destined to always remain the same. From the standpoint of the dynamic theory of entrepreneurship, any situation in which a public good appears to exist offers a clear opportunity for someone to discover and eliminate it through entrepreneurial creativity, and therefore from the dynamic perspective of free entrepreneurial processes, the set of public goods tends to be left empty. Thus one of the stalest alibis used to justify, in many spheres of society, systematic, institutional coercion against the free exercise of entrepreneurship disappears.

Finally, we mention the theories of the *public choice* school and of the *economic analysis of law* and of *institutions*. In these areas, theorists currently struggle to throw off the unhealthy influence of the static model based on complete information. This model is spawning a pseudoscientific analysis of many laws, an analysis grounded on methodological assumptions identical to those economists attempted to use at one time to justify socialism. Such assumptions totally bypass the dynamic, evolutionary analysis of the spontaneous social processes which entrepreneurship triggers and drives. It is manifestly inconsistent to strive to analyze guidelines and rules from a paradigm which presupposes the existence of complete information regarding the profits and costs derived from them, since such information, if it existed, would make the rules and guidelines unnecessary (it would be much more effective to replace them with simple orders), and if anything accounts for the evolutionary emergence of law, it is precisely the ineradicable ignorance in which humans are constantly immersed.

There are many other fields of research (the theory of population, the economic analysis of tax revenues and redistribution, environmentalism and so on), but the outline given above provides an adequate illustration of the direction in which economics will evolve in the future, once it has been rid of the theoretical and methodological defects the fall of socialism has exposed. As a result, hopefully a true social science at the service of humanity will emerge, a science which is much more wide-ranging, fruitful and instructive.

**The Reinterpretation and Historical Analysis of the Different Real Types of Socialism**

This line of research involves applying the economic analysis of socialism contained in this book to the redoing of work in the field of "comparative economic systems", most of which has until now been plagued with serious defects, due to a lack of the necessary analytical tools. The aim, therefore, is to conduct a detailed study consisting of the historical reinterpretation of each and every one of the different types of socialism that have existed or still persist in the real world. The purpose of such a study is not only to illustrate theory, but also to reveal the extent to which events appear to support it as they develop.

**The Formulation of a Theory on the Ethical Inadmissibility of Socialism**

It is necessary to consider whether or not efforts to find a theoretical basis for the idea of justice and for its implications are tainted with the methodological and analytical flaws that are criticized. In other words, we need to strive to reconstruct the theory of justice, while abandoning the static paradigm of complete information and focusing instead on the creative and uncertain reality of human action, so that we can study the degree to which socialism, besides being an intellectual error and a historic failure, is or is not also ethically unacceptable.

**The Development of a Theory on the Prevention and Dismantling of Socialism**

If it is concluded that socialism is ethically inadmissible, as well as a historic failure and an intellectual error, it will eventually be necessary to develop an entire tactical and strategic theory on the dismantling and prevention of it. The above will involve examining the concrete difficulties posed by the dismantling of each historical type of socialism ("real", social democratic, self-management and so on) and evaluating the advantages and disadvantages of the different alternatives or courses of action, particularly "gradualism versus revolution", according to the possible specific circumstances in each case. Finally, prevention takes on key importance, given the recurrent, deceptive and essentially corrupting nature of the mechanisms which at all times encourage the resurgence of socialism and necessitate unflagging alertness, not only in the scientific realm, but also with respect to the defense and development of the institutions, habits, principles and behavior patterns required by any healthy social framework free from systematic coercion.

## 4 CONCLUSION

It was necessary to outline the above considerations in order to place our study of socialism and institutional coercion in its proper context. Only an appropriate understanding of the general theory of human action can explain the consequences which invariably follow from any attempt to forcibly block the free exercise of entrepreneurship. Hence, our analysis centers on human beings, understood as creative, acting subjects who struggle tirelessly throughout history to express and act according to their most intimate nature, free from the fetters and coercion which would be systematically imposed on them under the most varied and unjustified pretexts.

## NOTES

1. Now that it has become clear that economists had conducted little or no research in this field, which until recently was excluded from nearly all scientific research programs, it actually seems relatively unimportant that economic science was again found wanting when its help was required to accomplish the transition to market economies in the collapsed systems.
2. The leading economists of Eastern Europe have not followed suit, and we shall take an

3. These were the only explanations offered by Gary Becker in the "Presidential Address" he delivered at the regional meeting of the Mont-Pèlerin Society which took place in Prague, Czechoslovakia, November 3–6, 1991 under the general title "In Search of a Transition to a Free Society".
4. Worthy of special mention among the works of these professionals is Don A. Lavoie's *Rivalry and Central Planning: The Socialist Calculation Debate Reconsidered* (1985c), which has become required reading for all experts on the subject.
5. This is the thesis that Hayek presents in his book, *Fatal Conceit: The Errors of Socialism* (Hayek, 1988).
6. Hayek (1952, 31). (See also the 1979 reprint from Liberty Press, Indianapolis.) In footnote 24, on pages 209–10, Hayek adds that subjectivism "has probably been carried out most consistently by L. v. Mises and I believe that most peculiarities of his views which at first strike many readers as strange and unacceptable are due to the fact that *in the consistent development of the subjectivist approach he has for a long time moved ahead of his contemporaries*. Probably all the characteristic features of his theories, from his theory of money to what he calls his *apriorism*, his views about mathematical economics in general, and the measurement of economic phenomena in particular, and his criticism of planning all follow directly from his central position." (As in the rest of the notes of this book, in the absence of an explicit comment to the contrary, the italics have been added and do not appear in the original text. Also, whenever possible, the direct quotes have been provided in the language in which they were originally published, though for convenience, an English translation is often supplied.)
7. The static argument is totally unrelated to the analysis of equilibrium or the static conception which is so strongly criticized in Chapter 4 and, in general, throughout the entire book. However, the term "static" is used for want of a better one, since this argument deals with the *dispersed* nature of information which has hypothetically *already been created*, as opposed to the "dynamic" argument, which refers to the process by which *new* information is generated. Later it will be shown that from our perspective both arguments are equally dynamic and thus equally incompatible with equilibrium theory. In fact, both arguments refer to simultaneous, indistinguishable social processes which are discussed separately for educational purposes only.
8. The list is not meant to be exhaustive, as is clear, and corresponds to the outline of a second volume on socialism, a possible follow-up to this one.
9. Such is the case with the scientistic economist Wasily Leontief, who, always desirous of finding new "applications" for his "intellectual creature" (input–output tables), does not hesitate to propose continual plans for intervention on society. See Lavoie (1985b, 93–124).
10. For an example of this line of research, see Lavoie's fascinating paper, "A critique of the standard account of the socialist calculation debate" (Lavoie, 1981).
11. Israel M. Kirzner has revealed the key importance this debate has taken on as a catalyst for the development, refinement and proper articulation of Austrian school theories, in general, and for the thorough analysis and comprehension of the theory of entrepreneurship and of the dynamic market processes of creativity and discovery, in particular. See Kirzner (1988).
12. "The operation of the money and credit structure has, with language and morals, been one of the spontaneous orders most resistant to efforts at adequate theoretical explanations, and it remains the object of serious disagreement among specialists . . . The selective processes are interfered with here more than anywhere else: selection by evolution is prevented by government monopolies that make competitive experimentation impossible" (Hayek, 1988, 102–3). See also Huerta de Soto (2006).
13. Huerta de Soto (2009a).

## 2. Entrepreneurship

As it is impossible to grasp the concept of socialism without a prior understanding of the essence of entrepreneurship, this chapter will be devoted to a study of the notion, characteristics and basic elements of entrepreneurship. Our idea of entrepreneurship is at once broad and precise. It is closely related to the conception of human action as an integral and fundamentally creative feature of all human beings, and also as the set of coordinating abilities which spontaneously permit the emergence, preservation and development of civilization. Finally, our analysis of entrepreneurship will allow us to propose an original definition of socialism, understood as a "social illness", the most characteristic symptoms of which are widespread maladjustment and extensive discoordination between the individual behaviors and social processes that make up life in society.

### 1 THE DEFINITION OF ENTREPRENEURSHIP

In a broad or general sense, entrepreneurship actually coincides with *human action*. In this respect, it could be said that any person who *acts* to modify the present and achieve his objectives in the future exercises entrepreneurship. Although at first glance this definition may appear to be too broad and to disagree with current linguistic uses, let us bear in mind that it coincides with a conception of entrepreneurship which economists are increasingly studying and developing.[1] Moreover, this conception fully agrees with the original etymological meaning of the term "enterprise" (*empresa* in Spanish). Indeed, both the Spanish word *"empresa"* and the French and English expression "entrepreneur"[2] derive etymologically from the Latin verb *in prehendo-endi-ensum*, which means to discover, to see, to perceive, to realize, to attain; and the Latin term *in prehensa* clearly implies action and means to take, to catch, to seize. In short, *empresa* is synonymous with action. In France, the term *"entrepreneur"* has long been used, and during the High Middle Ages it designated people in charge of performing important and generally war-related deeds,[3] or entrusted with executing the large cathedral-building projects. The *Diccionario* of the Real Academia Española (Royal Academy of the Spanish Language) gives

*15*

one meaning of *empresa* as "arduous and difficult *action* which is valiantly undertaken".[4] *Empresa* also came into use during the Middle Ages to refer to the insignias borne by certain orders of knighthood to indicate their pledge, under oath, to carry out a certain important action.[5] The conception of an enterprise as an action is necessarily and inexorably linked to an *enterprising* attitude, which consists of a continual eagerness to seek out, discover, create, or identify new ends and means (all of which is in accordance with the above-mentioned etymological meaning of *in prehendo*).

**Human Action: Ends, Value, Means and Utility**

Now that we have defined entrepreneurship in terms of human action, we need to explain what we mean by this term. Human action is any deliberate behavior or conduct.[6] In acting, all men seek to accomplish certain *ends* which they have discovered are important to them. "Value" is the subjective and more or less psychically intense appreciation that the actor assigns to his end. The *means* is any method the actor subjectively believes suitable for achieving his end. "Utility" indicates the subjective appreciation the actor assigns to the means, depending upon the value of the end he believes the means will permit him to accomplish. In this sense, value and utility are two sides of the same coin, since the actor projects the subjective value he attaches to his end onto the means he believes useful for achieving it, and this is done precisely through the concept of utility.

**Scarcity, Plans of Action and Acts of Will**

By definition, means must be scarce, because if they were not scarce, the actor would not even take them into account when acting. In other words, where there is no scarcity, there is no human action.[7] Ends and means are never given; on the contrary, they result from the essential entrepreneurial activity which consists precisely of creating, discovering, or simply recognizing the ends and means that are relevant for the actor in each set of circumstances he encounters in his life. Once the actor feels he has discovered which ends are worthwhile to him and which means are available to enable him to reach those ends, he incorporates both, almost always tacitly,[8] into a *plan* of action,[9] which he adopts and implements owing to a personal act of *will*.[10]

**The Subjective Conception of Time: Past, Present and Future**

All human action takes place in time, however not in the deterministic, Newtonian, physical, or analogical sense, but in the subjective sense; that is, 'time' as the actor subjectively perceives and experiences it within the context of each action.[11] According to this subjective notion of time, the actor perceives and experiences its passage as he acts; that is, as he creates, discovers, or simply becomes aware of new ends and means, in line with the essence of entrepreneurship as has been explained. In this way, the past experiences stored in the actor's memory continuously fuse in his mind with his simultaneous, creative view of the future in the form of mental images or expectations. This future is never determined, but instead the actor imagines and creates it step by step.

**Creativity, Surprise and Uncertainty**

Therefore, the future is always uncertain, in the sense that it has yet to be built, and concerning it the actor has only certain ideas, mental images, or expectations which he hopes to realize via his personal action and interaction with other actors. Moreover, the future is open to all of man's creative possibilities, and thus each actor faces it with permanent uncertainty, which can be reduced through behavior patterns of his own and others (institutions) and through action and the alert exercise of entrepreneurship. Nevertheless, he will not be able to totally eliminate this uncertainty. The open and unlimited nature of such uncertainty renders both traditional notions of objective and subjective probability, and the Bayesian conception of the latter, inapplicable to the field of human action. This is so for two reasons: first, actors are not even conscious of every possible alternative or case; and second, the actor only possesses certain subjective beliefs or convictions – called by Mises "case probabilities" (of unique events)[12] – which, as they are modified or broadened, tend to change by surprise, that is, in a radical, divergent manner, the actor's entire "map" of beliefs and knowledge. In this way, the actor constantly discovers totally new situations of which previously he had not even been able to conceive.[13]

**Cost as a Subjective Concept: Entrepreneurial Profit**

Whenever the actor realizes that he desires a particular end and discovers and selects certain means by which to achieve it, he simultaneously forgoes the opportunity to accomplish other, different ends which, *ex ante*, he values less yet believes he could achieve by using the means available to him in a different way. The term "cost" will be used to indicate the subjective value the actor places on the ends he gives up when he decides to continue and embarks on a certain course of action. In other words, action always implies a sacrifice; the value the actor attaches to what he relinquishes is his cost, and this in essence consists of a purely subjective valuation, estimate, or judgment.[14] As a rule, all people act because they subjectively estimate that the value of the proposed end will be greater than the cost they plan to incur; in other words, because they hope to obtain an entrepreneurial *profit*.[15] Therefore, profit is the gain acquired through human action, and it constitutes the *incentive* which drives or motivates people to act. In actions which do not involve a cost, the subjective value of the end coincides with the profit. It will later be argued that all human action includes, without fail, a pure and fundamentally creative entrepreneurial component which does not entail any cost, and that this element is precisely what has led us, in a broad sense, to identify the concepts of human action and entrepreneurship. Furthermore, given that the value of the end always incorporates the profit or gain, from now on, on many occasions, "end" will be considered to be almost synonymous with "profit", without continually stopping to clarify the aforestated distinction between them.

**Rationality and Irrationality: Entrepreneurial Error and Loss**

Human action is by definition always rational,[16] in the sense that, *ex ante*, the actor invariably seeks and chooses the means he believes most suited to accomplishing the ends he finds worthwhile. The above is undoubtedly compatible with an *ex post* discovery by the actor that he has committed an entrepreneurial error; in other words, that he has incurred entrepreneurial losses by selecting certain ends or means without noticing the existence of others more valuable to him. Nevertheless, the outside observer can never objectively classify an action as irrational, given the essentially subjective nature of ends, costs and means. Hence, in the field of economics, we can affirm that human action is an ultimate given in the sense that it is an axiomatic concept which does not require a reference to any other or any further explanation. The axiomatic character of the concept of human action is also manifest, since to criticize or doubt it involves an insoluble logical contradiction, as criticism can only be expressed through (human) action.[17]

**Marginal Utility and Time Preference**

Finally, considering that means are scarce by definition, the actor will tend to first accomplish those ends he values more, and then those which are relatively less important to him. As a result, each unit of means which is available to the actor, and is interchangeable and relevant within the context of his action, he will tend to value in terms of the least important end he believes he can achieve with it (*law of marginal utility*). Moreover, given that action is undertaken with a view to attaining a certain end and that all action takes place in time and thus has a certain duration, the actor will try, *ceteris paribus*, to achieve his end as soon as possible. To put it another way, other things being equal, the actor will always place a higher value on the ends closer to him in time, and he will only be willing to undertake actions of a longer duration if he believes that by doing so he will be able to accomplish ends of greater value to him (*law of time preference*).[18]

## 2  CHARACTERISTICS OF ENTREPRENEURSHIP

**Entrepreneurship and Alertness**

Entrepreneurship, in a strict sense, consists basically of discovering and perceiving (*prehendo*) opportunities to achieve an end, or to acquire a gain or profit, and acting accordingly to take advantage of these opportunities which arise in the environment. Kirzner holds that the exercise of entrepreneurship entails a special alertness; that is, a constant vigilance, which permits a person to discover and grasp what goes on around him.[19] Perhaps Kirzner uses the English term "alertness" because "entrepreneurship" originates from French and in English does not imply the idea of *prehendo* that it does in the continental romance languages. In any case, the Spanish adjective *perspicaz* (perceptive, shrewd) is quite appropriate to entrepreneurship, since, as the *Diccionario* of the Real Academia Española informs us, it applies to "vision or a gaze which is far-sighted and very sharp".[20] This idea fits in perfectly with the activity the entrepreneur engages in when he decides which actions he will carry out and estimates the future effect of those actions. In addition, the word "speculator" derives etymologically from the latin word *specula*, which denoted certain towers from which lookouts could view from a distance all who approached. Though *el estar alerta* may also be an acceptable indication of entrepreneurship, since it involves the notion of attention or vigilance, at any rate, it is somewhat less fitting than *perspicaz*, perhaps because the former clearly suggests a rather more static approach. At the same time, we must also keep in mind that a striking similarity exists between the alertness a historian must show when selecting and interpreting the important past events which interest him, and the alertness an entrepreneur must show concerning the events he believes will occur in the future. This is why Mises asserts that historians and entrepreneurs employ very similar approaches, and he goes so far as to define "entrepreneur" as someone who looks into the future with the eyes of a historian.[21]

## Information, Knowledge and Entrepreneurship

In order to thoroughly understand the nature of entrepreneurship as we have been approaching it, one must first comprehend the way it modifies or changes the information or knowledge the actor possesses. The perception or recognition of new ends and means implies a modification of the actor's knowledge, in the sense that he discovers new information. Moreover, this discovery modifies the entire map or context of information or knowledge the subject possesses. Let us ask the following fundamental question: what are the characteristics of the information or knowledge which is relevant to the exercise of entrepreneurship? We shall study in detail six basic features of this type of knowledge: (i) it is subjective and practical, rather than scientific, knowledge; (ii) it is exclusive knowledge; (iii) it is dispersed throughout the minds of all men; (iv) it is mainly tacit knowledge, and therefore not expressed in words; (v) it is knowledge created *ex nihilo*, from nothing, precisely through the exercise of entrepreneurship; and (vi) it is knowledge which can be transmitted, for the most part unconsciously, via extremely complex social processes, the study of which is the object of research in economics.

### Subjective and Practical, rather than Scientific, Knowledge

The knowledge we are analyzing, that most crucial to the exercise of human action, is above all subjective and practical, not scientific. Practical knowledge is any that cannot be represented in a formal manner, and that is instead progressively acquired by the subject through practice, that is, through human action itself in its different contexts. As Hayek maintains, it is knowledge that is significant in all sorts of particular circumstances, or different sets of specific, subjective coordinates of time and place.[22] In short, we are referring to knowledge in the form of concrete human appraisals, information regarding both the ends the actor pursues and those ends he believes other actors pursue. This knowledge also consists of practical information on the means the actor believes are available to him and can enable him to attain his ends, especially information about all of the conditions, whether personal or otherwise, which the actor feels may be of importance within the context of any concrete action.[23]

### Exclusive and Dispersed Knowledge

Practical knowledge is exclusive and dispersed. This means that each actor possesses only a few "atoms" or "bits" of all of the information generated and transmitted in society,[24] and that paradoxically, only he

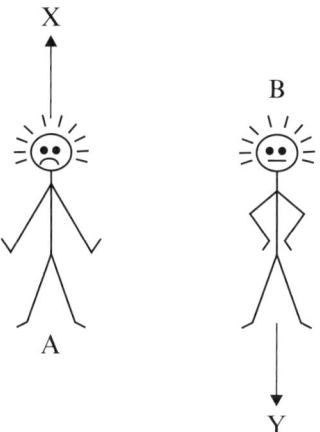

*Figure 2.1*

possesses these bits; in other words, only he accesses and interprets them consciously. Hence, each man who acts and exercises entrepreneurship does so in a strictly personal and unrepeatable manner, since he begins by striving to achieve certain ends or objectives that correspond to a vision of the world and a body of knowledge concerning it, both of which only he possesses in all of their richness and diverse nuances, and which no other human being can possess in identical form. Therefore, such knowledge is not *given* and accessible to everyone via some material means of storing information (newspapers, journals, books, computers and so on). On the contrary, the knowledge relevant to human action is fundamentally practical and strictly exclusive, and it is only "found" diffused throughout the minds of each and every one of the men and women who act and comprise society. Figure 2.1 introduces some amiable stickmen who will accompany us all through this book with the sole purpose of helping to more graphically illustrate our analysis.[25]

The stickmen in this figure are intended to symbolize two *real*, flesh-and-blood human beings, A and B. Each of the people A and B represent possesses some personal or exclusive knowledge, that is, knowledge the other does not have. In fact, we can see from our viewpoint as outside observers in this case that knowledge "exists" which an outside observer does not possess, and which is dispersed between A and B, in the sense that A has one part of it, and B has the other. For example, let us suppose that the information A possesses is that he plans to achieve an end, X (represented by the arrow that points toward X above his head), and to help him accomplish this end, he has certain practical knowledge relevant within the context of his action (a body of practical knowledge or information represented by the halo of short lines which surrounds the head of A). The case of B is similar, except that he pursues a completely different goal, Y (represented by an arrow at his feet which points toward Y). The body of practical information which actor B considers relevant in the context of his action, an action he performs to achieve Y, is likewise represented by a halo surrounding his head.

In the case of many simple actions, an actor individually possesses the information necessary to reach his goal without needing to involve other actors at all. In such situations, whether or not an action is undertaken depends upon an economic calculation or appraisal the actor makes by directly comparing and weighing the subjective value of his end against the cost, or the value he attaches to that which he would relinquish should he pursue the chosen end. The actor is able to make this type of decision directly with respect to only a few, very simple actions. Most of the actions in which we are involved are much more complex and of the sort that will now be described. Let us imagine, just as we have shown in Figure 2.1, that A fervently wishes to achieve the objective X, but to do so he requires a means, R, which is unavailable to him and which he does not know where or how to obtain. Let us also suppose that B is in another place, that he strives for a very different goal (the end Y), to which he dedicates all of his efforts, and that he knows or "knows of" or has available to him a large quantity of the resource R, which he does not find useful or suitable for achieving his end, but which happens to be what A would need to reach his desired objective (X). In fact, X and Y are contradictory, as in most real cases; that is, the actors pursue different ends, with different levels of intensity, and with disparate or maladjusted relative knowledge about these ends and about the means at their disposal (which explains the dejected expressions that are drawn on the faces of the stick figures). Later it will be seen how the exercise of entrepreneurship makes it possible to overcome these contradictory or discoordinated behaviors.

**Tacit Knowledge which cannot be Articulated**

Practical knowledge is mainly tacit knowledge which cannot be articulated. This means that the actor knows how to perform certain actions (*know how*), but he cannot identify the elements or parts of what he is doing, or whether they are true or false (*know that*).[26] For example, when someone learns to play golf, he does not learn a set of objective, scientific rules which allow him to make the necessary movements through the application of a series of formulae from mathematical physics. Instead, the learning process consists of conforming to a number of practical behavior patterns. We could also cite, following Michael Polanyi, the example of a person who, learning to ride a bicycle, attempts to maintain his balance by moving the handlebars to the side toward which he begins to fall and creating in this way centrifugal force which tends to keep the bicycle upright, yet almost no cyclist is aware of or familiar with the physical principles behind his ability. On the contrary, what the cyclist actually uses is his "sense of balance", which in some way tells him how to behave at each moment to keep from falling. Polanyi goes so far as to assert that tacit knowledge is in fact the dominant principle of all knowledge.[27] Even the most highly formalized and scientific knowledge invariably follows from an intuition or an act of creation, which are simply manifestations of tacit knowledge. Moreover, the new formalized knowledge we can acquire through formulae, books, charts, maps and so on is important mainly because it helps us to reorganize our entire framework of information from different, richer and more valuable perspectives, which in turn opens up new possibilities for the exercise of creative intuition. Therefore, the impossibility of articulating practical knowledge is expressed not only "statically", in the sense that any apparently articulated statement contains information only insofar as it is interpreted through a combination of beliefs and knowledge that cannot be expressed in words, but also "dynamically", since the mental process used in any attempt at articulation is itself essentially tacit knowledge which cannot be articulated.[28]

We must emphasize that all tacit knowledge is, by its own nature, difficult to articulate. If we ask a young woman who has just purchased a skirt of a certain color why she chose it, she will most likely answer, "just because", or simply, "because I liked it", without being able to offer us a more detailed and formalized explanation for her choice. Another type of knowledge that cannot be articulated and that plays an essential role in the functioning of society is represented by the set of habits, traditions, institutions and juridical rules which comprise the law, which make society possible, and which human beings learn to follow, though they cannot theorize about them or detail the precise function these rules and institutions perform in the various situations and social processes in which they are involved. The same can be said about language and also, for instance, about the financial and cost accounting which entrepreneurs use as a guide for their actions and which consists simply of practical knowledge or techniques that, in the context of a specific market economy, provide entrepreneurs with common guidelines for reaching their goals, even though most entrepreneurs are unable to formulate a scientific theory of accounting, let alone explain how it helps in the complicated processes of coordination which make life in society possible.[29] Hence, we may conclude that the exercise of entrepreneurship as we have defined it (the capacity for discovering and perceiving opportunities for profit and consciously acting to take advantage of them) essentially amounts to tacit knowledge which cannot be articulated.

**The Fundamentally Creative Nature of Entrepreneurship**

The exercise of entrepreneurship does not require any means. That is to say, entrepreneurship does not entail any costs and is therefore essentially creative.[30] This creative aspect of entrepreneurship is embodied in its production of a type of profit which, in a sense, arises out of nothing, and which we shall refer to as "pure entrepreneurial profit". To derive entrepreneurial profit, one needs no prior means, but only to exercise entrepreneurship well. To illustrate this point, let us go back to the situation Figure 2.1 represented. The simple realization that a state of maladjustment or discoordination exists between A and B is enough to immediately spark an opportunity for pure entrepreneurial profit.[31] In Figure 2.2, we suppose that a third party, in this case C, is the one who exercises entrepreneurship, and that he does so upon discovering the profit opportunity inherent in the maladjustment or discoordination present in Figure 2.1. (A light bulb is used to show that C recognizes this opportunity. As is logical, in practice, entrepreneurship could be exercised by A or B or both simultaneously,

Figure 2.2

with the same or differing intensities, though for our purposes it is more illustrative to consider the third party C to be the one who exercises entrepreneurship in this case.)

In fact, C needs only to contact B and offer to buy for a certain quantity, let us say three monetary units, the resource so abundantly available to B, who attaches practically no importance to it. B will be enormously pleased, since he never could have imagined receiving so much for his resource. Following this exchange, C can contact A and sell him this resource, which A so urgently needs to achieve the end he is pursuing. C might sell A the resource for nine monetary units, for instance. (If C lacks money, one way for him to obtain it would be to convince someone to lend it to him temporarily.) Thus, through the exercise of entrepreneurship, C derives, *ex nihilo*, a pure entrepreneurial profit of six monetary units.[32]

It is particularly important at this point to emphasize that the above act of entrepreneurship has produced three extraordinarily significant effects. First, entrepreneurship has created new information which did not exist before. Second, this information has been transmitted throughout the market. Third, the above entrepreneurial act has taught the economic agents involved to tune their behavior to that of the others. These consequences of entrepreneurship are so important that they are each worth studying closely.

**The Creation of Information**

Each entrepreneurial act entails the *ex nihilo* creation of new information. This creation takes place in the mind of the person, represented by stick figure C in our example, who first exercises entrepreneurship. Indeed, when C realizes that a situation such as the one described exists involving A and B, new information that he did not possess before is created in his mind. Furthermore, once C acts and contacts A and B, new information is also created in the minds of A and B. Thus, A realizes that the resource he lacked and needed so urgently to accomplish his end is available elsewhere in the market in greater quantities than he thought, and that therefore he can now readily undertake the action he had not initiated before due to the absence of this resource. For his part, B realizes that the resource he so abundantly possesses yet did not value is keenly desired by other people, and that therefore he can sell it at a good price. Moreover, part of the new practical information which originates in the mind of C with the exercise of entrepreneurship, and which later springs up in the minds of A and B, is collected in a highly summarized or compressed form in a series of prices or historical ratios of exchange (that is, B sold for three monetary units and A bought for nine).

### The Transmission of Information

The entrepreneurial creation of information implies its transmission in the market. Indeed, to transmit something to someone is to cause that person to generate in his mind part of the information which we create or discover beforehand. Strictly speaking, though our example has contained the transmission to B of the idea that his resource is important and that he should not waste it, and to A of the idea that he can go ahead in the pursuit of the goal he had set himself yet failed to work toward due to the lack of this resource, more has been communicated. In fact, the respective prices, which constitute a highly powerful system of transmission, since they convey a large amount of information at a very low cost, communicate in successive waves to the entire market or society the message that the resource in question should be saved and husbanded, since there is a demand for it, and at the same time, that all those who, owing to a belief that this resource does not exist, are refraining from undertaking certain actions, can obtain the resource and go ahead with their corresponding plans of action. As is logical, the important information is always subjective and does not exist beyond the people who are capable of interpreting or discovering it, so it is always human beings who create, perceive and transmit information. The erroneous notion that information is objective stems from the fact that part of the subjective information which is created via entrepreneurship is expressed objectively in signs (prices, institutions, rules, "firms" and so on) which can be discovered and subjectively interpreted by many within the context of their particular actions, thus facilitating the creation of new, richer and more complex subjective information. Nevertheless, despite appearances, the transmission of social information is basically tacit and subjective; that is, the information is not expressly articulated, and it is conveyed in a highly abridged manner. (Indeed, the minimum amount essential for coordinating the social process is subjectively communicated and received.) The above enables people to make the best possible use of the human mind's limited capacity to constantly create, discover and transmit new information.

### The Learning Effect: Coordination and Adjustment

Finally, attention must be drawn to the way in which agents A and B have learned to act in tune with each other. B, as a result of the entrepreneurial action originally undertaken by C, no longer squanders the resource available to him, but conserves it instead, acting in his own interest. As A can then count on employing this resource, he is able to achieve his end, and he embarks on the action he had refrained from performing before.

Hence, both learn to act in a coordinated manner; that is, to discipline themselves and modify their behavior in terms of each other. Moreover, they learn in the best way possible: without realizing they are learning and *motu proprio*; in other words, voluntarily and within the context of a plan in which each pursues his particular ends and interests. This alone is the core of the simple, effective, and marvelous process which makes life in society possible.[33] Finally, we observe that the exercise of entrepreneurship by C not only permits a coordinated action previously absent between A and B, but also allows both to make an economic calculation within the context of their respective actions, using data or information which was unavailable to them before and which makes them much more likely to successfully reach their objectives. In short, the information generated in the entrepreneurial process is precisely what enables each actor to make an economic calculation. Without the exercise of entrepreneurship, the information necessary for the actors to properly calculate or estimate the value of each alternative course of action is not created. In brief, without entrepreneurship, economic calculation is impossible.[34]

The above observations constitute both the most important and the most fundamental teachings of social science, and they allow us to conclude that entrepreneurship is undoubtedly the quintessential social function, given that it makes life in society possible by adjusting and coordinating the individual behaviors of its members. Without entrepreneurship, it is impossible to conceive of the existence of any society.[35]

**Arbitration and Speculation**

From a temporal standpoint, entrepreneurship can be practiced in two different ways: synchronically or diachronically. The first is called "arbitration" and is entrepreneurship exercised in the present (understood as the temporal present from the actor's point of view)[36] between two distinct places or situations in society. The second is called "speculation" and consists of the exercise of entrepreneurship between the present and the future. One might think that entrepreneurship, in the case of arbitration, amounts to discovering and transmitting information which already exists but which is dispersed, while in the case of speculation, "new" information is created and transmitted. Nevertheless, this distinction is purely artificial, because discovering what "already existed", though no one knew it existed, is synonymous with creating. Thus, qualitatively and theoretically speaking, there is no difference between arbitration and speculation. Both types of entrepreneurship give rise to social coordination (*intratemporal* in the case of arbitration and *intertemporal* in the case of speculation) and create the same sort of trends toward adjustment and coordination.

## Law, Money and Economic Calculation

In our illustrated example, C could not easily have exercised his creative entrepreneurship if any person had had the power to seize the result of it by force; or, for example, if A or B had deceived him and failed to turn over the resource or the promised monetary units. This means that the exercise of entrepreneurship, and of human action in general, requires of the people involved a constant and repetitive adherence to certain standards or rules of conduct; in other words, they must comply with the law. This law is composed of a series of behavior patterns which have evolved and become more refined through custom. These patterns basically define property rights ("several property", in Hayekian terminology[37]), and they can be reduced to the following essential principles: respect for life, stability of peacefully acquired possession, transference by consent, and fulfillment of promises.[38] We could adopt three different but complementary viewpoints to examine the foundation of the legal rules which make life in society possible: utilitarianism, evolutionism and custom, and the theory of the social ethics of property rights. Nevertheless, this type of analysis far exceeds the scope of this project, and therefore it will simply be pointed out that, while the law makes possible the exercise of human action, and hence also the emergence and development of society and civilization, the law is at the same time an evolutionary product of the exercise of entrepreneurship itself and is consciously designed by no one. Juridical institutions, and in general all social institutions (language, money, the market and so on), arise from evolutionary processes in which a vast number of people individually contribute throughout history their own small bit of practical information and entrepreneurial creativity and thus spontaneously give rise, in accordance with Carl Menger's well-known theory, to institutions[39] which are without a doubt the product of the interaction between many people, though these institutions have not been consciously designed or organized by any person.[40] This is so because no human mind or organized group of human minds possesses the intellectual capacity necessary to take in or to understand the enormous volume of practical information which has come into play in the gradual formation, consolidation and later development of these institutions. Thus the paradoxical truth that those institutions (linguistic, economic, legal and moral) which are most important and essential to the life of man in society could not be deliberately created by man himself, since he lacks the necessary intellectual capacity. Instead they have gradually emerged from the entrepreneurial process of human interaction, and they have spread to broader and broader groups through the unconscious mechanism of learning and imitation explained above. Moreover, the emergence and refinement of institutions makes possible, through a typical feedback process, an increasingly rich and complex entrepreneurial process of human interaction. For the same reason man has been unable to deliberately create his institutions,[41] he is also unable to fully comprehend the overall role which the existing ones play at any point in history. Institutions and the social order which gives rise to them become progressively more abstract in the sense that it is impossible to discern or identify the infinite variety of particular knowledge and individual ends possessed or pursued by the human beings who act within the scope of an institution. Institutions are highly powerful signs, since they all consist of behavioral rules or customs and thus guide people's actions.

Of all of these institutions, perhaps the most abstract, and therefore the most difficult to understand, is that of money. Indeed, money, or a generally accepted medium of exchange, is one of the institutions most vital to the existence and development of our civilization. However, few people come to even intuit the way in which money permits an exponential increase in the possibilities of social interaction and entrepreneurial creativity, and the role money plays by facilitating and making possible the extremely complex and increasingly difficult economic calculations a modern society demands.[42]

In our elementary model of the exercise of entrepreneurship, it has been taken for granted that money exists and that therefore A, B and C are willing to carry out certain exchanges in return for a quantity of monetary units. Money is very important, because, as Mises has demonstrated, it constitutes a common denominator that makes economic calculation possible in connection with all of those goods and services which are objects of trade or exchange among people. Therefore, the term "economic calculation" is taken to mean any calculation, in monetary units, of the value in terms of market prices of the results of different courses of action. Such an economic calculation is made by each actor whenever he exercises entrepreneurship and is made possible only by the existence of money and by the practical information which the exercise of entrepreneurship constantly generates and transmits in a free market.[43]

**The Ubiquity of Entrepreneurship**

All men, when they act, exercise entrepreneurship. They do so to a greater or lesser extent, and with varying degrees of success. In other words, entrepreneurship, in its purest state, it ubiquitous. Thus, for example, a *worker* exercises it when he is on the lookout and decides whether or not to change jobs, to accept one offer, to reject another one and so on. If he makes wise choices, he will find a more attractive job than he would have under other circumstances. If he chooses poorly, his work conditions may be less favorable than they would be otherwise. In the first case, he will obtain entrepreneurial profits; in the second, he will incur losses. A *capitalist* also exercises entrepreneurship constantly. He exercises it when, for example, he decides to hire one manager instead of another, or he studies the possibility of selling one of his companies, or entering into a certain sector, or including in his portfolio a particular combination of fixed-income and variable-yield securities and so on. Finally, a *consumer* also acts in an entrepreneurial manner continually. He does so when he tries to decide which consumer good he likes best, when he is on the watch for new products in the market, or, on the contrary, when he decides to stop wasting time in the search for new opportunities and so on. Thus, each day in real life, in all specific actions and enterprises, entrepreneurship is constantly exercised to one degree or another, and with more or less success. All who act in the market exercise entrepreneurship, regardless of the capacity in which they act, and consequently, in practice, pure entrepreneurial profits and losses almost invariably appear mixed with income from other economic categories (wages, land rent, interest and so on). Detailed historical research alone will permit us to identify, in each case, where such profits and losses occur, and who has exercised entrepreneurship most significantly in the context of each specific action or enterprise.

**The Essential Principle**

From a theoretical standpoint, what is truly important is not who specifically exercises entrepreneurship (though in practice this is precisely the most important question), but a situation in which there are no institutional or legal restrictions on the free exercise of entrepreneurship, and hence each person is free to use his entrepreneurial abilities in the best way possible to create new information and to take advantage of the exclusive, practical information he has discovered in any particular instance.

It does not fall to the economist, but rather to the psychologist, to study in greater depth the origin of the innate strength which motivates man to act in an entrepreneurial manner in all areas. At this point, we shall merely underline the following essential principle: man tends to discover the information which interests him, and hence, if he is free to accomplish his ends and promote his interests, both will act as an incentive[44] to motivate him in the exercise of entrepreneurship and will permit him to constantly perceive and discover the practical information which is important for the achievement of his objectives. The opposite is also true. If, for whatever reason, the scope for the exercise of entrepreneurship is limited or closed in a certain area of life in society (via coercive legal or institutional restrictions), then humans will not even consider the possibility of accomplishing ends in that prohibited or limited area, and therefore, since the ends will not be achievable, they will not act as an incentive, and the actor will not perceive or discover the practical information relevant to the achievement of them. Furthermore, under such circumstances, not even the people affected will be aware of the great value and large number of goals which cease to be realizable as a result of these institutional restrictions.[45] In the stick figure model presented in Figures 2.1 and 2.2, we see that if people are at liberty to exercise human action, the "entrepreneurial light bulb" can light up freely in any case of social maladjustment or discoordination and thus trigger the process of the creation and transmission of information, a process which will lead to the coordination of the maladjustment; such coordination is what makes life in society possible. However, if the exercise of entrepreneurship is prevented in a certain area, then it becomes impossible for the entrepreneurial light bulb to light up in any case. In other words, the entrepreneur cannot possibly discover the existing maladjustment which may therefore continue unchanged indefinitely or even worsen. From this perspective, it is easy to grasp the great wisdom behind the old Spanish proverb, *"ojos que no ven, corazón que no siente"* (out of sight, out of mind), which applies directly to the situation we are considering. We see this paradox: man is incapable of feeling or perceiving what he loses when he is unable to freely act or exercise his entrepreneurship.[46]

Finally, let us remember that each man-actor possesses some bits of practical information which, as we have seen, he tends to discover and use to accomplish an end. Despite its social implications, only the actor has this information; that is, only he possesses and interprets it consciously. It is clear that we are not referring to the information published in specialized magazines, books, newspapers, computers and so on. The only information or knowledge relevant to society is that which someone is aware of, though in most cases only tacitly, at each point in history. Therefore, each time man acts and exercises entrepreneurship, he does so in a characteristic, personal, and unrepeatable manner all his own, a manner which arises from his attempt to gain certain objectives or arrive at a particular vision of the world, all of which act as incentives and which, in their particular form and circumstances, only he possesses. The above enables each human being to obtain certain knowledge or information which he discovers only depending on his ends and circumstances and which no other person can possess in an identical form.[47]

Thus it is of vital importance not to disregard anyone's entrepreneurship. Even the humblest people, those of the least social status, and the most lacking in formal knowledge, will exclusively possess at least small bits or pieces of subjective knowledge or information which could be of decisive value in the course of historical events.[48] From this standpoint, it is obvious that our concept of entrepreneurship is of an essentially humanistic nature, a concept which makes economics the quintessential humanistic science.

**Competition and Entrepreneurship**

By its very nature and definition, entrepreneurship is always competitive.[49] This means that once an actor discovers a certain profit opportunity and acts to take advantage of it, the opportunity disappears and no one else can perceive and seize it. Likewise, if an actor only partially discovers an opportunity for profit, or, having discovered it completely, takes only partial advantage of it, then a portion of that opportunity will remain latent for another actor to discover and grasp. Therefore, the social process is markedly competitive, in the sense that different actors compete with each other, either consciously or unconsciously, to be the first to perceive and embrace profit opportunities.[50] In our model, illustrated by the stickman diagrams, we should consider entrepreneurship to be represented not by one single light bulb, as we have depicted it for simplicity, but by the simultaneous and successive appearance of multiple light bulbs, each one symbolizing the many, varied entrepreneurial acts of diagnosis and of experimentation with the newest and most diverse solutions to problems of social discoordination, solutions which are matched against each other and of which not all can succeed and predominate.

Every entrepreneurial act uncovers, coordinates and eliminates social maladjustments, and the fundamentally competitive nature of entrepreneurship makes it impossible for any actor to perceive and eliminate those maladjustments anew once they have been previously discovered and already coordinated. One might mistakenly think that the social process driven by entrepreneurship could lose momentum and come to a stop or disappear, once the force of entrepreneurship had revealed and exhausted all of the existing possibilities of social adjustment. However, the entrepreneurial process of social coordination never stops, nor is it exhausted. This is because the essential coordinating act, which has been explained in Figures 2.1 and 2.2, amounts to the creation and transmission of new information which necessarily modifies among all of the actors involved the general perception of ends and means. This shift in turn gives rise to the appearance of a limitless number of new maladjustments which represent new opportunities for entrepreneurial profit, and this dynamic process spreads, never comes to a halt, and results in the constant advancement of civilization. In other words, entrepreneurship not only makes life in society possible by coordinating the maladjusted behavior of its members, but it also permits the development of civilization by continually leading to the creation of new objectives and knowledge which spread in consecutive waves throughout all of society. Furthermore, it performs the very important function of enabling this development to be as adjusted and harmonious as humanly possible under each set of historical circumstances, because the maladjustments which are constantly created as civilization evolves and new information emerges tend in turn to be discovered and eliminated by the very entrepreneurial force of human action.[51] That is, entrepreneurship is the force which unites society and permits its harmonious advancement, since it tends to coordinate the inevitable and necessary maladjustments which this process of advancement brings forth.[52]

## The Division of Knowledge and the "Extensive" Order of Social Cooperation

Given the limited capacity of the human mind for assimilating information, and the growing volume of new information which is constantly created through the social process entrepreneurship drives, it is clear that the development of society requires that the division of knowledge continuously spread and deepen. This idea, which in its original formulation was awkward and objectivist and known as the "division of labor",[53] simply means that the process of development implies, from a vertical standpoint, knowledge which is increasingly deep, specialized and detailed, and which, to spread horizontally, demands a constantly increasing human population. Population growth both follows from and is a necessary condition for the advancement of civilization, given that the capacity of the human mind is quite limited and is incapable of reproducing the enormous volume of practical information which would be necessary if people constantly created new information through the entrepreneurial process without a parallel increase in the number of people and human minds. Figure 2.3 illustrates the process through which the division of practical and dispersed knowledge deepens and spreads, a process which, driven by entrepreneurship, constitutes the advancement of society.[54]

The numbers in Figure 2.3 serve to identify the different human beings. The letters represent the practical knowledge each human being applies to specific ends. The lit bulbs above the arrows in the center of the figure denote the entrepreneurial act of discovering the advantages of trade and of the horizontal division of knowledge: indeed, in the second line we observe that each person no longer reproduces the knowledge ABCD possessed by every other person, but instead 2 specializes in AB, and 3 and 4 in CD, and they all trade with each other the product of their entrepreneurial

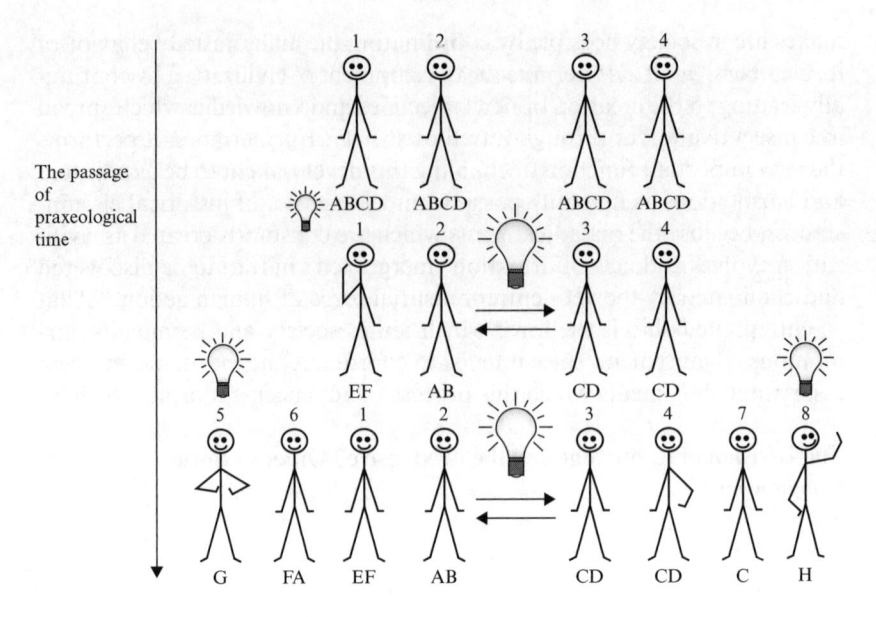

*Figure 2.3*

action. The light bulbs at the sides represent the entrepreneurial creation of new information which triggers an increase in the vertical division of knowledge. In fact, new ideas arise because each actor no longer needs to reproduce all of the dispersed knowledge held by the other actors. Moreover, the increasing depth and complexity of knowledge requires a rise in the population; that is, the appearance of new people (numbers 5, 6, 7 and 8) who in turn can create new information and learn that communicated to them by their "parents", information they spread to all of society through trade. In short, it is impossible to possess increasing knowledge in a greater number of specific areas if the number of human beings does not increase. In other words, the main limit to the advancement of civilization is a stagnant population, since it holds back the process by which the practical knowledge necessary for economic development becomes deeper and more specialized.[55]

**Creativity versus Maximization**

Entrepreneurship, or human action, does not fundamentally consist of the optimal allocation of given means to ends which are also given. Instead, as we have already seen, it basically involves perceiving, determining, and recognizing the ends and means; that is, actively and creatively seeking and discovering new ends and means. Hence, we should be particularly critical of the awkward and narrow conception of economics which originated with Lionel Robbins and his well-known definition of the discipline as a science that studies the use of scarce means which could be put to alternate uses to satisfy human needs.[56] This view presupposes given knowledge of the ends and means, and thus it reduces the economic problem to a technical problem of simple allocation, maximization or optimization. From the Robbinsian perspective, man is an automaton or a human caricature limited to passively reacting to events. In contrast to this view, let us consider that of Mises, according to whom man, even more than *homo sapiens*, is *homo agens* or *homo empresario*, since he acts. Rather than merely allocate given means to given ends, what man really does is to constantly seek out new ends and means, while learning from the past and using his imagination to discover and create the future step by step.[57] In fact, as Kirzner has convincingly shown, even actions which appear to be solely maximizing or optimizing invariably possess an entrepreneurial component, since the actor involved must first realize that such a course of action, one so automatic, mechanical and reactive, is the most advantageous.[58] In other words, the Robbinsian conception is simply a particular and relatively unimportant case within the Misesian model, which is much richer and more general and explains social reality much more satisfactorily.

**Conclusion: Our Concept of Society**

We shall conclude by defining society[59] as a *process* (that is, a dynamic structure) which is: *spontaneous* and thus not consciously designed by anyone; highly *complex*, since it comprises billions of people with an infinite range of goals, tastes, valuations and practical knowledge; and composed of human *interactions* (which basically consist of *exchange* dealings that often yield monetary prices and are always carried out according to certain *rules*, habits or standards of conduct); all such human interactions are driven by the force of *entrepreneurship*, which continually *creates*, discovers, and transmits information, as it adjusts and *coordinates* the contradictory plans of the different individuals through *competition* and enables them to *live* and coexist in an increasingly rich and complex environment.[60]

# 3 ENTREPRENEURSHIP AND THE CONCEPT OF SOCIALISM

Our definition of socialism rests on the concept of entrepreneurship, as we shall see, and consequently, it was important that we carry out a relatively detailed and in-depth analysis of entrepreneurship, as we have done here. Indeed, throughout this book, "socialism" will be defined as any institutional restriction or aggression on the free exercise of human action or entrepreneurship. The following chapter will be devoted to a thorough analysis of this definition and all of its implications. For now it will simply be pointed out that the institutional restriction or aggression often springs from a deliberate desire to improve the process of social coordination and achieve certain ends or objectives. In some cases, socialism's institutional attack on human action may have its origins in tradition or history, as in certain precapitalist societies anchored in, for example, the caste system. However, socialism as a modern phenomenon, regardless of its specific type, arises as a deliberate attempt to achieve the following goals through the use of institutional coercion: the "improvement" of society, an increase in the efficiency of its development and functioning, and the accomplishment of particular ends considered "just". Hence, we can complete in the following manner the definition of socialism offered above: socialism is any system of institutional restriction or aggression on the free exercise of human action or entrepreneurship which ordinary people, politicians, and scientists usually justify as one capable of improving the functioning of society and of achieving certain ends and objectives considered good. An in-depth study of socialism as it has just been defined requires a theoretical analysis of the concept and its implications, an analysis which permits us to clarify whether or not an intellectual error is involved in the belief that it is possible to improve the system of social coordination via the institutional coercion that socialism always entails. Also called for is an empirical or historical interpretative study of the different instances of socialism identifiable in the real world, an interpretation to complete and enrich the conclusions drawn from the theoretical examination. Finally, it will be necessary to embark on an analysis in the field of the theory of social ethics, with the purpose of clarifying whether or not it is ethically admissible to attack the most intimate and essential characteristic of man: his ability to act creatively. As indicated in the introduction, the subsequent chapters of this book will be devoted to addressing *in extenso* the first of these questions, and the necessary historical and ethical analyses will be left for future research.

## NOTES

1. The primary writer on entrepreneurship as conceived in this book is Israel M. Kirzner, former Professor of Economics at New York University. Kirzner authored a trilogy (*Competition and Entrepreneurship*, 1973; *Perception, Opportunity, and Profit*, 1979;

and *Discovery and the Capitalist Process*, 1985), in the first work of which he does an impeccable job of delving into and elaborating on the different aspects of the conception which his teachers, Ludwig von Mises and Friedrich A. Hayek, initially developed of entrepreneurship. In addition, Kirzner brought out a fourth book (*Discovery, Capitalism, and Distributive Justice*, 1989), which he devotes entirely to a study of the implications which his idea of entrepreneurship has in the area of social ethics. Finally, when this chapter had already been written, Kirzner published another notable book (*The Meaning of Market Process: Essays in the Development of Modern Austrian Economics*, 1992), which contains his then most recent contributions, as well as a series of previously published papers which have been taken into account here whenever possible. In Spain, apart from my own work, the following writings, among others, contain an economic analysis based on entrepreneurship: Schwartz (1981, esp. ch. 3, 107–48); Raga (1982); and Marcos de la Fuente (1983).

2. Curiously, English has incorporated the French word *entrepreneur* in its literal sense. It did so rather belatedly though, as we can see from the 1821 English translation of Jean-Baptiste Say's *Traité d'Économie Politique*, the translator, C.R. Prinsep, was obliged to awkwardly render the French term "*entrepreneur*" as "adventurer" in English, which shows that the transfer of terminology had not yet occurred. On this topic, see, for example, pp. 329 and 330 of the above English edition, republished in 1971. John Stuart Mill, for his part, lamented the lack of an English expression equivalent to the French word *entrepreneur* and stated in 1871 that "it is to be regretted that this word – undertaker – is not familiar to an English ear. French political economists enjoy a great advantage in being able to speak currently of: *les profits de l'entrepreneur*" (1976, footnote, 406). Mill refers here, almost word for word, to the title of section 3 of ch. 7 of book 2 of the 16th edition of *Traité d'Économie Politique*, by Say (1803, reprinted in Geneva: Slatkine, 1982, 368).

3. Hoselitz (1956).

4. "*Acción ardua y dificultosa que valerosamente se comienza.*"

5. For example, at the beginning of ch. 2, part 1 of Cervantes's immortal work, we read the following of Don Quixote: "But scarcely did he find himself upon the open plain, when a terrible thought struck him, one all but enough to make him abandon the *enterprise* at the very outset. It occurred to him that he had not been dubbed a knight, and that according to the law of chivalry he neither could nor ought to bear arms against any knight; and that even if he had been, still he ought, as a novice knight, to wear white armour, without a device [*empresa*] upon the shield until by his prowess he had earned one" (italics added; Cervantes, *Don Quixote*, 1885).

6. On the concept of human action and its main components, see especially Mises (1966, 11–29 and 251–6). Mises states precisely: "Every *actor* is always an *entrepreneur* and speculator" (p. 252), and "*Entrepreneur means acting man* in regard to the changes occurring in the market" (p. 254). See also Richard Taylor (1980), although he fails to emphasize as he should the fact that human action in essence consists of apprehending or discovering new ends and means, more than it does efficiently allocating given means to pre-established ends. Tadeusz Kotarbinski (1965) takes the same error even further.

7. In this sense, to define economics as "the science which studies human action influenced by scarcity" (García Villarejo and Salinas Sánchez, 1985, 25) is a clear pleonasm, since all human action presupposes scarcity. As Mises eloquently puts it (1966, 93), "Where man is not restrained by the insufficient quantity of things available, there is no need for any action".

8. Later it will be explained that the information or knowledge most relevant to human action is very difficult to articulate and is generally of a *tacit*, rather than an explicit, nature.

9. The *plan* is the prospective mental picture that the actor conjures up of the different stages, elements and circumstances which may have a bearing on his action. Therefore, the plan consists of a personal arrangement of the practical information the actor possesses and progressively discovers within the context of each action. In this sense, as the

actor generates new information, each action entails a continuous process of individual or personal planning. Central planning is different, and as we shall see, serves the need of the governing body in a socialist system to organize, in a manner as official and coordinated as possible, the means it can make coercive use of to achieve its proposed goal. Central planning fails because the authorities are incapable of obtaining the necessary practical information. Hence, the issue is not whether to plan or not; on the contrary, assuming that *planning* is essential to all human action, the question is who should plan, whether the individual actor, who is the only one who possesses the necessary practical information, or an unrelated, coercive body which lacks this information. See Hayek (1978c, 232–46). Different types of planning can also be categorized as integral, partial, indicative, or individual, and all, with the exception of individual planning, pose an epistemological contradiction which cannot be eliminated, and which we shall call "the paradox of planning" (see, in Chapter 3, note 11 and Section 6, item 3 under "Discoordination and Social Disorder").

10. According to Saint Thomas Aquinas, "voluntatis autem motivum et obiectum est finis" (that is, "the end is the cause and the object of the will"). *Summa Theologiae*, pt. 1–2, ques. 7, art. 4, Vol. 4 (1954, 301).

11. On the idea that only a subjective, practical and dynamic concept of time is applicable to the field of human action and economic science, see O'Driscoll and Rizzo (1985, ch. 4, 52–70). This conception of time had already been advanced by Henri Bergson, for whom "La durée toute pure est la forme que prend la succession de nos états de conscience quand notre moi se laisse vivre, quand il s'abstient d'établir une séparation entre l'état présent et les états antérieurs" ("Essai sur les Donnés Inmédiates de la Conscience" in Bergson, 1959, 67).

12. Mises (1966, 110–18). The following table reflects the chief differences which, according to Mises, exist between the concepts of probability applicable to the field of natural science and those applicable to the field of human action:

| The Field of Natural Science | The Field of Human Action |
|---|---|
| 1. *Class probability*: The behavior of the class is known or knowable, while the behavior of its individual elements is not | 1. *"Probability"* of a unique case or event: class does not exist, and while some of the factors which affect the unique event are known, others are not. Action itself brings about or creates the event |
| 2. A situation of *insurable risk* exists for the whole class | 2. Permanent inerradicable *uncertainty* exists, given the creative nature of human action. Uncertainty is not insurable |
| 3. Probability can be expressed in *mathematical terms* | 3. Probability cannot be expressed in *mathematical terms* |
| 4. Probability is gauged through logic and *empirical research*. Bayes's theorem makes it possible to estimate the probability of class as new information appears | 4. Probability is discovered through insight ("understanding") and *entrepreneurial estimation*. Each new bit of information modifies *ex novo* the entire map of beliefs and expectations (concept of surprise) |
| 5. An object of research to the natural *scientist* | 5. A concept typically used by the *actor–entrepreneur* and by the historian |

13. "Surprise is that dislocation and subversion of received thoughts, which springs from an actual experience outside of what has been judged fully possible, or else an experience of a character which has never been imagined and thus never assessed as either possible or impossible; a *counter-expected* or else an *unexpected* event" (Shackle, 1972, 422). Anglo-

Saxons use the term "serendipity" to describe the typically entrepreneurial capacity for recognizing opportunities which crop up by surprise, without being deliberately sought. The word derives etymologically from the Arab term "*sarandib*", as Sri Lanka (also previously Ceylon) was formerly known, and Horace Walpole gave the word its current meaning. Walpole first used the term in the eighteenth century and drew his inspiration from the fortuitous discoveries often made by the heroes of "The Three Princes of Serendip", a story of Persian origin. See the letter from Horace Walpole to Mann dated January 28, 1754, in which Walpole points out that the heroes of this story "were always making discoveries, by accidents and sagacity, of things they were not in quest of". He concludes, "this discovery, indeed, is almost of that kind which I call Serendipity". See the *Oxford English Dictionary*, 2nd edn (Oxford: Clarendon Press, 1983, 15: 5). Gregorio Marañón refers to the same idea when he states: "The creation of a genius differs from one of ordinary men in that what he *creates* is something *unexpected* and *surprising*" (1971b, 421).

14. See Buchanan and Thirlby (1981, esp. 14 and 15).
15. "Profit, in a broader sense, is the gain derived from action; it is the increase in satisfaction (decrease in uneasiness) brought about; it is the difference between the higher value attached to the result attained and the lower value attached to the sacrifices made for its attainment; it is, in other words, yield minus cost. To make profit is invariably the aim sought by any action" (Mises, 1966, 289). In Mises's view, losses sustained by a company reveal that it is making unsuitable use of scarce resources which are more urgently needed in other lines of production. John Paul II finally appears to have understood this idea perfectly. He states: "When a firm makes a profit, this means that productive factors have been properly employed and corresponding human needs have been duly satisfied" (John Paul II, 1991, ch. 4, section 35).
16. Therefore, economics is not a theory on choice or decision making (which is, *ex ante*, always rational by definition), but on the social processes of creativity and coordination which, regardless of the rational nature of all decisions involved in them, can be well or poorly adjusted, depending upon the awareness the different actors show in their exercise of entrepreneurship. See Kirzner (1992, 201–8). Furthermore, it must be stressed that the essentially *subjective* character of the components of human action (ends, means and costs) is precisely what gives economics, in a sense only apparently paradoxical, complete objectivity, in that it is a theoretical science with conclusions that are applicable to any sort of action (praxeology).
17. Mises (1966, 19–22). Mises makes an unnecessary concession atypical of him when he asserts that human action will continue to be an ultimate given until it is discovered how the natural outside world determines human thoughts. I not only agree with Hayek that it is impossible for the human mind to come to explain itself (1952 [1976], 184–91), but also maintain that all determinists fall into an insoluble logical contradiction: as the knowledge they aspire to obtain of how the outside world determines thought is itself determined, then according to their own criteria, it could not be reliable. See Rothbard (1980, 5–10).
18. That is, neither the law of marginal utility nor that of time preference is an empirical or psychological law; instead, both are logical implications of the fundamental concept of human action. According to Mises, "the Law of Marginal Utility is already implied in the category of action" and "time preference is a categorical requisite of human action" (1966, 124 and 484).
19. Kirzner (1973, 65 and 69).
20. "*La vista or mirada muy aguda y que alcanza mucho.*"
21. "Acting man looks, as it were, with the eyes of a historian into the future" (Mises, 1966, 58).
22. Saint Thomas Aquinas defines particular circumstances as "accidentia individualia humanorum actuum" (that is, the individual accidents of human acts), and he affirms that, besides time and place, the most significant of these particular circumstances is the end the actor seeks to accomplish ("principalissima est omnium circunstantiarum

illa quae attingit actuum ex parte finis"). See *Summa Theologiae*, pt. 1–2, ques. 7, art. 1 and 2, Vol. 4 (1954, 293–4, 301). Furthermore, credit goes to Michael Oakeshott for drawing the distinction between "practical knowledge" and "scientific knowledge" (see *Rationalism in Politics*, 1962). This book has been republished in an expanded version entitled *Rationalism in Politics and Other Essays* (1991; see esp. pp. 12 and 15). See also Oakeshott's *On Human Conduct* (1975 [1991], 23–5, 36, 78–9, 119–21). Oakeshott's distinction parallels the one Hayek notes between "dispersed knowledge" and "centralized knowledge", the one Michael Polanyi emphasizes between "tacit knowledge" and "articulate knowledge", and the aforementioned one Mises makes between knowledge of "unique events" and knowledge of the behavior of an entire "class of phenomena". The following table summarizes the various approaches of these four authors to the two different basic types of knowledge:

Two Different Types of
KNOWLEDGE

|  | Type A | Type B |
|---|---|---|
| Oakeshott | Practical (Traditional) | Scientific (or Technical) |
| Hayek | Dispersed | Centralized |
| Polanyi | Tacit | Articulate |
| Mises | of "Unique Events" | of "Classes" |

ECONOMICS
(Type B knowledge on type A knowledge)

The relationship between the two sorts of knowledge is complex and has been little studied. All scientific knowledge (type B) rests on a foundation of tacit knowledge that cannot be expressed in words (type A). Moreover, scientific and technical advances (type B) promptly result in new, more productive and powerful practical knowledge (type A). Likewise, economics amounts to type B (scientific) knowledge of the processes of creation and transmission of practical knowledge (type A). Now it is clear why Hayek maintains that the main risk in economics as a science lies in the danger that, as it consists of theorizing about type A knowledge, people could come to believe that those who practice it ("economic scientists") are somehow capable of gaining access to the specific content of type A practical knowledge. Scientists could even go so far as to completely disregard the specific content of practical knowledge, as has been so rightly criticized by Oakeshott, for whom the most dangerous, exaggerated and erroneous version of rationalism would consist of "the assertion that what I have called practical knowledge is not knowledge at all, the assertion that, properly speaking, there is no knowledge which is not technical knowledge" (Oakeshott, 1991, 15).

23. See especially Hayek's seminal articles, "Economics and knowledge" (1937) and "The use of knowledge in society" (1945), which appear in the book *Individualism and Economic Order* (1972). It is necessary to point out that these two articles of Hayek's are among the most important in economics. Nevertheless, particularly the first one reveals that when it was written a certain confusion still existed in the mind of its author as to the nature of economics as a science. Indeed, it is one thing to maintain that economics basically studies the processes involved in the transmission of practical information, the concrete content of which depends on the circumstances specific to each point in time and to each place, and it is quite another to suggest, as Hayek appears to mistakenly do

in some places, that economics is therefore a science with a certain empirical content. Quite the opposite is true: the fact that the scientist can never gain access to the dispersed practical information those observed possess is precisely what makes economics essentially and inevitably a theoretical, rather than empirical, science. It is a science which studies the form but not the specific content of the entrepreneurial processes by which practical information is created and transmitted (processes which, as an object of estimation and research, correspond to the historian or the entrepreneur, depending upon whether the past or the future is of interest). Kirzner, in his article, "Hayek, knowledge and market processes" (in Kirzner, 1979, 13–33), makes the same critical observation of Hayek from a slightly different perspective.

24. See Thomas Sowell (1980, 3–44). We should mention, however, that in our opinion, Sowell is still heavily influenced by the neoclassical conception of equilibrium and has not yet properly understood the role of entrepreneurship. On this topic, see Kirzner, "Prices, the communication of knowledge and the discovery process" (1984).

25. Without doubt, when he wrote the following, Adam Smith was aware that practical knowledge is basically diffuse or dispersed knowledge: "What is the species of domestick industry which his capital can employ, and of which the produce is likely to be of the greatest value, *every individual, it is evident, can, in his local situation, judge much better than any statesman or lawgiver can do for him*" (italics added). However, Smith failed to express the idea with total clarity (each individual not only knows "much better," but is the *only one* perfectly familiar with his own particular circumstances). Furthermore, Smith was unable to carry his idea to its logical conclusion with respect to the impossibility of safely entrusting a central authority with all human affairs. (Smith believed that any statesman who attempted to assume such responsibility would "load himself with a most unnecessary attention", though he would not face a logical impossibility.) See Smith, *An Inquiry into the Nature and Causes of the Wealth of Nations* (1981, 1: 456, para. 10). It is very difficult to graphically illustrate the processes by which practical and dispersed information is transmitted, and these processes are depicted here using the stick figures from the text.

26. This distinction has become common since Gilbert Ryle drew it back in 1949 in his article, "Knowing how and knowing that" (1949).

27. Polanyi, *The Study of Man* (1959, 24–5). All economics scholars should read this little book, which is a true jewel of social science. Other important works by Polanyi include *The Logic of Liberty* (1951), *Personal Knowledge* (1958), and *Knowing and Being* (1969a). Michael Polanyi (1891–1976) – the brother of Karl Polanyi (1886–1964) – was a man of very broad horizons, and he carried out his scientific work in the fields of chemistry, philosophy, politics, sociology and economics. The bicycle example is found on page 144 of *Knowing and Being*. Polanyi traces the idea of a limited capacity to articulate human thought back to certain contributions originally made in the field of mathematics, and especially to the work of Kurt Gödel. See *Personal Knowledge*, 259. For his part, Hayek affirms that "Gödel's theorem is but a special case of a more general principle applying to all conscious and particularly all rational processes, namely the principle that among their determinants there must always be some rules which cannot be stated or even be conscious" ("Rules, perception and intelligibility", in Hayek, 1969, 62). Gödel develops his theorem in "Über formal unentscheidbare Sätze der *Principia Mathematica* und verwandter Systeme I" (1931).

28. In the same line of thought, great satisfaction is to be derived from reading Roger Penrose's book, *The Emperor's New Mind: Concerning Computers, Minds and the Laws of Physics* (1989), in which he explains in detail, in several instances, how very important thought which cannot be expressed in words is even for the most illustrious scientific minds (for example, see pp. 423–5). Gregorio Marañón, the brilliant Spanish doctor and writer, presented this idea years ago when relating a private conversation he had with Bergson shortly before his death, a conversation in which the French thinker stated: "I am sure that Cajal's great discoveries were no more than the objective verification *of facts that his brain had foreseen* as actual realities" (1971a, 7: 331). For his part,

K. Lorenz asserts that "No important scientific fact has ever been 'proved' that has not previously been simply and immediately seen by intuitive *Gestalt* perception" (see "The role of Gestalt perception in animal and human behaviours", in *Aspects of Form*, 1951, 176).

29. Lavoie (1985c). Lavoie adds that if costs could be established objectively, scientifically and universally, decision making in economic life could be limited to obedience to a set of wholly articulated and specific rules. However, given that costs are subjective and can only be known by the actor in the context of each specific action, the practice of entrepreneurship cannot be articulated in detail or replaced by any objective scientific criterion (ibid., 103–4).

30. According to Saint Thomas Aquinas, "creare est aliquid ex nihilo facere" (that is, to create is to make something out of nothing). *Summa Theologiae*, pt. 1, ques. 45, art. 1 and following, Vol. 2 (1948, 740). I cannot agree with the Thomist thesis that only God is capable of creating, since human beings also create constantly whenever they exercise entrepreneurship. Aquinas uses the term *ex nihilo* in an excessively materialistic sense, whereas I consider that *ex nihilo* creation takes place each time someone perceives or realizes something he had not even conceived of before (ibid., 756). Although he sometimes confuses the concept of human action with that of "work" (see also note 32), Pope John Paul II appears to favor my interpretation in his encyclical *Laborem Exercens*, when he states that man "reflects the very action of the Creator of the universe" (nos 4 and 25, 1981).

31. I believe that all human action has an essentially creative component and that no basis exists for distinguishing between entrepreneurial creativity in the economic realm and creativity in other human spheres (artistic, social and so on). Robert Nozick mistakenly draws just such a distinction, as he fails to realize that the essence of creativity is the same in all areas, and that the concept and characteristics of entrepreneurship, both of which we are analyzing, apply to all human action, regardless of the type (Nozick, 1989, 40).

32. The fact that entrepreneurship is distinctly creative and that therefore pure entrepreneurial profits arise from nothing can lead us to the following theological digression: if we accept for the sake of argument that a Supreme Being exists, one who created all things from nothing, then when we suppose entrepreneurship to be an *ex nihilo* creation of pure entrepreneurial profits, it seems clear that man resembles God precisely when man exercises pure entrepreneurship! This means that man, more than *homo sapiens*, is *homo agens* or *homo empresario*, and that more than when he thinks, he resembles God when he acts, that is, when he conceives and discovers new ends and means. We could even construct an entire theory of happiness, a theory which would suggest that man is happiest when he resembles his Creator. In other words, the cause of the greatest happiness in man would be to recognize and reach his objectives (which implies action and the exercise of entrepreneurship). Nevertheless, at times we undoubtedly commit multiple entrepreneurial errors, above all with respect to the choice of ends to pursue. (Fortunately, man is not lost but has certain guides, such as ethics and religion, to help him in this area.) I hope this digression will not appear to Professor Kirzner, a man of profound religious convictions, as "a sacrilegious use of theological metaphor" (Kirzner, 1989, 40). As mentioned in note 30, Pope John Paul II, in his encyclical *Laborem Exercens*, appears to lean toward our interpretation when he affirms that man imitates and "reflects the very action of the Creator of the universe", that he truly cooperates with God and participates in the divine plan and in the work of the Creator. Nevertheless, John Paul II sometimes seems to confuse the concept of "human action" with that of "work", thus introducing a nonexistent dichotomy of human actions (those related to "work" *stricto sensu* and those related to "capital"). The true social issue is not the contradiction between "work" and "capital", but the question of whether it is legitimate to systematically commit institutional aggression or violence against the creative capacity man exercises when he acts, and the matter of what type of rules and laws should govern all action. Moreover, the author of the encyclical fails to realize that

if he is referring to human action in general, it makes no sense to speak (as he does in no. 19) of the right to receive "just remuneration", since every actor has the right, as we shall see, to the complete outcome (whether profit or loss) of his entrepreneurial creativity or action; and if the author is referring to work in a strict sense, as a factor of production, any creative possibility related to it is theoretically eradicated. In preparing these reflections, of great use was an article by Fernando Moreno entitled "El Trabajo según Juan Pablo II" (1988). The conception John Paul II has of entrepreneurial ability or creative human action as a decisive factor in life in society, or at least his language and articulation on the topic, improved notably in his later encyclical, *Centesimus Annus*, where he expressly states that the determining factor is "man himself, that is, his *knowledge*", both scientific knowledge and practical knowledge (that necessary to "perceive the needs of others and to satisfy them"). These types of knowledge enable humans to "express their creativity and develop their potential", as well as to enter that "network of knowledge and intercommunication" which constitutes the market and society. John Paul II concludes: "The role of disciplined and *creative* human work [I prefer 'human action'] and, as an essential part of that work, [of] *initiative* and *entrepreneurial* ability becomes increasingly evident and decisive" (John Paul II, 1991, chap. 4, sections 31, 32 and 33). Without a doubt, the encyclical *Centesimus Annus* reveals that the Supreme Pontiff has enormously modernized his conception of economics and has taken a large qualitative step forward from a scientific standpoint, thus rendering outdated much of the Church's former social doctrine. His updated perspective even surpasses broad sectors within economic science itself, groups which remain anchored to mechanicism and have not been able to introduce into their "models" the essentially creative and dynamic nature of entrepreneurship. See Novak (1993).

33. It will be seen when we cover arbitration and speculation that human beings learn through entrepreneurship to condition their behavior even upon the circumstances and needs of future people not yet born (*intertemporal coordination*). Furthermore, this process could not be reproduced even if human beings, either obeying the coercive orders of a benevolent dictator or through their own philanthropic desire to help humanity, were to try to deliberately adjust all situations of social discoordination, yet refrain from seeking and taking advantage of any profit or gain. In fact, in the absence of gain or profit to serve as an incentive, the practical information necessary for people to act and coordinate situations of social maladjustment does not even appear. (This is independent of an actor's possible decision to use his entrepreneurial profit for charitable purposes, once it has been sought and obtained.) A society whose members dedicated most of their time to "deliberately helping their fellow man" and not to exercising entrepreneurship would be a tribal, precapitalist society, one incapable of supporting a fraction of the population that inhabits the world today. Thus, it is theoretically impossible for the principles of "solidarity" and altruism to serve human beings as a guide for action in an order which, like the social one, rests on a series of abstract relationships with multiple other individuals whom one can never come to know and about whom one only perceives dispersed information and signs in the form of prices, substantive or material rules, and institutions. The principles of solidarity and altruism are therefore tribal atavisms which can only be applied in small primary groups and between a very limited number of participants, who share an intimate knowledge of each other's personal circumstances. Although nothing can be said against the activities many people engage in within society to satisfy their more or less atavistic or instinctive need to appear supportive or altruistic toward their "fellow man", we can categorically affirm that not only is it theoretically impossible to coercively organize society based on the principles of solidarity and altruism, but such an attempt would do away with civilization as we now know it and eliminate fellow men, both close and distant, such that very few potential recipients of help would remain. See Hayek (1988, 13).

34. The term "calculation" derives etymologically from the Latin expression *calx-calcis*, the meanings of which include the lime chalk which was used in Greek and Roman

abacuses. A more precise definition of economic calculation appears ahead (in the section entitled "Law, Money and Economic Calculation").

35. Kirzner maintains that entrepreneurship permits the discovery and elimination of the "errors" which occur in society and go unnoticed. However, we find this conception of error less than completely satisfactory, since it implies a judgment from the position of a hypothetical omniscient being familiar with all of the situations of maladjustment that arise in society. From our point of view, it only makes sense to speak of error in subjective terms; in other words, whenever the actor realizes, *a posteriori*, that he should not have striven for a certain goal, or that he should not have used certain means, since by acting he has incurred costs. He has forgone the achievement of ends of higher value to him than those he has accomplished (that is, he has sustained entrepreneurial losses). Moreover, we must remember that the elimination of an error in Kirzner's objectivist sense is generally perceived by an actor as a fortunate, wise decision which leads to significant gains or entrepreneurial profits. "Economics and error", in Kirzner (1979, 120–37).

36. "The present qua duration is the continuation of the conditions and opportunities given for acting. Every kind of action requires special conditions to which it must be adjusted with regard to the aims sought. The concept of present is therefore different for various fields of actions" (Mises, 1966, 101).

37. Hayek (1988, 12).

38. "We have now run over the three fundamental laws of nature, *that of the stability of possession, of its transference by consent*, and *of the performance of promises*. 'Tis on the strict observance of those three laws, that the peace and security of human society entirely depend; nor is there any possibility of establishing a good correspondence among men, where these are neglected. Society is absolutely necessary for the well-being of men; and these are as necessary to the support of society" (Hume, 1981, bk. 3, pt. 2, sec. 6, 526).

39. An institution is considered to be any repetitive pattern, rule, or model of conduct, regardless of its sphere – linguistic, economic, legal and so on.

40. Menger (1883). The term Menger uses to express the "unintended consequences of individual actions" is *Unbeabsichtigte Resultante*. Specifically, Menger states that the social phenomenon is characterized by the fact that it arises as "die unbeabsichtigte Resultante individueller, d.i. individuellen Interessen verfolgender Bestrebungen der Volksglieder . . . die unbeabsichtigte soziale Resultante individuell teleologischer Faktoren" (p. 182). See Lawrence H. White's prologue to the English edition of Menger's book, *Investigations into the Method of the Social Sciences with Special Reference to Economics* (1985, vii–viii, 158, where we find page 182 of the original German edition translated into English). See also "The results of human action but not of human design", in Hayek (1969, 96–105). Sometimes Adam Ferguson is recognized as the first to explicitly refer to this spontaneous type of social phenomena. In fact, on page 187 of his *An Essay on the History of Civil Society* (1767), we read: "Nations stumble upon establishments, which are indeed the result of human action, but not the execution of any human design". He adds the famous phrase attributed by Cardinal de Retz to Oliver Cromwell, according to whom man never reaches greater heights than when he does not know where he is going ("on ne montait jamais si haut que quand on ne sait pas où l'on va"). However, Ferguson is following a much older tradition, which through Montesquieu, Bernard de Mandeville, and the sixteenth-century Spanish scholastics, dates back even to an entire school of classical Roman and Greek thought, as will be seen at the beginning of Chapter 4.

41. Therefore, we cannot agree with Saint Thomas Aquinas's concept of the law, which he defines as "rationis ordinatio ad bonum commune, ab eo qui curam communitatis habet promulgata" (*Summa Theologiae*, pt. 1–2, ques. 90, art. 4, Vol. 6 (1955, 42) and thus considers it a deliberate product of human reasoning. In this sense, Aquinas is a forerunner of the "false rationalism" Hayek criticizes, as Saint Thomas supposes that through human reason, man can know much more than he is capable of knowing. This

extreme rationalism would culminate in the French Revolution, the triumph of utilitarianism, and, in the field of law, Kelsenian positivism and the views of A.F.J. Thiebaut. See "Kinds of rationalism", in Hayek (1969, ch. 5, 82–96). Hayek also criticized the fact that Aristotle, though he did not go to the socialist extremes Plato did, was never able to fully understand the existence of spontaneous social orders or the essential idea of evolution (1988, 45–7), and hence he sparked the emergence of a naively scientific trend which has encumbered or rendered useless much of the social science developed up to our time.

42. In fact, in his theory on the origin of money, Menger refers to money as one of the most important and paradigmatic illustrations of his theory on the emergence, development and spontaneous evolution of social institutions. See pages 152 and following of the English edition of *Untersuchungen* (1883), cited in note 40.

Another institution of economic interest and an example of economic organization is the entity unfortunately referred to in Spanish as an *empresa*, when, following the Anglo-Saxon example, it should be called simply a *firma* (firm), in order to avoid confusion between the concept of human action or entrepreneurship and the concept of a firm, which is just another institution, of relative importance, and which emerges in the market because actors find that a certain amount of organization often helps to promote their interests. There seems to be an entire school of economic thought which tends to exaggerate the importance of firms or business enterprises as an object of research in economics. The firm is merely one of many institutions which arise from human interaction, and one can only understand its emergence and evolution from the standpoint of the theory of entrepreneurship put forward here. Often, the theorists of the firm or business enterprise not only disguise, confuse and overlook the subjective nature of entrepreneurship, but they also tend to objectify the field of economic research and inappropriately limit it to the firm. See, for example, Coase (1937 [1988]). See also Alchian (1969). A detailed critique of this school of thought appears in Kirzner (1973, 52ff.). See also Chapter 4, note 50.

43. According to Mises, "Economic calculation is either an estimate of the expected outcome of future action or the establishment of the outcome of past action" (1966, 210, 198–231). Rothbard does not seem to understand that economic calculation always poses a problem of the creation and transmission of dispersed, exclusive information without which such an estimate cannot be made. The observations about the economic calculation controversy which appear in his work, *Ludwig von Mises: Scholar, Creator and Hero* (1988, ch. 5, 35–46), make this clear. Rothbard's position seems to derive from an almost obsessive desire to emphasize Mises and Hayek's differences more than their similarities. Though it is true, as Rothbard points out, that Hayek's view has at times been interpreted too strictly, as if he merely referred to a problem arising from the dispersed nature of existing knowledge, and as if uncertainty and the future generation of knowledge, issues Mises particularly stressed, posed no difficulty, both viewpoints can be easily combined, since they are closely related. In the next chapter, these two points of view will be joined and they will be presented as, respectively, the *static* argument and the *dynamic* argument against the possibility of socialist economic calculation. See especially Rothbard (1991, 66) and Salerno (1990a, 36–48, and 1990b). See also the end of note 16, Chapter 4.

44. According to *Merriam-Webster's Collegiate Dictionary* (11th edn), an incentive is "something that incites or has a tendency to incite to determination or action", a definition which coincides with the one we have given for profit or gain. The subjective profit or gain an actor attempts to acquire with a human action is precisely the incentive or stimulus that motivates him to act. In principle, and granting that this is not the appropriate place to explain in greater depth the psychic essence of entrepreneurship, the more clearly an actor visualizes his objective, and the greater the psychic intensity with which he pursues it, the stronger will be the influx of creative ideas relevant to achieving the objective, and the more easily the actor will distinguish and reject the mire of irrelevant information which could distract him. See also, in Chapter 7, the

section entitled, "Henry Douglas Dickinson's Book, *The Economics of Socialism*". In this section, two different meanings of the term "incentive" are explained: a static and a dynamic meaning.

45. For many, many years, students in the countries of Eastern Europe, especially in the former Soviet Union, spent thousands upon thousands of hours copying their notes by hand from library reference books, without being aware that photocopiers could have lightened or completely eliminated this work. Only when they discovered the widespread use of these machines in the West and their direct application to the field of study and research, among others, did they begin to feel the need for photocopiers and to demand their availability. Such cases are more obvious in comparatively more controlled societies than in those of western countries. Nevertheless, we must not become self-satisfied or commit the error of considering western societies free of similar cases, since the lack of other, systematically less restrictive societies to serve us as a comparative model keeps us from being aware of how much is lost in the West as a result of interventionism.

46. Samuel Bailey stated that every action requires "minute knowledge of a thousand particulars *which will be learnt by nobody but him who has an interest in knowing them*" (1840: 3). And even earlier, Turgot (1844) explained the same idea in 1759. See also, in Chapter 3, the section entitled, "Socialism as the 'Opium of the People'".

47. León Felipe, in one of his most inspired moments, said:

| | |
|---|---|
| *Nadie fue ayer* | No one traveled yesterday |
| *ni va hoy* | Nor travels today |
| *ni irá mañana* | Nor will travel tomorrow |
| *hacia Dios* | Toward God |
| *por este mismo camino que yo voy.* | By this same path I'm travelling. |
| | |
| *Para cada hombre* | For each man |
| *guarda un rayo nuevo de luz el sol* | The sun saves a new ray of light |
| *y un camino virgen Dios.* | And God a virgin path. |

(León Felipe, prologue to *Obras Completas*, 1963: 25).

48. "Each living person, even the most humble, creates merely by being alive" (Marañón, 1971b, 7: 421).

49. The term "competition" derives etymologically from the Latin word *cumpetitio* (the concurrence of multiple requests for the same thing, which must be allotted to an owner), which comprises two parts: *cum*, with; and *petere*, to request, attack, seek. *Merriam-Webster's Collegiate Dictionary* (11th edn) defines *competition* as "a contest between rivals". Thus, competition consists of a dynamic process of rivalry, and not the so-called "model of perfect competition", in which multiple suppliers produce the same thing and all sell it at the same price; that is, a situation in which, paradoxically, no one competes. See Huerta de Soto (1990b, 36).

50. See Kirzner (1973, 12–13, and 1985, 130–31). Kirzner emphasizes that all that is necessary to guarantee the competitiveness of the social process is freedom of entry; that is, the absence in all social areas of legal or institutional restrictions on the free exercise of entrepreneurship.

51. Therefore, the entrepreneurial process gives rise to a sort of continuous social "Big Bang" which permits the boundless growth of knowledge. According to Frank J. Tipler, Professor of Mathematics and Physics at Tulane University, the limit to the expansion of knowledge on earth is $10^{64}$ bits (and thus it would be possible to multiply by 100 billion the physical limits to growth which have been considered up to now), and it can be mathematically demonstrated that a human civilization based in space could expand its knowledge, wealth, and population without limit. Tipler concludes: "Much nonsense has been written on the physical limits to economic growth by physicists who are ignorant of economics. A correct analysis of the physical limits to growth is possible

*Entrepreneurship* 47

only *if one appreciates Hayek's insight that what the economic system produces is not material things, but immaterial knowledge*" (Tipler, 1988–89, 4–5). See also the remarkable book by Barrow and Tipler, *The Anthropic Cosmological Principle* (1986, esp. 658–77).

52. In the figure below, we encounter a basic situation like that described in the text. Indeed, A can undertake his action because the entrepreneurship C exercises informs A that a sufficient quantity of resource R is available. Subsequently, in view of the action A performs, it occurs to a fourth subject, D, that he could in turn pursue objective Z if he had resource S, which he does not know where to find, but which is available to agent E elsewhere in the market. Therefore, as a result of the information generated in the first entrepreneurial act, a new maladjustment between D and E emerges and creates a new profit opportunity which awaits discovery and use by someone. And so the process continues.

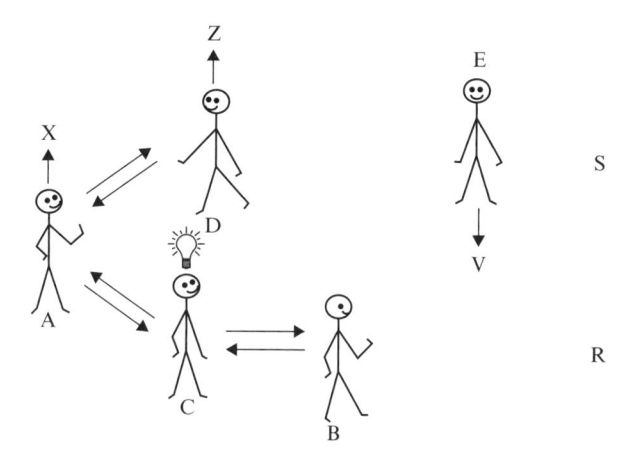

53. On the "law of the division of labor" and David Ricardo's more general "law of association", see the remarks Mises makes in his *Human Action* (1966, 157–65). See also Mises (1940 [1980], 126–33). (Here Mises uses the expression "Vergesellschaftungsgesetz" to refer to the "law of association".) As Robbins states (1963, 141), it is to Mises's credit that he recognized Ricardo's "law of comparative costs" as merely a particular case within a much broader law, the "law of association", which explains how cooperation between the most highly skilled and the least skilled benefits both, whenever each person makes the entrepreneurial discovery that he profits by specializing in that activity at which he has a greater relative comparative advantage. Nevertheless, not even here does Mises manage to weed out all of the objectivist remains which from the time of Adam Smith have pervaded the theory of the law of the division of labor. Not until page 709 of his *Human Action* does he expressly mention the intellectual division of labor, which in the text we have termed the "division of knowledge" or of information.

54. Note that it is nearly impossible for us to graphically illustrate even the salient characteristics of the social process driven by entrepreneurship, a process Hayek believes may be the most complex structure in the universe. ("The extended order is probably the most complex structure in the universe", 1988, 127.) This "extensive order of social cooperation", which has been described in this chapter, is at the same time the quintessence of a spontaneous, evolutionary, abstract and unplanned order. Hayek refers to it as *Cosmos* and contrasts it with a deliberate, constructivist, or organized order (*taxis*) (1973, Vol. 1, ch. 2, 35–55).

55. "We have become civilised by the increase of our numbers just as civilisation made that increase possible: we can be few and savage, or many and civilised. If reduced to its population of ten thousand years ago, mankind could not preserve civilisation. Indeed, even if knowledge already gained were preserved in libraries, men could make little use of it without numbers sufficient to fill the jobs demanded for extensive specialisation and division of labor. All knowledge available in books would not save ten thousand people spared somewhere after an atomic holocaust from having to return to a life of hunters and gatherers" (Hayek, 1988, 133). Therefore, the process, which we have described as a marvelous and surprising social "big bang", is based on an extremely important feedback phenomenon: it makes a growing population sustainable, the members of which, in turn, feed and provide even more vigorous impetus for the future development and spread of the social *big bang*, and so the process continues. Thus, after thousands of years, we have finally been able to explain in rational and scientific terms this biblical commandment in *Genesis* (1: 28 New International Version): "Be fruitful and increase in number; fill the earth and subdue it".
56. Robbins (1972, 16). Robbins, in his acknowledgment of Mises in the prologue to this book, reveals his poor and confused assimilation of Mises's teachings.
57. As a result, Mises sees economics as part of a much broader and more general science, a general theory of human action or entrepreneurship he calls "praxeology". See part one of *Human Action* (1966, 11–200). For his part, Hayek states that if for the new science which emerges as we broaden our view of economics "a name is needed the term 'praxeological' sciences . . . now clearly defined and extensively used by L.v. Mises would appear to be most appropriate" (1952, 209).
58. Kirzner (1989, 36ff.). Kirzner also thoroughly criticizes failed attempts to confine the concept of entrepreneurship to the methodological framework of equilibrium and the neoclassical paradigm.
59. In a broad sense, the concepts of "society" and "market" coincide, and thus the above definition of "society" fully applies to the market. Moreover, the *Diccionario* of the Real Academia Española defines "market" as "a gathering of people" ("*concurrencia de gente*"), and hence it appears that the Real Academia shares this point of view and considers the terms "society" and "market" to be synonymous.
60. Economic science should center precisely on the study of this social process as described above. Hayek feels that the essential purpose of economics is to analyze how the spontaneous social order enables us to take advantage of an enormous volume of practical information which is not available anywhere in a consolidated form, but rather is dispersed throughout the minds of millions of individuals. He maintains that the object of economics is to study this dynamic process by which information is created and transmitted, a process which entrepreneurship perpetually drives and which tends to adjust and coordinate individual plans, and thereby makes life in society possible. This and this alone constitutes the fundamental economic problem, and thus Hayek is especially critical of the study of equilibrium. He deems such a focus devoid of scientific interest, since it is premised on the assumption that all information *is given* and that therefore the fundamental economic problem has already been resolved. See Hayek, "Economics and knowledge" (1937 [1972], 51) and "The use of knowledge in society" (1945 [1972], 91).

# 3. Socialism

The last chapter analyzed the concept of entrepreneurship, and this one begins with a detailed explanation of the nature of socialism and how it precludes the emergence of the coordinating tendencies necessary to life in society. Specifically, we shall study the effects socialism exerts on incentives and on the generation of information, as well as the perverse deviation it provokes in the exercise of entrepreneurship. In addition, we shall explain the sense in which socialism constitutes an intellectual error and always has the same essential nature, despite the fact that historically it has emerged in different types or forms, the main characteristics of which we shall attempt to isolate. The chapter will conclude with a critical analysis of the traditional alternative concepts of socialism.

## 1 THE DEFINITION OF SOCIALISM

We shall define "socialism" as any system of institutional aggression on the free exercise of entrepreneurship. By "aggression" or "coercion" we mean all physical violence or threats of physical violence which another person or group of people initiates and employs against the actor. As a result of this coercion, the actor, who otherwise would have freely exercised his entrepreneurship, is forced, in order to avoid greater evils, to act differently than he would have acted in other circumstances, and thus to modify his behavior and adapt it to the ends of the person or persons who are coercing him.[1] We could consider aggression, when defined in this way, to be the quintessential antihuman action. This is so because coercion keeps a person from freely exercising his entrepreneurship. In other words, as we read in the definition from the last chapter, it prevents a person from pursuing those objectives he discovers and from employing the means he deems within his reach, according to his information or knowledge, to help him achieve them. Therefore, aggression is an evil, because it precludes man from engaging in the activity which is most characteristic of him and which by its essence most intimately befits his nature.

Aggression can be of two types: systematic or institutional; or asystematic or non-institutional. This second type of coercion, which is dispersed,

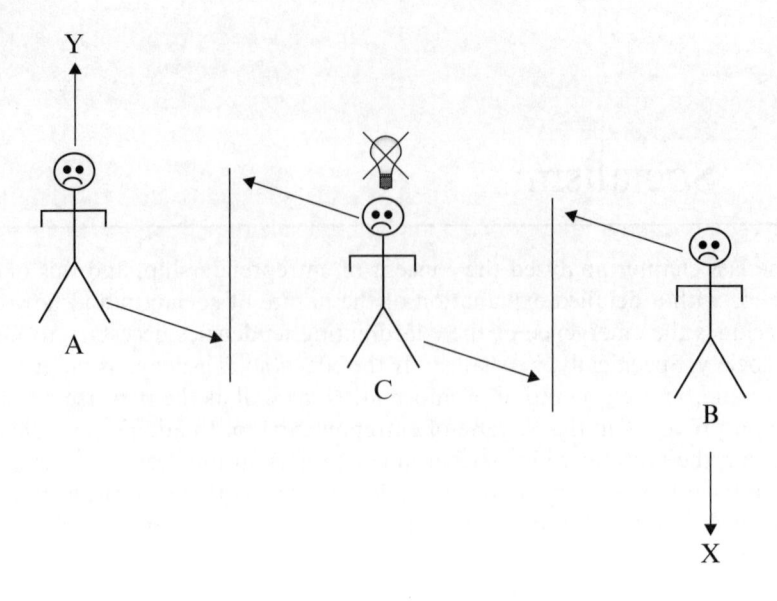

*Figure 3.1*

arbitrary and more difficult to predict, affects the exercise of entrepreneurship to the extent that the actor considers it more or less probable that within the context of a specific action he will be coerced in the exercise of his entrepreneurship by a third party, who could even wrest away by force the product of the actor's own entrepreneurial creativity. While the effects of asystematic outbreaks of aggression on the coordinated exercise of human interaction are of varying seriousness, depending on the circumstances, institutional or systematic aggression, which constitutes the core of our definition of socialism, exerts a much more harmful influence. Indeed, institutional coercion is characterized by a highly predictable, repetitive, methodical and organized nature.[2] The main consequence of this systematic aggression against entrepreneurship is that it thwarts to a high degree, and causes a perverse deviation in, the exercise of entrepreneurship in all areas of society in which such aggression is effective. Figure 3.1 reflects the situation which typically results from the systematic exercise of coercion.

Let us suppose that in Figure 3.1, the free human action of C in relation to A and B is prevented in a systematic and organized manner, via coercion, in a specific sphere of social life. We represent this situation using the vertical bars which separate C from A and B. The above systematic coercion presents a threat of serious harm and thus makes it impossible for C to discover and take advantage of the profit opportunity he would have if he could freely interact with B and A. It is very important to clearly understand that aggression not only keeps actors from grasping opportunities for profit; it precludes even the discovery of such opportunities.[3] As explained in the last chapter, the chance of making a profit acts as an incentive for the actor to discover an opportunity. Therefore, if systematic coercion restricts a certain area of social life, actors tend to adapt to this situation and take it for granted, and hence they do not even create, discover, or recognize the latent opportunities for profit. This situation is illustrated in Figure 3.1 by crossing out the bulb used to represent the creative act of pure entrepreneurial discovery.

Logically, if the aggression consists of a systematic assault on a social sphere and actors cannot exercise entrepreneurship in that area as a result, then none of the other typical effects we studied with respect to the entrepreneurial act will appear. First, new information will not be created or transmitted between actors; and second, the necessary adjustment in cases of social discoordination will not be made. (The second of the above consequences is even more worrying than the first.) Indeed, as actors will be unable to freely seize profit opportunities, they will have no incentive to recognize the situations of social maladjustment or discoordination which emerge. In short, information will not be created; it will not be transmitted among agents; and individuals will not learn to key their behavior to that of their fellow men.

Thus, we see in Figure 3.1 that the inability of C to exercise entrepreneurship keeps the system permanently discoordinated: A cannot pursue the end Y due to the lack of a resource which B has in abundance yet has no use for; and B, unaware that A exists and urgently needs the resource, squanders it. According to our analysis, we can therefore conclude that the main effect of socialism as it has been defined is to inhibit the action of the creative and coordinating forces which make life in society possible. Does this mean that proponents of socialism fight for a chaotic or discoordinated society? Quite the opposite is true. Barring rare exceptions, defenders of the socialist ideal defend it because they tacitly or explicitly believe or assume that not only will the system of social coordination not be disturbed by the institutional or systematic aggression they advocate, but that on the contrary, it will become much more effective, since the systematic coercion is to be committed by a governing body which is supposed to make assessments and possess knowledge (regarding both ends and means) quantitatively and qualitatively far superior to those possible on an individual level for the coerced actors. From this perspective, we can now complete the definition of socialism offered at the beginning of this section: socialism is any systematic or institutional coercion or aggression which restricts the free exercise of entrepreneurship in a certain social sphere and which is exercised by a governing body responsible for the necessary tasks of social coordination in this area. The following section will consider the extent to which socialism, as just defined, is or is not an intellectual error.

## 2   SOCIALISM AS AN INTELLECTUAL ERROR

In the last chapter, we saw that social life is possible because individuals, spontaneously and without realizing it, learn to tune their behavior to the needs of others. This unconscious learning process springs naturally from man's exercise of entrepreneurship. Thus, as each person interacts with others, he spontaneously initiates a process of adjustment or coordination in which new tacit, practical and dispersed information is continually created, discovered and transmitted between people. We know that socialism consists chiefly of institutional aggression against the free exercise of human action or entrepreneurship. Hence, the question socialism poses is this: can the coercive mechanism possibly instigate the process which adjusts and coordinates the behavior of different people and is essential to the functioning of life in society, and can it do so within an environment in which people constantly discover and create new practical information that permits the advancement of civilization? Socialism establishes a highly daring and ambitious ideal,[4] since it involves the belief that not only can the mechanism of social coordination and adjustment be set in motion by the governing body that applies institutional coercion in the social sphere in question, but also that this coercive procedure can even result in a more proper adjustment.

Figure 3.2 represents the concept of socialism as defined. On the "lower" level of this figure we find human beings, who possess practical knowledge or information and therefore try to freely interact with each other, even though institutional coercion precludes this interaction in certain areas. This coercion is illustrated via the vertical bars that separate the stickmen of each group of three. On the "higher" level is the governing body, which exercises institutional coercion in certain spheres of social life.[5] The vertical arrows which point up and down from the stickmen at the left and right of each group of three represent the existence of maladjusted personal plans, a typical sign of social discoordination. Such cases of discoordination cannot be discovered and eliminated through entrepreneurship, because institutional coercion has erected barriers to it. The arrows drawn from the head of the governing stickman toward each of the human beings indicated on the lower level stand for the coercive commands which embody the institutional aggression typical of socialism and which are intended to

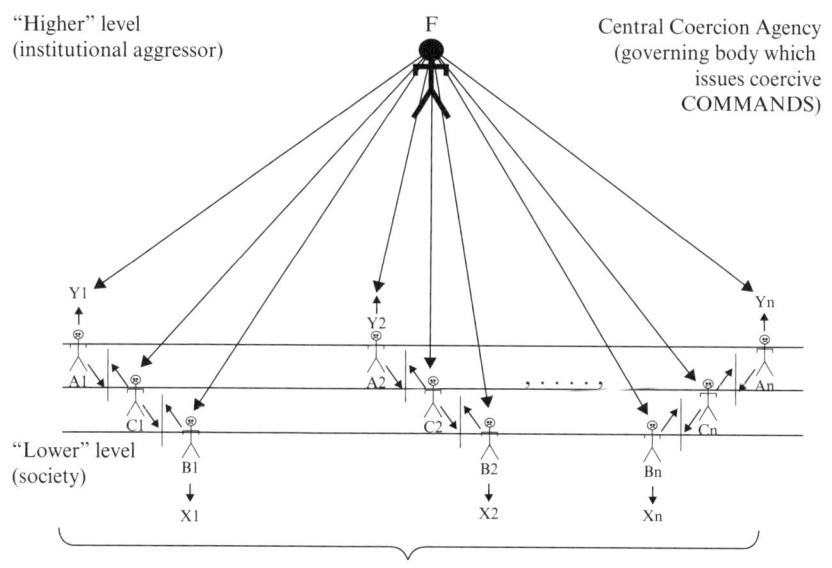

## Socialism

| "Higher" level (institutional aggressor) | F | Central Coercion Agency (governing body which issues coercive COMMANDS) |

[Diagram showing F at top connected by arrows down to multiple actors A1, A2,...,An; B1, B2,...,Bn; C1, C2,...,Cn; with Y1, Y2,...,Yn and X1, X2,...,Xn]

"Lower" level (society)

Specific sphere of society upon which institutional coercion is used

*Figure 3.2*

compel citizens to act in a coordinated manner and pursue end "F" which the governing body considers "just".

A command can be defined as any specific instruction or rule which has an explicit content and which, regardless of its formal legal appearance, forbids, orders or compels people to carry out certain actions under particular circumstances. A command is characterized by the fact that it prevents human beings from freely exercising their entrepreneurship in a given social area. Furthermore, commands are deliberate creations of the governing body which applies institutional coercion, and they are designed to force all actors to realize or pursue not their own objectives, but those of the authorities.[6]

Socialism is an intellectual error, because it is theoretically impossible for the agency in charge of applying institutional aggression to gain access to enough information to allow it to issue commands capable of coordinating society. This simple argument, which we shall study in some depth, can be developed from two distinct but complementary points of view: first, from the standpoint of the group of human beings which make up society and are coerced; and second, from the perspective of the coercive organization which systematically exercises aggression. Next, we shall analyze the problem socialism poses from each of these points of view.

## 3 THE IMPOSSIBILITY OF SOCIALISM FROM THE STANDPOINT OF SOCIETY

### The "Static" Argument

Each of the human beings who interact with each other and comprise society (the "lower" level in Figure 3.2) possesses some exclusive bits of practical and dispersed information which for the most part is tacit and thus cannot be articulated. Therefore it is logically impossible for this information to be transmitted to the governing body (the "higher" level in Figure 3.2). The total volume of all practical information perceived and managed in dispersed form and on an individual level by all people is of such magnitude that it is inconceivable that the governing body could consciously acquire it. Furthermore, and more importantly, this information is dispersed throughout the minds of all men in the form of tacit knowledge which cannot be articulated, and hence it cannot be formally expressed or explicitly transmitted to any governing agency.

We saw in the last chapter that social agents create and transmit the information important to social life in an implicit, decentralized and dispersed manner; in other words, they do so unconsciously and unintentionally. Indeed, the different agents learn to discipline their behavior in terms of others, but without explicitly realizing that they are doing so or that they are playing a key role in this learning process: they are simply aware that they are acting; that is, trying to achieve their own particular ends by employing the means they believe available to them. Therefore, the knowledge in question is only available to the human beings who act in society, and by its very nature, it cannot be explicitly transmitted to any coercive central body. As this knowledge is essential to the social coordination of the different individual behaviors which makes society possible, and because it cannot be articulated and thus cannot be transmitted to the governing body, the belief that a socialist system can work is logically absurd.[7]

### The "Dynamic" Argument

Socialism is impossible, not only because the information actors possess is by its very nature explicitly non-transmissible, but also because, from a dynamic standpoint, when people exercise entrepreneurship, that is, when they act, they constantly create and discover new information. Moreover, it is hardly possible to transmit to the governing body information or knowledge which has not yet been created, but which gradually emerges as a result of the social process itself, to the extent that this process is not assaulted.

Socialism 55

"Higher" level (institutional aggressor)

"Lower" level (society)

a) When commands do not penetrate the "capsule" – points t2 and tn – the governing body cannot obtain the practical information it needs to deliberately coordinate society

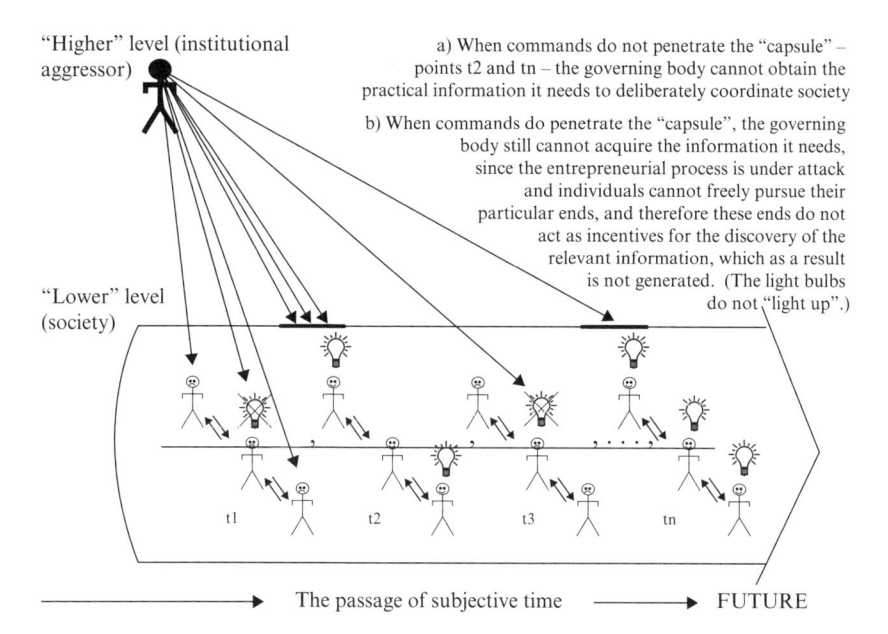

b) When commands do penetrate the "capsule", the governing body still cannot acquire the information it needs, since the entrepreneurial process is under attack and individuals cannot freely pursue their particular ends, and therefore these ends do not act as incentives for the discovery of the relevant information, which as a result is not generated. (The light bulbs do not "light up".)

⟶ The passage of subjective time ⟶ FUTURE

*Figure 3.3*

Figure 3.3 depicts the actors who create and discover new information throughout the social process. As time passes (time understood, as we saw, in the subjective or Bergsonian sense), those who exercise entrepreneurship in interaction with other people constantly recognize new profit opportunities which they attempt to seize. As a result, the information each of them possesses changes continuously. This is represented in the diagram by the different light bulbs which light up as time passes. It is clear that the governing body cannot possibly obtain the information necessary to coordinate society via commands, not only because this information is dispersed, exclusive and cannot be articulated, but also because it constantly changes and emerges *ex nihilo* as time passes and actors freely exercise entrepreneurship. In addition, it would hardly be possible to transmit to the governing body the information essential at all times to coordinate society, when this information has not yet even been generated by the entrepreneurial process itself, nor can it ever be generated if institutional coercion is applied to the process.

For example, when the day dawns with signs of a change in the weather, a farmer realizes he should alter his plans regarding the particular tasks it most behooves him to perform that day, though he cannot formally articulate the reasons behind his decision. Thus, it would not be possible for the farmer to transfer that information, a product of many years of experience and work on the farm, to a hypothetical governing agency (a ministry of agriculture in the capital, for instance) and then wait for instructions. The same can be said for any other person who exercises entrepreneurship in a given setting, whether it be to decide between investing or not in a certain company or sector, buying or selling certain securities or stocks, or hiring or not certain people to collaborate on one's work and so on. Hence, we can consider practical information to be encapsulated, so to speak, in the sense that it is not accessible to the higher authority which engages in institutional aggression. Moreover, this information is constantly changing and emerging in new forms as actors create the future step by step.

Finally, let us recall that the more continuous and effective socialist coercion is, the more it will preclude the free pursuit of individual ends and therefore keep these ends from acting as an incentive and actors from discovering or producing, through the entrepreneurial process, the practical information necessary to coordinate society. The governing body thus faces an inescapable dilemma. It definitely needs the information the social process generates, yet it can never acquire this information: if the governing body intervenes coercively in this process, it destroys the capacity of the process to create information, and if it does not intervene, it does not obtain any information either.

In short, we conclude that from the standpoint of the social process, socialism is an intellectual error, since the governing body in charge of intervening via commands cannot conceivably glean the information necessary to coordinate society. It cannot do so for the following reasons. First, it is impossible for the intervening body to consciously assimilate the enormous volume of practical information spread throughout the minds of human beings. Second, as the necessary information is of a tacit nature and cannot be articulated, it cannot be transferred to the central authority. Third, the information actors have not yet discovered or created, and which emerges only from the free process of entrepreneurship, cannot be transmitted. Fourth, the exercise of coercion prevents the entrepreneurial process from provoking the discovery and creation of the information necessary to coordinate society.

## 4 THE IMPOSSIBILITY OF SOCIALISM FROM THE PERSPECTIVE OF THE GOVERNING BODY

From the standpoint of what in our figures is called the "higher" level, that is, the more or less organized person or group of people who commit systematic and institutional aggression against the free exercise of entrepreneurship, we can make a series of observations which confirm, to an

## Socialism

even greater extent if possible, the conclusion that socialism is simply an intellectual error.

We shall begin by assuming for the sake of argument, as Mises does,[8] that the governing entity (be it a dictator or military leader, an elite, a group of scientists or intellectuals, a cabinet ministry, a group of representatives elected democratically by the "people", or, in short, any combination, of any level of complexity, of all or some of these elements) is endowed with the maximum technical and intellectual capacity, experience, and wisdom, as well as the best intentions humanly conceivable (though we shall soon see that these assumptions are not justified in reality and why). Nevertheless, we cannot possibly suppose that the governing body has superhuman abilities or, to be specific, the gift of omniscience, that is, the ability to simultaneously gather, assimilate and interpret all of the dispersed, exclusive information spread throughout the minds of all of the people who act in society, information which these people constantly generate *ex novo*.[9] The truth is that the governing authority, sometimes called the central or partial planning agency, for the most part lacks or has only very vague indications of the knowledge available in dispersed form in the minds of all of the actors potentially subject to its orders. Thus, it is a remote or non-existent possibility that the planner will come to know what or how to seek and where to find the bits of dispersed information generated by the social process, information the planner so desperately needs to control and coordinate the process.

Moreover, the coercive body is unavoidably composed of flesh-and-blood people, with all of their faults and virtues, human beings who, like all other actors, have personal goals which act as incentives that lead them to discover the information essential to their particular interests. Therefore, it is most probable that if those who comprise the governing agency are adept at exercising their entrepreneurial intuition, then they will promote their own ends and interests and generate the information and experience they need, for example, to stay in power indefinitely and to justify and rationalize their acts to themselves and others, to apply coercion in an increasingly sophisticated and effective manner, to present their aggression to citizens as inevitable and attractive and so on. In other words, though at the beginning of the last paragraph it was assumed that the authorities had good intentions, the above incentives will normally be the most common, and they will prevail over others, especially the interest in discovering the important, specific practical information that exists in society at all times in dispersed form and which is necessary to make society function in a coordinated way via commands. These peculiar incentives will also keep the directing authorities from even being aware of their degree of inevitable ignorance, and they will sink more and more into a process which progressively distances them from precisely those social realities they aim to control.

Furthermore, the governing agency will be incapable of making any economic calculation,[10] in the sense that, regardless of the agency's ends (and even assuming they are the most "human" and "moral"), these authorities will have no way of knowing whether the cost to them of pursuing those ends is higher than the value they subjectively attach to them. The cost is simply the subjective value the actor places on what he gives up when he acts, and works toward a certain end. Clearly, the governing body cannot obtain the knowledge or information it needs to perceive the true cost it incurs according to its own value scales, since the information about the specific circumstances of time and place that is necessary to estimate costs is dispersed in the minds of all of the people or actors who comprise the social process and who are coerced by the governing body (democratically elected or not) in charge of committing systematic coercion in society.

If we define responsibility as the quality of an action performed by one who has become aware, through economic calculation, of the action's cost, we can conclude that the directing authority, regardless of its structure, method of selection, and value judgments, will invariably tend to act irresponsibly, because it is unable to see and determine the costs it incurs. Thus arises this unsolvable paradox: the more the governing authority insists on planning or controlling a certain sphere of social life, the less likely it is to reach its objectives, since it cannot obtain the information necessary to organize and coordinate society. In fact, it will cause new and more severe maladjustments and distortions insofar as it effectively uses coercion and limits people's entrepreneurial capacity.[11] Hence, we must conclude that it is a grave error to believe the governing body capable of making economic calculations in the same way the individual entrepreneur makes them. On the contrary, the higher the rung in the socialist system, the more first-hand, practical information essential for economic calculation is lost, to the point that calculation becomes completely impossible. The agency of institutional coercion obstructs economic calculation precisely to the extent that it effectively interferes with free human action.

## 5  WHY THE DEVELOPMENT OF COMPUTERS MAKES THE IMPOSSIBILITY OF SOCIALISM EVEN MORE CERTAIN

Different people without a clear understanding of the peculiar nature of the knowledge crucial to the functioning of society have often argued that extraordinary advances in the field of computer science could make it possible, both theoretically and practically, for the socialist system to operate. However, a simple theoretical argument will permit us to show that the development of computer systems and capacity will never make it possible to remedy the ignorance inherent in socialism.

Our argument rests on the assumption that the benefits of any technological development in the field of computer science will be available to both the governing body and the different human actors who take part in the social process. If this is so, then in all contexts in which actors exercise their entrepreneurship, the new computer tools available to them will tremendously increase their ability to create and discover new practical, dispersed and tacit information. There will be a dramatic rise in the quantity and quality of the information generated through entrepreneurship with the help of new computer tools, and this information will become progressively deeper and more detailed, to an extent inconceivable to us today, based on the knowledge we now have. Moreover, as is logical, it will still be impossible for the governing body to acquire this dispersed information, even if it has available to it at all times the most modern, capable and revolutionary computers.

To put it another way, the important entrepreneurial knowledge generated in the social process will always be tacit and dispersed, and thus not transmissible to any governing agency, and the future development of computer systems will further complicate the problem for the directing authority, since the practical knowledge produced with the help of such systems, as is now evident with the internet, will become progressively more vast, complex and rich.[12] Therefore, the development of computers and computer science not only fails to alleviate the problem of socialism, but makes it much more difficult, since computers enable actors to entrepreneurially create a much larger volume of increasingly complex and detailed practical information, data which will always be richer and more profound than that the governing body can assimilate with its own computers. Figure 3.4 illustrates this argument.

Furthermore, we should note that the machines and computer programs produced by man will never be capable of acting or exercising entrepreneurship; they will never be able to create new practical information from nothing, to discover and seize new profit opportunities unnoticed up to that point.[13]

The information stored on computers is not "known", that is, consciously assimilated or interpreted by human minds and capable of turning into practical information that is significant from a social standpoint. The information stored on a computer disk or any other computer medium is identical to the information included in books, charts, maps, newspapers and journals, simple instruments to be used by the actor within the context

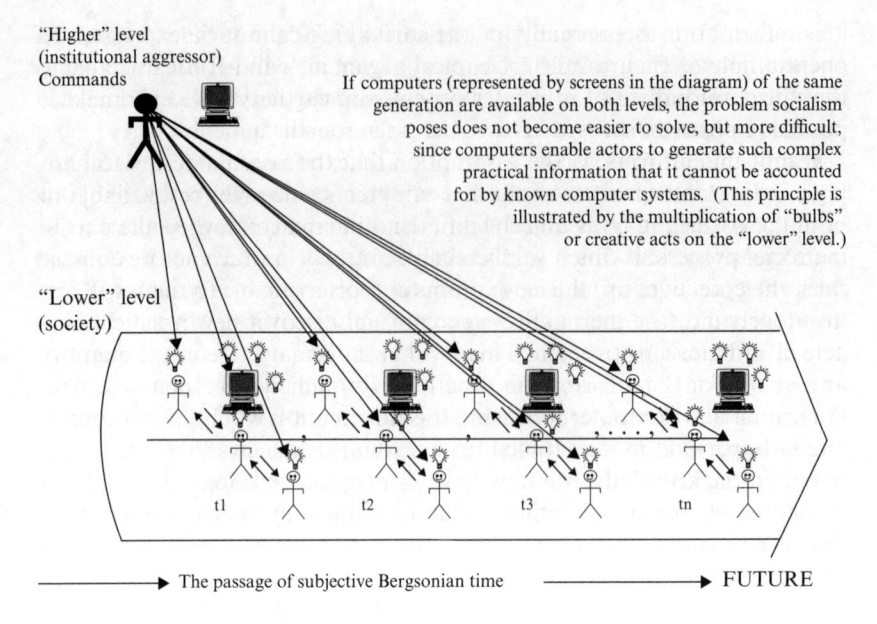

"Higher" level
(institutional aggressor)
Commands

If computers (represented by screens in the diagram) of the same generation are available on both levels, the problem socialism poses does not become easier to solve, but more difficult, since computers enable actors to generate such complex practical information that it cannot be accounted for by known computer systems. (This principle is illustrated by the multiplication of "bulbs" or creative acts on the "lower" level.)

"Lower" level
(society)

t1    t2    t3    tn

⟶ The passage of subjective Bergsonian time ⟶ FUTURE

*Figure 3.4*

of specific actions that are important for the achievement of his particular ends. In other words, the "stored information" is not information in the sense we have attributed to the word: important practical knowledge which the actor knows, interprets, and uses in the context of a specific action.

Moreover, clearly there is no way to computer process the practical information which, because it has not yet been entrepreneurially discovered or created, does not exist. Thus, computer systems are of no use in coordinating the process of social adjustment via commands; the fundamentally creative nature of human action is the only catalyst to initiate and further this process. Computers can only process information that has already been created and articulated, and without a doubt, they are a highly useful and powerful tool for the actor, but they are incapable of creating, discovering or recognizing new profit opportunities; that is, they cannot act entrepreneurially. Computers are instruments at the actor's disposal, but they do not act, nor will they ever act. They can only be used to manage articulate, formalized and objective information, and the information significant on a social level essentially cannot be articulated and is always subjective. Hence, computers are not only incapable of creating new information; they are also fundamentally incapable of processing information that has already been created if, as occurs in social processes, this information is essentially of the sort which cannot be expressed. In the example of Figure 2.2, in Chapter 2, even if A and B became able to verbalize, formally and in detail, those resources they lacked and needed to accomplish their respective goals, and even if somehow they could transmit this information to a gigantic and extremely modern database, the act by which a human mind (that of C) realizes that the resource of one could be used to gain the objectives of the other is an entrepreneurial act of pure creativity, one which is essentially subjective and cannot be equated with the objective, formalized patterns characteristic of a machine. For a computer to direct action effectively, not only must it first receive articulate information, but someone must program it as well. In other words, it is first necessary to thoroughly and formally indicate the rule of action, for example: whenever a person possesses a certain amount of resource R, the resource will be used by the person who is pursuing objective X. The formal existence of this rule presupposes the prior discovery of the course of action appropriate from an entrepreneurial standpoint, regarding the use of resources R for the accomplishment of goals X. Thus, it is evident that computer systems can only apply previously discovered knowledge to given situations; they can never create new information with respect to situations that have not yet been discovered and in which the *ex novo* creation of the subjective, tacit and dispersed knowledge typical of the social process predominates.

Therefore, trusting in computers as instruments which can make socialism possible is just as absurd as believing that in a much less advanced society, the invention of the printing press and other simpler methods of gathering and handling articulate information could make available the practical and subjective knowledge crucial to society. The outcome of the discovery of books and printing was just the opposite: it made society even richer and more difficult to control. It would only be conceivable that the problem of socialism could be somewhat alleviated quantitatively, yet never resolved, if the governing authority could apply the most modern computers to a society in which the continuous generation of new practical information had been reduced to a minimum. This state of affairs could only be achieved through an extremely rigid system which would forcibly hinder, to the greatest extent possible, the exercise of entrepreneurship, while prohibiting people from using any type of computers, machines, calculating instruments, books and so on. Only in this hypothetical society of "enslaved brutes'" could the problem of economic calculation in socialism appear somewhat less complex. Nevertheless, not even in such extreme circumstances could the problem be resolved theoretically, since even under the most adverse conditions, human beings have an innate, creative entrepreneurial capacity[14] which is impossible to control.

Finally, in light of the above considerations, it should not surprise us that the most qualified computer scientists and software programmers are precisely the most skeptical professionals in terms of evaluating the possibilities of using computers to regulate and organize social processes. In fact, not only do they clearly grasp the principle that imprecise information entered into a machine yields results which in turn multiply errors ("garbage in, garbage out"), but also, they constantly find in their daily experience that as they attempt to develop increasingly extensive and complicated programs, they encounter more and more difficulties in ridding them of logical defects to make them operational. Hence, programming a social process to such a degree of complexity as to incorporate man's most fundamental creative capacities is out of the question. Moreover, computer science has not come to the aid of interventionists, as many "social engineers" naively hoped and expected, but instead the latest advances in computer science have taken place due to the reception in that field of the intuitions and knowledge developed by theoretical economists who focus on spontaneous social processes, specifically Hayek, whose ideas are today considered to be of great practical importance in promoting and facilitating the design and development of new computer programs and systems.[15]

## 6  OTHER THEORETICAL CONSEQUENCES OF SOCIALISM

In the preceding sections, we showed that socialism is an intellectual error which stems from the "fatal conceit"[16] of supposing that man is intelligent enough to organize life in society. This section will succinctly and systematically analyze the inexorable consequences which follow when man overlooks the logical impossibility socialism represents and insists on establishing an institutional system of coercion which restricts the free exercise of human action.

### Discoordination and Social Disorder

1. We have already seen that when its exercise is impeded, entrepreneurship can no longer uncover the maladjustment situations which arise in society. When coercion is used to keep actors from seizing the profit opportunities every maladjustment creates, the actors fail to even perceive the opportunities, which go unnoticed. Moreover, if, by chance, a coerced actor should recognize an opportunity for profit, it would be irrelevant, since institutional coercion itself would preclude him from acting to benefit from the opportunity.

Furthermore, the governing body in charge of applying institutional coercion cannot conceivably coordinate social behavior via orders and commands. To do so, it would have to have access to information it cannot possibly obtain, given that this information is scattered throughout the minds of all of the actors in society, and each one has exclusive access to his own part of it.

Therefore, according to theory, the first consequence to follow from any attempt to establish a socialist system will be widespread social "discoordination" or "maladjustment", characterized by the systematically conflicting actions of multiple agents, who will not adapt their behavior to that of others nor realize they are committing systematic errors on a broad scale. As a result, a very large number of human actions will be thwarted, as maladjustments will prevent them. This generalized frustration of plans or discoordination strikes at the very heart of social life and is apparent both intra- and intertemporally. That is, it affects both current actions as well as the vital coordination between present and future actions in any social process.

Hayek considers "order" to be any process in which a multitude of diverse elements interact in such a way that knowledge of one part permits the formulation of correct expectations concerning the whole.[17] This definition exposes socialism as a producer of social disorder; to the extent that it hampers and even blocks the necessary adjustment between discoordinated individual behaviors, it also hampers and even blocks potential human actions based on unfrustrated expectations of others' behavior, since the social maladjustments which invariably emerge whenever the free exercise of entrepreneurship is obstructed persist and remain hidden. Hence, the voluntaristic desire to "organize" society via coercive commands essentially creates disorder, and the more complex a social order is in Hayekian terms, the more clearly impossible the socialist ideal will be, since a complex order will require the delegation of many more decisions and activities, which will depend on circumstances completely unknown to those bent on controlling society.

2. Paradoxically, widespread social discoordination is very often cited as a pretext for administering subsequent doses of socialism; in other words, institutional aggression which is unleashed in new areas of social life or is even more involved or stringent than before. The above usually occurs because the directing authority, though it cannot perceive in detail the particular conflicting and maladjusted actions its intervention provokes, does sooner or later become aware that the social process in general is not working. From the perspective of its extremely limited power of appraisal, the directing authority interprets

this situation as the logical result of the "lack of cooperation" shown by those citizens who do not wish to strictly obey its orders and commands, which therefore become increasingly broad, detailed and coercive. This increase in the degree of socialism will infuse the social process with even greater discoordination or maladjustment, which will in turn be used to justify new "doses" of socialism and so on. Thus, we see socialism's overwhelming tendency toward totalitarianism, understood as a regime in which the government tends to "forcefully intervene in all areas of life".[18] In other cases, this totalitarian process of progressive increases in coercion is accompanied by continuous jolts or sudden changes in policy, radical modifications of the content of commands or the area to which they apply, or both, and all in the vain hope that asystematic "experimentation" with new types and degrees of interventionism will provide a solution to the insoluble problems considered.[19]

3. The coercive interventionary measures socialism embodies exert effects on society which are generally the exact opposite of those the governing body itself intends. This authority aims to achieve its ends by directing coercive commands to the social spheres most connected with these ends, and the paradoxical result is that the commands prevent the exercise of human action in those areas and do so with particular effectiveness. In other words, the governing body immobilizes the force of entrepreneurship precisely where it is most necessary, considering that this force is essential to the coordination of the social sphere in question and hence to the accomplishment of the goals pursued. In short, the necessary adjustment process is not triggered and in fact becomes more remote, and the social process becomes less likely to produce the desired ends. The more effectively imposed the commands are, the more they distort the exercise of entrepreneurship. Not only do commands fail to incorporate the necessary practical information, but they also deter people from creating it, and economic agents cannot rely on them as a guide to creativity and coordination. Theorists have long been familiar with this self-destructive effect socialism exerts, also known as the "paradox of planning or interventionism", but only recently have they managed to explain it in the precise terms of the theory of entrepreneurship.[20]

4. Though the inhibiting effect socialism has on the creation of practical information appears in all social spheres, perhaps it is most obvious in the economic sphere. First, for example, poor quality in the goods and services produced is one of the most typical signs of socialist discoordination, and it stems precisely from the lack of incentives for actors in the social process and members of the directing authority to

generate information and discover people's true desires with respect to quality standards.

Second, in a socialist system, investment decisions become purely arbitrary, both quantitatively and qualitatively, due to the absence of the information necessary to make even rough economic calculations. In fact, in a socialist environment it is impossible to know or estimate the opportunity cost of each investment, and these difficulties emerge even when the governing body imposes its rate of time preference on all of society. Moreover, the governing body's lack of information also precludes the calculation of even minimally reliable depreciation rates for capital equipment. Thus, socialism provokes and maintains the widespread malinvestment of resources and factors of production, and to make matters worse, this malinvestment often develops a somewhat erratic, cyclical quality, due to the sudden changes in policy which are typical of this system and which we covered at the end of the last section.

Third, socialism gives rise to severe, generalized scarcity at all levels of society, mainly because institutional coercion eradicates the opportunity for the enormous force of human entrepreneurial ingenuity to systematically discover states of scarcity and seek new, more effective ways of eliminating them. In addition, the impossibility of economically calculating costs leads, as we have seen, to the squandering of a large share of the productive resources on senseless investments, which aggravates even further the problem of scarcity.[21] Moreover, this scarcity goes hand in hand with an inefficient excess of certain resources which springs not only from production errors, but also from the fact that economic agents hoard all of the goods and resources they can, since systematic scarcity makes people unable to depend on an adequate supply of goods, services and factors of production.

Finally, in the case of labor, errors in the allocation of resources are particularly grave. Labor tends to be systematically misused, and a high level of unemployment results and is concealed to a greater or lesser extent, depending upon the specific type of socialism in question. In any case, a high level of unemployment is one of the most typical effects of institutional coercion against the free exercise of entrepreneurship in the social processes connected with the labor market.

**Erroneous Information and Irresponsible Behaviors**

Socialism is characterized not only by its hindrance of the creation of information, but also by its triggering of processes that systematically attract and generate erroneous information and thus encourage widespread irresponsible behavior.

1. There is no guarantee that the governing body which exercises systematic coercion will be able to recognize the specific profit opportunities that emerge in the social process. Given the authority's lack of the practical information relevant to the coerced individuals, we cannot imagine it being capable of discovering the current social maladjustments, except in very isolated cases or by mere accident or coincidence. In fact, even if by chance a member of the governing body discovers a maladjustment, the "find" will most likely be covered up or hidden by the very inertia of the coercive organization, which, except on very few occasions, will have no interest at all in exposing unpopular problems that will invariably require, in order to solve them, "bothersome" changes and measures. At the same time, members of the directing authority will not even be aware of their grave, ineradicable ignorance. Therefore, the information generated via commands will be riddled with errors and fundamentally irresponsible, since members of the governing body cannot obtain the practical, dispersed information pertaining to the alternatives they give up when they decide to follow a certain course of action, and hence they will be unable to consider the true cost or value of these alternatives in their decision-making process.[22]

2. The fact that the governing body is inexorably separated from the social process by a permanent veil of ignorance, through which it can only discern the most obvious, basic particulars, invariably compels it to focus on the accomplishment of its goals in an extensive and voluntaristic manner. Voluntaristic in the sense that the governing body expects to achieve its ends through mere coercive will, in the shape of commands. Extensive in the sense that only the parameters which are the easiest to define, articulate and transmit are used to measure or judge the achievement of those ends. In other words, the governing body concentrates merely on statistical or quantitative parameters which exclude or fail to sufficiently incorporate all of the subjective and qualitative nuances that are precisely the most valuable and distinctive part of the practical information dispersed throughout human minds.

Thus, the proliferation and excessive use of statistics is another characteristic of socialism, and it is not at all surprising that the word "statistic" derives etymologically from precisely the term for the quintessential organization of institutional coercion.

3. When the systematic generation of inaccurate information leads to widespread irresponsible behaviors, and the coercive governing body

pursues its ends in a voluntaristic and extensive manner, the consequences which ensue are tragic for the environment. As a general rule, the environment will deteriorate precisely in those geographical areas in which socialism is most prevalent (that is, where the greatest constraints are placed on the exercise of entrepreneurship), and the more generalized and far-reaching the coercive intervention is, the more severe this deterioration will be.[23]

**The Corruption Effect**

Socialism has the effect of corrupting or perversely deflecting the force of entrepreneurship, which is the manifestation of all human action. The *Diccionario* of the Real Academia Española defines "to corrupt" as "to spoil, deprave, damage, rot, pervert, destroy, or warp",[24] and it specifically indicates that this destruction applies mainly to social institutions, understood as behavior patterns. Corruption is one of the most typical and fundamental consequences of socialism, as this system tends to systematically pervert the process by which information is created and transmitted in society.

1. First, coerced or managed human beings soon make the entrepreneurial discovery that they stand a better chance of achieving their ends if, rather than try to discover and coordinate social maladjustments by seizing the profit opportunities they yield, they devote their time, efforts and human ingenuity to influencing the decision-making processes of the governing body. Thus, an impressive volume of human ingenuity – and the more intense the socialism, the larger the volume – will be constantly devoted to thinking up new and more effective ways to influence the governing body, with the real or imaginary hope of gaining personal advantages. Therefore, socialism not only prevents each member of society from learning to tune his behavior to that of the other members, but it also provides an unavoidable incentive for different individuals and groups to try to influence the governing body, with a view to using its coercive commands to forcibly acquire personal privileges or advantages at the expense of the rest of society. Hence, the spontaneous and coordinating social process is corrupted and replaced by a power struggle process, in which systematic violence and conflict between the different individuals and social groups that vie for power or influence become the leitmotif of life in society. Thus, in a socialist system, people lose the habit of behaving morally (that is, according to customs or principles) and gradually alter their personalities and their behavior, which becomes increasingly amoral (that is, less subject to principles) and aggressive.[25]

2. Second, we see another sign of the corrupting effect of socialism when those groups or individuals who have not managed to acquire power are forced to devote a major part of their entrepreneurial ingenuity or activity to an attempt to divert or avoid, in their own circumstances, the effects of coercive commands, which for them are more damaging or drastic, by conferring privileges, advantages and certain goods and services on the people in charge of monitoring and enforcing the fulfillment of those commands. This corrupting activity is of a defensive nature, since it acts as a true "escape valve" and permits a certain alleviation of the harm socialism causes in society. It can have the positive effect of enabling people to maintain some minimally coordinating social connections, even in the severest cases of socialist aggression. At any rate, the corruption or perverse deflection of entrepreneurship will always be superfluous and redundant, as Kirzner indicates.[26]

3. Third, the members of the governing body, that is, the more or less organized group which systematically exercises coercion, will also tend to use their entrepreneurial capacity, their own human ingenuity, in a perverse manner. The chief object of their activity will be to hold onto power and to justify their coercive action before the rest of the actors in society. The details and peculiar characteristics of the corrupting activity of those in power will vary depending upon the specific type of socialism in question (totalitarian, democratic, conservative, scientistic and so on). What we should emphasize at this point is that the perverse entrepreneurial activity of those who ultimately control the governing body will tend to creatively bring about situations in which this power can increase, spread and appear justified.[27] Thus, for example, those in power will encourage the establishment of privileged special interest groups that back the governing body in exchange for benefits and privileges it can grant them. Also, any socialist system will tend to overindulge in political propaganda, by which it will invariably idealize the effects on the social process of the governing body's commands, while insisting that the absence of such intervention would produce very negative consequences for society. The systematic deception of the population, the distortion of facts, the fabrication of false crises to convince the public that the power structure is necessary and should be maintained and strengthened, and so on are all typical characteristics of the perverse and corrupting effect socialism exerts on its own governing bodies or agencies.[28] Furthermore, these characteristics will be common to the supreme decision-making authorities in charge of institutional aggression and to the intermediate bureaucratic bodies which are necessary to issue coercive commands and supervise their fulfillment. These secondary

bureaucratic organizations will always tend to overexpand, to seek the support of specific interest groups, and to create the artificial need for their existence by exaggerating the beneficial results of their intervention and systematically concealing its perverse effects.

Finally, the megalomaniacal nature of socialism becomes obvious. Not only do bureaucratic organizations tend toward unlimited expansion, but those who control them also instinctively try to reproduce the macrostructures of these bodies in the society they act upon, and, under all sorts of false pretexts, these authorities force the creation of increasingly large units, organizations and firms. Their reason for this action is twofold: first, they instinctively believe that such structures make it easier for them to supervise the execution of the coercive commands issued from above; and second, such structures provide the bureaucratic authorities with a false sense of security against genuine entrepreneurial effort, which always originates from an essentially individualistic and creative microprocess.[29]

## The Underground or "Irregular" Economy

Another typical consequence of socialism is that it triggers an inexorable social reaction in which the different actors, to the best of their abilities, systematically disobey the coercive commands of the governing body by undertaking a series of actions and interactions outside of the regular framework the commands are intended to establish. Thus an entire social process begins behind the backs of those the governing body considers "regular", and this process reveals the extent to which institutional coercion is condemned to failure in the long run, since it goes against the fundamental essence of human action. Therefore, often the governing body has no choice but to exercise its power while implicitly tolerating "irregular" social processes that survive alongside the rigid structures it devises. Hence, the emergence of a hidden, "irregular", or "underground" economy or society is an integral feature of socialism, and one that appears without exception in spheres of coercive activity and varies in intensity with that activity. The basic characteristics of corruption and of the underground economy are the same in both real-socialist countries and mixed economies. The only difference is that in the latter, corruption and the underground economy are present precisely in those areas of social life in which the state intervenes.[30]

## A Lag in Social (Economic, Technological, Cultural) Development

1. Socialism patently entails an assault on human creativity and hence on society and the advancement of civilization. In fact, to the extent that

the free exercise of human action is forcibly impeded via coercive commands, actors are unable to create or discover new information, and the advancement of civilization is blocked. To put it another way, socialism implies the systematic establishment of a series of barriers to free human interaction, and these barriers freeze the development of society. This effect is felt in all areas of social development, not just in those which are strictly economic. One of the most typical characteristics of the socialist system is its slowness to innovate and to introduce current technological innovations, and as a consequence, socialist systems invariably trail behind their competitors in the development and practical application of new technologies.[31] This is so even though socialists, in an extensive and voluntaristic manner as always, strive to force society's technological development by issuing commands and creating pretentious ministries, institutes or councils devoted to scientific research and to planning the future development of new technologies. Nevertheless, the very creation of these bureaucratic agencies for the development of innovations is the clearest and most obvious sign that the system is blocked with respect to scientific and technological development. The fact is, it is impossible to plan the future development of knowledge which has not yet been created and can only emerge in an environment of entrepreneurial liberty that commands cannot simulate.

2. The above remarks also apply to any other sphere in which spontaneous and constant social development or evolution takes place. Specifically, we are referring to cultural, artistic and linguistic areas, and in general, to all areas rooted in the spontaneous evolution and development of social habits and customs. Culture is simply the spontaneous result of a social process in which multiple actors interact, and each one makes his own small contribution of experience, originality and vision. If the authorities apply systematic coercion to this process, they cripple and corrupt it, if they don't stop it altogether. (Again the governing body will seek to appear as the "champion" of the cultural impetus by establishing all sorts of agencies, ministries, councils, and commissions entrusted with boosting and "fostering" cultural "development" using commands.)[32]

3. The evolution or development of new social habits is key as well, since they teach people how to behave with respect to the new circumstances, products, services and so on that emerge in the process of social development. There is nothing more tragic than a society which has stagnated due to institutional aggression against the interaction of its members, an assault that hampers the learning process necessary to confront the new challenges and make the most of the new opportunities which constantly arise.[33]

## The Prostitution of the Traditional Concepts of Law and Justice: The Moral Perversion Socialism Creates

1. In the last chapter, we saw that the social process, propelled by the force of entrepreneurship, is made possible by a set of customary rules which also spring from it. These behavioral habits are the substance of private contract law and criminal law, and no one deliberately designed them. Instead, they are evolutionary institutions which emerged as a result of the practical information contributed to them by a huge number of actors over a very lengthy period of time. From this viewpoint, the law is composed of a series of substantive laws or rules which are general (as they apply equally to all) and abstract (as they only establish a broad framework for personal conduct, without predicting any concrete result of the social process).

   Because socialism rests on institutionalized, systematic aggression (in the form of a series of coercive orders or commands) against human action, socialism entails the disappearance of the above traditional concept of law and its replacement with a spurious sort of "law", composed of a conglomeration of administrative orders, regulations and commands which spell out how each person should behave. So, as socialism spreads and develops, laws in the traditional sense cease to act as guidelines for personal behavior, and their role is usurped by the coercive orders or commands which emanate from the governing body (whether democratically elected or not). In this way, the law's scope of practical application is gradually restricted to those regular or irregular spheres not directly and effectively influenced by the socialist regime.

   In addition, a very important secondary effect appears: when actors lose the yardstick that substantive law provides, they begin to change their personalities and drop their habits of adjustment to abstract general rules, and hence, the actors become progressively worse at assimilating traditional rules of conduct, and they abide by them less and less. In fact, given that on many occasions dodging commands is necessary to satisfy one's own need to survive, and that on others it is a sign that the corrupt or perverse entrepreneurship socialism always provokes is successful, in general the population comes to view the infringement of the rules more as a commendable manifestation of the human ingenuity which should be sought and encouraged, than as a violation of a system of standards and a threat to life in society. Therefore, socialism induces people to violate the law, drains it of its content, and corrupts it, by completely discrediting it in society and as a result, causing citizens to lose all respect for it.

2. The prostitution of the concept of law, which was explained in the last section, is invariably accompanied by a parallel corruption of the concept and application of justice. Justice, in the traditional sense, consists of the equal application to everyone of the substantive, abstract rules of conduct which make up private law and criminal law. Therefore, it is no coincidence that justice has been portrayed as blindfolded, since above all she must be blind, in the sense that she must not allow herself to be influenced in her application of the law by the gifts of the rich, or by the tears of the poor.[34] Because socialism systematically corrupts the traditional concept of law, it also modifies this traditional idea of justice. In fact, in the socialist system, justice primarily consists of the arbitrary judgment of the governing body, based on the more or less emotional impression its members derive from the concrete "final result" of the social process which they believe they perceive and which they daringly attempt to organize from above via coercive commands. Thus, it is no longer human behaviors which are judged, but the perceived "result" of them within a spurious context of "justice", to which the adjective "social" is added to make it more attractive to those who suffer it.[35] From the opposite perspective of traditional justice, there is nothing more unjust than the concept of social justice, since it hinges on a view, impression, or estimate of the "results" of social processes, regardless of the particular behavior of each actor from the standpoint of the rules of traditional law.[36] The role of the judge in traditional law is of a merely intellectual nature, and he must not allow himself to be swayed by his emotional inclinations or by his personal assessment of the effect the ruling will have on each party. If, as occurs in socialism, the objective application of the law is impeded and legal decision making based on more or less subjective and emotional impressions is permitted, all legal certainty vanishes, and soon actors begin to perceive that any desire can obtain judicial protection if only a favorable impression can be made on the judge. Consequently, an extremely strong incentive to litigate is created and, together with the chaotic situation produced by the increasingly imperfect and contradictory jumble of coercive commands, it overloads judges to the extent that their job becomes more and more unbearable and inefficient. So the process continues, a progressive breakdown which comes to an end only with the virtual disappearance of justice in its traditional sense, and of judges, who turn into ordinary bureaucrats at the service of the authorities and are in charge of supervising the fulfillment of the coercive commands they issue. Table 3.1 lists the most significant differences between the spontaneous process based on entrepreneurship and free human interaction,

and the system of organization based on commands and institutional coercion (socialism). In the table, note the opposite effects that the two exert on the concepts and application of law and justice.

3. Another of the most typical characteristics of socialism is the loss of the habits of adapting one's own behavior to general standards which have formed through tradition, and whose essential social role is not fully grasped by any one individual. Morality is weakened at all levels and even disappears and is replaced by a reflection of the governing body's mystic approach to social organization, a mysticism that tends to reproduce on the level of each individual actor's behavior. Hence, on an individual level as well, the wishful thinking typical of socialism is sure to prevail with respect to the achievement of ends a subject pursues more through caprice or personal "commands" fed by his own desires and instincts, which he declares *ad hoc* in each particular case, than by the exercise of human interaction subject to general moral and legal guidelines.

A leading exponent of this moral perversion socialism begets was Lord John Maynard Keynes, one of the most conspicuous forces behind systematic coercion and interventionism in the monetary and fiscal sphere. Keynes offered the following explanation of his "moral" position:

> We entirely repudiated a personal liability on us to obey general rules. We claimed the right to judge every individual case on its merits, and the wisdom, experience, and self-control to do so successfully. This was a very important part of our faith, violently and aggressively held, and for the outer world it was our most obvious and dangerous characteristic. We repudiated entirely customary morals, conventions and traditional wisdom. We were, that is to say, in the strict sense of the term, immoralists . . . We recognized no moral obligations, no inner sanction, to conform or obey. Before heaven we claimed to be our own judge in our own case . . . So far as I am concerned, it is too late to change. I remain, and always will remain, an immoralist.[37]

Thus, socialism appears to be both a natural product of the false, exaggerated rationalism of the so-called Enlightenment and a result of the basest and most atavistic human instincts and passions. In fact, by believing there are no limits to the capacity of the human mind, the naive rationalists rebel, like Keynes, Rousseau and so many others, against the institutions, habits and behaviors which make the social order possible; cannot, by definition, be completely rationalized; and are irresponsibly labeled as repressive and inhibitory social traditions. The paradoxical outcome of this "deification" of human reason is simply the elimination of the moral principles, rules, and behavioral

*Table 3.1*

| Spontaneous social process based on entrepreneurship (unassaulted social interaction) | Socialism (systematic institutional aggression against entrepreneurship and human action) |
|---|---|
| 1. Social coordination occurs spontaneously, due to entrepreneurship, which constantly discovers and eliminates social maladjustments, which emerge as profit opportunities. (Spontaneous order) | 1. Attempts are made to deliberately impose social coordination from above via *coercive commands, orders and regulations* which emanate from the authorities. (An organized hierarchy – from *hieros*, sacred, and *archein*, to command) |
| 2. The protagonist of the process is *man*, who acts and exercises creative entrepreneurship | 2. The protagonists of the process are the *leader* (democratic or not) and the *public official* (that person who acts in compliance with the administrative orders and regulations which emanate from the authorities) |
| 3. The links of social interaction are *contractual*, and the parties involved exchange goods and services according to substantive legal rules. (Law) | 3. The links of social interaction are *hegemonic*; some people command and others obey. In a "social democracy", the "majority" coerces the "minority" |
| 4. *The traditional, substantive concept of law, understood as an abstract, general rule* predominates and is applied equally to all regardless of particular circumstances | 4. *Commands and regulations* predominate and, notwithstanding their appearance as formal laws, are specific, concrete orders which command people to do certain things in particular circumstances and are not applied equally to all |
| 5. The laws and institutions which make the social process possible have not been deliberately created, but have *evolved* from *custom*, and they incorporate an enormous volume of practical experience and information which has accumulated over many generations | 5. Commands and regulations are deliberately issued by the *organized authorities* and are highly imperfect and unsound, given the ineradicable ignorance in which the authorities are always immersed with respect to society |
| 6. The spontaneous process makes *social peace* possible, since each actor, within the framework of the law, takes advantage of his | 6. One end or set of ends must *predominate* and be imposed on all through a system of commands. This results in unresolvable and |

*Table 3.1* (continued)

| Spontaneous social process based on entrepreneurship (unassaulted social interaction) | Socialism (systematic institutional aggression against entrepreneurship and human action) |
|---|---|
| practical knowledge and *pursues his own particular ends*, through pacific cooperation with others and by spontaneously adapting his behavior to that of others, who pursue different goals | interminable social conflict and violence, which obstruct social peace |
| 7. *Freedom* is understood as the absence of coercion or aggression (both institutional and asystematic) | 7. "Freedom" is understood as the ability to achieve the specific ends desired at any moment (through a simple act of will, a command, or caprice) |
| 8. The traditional meaning of *justice* prevails and indicates that the law in substantive form is applied equally to all, regardless of the concrete results of the social process. The only equality pursued is *equality before the law*, applied by a justice system blind to particular differences between people | 8. The spurious sense of "justice of the results" or "social justice" prevails; in other words, *equality of the results* of the social process, regardless of the behavior (whether correct or not from the standpoint of traditional law) of the individuals involved |
| 9. *Abstract, economic* and *commercial* relationships prevail. The spurious concepts of loyalty, "solidarity" and hierarchy do not come into play. Each actor disciplines his behavior based on substantive law rules and participates in a *universal social order*, in which there are no "friends" or "enemies", or people he is close to or distant from, but simply many human beings, the majority of whom he does not know, and with whom he interacts in a mutually satisfying, and increasingly far-reaching and complex, manner (correct meaning of the term "solidarity") | 9. The *political* predominates in social life, and the basic links are "tribal": (a) *loyalty* to the group and to the chief; (b) respect for the *hierarchy*; (c) help to the "fellow man" one knows ("solidarity") and forgetfulness or even contempt toward the "other" more or less unknown people, who are members of other "tribes" and are distrusted and considered "enemies" (spurious and short-sighted meaning of the term "solidarity") |

norms which allowed civilization to evolve, and the inevitable abandonment of man, who needs these vital guides and standards, to his most atavistic and primitive passions.[38]

### Socialism as the "Opium of the People"

Finally, socialism exerts the systematic effect of seriously hindering citizens' discovery of the negative consequences it produces. By its very essence, socialism obstructs the emergence of the important information necessary to criticize or eliminate it. When actors are forcibly blocked in the creative exercise of their own human action, they lack even the awareness of what they fail to create in the coercive, institutional environment in which their lives are immersed.

As the old saying goes, "What the eye does not see the heart does not grieve for".[39] Thus, a mirage appears, and the different actors identify the coercive agency with the existence of those goods and services which are considered crucial to life and which the agency provides. It does not even enter the actors' minds that the imperfect result of the coercive commands could be achieved in a much more creative, fruitful and effective manner via free, entrepreneurial human action. Therefore, complacency, cynicism and resignation spread. Only the underground economy and knowledge of what occurs in other, comparatively less socialist systems of government can trigger the mechanisms of civil disobedience necessary to dismantle, either through social development or revolution, the organized, institutional system of coercion against human beings. Furthermore, socialism, like any drug, is "addicting" and causes "rigidity"; as we have seen, its authorities tend to justify increasing doses of coercion, and the system makes it very painful and difficult for people who become dependent on it to return to entrepreneurial habits and behavior patterns not based on coercion.[40]

### Conclusion: The Essentially Antisocial Nature of Socialism

If we recall our definition of "society" from the end of the last chapter, it becomes obvious that nothing is more antisocial than socialism itself. Our theoretical analysis has revealed the ways in which, in the *moral sphere*, socialism corrupts the principles or behavioral rules essential to upholding the fabric of society and does so by discrediting and encouraging the violation of the law (the concept of which becomes perverted) and disposing of justice in its traditional sense. In the *political sphere*, socialism inevitably tends toward totalitarianism, since systematic coercion tends to spread to every social nook and cranny, while erasing freedom and personal responsibility. *Materially speaking*, socialism greatly impedes the production of goods and services, and thus it encumbers economic development. *Culturally speaking*, socialism shackles creativity by preventing the development and learning of new behavior patterns and interfering with the discovery and introduction of innovations. In the *field of science*, socialism is simply an intellectual error which originates from the belief that the human mind has a much greater capacity than it actually does, and hence, that it is possible to obtain the information necessary to improve society through coercion.[41] In short, socialism constitutes the quintessential antihuman and antisocial activity, since it is based on systematic coercion against the most intimate characteristic of human nature: the ability to act freely and creatively.

## 7 DIFFERENT TYPES OF SOCIALISM

Now that we have stated the theoretical definition of socialism, explained why this system is an intellectual error, and studied the theoretical consequences it produces, in this section we shall examine history's most salient cases of socialism. Initially, our theoretical analysis will be connected with the real world by using the analysis to interpret the main, distinctive characteristics of each type of socialism. All of the examples we shall mention share the trait of being socialist systems; in other words, they are all based on systematic, institutional aggression against the free exercise of entrepreneurship. As we will see, the differences between them lie in the general purposes or ends pursued, and particularly in the breadth and depth to which institutional aggression is exercised in each.

### Real Socialism, or that of Soviet-type Economies

This system is characterized by the great breadth and depth to which institutionalized aggression is exercised against individuals' human action, and specifically, by the fact that this aggression is always, and at least, expressed in an attempt to block the free exercise of entrepreneurship with respect to economic goods of higher order, or material factors of production. Material factors of production (capital goods and natural resources) are all economic goods which do not directly satisfy human needs, but require the intervention of other factors of production, especially human labor, in order for consumer goods and services to be produced, through a production process that always takes time. From the perspective of the theory of human action, material factors of production, or higher-order economic goods, are all of the intermediate stages, subjectively considered as such by the actor, which form part of an action process prior to its ultimate conclusion. Thus, we can now grasp the profound effect that institutionalized aggression will have if it spreads to the factors of production, since such aggression will necessarily, to a greater or lesser extent, influence all human actions on a fundamental level. This type of socialism has long been considered the purest, or socialism par excellence. It is also known as "real socialism", and for many theorists and thinkers unfamiliar with the dynamic theory of entrepreneurship, it is, in fact, the only type of socialism that exists. As for the motives behind it, real socialism is generally, and passionately, aimed at not only "freeing humanity of its chains", but also at achieving equality of the results, which is deemed to be the quintessential ideal of "justice". It is of great interest to carry out a detailed study of the development and chief characteristics of this first type of socialism, which is currently in a state of marked decline.

**Democratic Socialism, or Social Democracy**

Today, this is the most popular variety of socialism. Historically, it emerged as a tactical departure from real socialism and differs from it insofar as social democracy is meant to achieve the objectives of its advocates via the traditional democratic mechanisms which have formed in western countries. Later, mainly due to the development of social democracy in states like West Germany,[42] democratic socialists gradually abandoned the goal of "socializing" the means or factors of production, and they began to place more and more emphasis on focusing systematic or institutionalized aggression on the fiscal sphere, with the purpose of evening out "social opportunities" and the results of the social process.

Note that, contrary to the impression which socialism of the above sort is intended to make on the public, the difference between real socialism and democratic socialism is not one of category or class, but simply one of degree. In fact, institutional aggression in social democracies is quite profound and far-reaching; with regard to both the number of social spheres and processes affected, and the degree of effective coercion exercised against the action of millions of people, who witness the systematic expropriation, through taxes, of a very large share of the fruits of their own entrepreneurial creativity, and who are forced via commands and regulations to take part in multiple actions which they would not voluntarily undertake, or would perform differently.

Social democrats usually pursue ostensibly "noble" goals, such as the "redistribution" of income and wealth and, in general, the "improved functioning" of society. This system tends to create the illusion that, because its primary aim is precisely the "democratic" ideal and institutional aggression is ultimately exercised by democratically elected "representatives", such aggression poses no problem. In this way, the system obscures the fact that the theoretical consequences of socialism inexorably appear, regardless of whether the governing body is composed of democratically elected representatives of the people, for democratic elections have no bearing on the fundamental problem of the ineradicable ignorance which envelops the entire governing body in charge of applying systematic coercion. Whether or not it originates in a democratic chamber, aggression always hinders to some extent the human interaction based on creative entrepreneurship, and thus it prevents social coordination and gives rise to all of the other theoretical consequences of socialism we have already analyzed.

Hence, the basic issue involved in harmonious social relations is not whether or not they are "democratically" organized, but the breadth and depth of systematic coercion against free human interaction. For this reason, Hayek himself explains that, if the so-called "democratic ideal" means granting representatives the power of unlimited institutional aggression, he does not consider himself a democrat. He defends a system defined by limits on state power and distrust toward the institutional aggression typical of the state, a system which rests on a series of self-compensating bodies comprised of democratically elected representatives. Hayek suggests the name "demarchy" for this political system.[43]

Finally, the "mirage" effect described in the last section appears wherever democratic socialism prevails: since this system has spread to some degree throughout all countries where real socialism is absent, there is no comparative social system which reveals to citizens the adverse consequences of social-democratic institutional aggression, and which, as is now occurring with respect to real socialism, strengthens the necessary movements, whether revolutionary or not, in favor of its dismantling and reform. Nevertheless, ordinary people are becoming increasingly aware of the damaging consequences of the social-democratic aggressor state, due to the latest advances in the realms of both theory[44] and practice. (In fact, despite multiple attempts to the contrary, social democracy has not managed to remain perfectly undisturbed by the failure of real socialism.) In more and more societies, the above factors are creating certain trends, now more or less consolidated, toward a reduction in the scope and depth of the systematic coercion inherent in social democracy.

## Conservative or "Right-wing" Socialism

"Conservative" or "right-wing" socialism can be defined as that type in which institutional aggression is employed to maintain the social status quo and the privileges certain people or groups of people enjoy. The fundamental objective of right-wing socialism is to keep things as they are by preventing the free exercise of entrepreneurship and creative human action from disrupting the pre-established framework of social organization. To reach this objective, right-wing socialist systems rely on systematic, institutionalized aggression at all levels necessary. In this sense, conservative socialism and democratic socialism differ only in the motivations behind them and in the social groups each aims to favor.

Conservative or right-wing socialism is also characterized by its marked paternalism, understood as the attempt to freeze the behavior of human beings by assigning them the roles as consumers or producers which the conservative regulatory agency deems fitting. Moreover, in a socialist system of this kind, the authorities typically seek to dictate, via commands, certain behaviors considered moral or religious.[45]

Military socialism is closely related to conservative or right-wing socialism, and Mises defines it as socialism in which all institutions are designed with a view to making war and the value scale by which citizens' social status and income are determined depends primarily or exclusively on the position each person holds with respect to the armed forces.[46] Guild socialism and agrarian socialism can also be considered types of conservative or right-wing socialism. In the first of these two systems, authorities intend to organize society based on a hierarchy of experts, managers, overseers, officers and workers, and in the second, to forcibly divide up land among certain social groups.[47]

Finally, note that conservatism is a philosophy incompatible with innovation and creativity, rooted in past, distrustful of anything market processes might create, and fundamentally opportunistic and bereft of general principles, and hence it tends to recommend that the exercise of institutional coercion be entrusted to the *ad hoc* criteria of "wise and good" leaders. In short, conservatism is an obscurantist doctrine which overlooks the manner in which social processes driven by entrepreneurship function, and specifically, the problem of the ineradicable ignorance which envelops all leaders.[48]

## Social Engineering, or Scientistic Socialism[49]

Scientistic socialism is that type favored by the scientists and intellectuals who believe that because they possess articulate knowledge or information "superior" to that of the rest of society, they are authorized to recommend and direct the systematic use of coercion on a social level. Scientistic socialism is especially dangerous, since it legitimizes all other kinds of socialism from an intellectual standpoint and tends to accompany both democratic socialism and the enlightened despotism typical of right-wing socialism. Its origin lies in the intellectual tradition of Cartesian or constructivist rationalism, according to which the reason of intellectuals is capable of anything, and in particular, has been behind man's deliberate creation or invention of all social institutions and is thus sufficient for him to modify and plan them at will. Hence, champions of this "rationalism" acknowledge no limits to the potential of human reason, and, obsessed with impressive advances in the natural sciences, technology and engineering, they attempt to apply the methods used in these areas to the social sphere, and in this way to develop a sort of social engineering capable of organizing society in a more just and efficient manner.

The main error that the socialist intellectual or scientistic social engineer commits is to assume that it is possible, by scientific means, to centrally observe, articulate, store and analyze the dispersed practical information actors constantly generate and transmit in the social process. To put it another way, a scientistic individual believes he can and must occupy the upper rung of the socialist governing agency, by virtue of his superior knowledge and intellectual position with respect to the rest of society, and that these factors authorize him to coordinate society via coercive commands and regulations.[50]

Cartesian rationalism is simply a false rationalism to the extent that it neglects to recognize the limits of human reason itself.[51] It embodies a very grave intellectual error, which is especially significant since it comes from those who supposedly benefit from the best intellectual education and thus should be more humble when evaluating their own potential. This error of rationalists is that they assume that the social laws and institutions which make the process of human interaction possible are a product of man that was deliberately sought, created and designed. They fail to consider that these institutions and laws may be the result of an evolutionary process in which, over a very prolonged period of time, millions and millions of people have taken part, and each has contributed his own small store of practical information and experience generated throughout the social process. Precisely for this reason, these institutions cannot possibly have sprung from a deliberate act of creation by the human mind, which lacks the capacity necessary to take in all of the practical information or knowledge that these institutions incorporate.

Hayek has covered the litany of errors that all socialist scientists are guilty of, and he boils them down to the following four mistaken ideas: (i) the idea that it is unreasonable to follow a course of action that one cannot scientifically justify or confirm via empirical observation; (ii) the idea that it is unreasonable to follow a course of action that one does not understand (due to its traditional, habitual or customary nature); (iii) the idea that it is unreasonable to follow a certain course of action unless its purpose has been clearly specified a priori (a grave error made by intellects of the stature of Albert Einstein, Bertrand Russell and Keynes himself);

and (iv) the idea, which is closely related to those above, that it is unreasonable to embark on any course of action unless its effects have been fully predicted beforehand, are expected to be beneficial from a utilitarian standpoint, and are entirely observable once the action is undertaken.[52] These are the four basic errors that the socialist intellectual commits, and they all stem from the fundamental error of believing the intellectual observer capable of grasping, analyzing and "scientifically" improving the practical information which the observed create and use.

At the same time, whenever a social engineer believes he has discovered a danger or maladjustment in the social process and scientifically justifies or recommends the issuance of a command involving institutionalized coercion or aggression intended to resolve the maladjustment, he commits four additional types of errors: (i) he fails to realize that in all probability, his observation concerning the discovered social problem is mistaken, since he has not been able to incorporate all of the crucial practical information; (ii) he overlooks the fact that, if such a maladjustment does actually exist, it is extremely likely that certain spontaneous entrepreneurial processes have already been set in motion and will tend to eliminate it much faster and more effectively than the proposed coercive command; (iii) he does not see that if his advice prevails and the social "repair" is carried out using coercion, there is every likelihood that this typical manifestation of socialism will halt, obstruct, or render impossible the necessary entrepreneurial process by which the maladjustment could be discovered and eliminated, and therefore, instead of solving the problem, the social-engineering command will complicate it even further and make it impossible to eliminate; and (iv) the socialist intellectual specifically overlooks the fact that his behavior will modify the entire framework of human action and entrepreneurship and will render them superfluous and perverse and, as we have seen, will direct them toward areas which do not normally correspond to them (corruption, the purchase of favors from the government, the underground economy and so on).[53] Finally, we should add that social engineering rests on an unsound methodological approach to the science of economics and of sociology, an approach which focuses exclusively on final states of equilibrium and depends upon the arrogant presumption that all information necessary is given and available to the scientist, and this approach and assumption virtually pervade most modern-day economic analysis, leaving it useless.[54]

**Other Types of Socialism (Christian or Solidarity Based, Syndicalist . . .)**

Socialism based on Christianity or "solidarity" arises when certain results of the social process are judged unfavorably from a moral standpoint and the systematic, institutional use of coercion to modify such situations of injustice is defended. In this sense, Christian socialism founded on "holy coercion" is no different from the other types of socialism that have already been analyzed, and it is only mentioned separately due to the distinct, more or less religious grounds upon which people justify it. Also, Christian socialism typically rests on a lack of knowledge and awareness of the functioning of the social processes the force of entrepreneurship drives. In the moral judgments involved, a vague idea of solidarity toward one's neighbor or fellow man predominates, though it is unaccompanied by the knowledge that the social process of human interaction makes the development of civilization possible not only for one's neighbors, but also for those far away and unknown, and this occurs spontaneously by a process in which diverse people cooperate by pursuing their own particular ends, even though they do not know each other. Finally, Christian socialists do not consider coercion morally detrimental if it is aimed at achieving morally superior goals. Nevertheless, systematic coercion, even when "holy", is still antihuman coercion, and therefore constitutes socialism with all of the characteristic analytical consequences we have already noted.[55]

Syndicalist socialism is another variety of socialism, and its advocates seek to create, through the systematic and institutional exercise of coercion, a society in which the workers directly own the means of production. This variety, sometimes called "self-management socialism", is socialism nonetheless, to the extent that it relies on the widespread, systematic use of coercion and thus reproduces all of the features and consequences of socialism which have already been examined in this chapter. However, syndicalist socialism also gives rise to peculiar forms of discoordination which do not appear in other types of socialism, especially if it is not confined to a mere redistribution of wealth but is intended to become a lasting economic and social system. Theorists have analyzed these typical, distinctive characteristics in detail, and the theoretical conclusions they have drawn have been well illustrated by the few historical cases, like that of the former Yugoslavia, in which an attempt has been made to put syndicalist socialism into practice effectively.[56]

## 8 CRITICISM OF THE ALTERNATIVE CONCEPTS OF SOCIALISM

### The Traditional Concept and the Process by which the New Concept Developed

Socialism has traditionally been defined as that system of social organization based on state ownership of the means of production.[57] This meaning, which in practice coincides with the definition given earlier for "real socialism", has long been the most widely accepted for historical and political reasons. It is the definition Mises originally used in 1922 in his critical treatise on socialism,[58] and afterward he himself, and the others of his school, used it as a point of reference throughout the subsequent debate on the impossibility of socialist economic calculation, a debate we shall have the opportunity to study in detail in the forthcoming chapters.

Nevertheless, this traditional definition of socialism was clearly unsatisfactory from the start. To begin with, it was plainly of a static nature, since it was formulated in terms of the existence (or nonexistence) of a certain legal institution (property rights) in connection with a specific economic category (the means of production). The use of this definition required a prior explanation of property rights and their implications within the sphere of the economy. Furthermore, the very debate on the impossibility of socialism revealed that the different scientists involved had considerable difficulty communicating with each other, precisely due to the different meanings they considered implicit in the concept of property rights. Finally, the traditional definition appeared to exclude the interventionism and economic regulation which, though they did not require the complete nationalization of the means of production, did produce discoordinating effects which were qualitatively very similar. For all of these reasons, it seemed highly advisable to continue to search for and to find a definition of socialism which would go to the very heart of the matter, be as free as possible of concepts that could lend themselves to mistaken interpretations, and, like the social processes to which the definition would be applied, have a distinctly dynamic nature.

One of the most important consequences of the debate on the impossibility of socialist economic calculation was the development and elaboration by Austrian economists (Mises, Hayek, and particularly Kirzner) of a theory of entrepreneurship, a theory which portrayed entrepreneurship as the leading, creative force behind all social processes. The direction to be taken in the formulation of a truly scientific concept of socialism was ultimately determined by the discovery that man's innate entrepreneurial capacity, expressed in his own creative action, is precisely what makes life in society possible, since it uncovers social maladjustments and leads to the creation and transmission of the information necessary for each actor to learn to tune his behavior to that of others.

Hans-Hermann Hoppe took the next most important step in the process toward the formation of a suitable definition of socialism.[59] Hoppe revealed the essential characteristic of socialism to be its basis of institutionalized aggression against or interference with property rights. His definition is more dynamic, and therefore much more operative than the traditional definition. It does not deal with the existence or nonexistence of property rights, but instead with the question of whether coercion or physical violence is institutionally, that is, in an organized, repetitive manner, used to violate property rights. Although Hoppe's definition can be viewed as a breakthrough, it is not completely satisfactory, since it requires one to specify or define *ab initio* what is understood by "property rights", and it makes no mention whatsoever of the exercise of entrepreneurship as the leading force behind all social processes.

If we combine Hoppe's intuition, specifically that all socialism involves the systematic use of coercion, with the contributions of Professor Kirzner to the theory of entrepreneurship, we reach the conclusion that the most appropriate definition of socialism is that proposed and used in this chapter, namely, that socialism is any organized system of institutional aggression against entrepreneurship and human action. This definition offers the advantage of universal comprehensibility without the need for a detailed a priori explanation of the concept of property rights and what they should entail. It is obvious that human action can either constitute an attack on other human beings or not, and that as long as it does not, and does not specifically consist of a defense against arbitrary or asystematic outside aggression, this action is the most intimate and typical characteristic of human beings, and therefore, is completely legitimate and must be respected.

In other words, the definition of socialism proposed here is the most suitable because it has been formulated in terms of human action, man's most intimate and fundamental trait. Moreover, socialism is conceived as an institutionalized assault on precisely those forces which make life in society possible, and in this sense the assertion that nothing is more antisocial than the socialist system itself is only apparently paradoxical. One of the greatest advantages of this definition of socialism is that it brings to light this state of affairs. Without a doubt, the process of social interaction free of aggression demands adherence to an entire series of rules, laws or behavioral habits. Together these make up substantive law; that is, the framework within which human actions can be peacefully carried out. Nevertheless, the law does not precede the exercise of human action, but evolves in the form of custom from the very process of social interaction. Therefore, according to our definition, socialism is not a system of institutional aggression against an evolutionary result of entrepreneurship (property rights), but is a system of aggression against human action or entrepreneurship itself. This definition of socialism enables us to directly link the theory of society with a theory of law and its emergence, development and evolution. Furthermore, it leaves us entirely free to ask, on a theoretical level, what property rights emerge from the non-coercive social process, which property rights are just, and to what extent socialism is or is not ethically admissible.

## Socialism and Interventionism

Another advantage of this definition of socialism is that it includes within its scope the social system based on interventionism. In fact, whether one regards interventionism as a typical manifestation of socialism or, as is more common, an intermediate system between "real socialism" and the free social process,[60] it is clear that since all interventionary measures constitute a coercive, institutional assault on a certain social sphere, interventionism, regardless of the degree, type, or motivation involved, is socialism from the standpoint of our definition, and thus, it will inexorably produce all of the discoordinating effects examined in this chapter.

The equation of the term "socialism" with the term "interventionism" is far from an unjustified broadening of the meanings these words usually convey, and is actually an analytical requirement of the theory of social processes based on entrepreneurship. In fact, though the first Austrian theorists who dealt with interventionism initially considered it a conceptual category separate from socialism, as the debate on the impossibility of socialist economic calculation progressed, the boundaries between the two concepts began to blur, and they continued to do so up to the present day, when it has become clear to the proponents of the theory of entrepreneurship that no qualitative difference exists between socialism and interventionism,[61] though colloquially the terms are sometimes used to refer to different degrees of the same reality.

Furthermore, the proposed definition of socialism permits scientists to fulfill the important function of exposing attempts, which are very skillful today in many political, social and cultural areas, to immunize interventionism against the natural and inevitable effects necessarily exerted upon it by the economic, social and political collapse of none other than its closest antecedent and intellectual forerunner: real socialism. At most, real socialism and interventionism are simply two manifestations, of different degrees of intensity, of the same coercive, institutional reality, and they fully share the same essential intellectual error and pernicious social consequences.[62]

## The Inanity of the "Idyllic" Concepts of Socialism

It is vacuous and futile to define socialism based on subjective, idyllic assessments. This type of definition, which prevailed from the start, never disappeared completely and has recently gained fresh impetus as a by-product of the dismantling of real socialism and the stubborn desire of many "intellectuals" to salvage at least an idyllic concept of socialism capable of retaining some popular appeal. Thus, it is not uncommon to again encounter definitions which equate socialism with "social harmony", the "harmonious union of man with nature"[63] or the simple "maximization of the welfare of the population".[64] These are all empty definitions as long as they prevent one from discerning whether or not the author who proposes them intends to justify the systematic exercise of institutional coercion against free human interaction. Thus, it will be necessary to establish in each case whether we are faced with simple, blatant opportunism, with the deliberate desire to conceal institutional aggression behind an attractive façade, or simply, with intellectual confusion and hazy ideas.

**Could the Term "Socialism" Someday be Restored?**

Although not impossible, it is very doubtful and highly unlikely that the meaning of the term "socialism", which rests on such a gross intellectual error and arises from such fatal scientific conceit, will change in the future in a manner that permits the restoration of the word and its redefinition based on a theoretical analysis of social processes, an analysis free from scientific errors. The only possible way to renew the term "socialism" would be to redefine it based on the concept of society as a spontaneous order and process driven by man's innate entrepreneurial capacity, which was described in detail in the last chapter. In this way, people would no longer consider socialism fundamentally antisocial, as it is now viewed, and the word would come to denote any non-coercive system which respects the processes of free human interaction. "Socialism" would thus become synonymous with terms which, like "economic liberalism" and "free market economy", currently convey an idea of respect toward spontaneous social processes and minimization of the systematic coercion the state applies to them.[65] Nevertheless, the disenchantment caused by the intensive, continued pursuit of the socialist ideal, together with the essentially arrogant nature man demonstrates in all areas, but especially in science, politics and society, make it almost impossible to imagine that this positive semantic development could actually take place one day.

# NOTES

1. The *Diccionario* of the Real Academia Española (1984) defines "coercion" as "force or violence used to oblige someone to do something" ("*la fuerza o violencia que se hace a una persona para que ejecute alguna cosa*"). The term derives from the Latin

word *cogere*, to impel, and from *coactionis*, which referred to tax collection. On the concept of coercion and its effects on the actor, see Hayek's *The Constitution of Liberty* (1959 [1990], esp. pp. 20–21). For his part, Rothbard defines "aggression" this way: "Aggression is defined as the initiation of the use or threat of physical violence against the person or property of someone else." See Rothbard (1973, 8). There are three types of coercion or aggression: autistic, binary and triangular. Autistic aggression involves a command issued to one subject only, a command which modifies the behavior of the coerced actor without affecting any interaction between him and another person. In cases of binary aggression, the governing body coerces the actor to obtain something from him against his will; that is, the governing body forces an exchange in its favor between it and the coerced actor. Triangular coercion is that in which the command and coercion of the governing body are intended to force an exchange between two different actors. We owe this system of classification to Rothbard (1970b, 9, 10).

2. Of course, within our conception of systematic aggression, we do not include the minimum level of institutional coercion necessary to prevent and rectify the damaging effects which non-institutional or asystematic arbitrary aggression produces. Even the non-institutional aggressor desires this minimum level of institutional coercion outside of the context of his asystematic aggression, to allow him to peacefully take advantage of it. The solution to the problem every society addresses when it attempts to avoid and remedy the effects of asystematic or non-institutional aggression lies in the development of an ethical theory of property rights. This theory would be based on the idea that the actor is the rightful owner of all fruits of his entrepreneurial creativity, when he has exercised it without initiating any aggression or coercion against anyone. We view as socialism any widening of the scope of systematic coercion beyond the minimum necessary to uphold the juridical institutions which define and govern property rights. The state is the organization which most typically uses systematic or institutional coercion, and in this sense, whenever the minimum amount of coercion necessary to prevent and eradicate asystematic aggression is exceeded, the state and socialism become intimately linked concepts. This is not the place to cover the different arguments put forward in the interesting debate, within the field of libertarian theory, between those who defend a strictly limited system of government and supporters of an anarcho-capitalist system. Nevertheless, members of the latter group argue that it is utopian to expect an organization with a monopoly on systematic coercion to limit itself effectively, and in fact, all historical attempts to limit state power to the above-mentioned minimum have failed. (For this reason, anarcho-capitalist theorists propose a system of competitive organizations of voluntary membership which would tackle the problem of defining and defending property rights, as well as preventing and fighting crime.) Furthermore, if a strictly limited state is financed coercively by taxes; that is, by a systematic assault on the citizenry and their freedom of action in the definition and defense of property rights, then the limited state could be called socialist in a strict sense as well. For their part, defenders of a limited government argue that even the different private defense agencies would be forced to reach agreements on principles and organization, and thus a de facto state would inevitably reemerge as a result of the very process of social development. On the content of this stimulating debate, see the following works, among others: Rothbard (1973, and 1982, ch. 23); Nozick (1974); and Friedman (1989). Hayek has not voiced a definite opinion on the chances that an anarcho-capitalist system will develop in the future. Against this possibility, he mentions that no process of social development has in the past given rise to a stateless society. He then indicates that, in any case, the evolutionary process of social development has not yet come to an end, and thus it is impossible to know today if in the future the state will disappear and become a sad, dark historical relic, or if, on the contrary, it will survive in a minimal form with strictly limited power. (He rules out the long-term survival of an interventionist or real socialist state, given the theoretical impossibility of both models.) See Hayek (1988). John Paul II, for his part (1991, ch. 5, section 48), points out that the principal obligation of the state is to guarantee the safety of individual freedom and of property, "so that those

who work and produce can enjoy the fruits of their labors and thus feel encouraged to work efficiently and honestly". He adds that the state should intervene only under circumstances of exceptional urgency, that intervention should be of a temporary nature, and that the principle of subsidiarity with respect to civil society should be respected. Finally, we should mention that in many societies, not only is systematic aggression committed by the state directly, but in numerous areas, with the state's complicity and consent, this type of aggression is wielded by groups or associations which, like unions, in practice enjoy the "privilege" of being able to use systematic violence with impunity against the rest of the population.

3. "In fact where self-interest is violently suppressed, it is replaced by a burdensome system of bureaucratic control which *dries up the wellsprings of initiative and creativity*" (John Paul II, 1991, ch. 3, section 25, para. 3).

4. Mises affirmed: "The idea of socialism is at once grandiose and simple. We may say, in fact, that it is one of the most ambitious creations of the human spirit, so magnificent, so daring, that it has rightly aroused the greatest admiration. If we wish to save the world from barbarism we have to refute socialism, but we cannot thrust it carelessly aside" (1922 [1981], 41).

5. John Paul II uses the same terminology in his encyclical *Centesimus Annus*, where, in the context of his criticism of the "social assistance" or welfare state, he asserts: "A community of a *higher order* should not interfere in the internal life of a community of a *lower order*, depriving the latter of its functions" (1991, ch. 5, section 48, para. 4). The coercion typical of a higher order can be applied by one lone person, or, as is more common, by a group of people who usually act in an organized, though not necessarily consistent, manner. In both cases, aggression is used by a very small number of people in comparison with the size of the total coerced population, which comprises the lower-order social groups.

6. Hayek opposes the concept of command to that of substantive law, which we could define as an abstract rule which has a general content and applies to all people equally without regard for any particular circumstance. In contrast with what is stated about commands in the text, the law establishes a framework within which it is possible for each actor to create and discover new knowledge and to take advantage of it as he works toward his particular ends in cooperation with others, no matter what these ends are, as long as he abides by the law. In addition, laws, unlike commands, are not deliberate creations of the human mind, but rather are of customary origin. In other words, they are institutions which have developed over a very long period of time due to the participation of many individuals, each of whom, by his behavior, has contributed his own small store of experience and information. This clear distinction between law and command often goes unnoticed, as a result of changes in state legislation, most of which consists almost exclusively of commands enacted in the form of laws. See Hayek (1959, ch. 10). Table 3.1, later in this chapter, outlines the way in which socialism corrupts law and justice as it replaces them with arbitrary commands.

7. In the words of Hayek himself: "This means that the, in some respects always *unique*, combinations of individual knowledge and skills, which the market enables them to use, *will not merely, or even in the instance, be such knowledge of facts as they could list and communicate if some authority asked them to do so*. The knowledge of which I speak consists rather of a capacity to find out particular circumstances, which becomes effective only if possessors of this knowledge are informed by the market which kind of things or services are wanted, and how urgently they are wanted" see (Hayek, 1978a, 182). Also, on page 51 of the second chapter of the first volume, *Rules and Order*, of Hayek's *Law, Legislation and Liberty* (1973), we read the following: "This is the gist of the argument against *interference* or *intervention* in the market order. The reason why such isolated *commands* requiring specific actions by members of the spontaneous order can never improve but must disrupt that order is that *they will refer to a part of a system of interdependent actions determined by information and guided by purposes known only to the several acting persons but not to the directing authority*. The spontaneous order

arises from each element balancing all the various factors operating on it and by *adjusting all its various actions to each other, a balance which will be destroyed* if some of the actions are determined by another agency *on the basis of different knowledge and on the service of different ends*".

8. Mises (1966, 696).
9. What is the just or mathematical price of things? The Spanish scholastics of the sixteenth and seventeenth centuries asked this question and arrived at the conclusion that the "just price" depends on so many particular circumstances that only God can know it, and that consequently, for human purposes, the just price is the price spontaneously established by the social process; in other words, the market price. John Paul II expresses just this idea in his encyclical, *Centesimus Annus* (1991, ch. 4, section 32), where he states that the just price is that "mutually agreed upon through free bargaining". Perhaps within the very foundations of socialism lies a hidden, atavistic desire of man to be like God, or to put it more accurately, to believe he is God, and thus free to tap a much greater store of knowledge and information than would be humanly possible. Hence, the Jesuit cardinal Juan de Lugo (1583–1660) wrote that "pretium iustum mathematicum, licet soli Deo notum" (*Disputationes de Iustitia et Iure*, Lyon 1643, Vol. 2, D. 26, S. 4, N. 40). For his part, Juan de Salas, also a Jesuit and a professor of philosophy and theology at various universities in Spain and Rome, agreed with Lugo when he asserted, in reference to the possibility of knowing the just price, that "quas exacte comprehendere et ponderare Dei est, non hominum" (*Commentarii in Secundam Secundae divi Thomae de Contractibus*, Lyon 1617, Tr. Empt. et Vend., IV, number 6, p. 9). Other interesting quotations from Spanish scholastics of this period appear in Hayek (1973, Vol. 2, 178, 179). For a summary of the important contributions sixteenth- and seventeenth-century Spanish scholastics made to economics, see Rothbard (1976).
10. In 1920, Mises made an original and brilliant contribution when he called attention to the impossibility of carrying out economic calculations without the dispersed, practical information or knowledge only generated in the free market (Mises, 1920 [1975]). Mises's main idea appears on page 102, where he states: "The distribution among a number of individuals of administrative control over economic goods in a community of men who take part in the labour of producing them, and who are economically interested in them, *entails a kind of intellectual division of labour*, which would not be possible without some system of calculating production and without economy". The following chapter will be devoted in its entirety to an examination of all implications of the Misesian argument and to an analysis of the start of the ensuing debate.
11. "The paradox of planning is that it cannot plan, because of the absence of economic calculation. What is called a planned economy is no economy at all. It is just a system of groping about in the dark. There is no question of a rational choice of means for the best possible attainment of the ultimate ends sought. What is called conscious planning is precisely the elimination of conscious purposive action" (Mises, 1966, 700–701). On the "paradox of planning" and the concept of responsibility, see also Section 6 of this chapter.
12. There will always be a "lag" or "qualitative leap" between the degree of complexity the governing body can take on with its computer equipment and that which social actors create in a decentralized and spontaneous manner using equipment that is similar (or at least of the same generation). The latter will invariably be much greater. Perhaps Michael Polanyi explained this argument better than anyone when he stated: "Our whole articulate equipment turns out to be merely a tool box, a supremely effective instrument for deploying our inarticulate faculties. And we need not hesitate then to conclude that the tacit personal coefficient of knowledge predominates also in the domain of explicit knowledge and represents therefore at all levels man's ultimate faculty for acquiring and holding knowledge ... Maps, graphs, books, formulae, and so on offer wonderful opportunities for reorganizing our knowledge from ever new points of view. And this reorganization is itself, as a rule, a tacit performance" (1959, 24, 25). See also Rothbard's argument, which we remark on in note 84 of Chapter 6.

13. Also, as Hayek asserts, it is a logical contradiction to hold that the human mind will some day be able to explain itself, much less reproduce its ability to generate new information. Hayek's argument, which we advanced in Chapter 2, note 17, is that an order, composed of a certain conceptual system of categories, can explain simpler orders (those which comprise a simpler system of categories), but it is logically inconceivable that it ever account for or replicate itself, or explain more complex orders. See Hayek (1952 [1976], 185–8). See also, in Penrose's (1989) book cited in note 28 of the last chapter, Penrose's arguments against the chances of the future development of artificial intelligence. Finally, even if the blueprint for the model of artificial intelligence were to be successful in the future (which we deem impossible for the reasons stated), it would simply mean the creation of new "human" minds, which would have to be incorporated into the social process and would complicate and distance it even further from the socialist ideal. (I owe this argument to my good friend, Luis Reig Albiol.)
14. The argument offered in the text reveals the absurdity of the belief, held by many "intellectuals" not well versed in the functioning of society, that it is "obvious" that the more complex society becomes, the more necessary exogenous, coercive, and institutional intervention becomes. This idea originated with Benito Mussolini, who stated: "We were the first to assert that the more complicated the forms assumed by civilization, the more restricted the freedom of the individual must become" (cited by Hayek in *The Road to Serfdom* (1944 [1972]). However, as shown, the logical–theoretical reality is just the opposite: as the wealth of society and the development of civilization increase, socialism becomes much more difficult. The less advanced or more primitive a society is, and the more plentiful are the means the directing authority has available to handle information, the less complicated the problem of socialism appears (though from a logical and theoretical standpoint it is always impossible when applied to human beings endowed in their actions with an innate creative capacity).
15. Here we should mention an entire group of computer scientists who have introduced theorists in their field to the contributions of the Austrian school of economics and have actually developed a whole new scientific research program called "Agoric Systems" (a term that derives etymologically from the Greek word for "market"), which places key importance on the theory of market processes with respect to achieving new advances in computer science. In particular, Mark S. Miller and K. Eric Drexler, of Stanford University (see Miller and Drexler, 1988). See also the following article (including all sources cited therein), which summarizes the program: "High-tech Hayekians: some possible research topics in the economics of computation" (Lavoie et al., 1990).
16. This is precisely the title of Hayek's last work, *The Fatal Conceit: The Errors of Socialism*. See *The Collected Works of F.A. Hayek*, ed. W.W. Bartley III (Chicago: University of Chicago Press, 1989). Hayek himself, when interviewed in Madrid by Carlos Rodríguez Braun, stated that the essence of his book was to show that "it is arrogant, boastful, to believe one knows enough to organize life in society, life which is in fact the result of a process which draws on the dispersed knowledge of millions of individuals. To think we can plan that process is completely absurd" (see Rodríguez Braun, 1986).
17. Hayek (1973, 2: 35–54) and Ortega y Gasset (1947, 603).
18. Real Academia Española, *Diccionario*, s. v. "*totalitarismo*", second meaning.
19. Even the sagacious Michael Polanyi made the very common mistake of deeming this sort of experimentation with planning relatively harmless, due to its incapacity to produce practical results, yet he was overlooking the severe damage done to social coordination by attempts to carry out utopian programs of social engineering (see Polanyi, 1951, 111). Those responsible for the coercive agencies are unable to fathom how, despite all of their efforts, social engineering does not work or works increasingly poorly, and they often end up sinking into hypocrisy or desperation and attributing the unhappy direction of events either to divine judgment – as did the Count-Duke of Olivares, as we see in note 50 – or to the "lack of cooperation or harmful intentions of civil society itself" – as did Felipe González, in the speech he gave at the Universidad Carlos III in Madrid for the Day of the Constitution, December 6, 1991.

20. Perhaps the first to reveal this self-destructive result of institutional coercion was Böhm-Bawerk (1914). Specifically, on page 192 of the English version of this article we read that "any situation brought about by means of 'power' may again bring into play motives of self interest, tending to oppose its continuance". Mises later carried on this line of research in his *Kritik des Interventionismus: Untersuchungen zur Wirtschaftspolitik und Wirtschaftsideologie der Gegenwart* (1929). Mises concludes that "all varieties of interference with the market phenomena not only fail to achieve the ends aimed at by their authors and supporters, but bring about a state of affairs which – from the point of view of their authors' and advocates' valuations – is less desirable than the previous state of affairs which they were designed to alter". Also worthy of special mention is the subsequent work of Rothbard, *Power and Market: Government and the Economy* (1970b). Nevertheless, the most brilliant approach to this topic is the one adopted by Kirzner in his article, "The perils of regulation: a market process approach", in Kirzner (1985, 119, 149).

21. János Kornai coined the term "soft budget constraint" to describe this characteristic of socialism, namely decision making at all levels which is not properly restricted by cost considerations. Although this term has gained a certain currency, it focuses too much on the most obvious manifestations of the fundamental problem in industrial organizations (the impossibility, in the absence of free entrepreneurship, of generating the information required to calculate costs), and this has led many scholars to inappropriately overlook the problem or fail to do it justice. See Kornai (1980). More recently, however, Kornai has managed to express his theory in terms of entrepreneurship, thus demonstrating that he has finally fully grasped the essence of the Austrian argument on planning. See Kornai (1986). On this topic, see also the works of Jan Winiecki (esp. 1988 [1991], and 1987).

22. An action is viewed as "responsible" when the actor who undertakes it bears in mind the cost that both he and others connected with him incur as a result of the action. Cost is the subjective value that the actor assigns to that which he forgoes upon acting, and it can only be properly estimated by one who possesses the necessary subjective, tacit and practical information regarding his own personal circumstances, as well as those of the other individuals with whom he interacts. If, because the free exercise of entrepreneurship is not permitted (systematic coercion), or the corresponding property rights are not adequately defined and defended (asystematic coercion), this practical information cannot be created or transmitted, the actor cannot perceive the costs and thus tends to act irresponsibly. On the concept of responsibility, see Garret Hardin (1977, 67). The irresponsibility typical of socialism causes the "tragedy of the commons" phenomenon to spread in a socialist regime to all of the social areas it affects (Rothschild, 1990, ch. 2).

23. The quasi-religious reverence for statistics originated with Lenin himself, who stated: "Bring statistics to the masses, make it popular, so that the active population learn by themselves to understand and realise how much and what kind of work must be done" (translated from p. 33 of the *Die nächsten Aufgaben der Sowjetmacht* (Berlin, 1918) in Hayek, 1935a [1975], 128). On the overproduction of statistics that arises from interventionism, and the great social harm, cost, and inefficiency they yield, see Stephen Gillespie (1990). On socialism and the environment, see Anderson and Leal (1991).

24. *"Echar a perder, depravar, dañar, pudrir, pervertir, estragar o viciar"* (Real Academia Española, *Diccionario*, s. v. *"corromper"*).

25. Perhaps it was Hans-Hermann Hoppe who best described the corrupting effect of socialism when he stated: "The redistribution of chances for income acquisition must result in more people using aggression to gain personal satisfaction and/or more people becoming more aggressive, that is, *shifting increasingly from non aggressive to aggressive roles, and slowly changing their personality as a consequence of this;* and this change in the character structure, in the moral composition of society, in turn leads to another reduction in the level of investment in human capital" (1989, 16–17). See also Huerta de Soto's analysis (1991). Another sign of the corrupting effect of socialism is a

general increase in the "social demand" for coercive state commands and regulations, an increase which arises from a combination of the following factors: (i) the desire of each special interest group to obtain privileges at the expense of the rest of society; (ii) the impossible, naive illusion that greater doses of regulation will be able to reduce the generalized legal uncertainty that everywhere predominates due to the expanding and tangled web of contradictory legislation; and (iii) the prostitution of habits of personal responsibility, which subjectively and unconsciously reinforce acceptance of state paternalism and feelings of dependence on authority.

26. See Kirzner, "The perils of regulation: a market process approach", in Kirzner (1985, 144, 145). In a socialist regime, because people need to influence the coercive body while continuing to at least appear to obey its commands, and because this body is highly arbitrary and discretionary, the old-boy network is considered vital. In fact, a system is more interventionary, the more necessary and important this network is, and the more social spheres it touches (precisely the spheres where intervention is strongest). Personal contacts are depended upon to the detriment of the sort of interaction typical in the free world, interaction which is more abstract and impersonal, and thus relegates questions of friendship to the background, always subordinate to the essential object of achieving one's own ends by furthering as much as possible others' interests, as revealed by the market. Moreover, attempts to win the favor of those in power, and the servility which this entails, often provoke a curious sort of "Stockholm syndrome", which gives the coerced person surprising feelings of understanding and camaraderie toward those who institutionally coerce him and prevent him from freely realizing his innate creative potential.

27. See Thomas J. Di Lorenzo (1988). Although the contributions of the public choice school are highly significant with respect to its analysis of the functioning of bureaucracies and political bodies in charge of applying institutional coercion, I agree with Di Lorenzo that the analysis of this school has until now been seriously weakened by its excessive dependence on the methodology of neoclassical economics; that is, by its excessively static nature, the use of the formal instruments characteristic of the economic analysis of equilibrium, and the failure to fully accept the dynamic analysis based on the theory of entrepreneurship. The introduction of the conception of entrepreneurship leads us to conclude that coercive institutional activity is much more perverse even than the public choice school has traditionally revealed. This school has generally overlooked the capacity of the governing body to entrepreneurially create perverse, corrupting actions and strategies which are new and more effective. For a summary of the most important contributions of the public choice school in this area, see Tullock (1965); Mises's pioneering work, *Bureaucracy* (1969); Niskanen (1971); Migué and Bélanger (1974, 27–43); and Mitchel (1979). Huerta de Soto (1986) outlines in Spanish the main arguments of all of this literature.

28. Precisely because socialism generates corruption and immorality, it will always be the most corrupt, immoral and unscrupulous individuals, that is, those most experienced in breaking the law, exercising violence, and successfully deceiving people, who will tend to rise to power. History has time and again confirmed and illustrated this principle in a variety of contexts, and in 1944 Hayek analyzed it in detail in chapter 10 ("Why the worst get on the top") of his *The Road to Serfdom* (1944 [2008], 134–52). There is a Spanish translation by José Vergara, *Camino de Servidumbre* (1978). We consider the title, *El Camino hacia la Servidumbre*, to be more suitable. Valentín Andrés Álvarez proposed this translation in his 1945 review of Hayek's book ("El Camino hacia la Servidumbre del Profesor Hayek"), a review that nearly cost him his professorship in Madrid, due to the political intolerance in Spain at that time.

29. Jean-François Revel (1981). According to Camilo José Cela, winner of the Nobel prize for literature in 1989, "the state divorces nature and leaps above countries, blood, tongues. The dragon of Leviathan has opened its jaws to devour mankind . . . The thousand gears of the state teem with its worm-like servants; they crawl with the worms who *learned* the fateful lesson that they must preserve their host" (Cela, 1990, 4, 5).

30. For a summary of theory concerning the irregular economy and an outline of the most important literature on the subject, see Joaquín Trigo Portela and Carmen Vázquez Arango (1983) and Trigo Portela (1988). For an illustration of the theoretical argument offered in the text, yet applied to the specific case of Peru, see Hernando de Soto (1987).
31. Moreover, V.A. Naishul has pointed out that the socialist system does not tolerate changes and innovations, given the profound, multiple maladjustments they cause in the rigid organization of the economy (see "The birthmarks of developed socialism", in Naishul, 1991, ch. 5, 26–9, esp. p. 28, "Hostility to change".)
32. Jacques Garello is the author of a good analysis of the damaging effects socialism exerts on culture, with special reference to France (see "Cultural protectionism", presented at the Mont Pèlerin Society Regional Meeting, Paris, 1984).
33. One example which graphically illustrates the argument we have invoked in the text is that of the harmful effects which authorities' systematic aggression on the production, distribution and consumption of drugs exerts on the social process by which people learn how to behave in connection with drugs. In fact, historically many drugs have met with less aggression, and as a result, throughout the adjustment process entrepreneurship drives, society has been able to generate a large volume of information and experience which have taught people how to behave properly with respect to these substances. For example, in many societies, this is what has occurred in the case of drugs such as wine and tobacco. However, a similar process is impossible as regards more recently discovered substances which, from the beginning, have been subjected to a very rigorous system of institutional coercion, a system that, apart from failing utterly, has kept individuals from experimenting and learning what the appropriate behavior patterns should be. See Guy Sorman (1993, 327–37).
34. "Do not pervert justice; *do not show partiality to the poor or favoritism to the great*, but judge your neighbor fairly" (Lev. 19: 15). "So I have caused you to be despised and humiliated before all the people, because you . . . have shown partiality in matters of the law" (Mal. 2: 9 New International Version).
35. The word "social" completely alters the meaning of any term to which it is applied (justice, democracy and so on). Other terms also used to camouflage reality with attractive connotations are, for example, the adjectives "popular" and "organic", which often precede the term "democracy". Americans use the expression "weasel words" to refer to all such words employed to semantically deceive citizens and permit the continued use of enormously attractive words (like "justice" and "democracy") but with meanings that directly contradict those they traditionally convey. The term "weasel word" derives from the well-known line from Shakespeare that refers to the ability of the weasel to drain an egg without damaging its shell at all. ("I can suck melancholy out of a song, as a weasel sucks eggs", *As You Like It* in *The Riverside Shakespeare*, 1974, 2.5.11, p. 379.) For more on this topic, consult in detail all of chapter 7 of Hayek's *The Fatal Conceit* (1988). Another term whose meaning has been corrupted is "solidarity", which today is used as an alibi for state violence considered legitimate if it is reportedly employed to "help" the oppressed. Nevertheless, "solidarity" has traditionally meant something quite different and has referred to the human interaction which emerges in the spontaneous social process entrepreneurship drives. In fact, "solidarity" derives from the Latin term *solidare* (to solder or unite) and means, according to the *Diccionario* of the Real Academia Española, "circumstantial commitment to the enterprise of others". The market, as we have defined it, is therefore the quintessential mechanism or system of solidarity between human beings. In this sense, there is nothing more antithetical to solidarity than the attempt to forcibly impose, from above, principles of solidarity which are as short-sighted as they are biased. Furthermore, the problem of permanent ignorance which plagues the regulatory agency is inevitably shared by those who conceive solidarity strictly in the terms of helping the needy, and this help will be inefficient and superfluous if the state proffers it instead of the individuals interested in voluntarily helping others. John Paul II, in his encyclical *Centesimus Annus*, not only refers to the

market as a "progressively expanding chain of *solidarity*" (ch. 4, section 43, para. 3), but he also affirms that "needs are best understood and satisfied by people who are closest to them and who act as neighbours to those in need", and thus he criticizes the social assistance state: "By intervening directly and depriving society of its responsibility, the Social Assistance State leads to a loss of human energies and an inordinate increase of public agencies, which are dominated more by bureaucratic ways of thinking than by concern for serving their clients, and which are accompanied by an enormous increase in spending" (ch. 5, section 48, para. 5).

36. The best critical treatise on the spurious concept of social justice was written by Hayek. See *The Mirage of Social Justice*, Vol. 2 of *Law, Legislation and Liberty* (1976).
37. For this passage, see pp. 25 and 26 of Vol. 1 of Hayek's *Law, Legislation and Liberty*, where Hayek quotes from Keynes's book, *Two Memoirs* (1949, 97–8). See also Robert Skidelsky (1983, 142–3).
38. See Hayek (1988, ch. 1).
39. *Ojos que no ven, corazón que no siente*. Miguel de Cervantes (*El Quijote*, ch. 67) uses the form, "*Ojos que no ven, corazón que no quiebra*", and the version, "*Ojos que no ven, corazón que no llora*" is also acceptable. (See pp. 327–8 of the *Diccionario de Refranes*, by Juana G. Campos and Ana Barella, 1975.)
40. From this standpoint, the situation is even graver, if possible, in a social democracy than in "real socialism", because in the former, the examples and alternative situations which might open the eyes of the citizenry are almost non-existent, and the possibilities of concealing the harmful effects of democratic socialism through demagogy and *ad hoc* rationalizations are nearly overwhelming. Hence, now that the "paradise" of real socialism has been lost, the true "opium of the people" lies today in social democracy. On this point, see the preface to the Spanish edition of *The Fatal Conceit* (Huerta de Soto, 1990c, 26–7).
41. In the words of Hayek himself: "On the moral side, socialism cannot but destroy the basis of all morals, personal freedom and responsibility. On the political side, it leads sooner or later to totalitarian government. On the material side it will greatly impede the production of wealth, if it does not actually cause impoverishment" (1978d, 304).
42. On the emergence and development of social democracy in West Germany, see the pertinent remarks of Hoppe (1989, ch. 4, esp. 61–4).
43. Hayek, *The Political Order of a Free People*, Vol. 3 of *Law, Legislation and Liberty* (1979, 38–40). On page 39, Hayek explicitly states: "Though I firmly believe that government ought to be conducted according to principles approved by a majority of the people, and must be so run if we are to preserve peace and freedom, *I must frankly admit that if democracy is taken to mean government by the unrestricted will of the majority I am not a democrat, and even regard such government as pernicious and in the long run unworkable*". Next, Hayek explains his rejection of the term "democracy" by pointing out that the Greek root *kratos* derives from the verb *kratein* and incorporates an idea of "brute force" or "heavy handedness" which is incompatible with a democratic government subject to the law, understood in a substantive sense, and applied equally to all ("isonomy").
44. Specifically, this refers to the chief contributions of the public choice school and the theory of interventionism developed by the Austrian school. See the related comments and bibliography offered in note 27 of this chapter. A detailed outline of the reasons public, bureaucratic management is condemned to failure even when it rests upon a "democratic" foundation appears in Huerta de Soto (1986).
45. The theorist who has most brilliantly explained conservative or right-wing socialism is Hoppe (1989, ch. 5).
46. Mises (1922 [1981], 220). Nevertheless, Mises shows that military socialism cannot compete on its own martial ground against those societies in which the exercise of creative entrepreneurial activity is permitted, and in fact he explains that the great Incan communist military empire was very easily destroyed by a handful of Spaniards (pp. 222–3).

47. On guild and agrarian socialism, see Mises (1922 [1981], 229–32, 236–7).
48. Hayek, "Why I am not Conservative", in Hayek (1959, 397–411).
49. The Real Academia Española fails to recognize the term *cientismo* (scientism), which we use. The closest term we find in its dictionary is *cientificismo*, the fifth meaning of which is listed as "the tendency to attach excessive value to scientific or supposedly scientific notions". While Marañón did on occasion also use the term *cientismo*, ultimately he appears to have preferred *cientificismo*, which he views as a "caricature of science" and defines as the "excessive display of a science which is lacking". He concludes: "The crux of the matter is that the *cientificista* uncritically attaches excessive, dogmatic importance to all his vast knowledge; *he takes advantage of his position and reputation to lead followers and listeners alike down the garden path*" (see "La plaga del Cientificismo", in Marañón (1971a, ch. 32, 360–61)). However, the term *cientismo* is more precise than *cientificismo*, since in fact the former refers more to an abuse of science *per se* than to an improper manner of practicing science. (*Científico* derives from Latin: *scientia*, science, and *facere*, to do.) Also, the word *scientism* is used in English to denote the inappropriate application of the methods used in the natural sciences, in physics, technology and engineering, to the field of the social sciences. ("A thesis that the methods of the natural sciences should be used in all areas of investigation, including philosophy, the humanities, and the social sciences." See *Webster's Third New International Dictionary of the English Language Unabridged*, Vol. 3 (Chicago: G. & G. Merriam, 1981, 2033). Finally, Manuel Seco, in his *Diccionario de Dudas y Dificultades de la Lengua Española* (1990, 96), states that the terms *ciencismo* and *ciencista* are both acceptable, though we consider them inferior to *cientismo* and *cientista*, since the latter derive from the Latin term *scientia* (and not the Spanish word *ciencia*), which is also the root of the corresponding expressions in French and English.
50. This common arrogance of the socialist intellectual is well illustrated by a legend which tells of the Spanish King Alphonso X, the Wise or Learned, who "was so insolent and arrogant due to his great knowledge of the humanities and to the secrets of nature he was privy to, that he went so far as to say, in contempt of providence and the supreme wisdom of the universal Creator, that if God had asked him for advice at the time the world was created along with everything in it, and he was with God, some things that were made would have been constructed or formed better than they were, and other things would not have been made at all or would have been improved or corrected". According to legend, this blasphemy of the king was punished with a terrible thunder, lightning, and wind storm that started a fire in the alcazar of Segovia, where the king and his court dwelt, a fire which left several people dead and others injured, and from which the king himself miraculously escaped with his life and immediately repented of his overweening pride. This fierce summer storm which set fire to the alcazar of Segovia and nearly cost the king his life struck on August 26, 1258 and is a rigorously confirmed historical event. See the biography of *Alfonso X El Sabio*, written by Antonio Ballesteros Beretta (1984, 209–11), where we find a critical evaluation of all versions of this legend and its connection with related events that have been historically verified. Although this legend appears to be apocryphal, there is no doubt that the scientistic nature of the "wise" king manifested itself at least in the strict regulations he unsuccessfully imposed to control and fix prices, to prevent a natural, inevitable increase which he himself had caused by systematically devaluing the currency, as well as in the king's equally failed attempt to replace Castile's traditional law of inheritance with a code considered more "scientific", the *Siete Partidas*, all of which set him against his son and successor, Sancho, and gave rise to a civil war that spoiled the last years of his life. Another historical figure who perfectly illustrates the failure of scientistic constructivism in social matters is the Count-Duke of Olivares, who was the royal favorite of King Philip IV and during much of his reign, responsible for the fate of the Spanish empire. The good intentions, capacity for work, and efforts made by the count-duke were as excessive as they were futile. In fact, the main fault of the count-duke was that "by nature, he wished to organize everything", and he could not resist the ambition to dominate in all areas of

social life. In the final stage of his rule, he himself expressed his "deep discouragement that any remedy attempted *produced an effect which was precisely the opposite of that intended*". Nevertheless, the count-duke never came to understand that this was simply the natural, inexorable result of trying to forcibly control and organize all of society, and thus he never attributed the disastrous situation he left Spain in to his management, but rather to the anger of God at the moral depravity of the age. See the excellent study by J.H. Elliott (1986 [1990], esp. 296, 388). (The two above quotations from Elliott's book were translated from the Spanish version.)

51. Hayek, "Kinds of rationalism", in Hayek (1969, 82–95).
52. Hayek (1988, 61, 62). Utilitarianism rests on exactly the same intellectual error as socialism, since it involves the assumption that the utilitarian scientist will have available to him the information on costs and benefits that is necessary to make objective decisions. However, given that such information is not centrally available, utilitarianism is impossible as a political–social philosophy, and hence the only option is to act within the framework of the law and patterned behavioral principles (morality). In fact, it may seem paradoxical, but given man's ineradicable ignorance, there is nothing more useful and practical than to base one's actions on principles and give up all naive, myopic utilitarianism.
53. It was Israel M. Kirzner who pointed out the above four errors social engineers commit when they make pseudo-scientific recommendations of coercion. See "The perils of regulation: a market process approach", in Kirzner (1985, 136–45).
54. Norman P. Barry (1988). In the following chapters, we shall have the opportunity to see how it was that the scientistic theorists with an ingrained focus on equilibrium were unable to grasp the Misesian argument with respect to the impossibility of economic calculation in socialist economies, and we shall also study, as one of the most significant by-products of this controversy, the methodological inconsistencies of modern economic analysis based on equilibrium.
55. A particularly important source on Christian socialism and the so-called "liberation theology" is *Religion, Economics and Social Thoughts* (Block and Hexham, 1989). See also Mises (1922 [1981], 223–6).
56. On syndicalist socialism in general, and the attempt to apply it in the former Yugoslavia, see Svetozar Pejovich (1987) and the bibliography cited therein. See also Furubotn and Pejovich (1973). A "Hayekian" version of syndicalist socialism has been designed by Burzak (2006); see the critical symposium in the *Review of Austrian Economics*, **22** (3), September 2009.
57. Sure enough, the *Diccionario* of the Real Academia Española defines *socialismo* as precisely the "system of social and economic organization based on the collective, state ownership and management of the means of production" (*el "sistema de organización social y económica basado en la propiedad y administración colectiva y estatal de los medios de producción"*).
58. According to Mises, "the essence of socialism is this: all means of production are in the exclusive control of the organized community. This and this alone is socialism. All other definitions are misleading" (Mises, 1922 [1981], 211).
59. Hoppe (1989, 2). Hoppe affirms that "socialism, by no means an invention of XIX's century Marxism but much older, must be conceptualized as an institutionalized interference with or aggression against private property and private property claims".
60. This is the second meaning the *Diccionario* of the Real Academia Española offers for the term *intervencionismo*: "an intermediate system between individualism and collectivism which entrusts the state with the management and supplementation of private enterprise in the life of the country" (*"sistema intermedio entre el individualismo y el colectivismo que confía a la acción del Estado el dirigir y suplir, en la vida del país, la iniciativa privada"*). However, the dictionary's writers contradict themselves with this definition based on the "intermediate" nature of interventionism, since they adopt a position very close to the one in the text when, in the same dictionary, they refer to *socialismo* as "state regulation of economic and social activities and the distribution of goods"

("*regulación por el Estado de las actividades económicas y sociales, y la distribución de los bienes*"). This last definition is essentially very similar to the one the dictionary gives for *intervencionismo*, which gives the impression that its writers consider the two terms – *socialismo* and *intervencionismo* – virtually synonymous.

61. For example, with respect to "interventionism", Lavoie concluded: "*It can be shown to be self-defeating and irrational on much the same grounds on which Mises pronounced complete central planning impossible* . . . piecemeal government interference into the price system must be seen as similarly obstructive of this same necessary discovery procedure, and therefore as distortive of the knowledge which it generates. Thus the calculation argument may be used to explain many of the less-than-total failures resulting from government *tinkering* with the price system, in fundamentally the same way that it explains the utter economic ruin inevitably resulting from the attempted *abolition* of the price system". See "Introduction" (1981, 5). For his part, Kirzner has on various occasions referred to the "parallelism" between "socialism" and "interventionism" (1989, ch. 6, 121ff.). We must criticize the idea, which even Mises defended a time or two, that economic calculation is possible in the interventionist system, since such calculation is impossible precisely in the areas where intervention is present, and if in general some calculations are possible, it is because the system does not extend its interference to all of society (to the degree which characterizes real socialism).

62. Nevertheless, our definition of socialism is not as broad as that proposed by Alchian, who states that "*government is socialism, by definition*", and concludes that therefore, at least a minimum of socialism is essential to the preservation of a market economy. First, as we have already explained (see note 2), the minimum amount of institutional coercion necessary to prevent and quell isolated outbreaks of asystematic coercion cannot be considered socialism. Second, it is not clear that this minimum must necessarily be provided by a monopolistic, government organization. See Alchian and Allen (1971, 627–8). And also Huerta de Soto (2009b).

63. See Alec Nove's comments on these "idyllic" definitions in "Socialism" (1987b, 398). Nove ultimately concludes with a traditional definition of socialism, according to which "a society may be seen to be a socialist one if the major part of the means of production of goods and services are not in private hands, but are in some sense socially owned and operated, by state, socialized or cooperative enterprises". Incidentally, on p. 407 of this article, Nove betrays his lack of understanding of the dynamic theory of entrepreneurship when he groups together Mises and the "Chicago Utopia" and criticizes capitalism because it is quite different from the "perfect competition" models one finds in textbooks.

64. This is the definition suggested by Oskar Lange in 1942, during his most "liberal" period, before he turned to the more hard-lined Stalinism of his later years. In fact, during the lecture he gave at the Socialist Club of the University of Chicago on May 8, 1942, Lange asserted: "By a socialist society, I mean a society in which economic activities, particularly production, is carried on in such a way as to maximise the welfare of the population". He also added that in his definition, "the accent is rather on the purpose than on the means". See the lectures of Oskar Lange on "The economic operation of a socialist society: I and II" (1942 [1987], 3, 4).

65. This would be a case of a word being rehabilitated and given a scientifically coherent meaning by a process which would reverse the semantic corruption that the adjective "social" provokes whenever it is attached to a concept, as explained in note 35.

# 4. Ludwig von Mises and the start of the debate on economic calculation

In this and the following chapters, we propose to closely analyze the debate on the impossibility of economic calculation in socialist economies. The scientific stature of the figures involved in the debate, its theoretical depth, and the influence it has had on the subsequent development of our science make it one of the most portentous debates in the history of economic thought. The chapters will cover each author's most important contributions, along with the stages and most significant facets of the controversy. Also, there will be a critical analysis of the most widespread version (which this author believes is erroneous), of its content and development, and an attempt to offer various explanations for its predominance up until recent times. This initial chapter will begin by examining the historical background to the debate and studying in detail the essential contribution of Ludwig von Mises which sparked it.

## 1 BACKGROUND

Only the emergence of an adequate understanding of the workings of society and the market as a spontaneous order which arises from the constant interaction between millions of people could, in the history of economic thought, make it obvious that socialism is an intellectual error, and thus impossible in both theory and practice. Although the tradition of the view of society that has been presented in the last two chapters dates back more than two thousand years,[1] it is true that its development throughout the centuries has been a very arduous one in constant conflict with the constructivist rationalism which justifies systematic coercion and violence and toward which the human intellect is almost intuitively and inexorably oriented. From the ancient Greek *kosmos*, understood as a natural or spontaneous order created independently of the deliberate will of man, through the most time-honored Roman legal tradition[2] and the contributions, closer to us in history, of the Spanish scholastics, Cantillon, Turgot and Menger, to Mises, Hayek and the other contemporary classical-libertarian thinkers, runs a long road fraught with setbacks, and during many of its stages, completely flooded with the "black tide" of scientism.

The basic idea at the heart of our criticism of socialism is that no person or group of people can obtain the information or knowledge necessary to organize society in a coordinated manner via coercive commands. This idea arises as a natural corollary to the conception of society as a spontaneous order. Hence, it is not surprising that though this notion had not been formulated in detail until recently, at least in embryonic form people have been defending it for much longer. For example, Cicero tells us that Cato considered the Roman legal system very superior to the rest because it was "not due to the personal creation of one man, but of very many; it has not been founded during the lifetime of any particular individual, but through a series of centuries and generations. *For . . . there never was in the world a man so clever as to foresee everything and . . . even if we could concentrate all brains into the head of one man, it would be impossible for him to provide for everything at one time without having the experience that comes from practice through a long period of history"*.[3]

Many centuries later, Montesquieu and Turgot explored this idea further and expressed a view which bears even more directly on the issue that now concerns us. They found it contradictory to think the state capable of simultaneously devoting attention both to large-scale projects and to all of the minor details involved in organizing them.[4] A little over a century later, in 1854, Hermann Heinrich Gossen repeated this idea almost literally and had the merit of raising it, for the first time, with the intention of expressly criticizing the communist system. Gossen arrived at the conclusion that the central authority planned by communists with the purpose of coercively allocating the different kinds of labor and their compensation would soon discover it had undertaken a task far too difficult for any one person.[5] Twenty years later, another German economist, Albert Schäffle, Menger's immediate predecessor as chair of the economics department at the University of Vienna, showed that, without imitating the system of price determination found in market processes, it would be inconceivable that a central planning agency could efficiently, in terms of both quantity and quality, allocate society's resources.[6] At the close of the century, Walter Bagehot[7] made the shrewd observation that primitive, uncivilized man was incapable of carrying out even the simplest estimations of costs and benefits, and Bagehot concluded that in all industrial societies, accounting in monetary units is necessary for the estimation of production costs.

Next, we should mention the contribution of Vilfredo Pareto. We have an ambivalent assessment to make of Pareto's influence on the subsequent debate over socialist economic calculation. His influence was negative to the extent that he focused on the mathematical analysis of economic equilibrium, an approach which always presumes from the beginning that all information necessary to achieve equilibrium is available. This approach gave rise to the idea, which Enrico Barone later developed and many other economists repeated ad nauseam, that the problem of economic calculation in socialist economies could be mathematically resolved in the very same way it had been raised and resolved by mathematical equilibrium economists in the case of a market economy. Nonetheless, neither Pareto nor Barone is totally responsible for the incorrect interpretation just mentioned, since both explicitly drew attention to the impossibility of solving the corresponding system of equations without the information the market itself provides. Specifically, in 1897, Pareto went so far as to assert, in reference to solving the system of equations which describes equilibrium: "As a practical matter, that is beyond the power of algebraic analysis . . . In that case the roles would be changed; and it would no longer be mathematics which would come to the aid of political economy, but political economy which would come to the aid of mathematics. In other words, if all these equations were actually known, the only means of solving them would be to observe the actual solution which the market gives".[8] Pareto expressly denies the possibility of accessing the information necessary even to formulate the system of equations which would make it possible to describe equilibrium, and he simultaneously touches on a secondary problem: the algebraic impossibility of solving, in practice, the system of equations which formally describes equilibrium.

Following Pareto, Barone, in his well-known 1908 article devoted to the application of the paradigm Pareto initiated to the collectivist state, explicitly asserts that even if the practical difficulty of algebraically resolving the above system of equations could be overcome (which is not theoretically impossible), it would in any case be inconceivable (and therefore would be theoretically impossible) to obtain the information necessary to determine the technical coefficients required to formulate the corresponding system of equations.[9]

Despite these clear (though isolated) warnings, it was stated earlier that our assessment of Pareto's and Barone's contributions is ambivalent. In fact, though both authors explicitly refer to the practical obstacles to solving the corresponding system of equations, and they also mention the insurmountable theoretical impossibility of obtaining the information necessary to describe equilibrium, by initiating a new scientific paradigm in economics, one based on the use of the mathematical method to describe the equilibrium model at least in formal terms, they are inexorably forced to assume that, at least in these formal terms, the necessary information is available. Hence, regardless of the reservations Pareto and Barone voiced in passing, a very large number of the economists who have continued the paradigm they initiated still fail to understand that the mathematical analysis of equilibrium has, at most, a hermeneutical or interpretive value which adds not one iota to the possibility of theoretically solving the problem faced by all governing bodies which aim to acquire the practical information necessary to coercively plan and coordinate society.

The first article to systematically address the insoluble economic problem that would confront a collectivist society was written by the Dutch economist, Nicolaas G. Pierson.[10] Pierson's article is especially commendable, in light of the fact that it was written in 1902. Pierson reveals that the problem of value in general, and in particular, the problem posed by any human action with respect to the need to perceive ends and means, is inseparable from human nature and thus will always exist and cannot be erased by the establishment of a socialist system. Furthermore, Pierson mentions the great obstacle to calculating and evaluating in the absence of prices, and he criticizes the awkward plans for the practical establishment of communism which had been formulated up to that point; specifically, economic calculation in labor hours. Nevertheless, despite all of these significant contributions, Pierson had only brilliant intuitions and was unable to pinpoint the problem posed by the dispersed character of the practical information constantly generated and transmitted in the market, and it was not until Mises made his momentous contribution that this problem was for the first time clearly explained.[11]

Just prior to Mises, Friedrich Wieser also sensed the fundamental economic problem when he stated in 1914 that in economics the dispersed action of millions of individuals is much more effective than organization from above by a single authority, since the latter "could never be informed of countless possibilities".[12]

After Wieser, the German sociologist Max Weber, in his magnum opus, *Economy and Society*, published posthumously in 1922 following a lengthy period of preparation, expressly addresses the economic problems which would arise from an attempt to put socialism into practice. In particular, Weber stresses that calculation in kind, proposed by certain socialists, could not provide a rational solution to the problems. In fact, Weber specifically emphasizes that the preservation and efficient use of capital can only be ensured in a society built on free exchange and the use of money, and the widespread loss and destruction of economic resources which a socialist system (invariably without rational economic calculation) would provoke would render it impossible to maintain even the population levels which had been reached in Weber's day in the most densely populated areas.[13] We have no reason to doubt Weber when, in a footnote, he indicates that he learned of Mises's vital article only after his book had gone to press.

Finally, we should mention the Russian professor, Boris Brutzkus, whose contribution is intimately related to the works of Weber and Mises. In the early 1920s, Brutzkus's research on the practical problems posed by the establishment of communism in Soviet Russia lead him to some conclusions which closely resemble those of Mises and Weber, and he even expressly asserted that economic calculation is a theoretical impossibility in central-planning societies without market prices.[14]

In short, the above contributions are the most significant and comprise the prehistory of the debate on the impossibility of economic calculation in socialist economies. The common denominator among them is their authors' imperfect and intuitive perception of the essential problem socialism poses, which was analyzed in detail in the last chapter and which consists of the theoretical impossibility of the central planning agency's obtaining the practical information necessary to organize society. Furthermore, none of these contributions was sufficient to awaken socialist theorists from their lethargic state, where, in the purest Marxist tradition, they usually confined themselves to criticizing the capitalist system, without shedding any light on the fundamental problem of how socialism should actually work. Only Karl Kautsky, spurred on by Pierson's abovementioned article, dared to violate the tacit agreement between Marxists on the issue and attempt to describe the future socialist organization, though in doing so he only managed to reveal his utter confusion about the essential economic problem Pierson had raised.[15] Afterwards, it was not until Mises made his fundamental contribution that analyses of much interest were carried out from the socialist point of view. The only exception is Otto Neurath,[16] who in 1919 published a book in which he argued that the events of the First World War had "proven" that it would be entirely possible to carry out central planning *in natura*. It was Neurath's book that evoked Mises's brilliant response, embodied in a lecture he gave in 1919, a lecture which provided the foundation for the landmark article he published in the spring of the following year, 1920.[17]

## 2 THE ESSENTIAL CONTRIBUTION OF LUDWIG VON MISES

If there is one point on which all of the participants in the debate over socialist economic calculation agree, it is that the debate officially began with Mises's famous 1920 article, "Die Wirtschaftsrechnung im Sozialistischen Gemeinwesen", or, "Economic calculation in the socialist commonwealth".[18] This article reproduces the content of the lecture Mises delivered the previous year (1919) before the Nationalökonomische

Gesellschaft (Economics Society), a lecture in which he responded to the thesis of Neurath's book, published that same year. It would be difficult to exaggerate the powerful impact Mises's article had among his professional economist colleagues and among socialism theorists. His cold, strict logic, the clarity of his explanations, and his provocative spirit made it impossible for his arguments to remain overlooked, as had occurred with the arguments of the theorists who preceded him. Thus, Otto Leichter emphasizes that the credit goes to Mises for having been the first to vigorously direct the attention of socialist theorists to the necessity of resolving the problem of economic calculation.[19] The socialist economist Oskar Lange, of whom we shall speak *in extenso* later on, ironically wrote that Mises had done such a service to socialist theory that a statue of him should be erected in a place of honor in the most important hall of the central planning bureau in every socialist country.[20] Perhaps, in light of historical events in the Eastern bloc countries, it would come as no surprise after all if Lange's sarcastic remarks were to backfire on him, and many plazas in the capitals of former communist nations were to see the raising of a statue of young Ludwig von Mises, in place of the obsolete, crumbling representations of the old Marxist leaders.[21]

### The Nature and Basic Content of Mises's Contribution

For the first time, Mises limited his focus to the theoretical analysis of the processes by which practical information is created and transmitted, processes which make up life in society and which were examined in Chapters 2 and 3. Mises's use of terms was still quite awkward, and rather than speaking of dispersed practical information, he referred to a certain 'intellectual division of labor', which according to him constituted the essence of the market and provided and generated the information that permits the economic calculation or estimation all entrepreneurial decisions require. Specifically, Mises states: "The distribution among a number of individuals of administrative control over economic goods in a community of men who take part in the labour of producing them, and who are economically interested in them, entails a kind of intellectual division of labour, which would not be possible without some system of calculating production and without economy".[22] Two years later, in 1922, in his systematic treatise on socialism, Mises repeated the same idea even more explicitly: "In societies based on the division of labour the distribution of property rights effects a kind of mental division of labour, without which neither economy nor systematic production would be possible".[23] Moreover, five years later, in his 1927 work, *Liberalism*, Mises expressly concluded that his analysis rests on the impossibility within a socialist system of generating the practical information, in the form of market prices, that is necessary for the intellectual division of knowledge which a modern society requires and which only arises from the creative capacity of human action or entrepreneurship: "The *decisive objection* that economics raises against the possibility of a socialist society is that it must forgo the *intellectual division of labour* that consists in the cooperation of all entrepreneurs, land owners and workers as producers and consumers in the formation of *market prices*".[24]

Another of Mises's fundamental contributions was his discovery that the information the market constantly generates springs from the exercise of entrepreneurship, keyed to the particular circumstances of time and place which can only be perceived by each individual within the context in which he acts. Thus, practical, entrepreneurial knowledge originates in the market as a result of the unique position each actor occupies in the production process. If the free exercise of entrepreneurship is obstructed, and an attempt is made to coercively organize all of society from above, entrepreneurs will be unable to act freely and will therefore cease to be entrepreneurs. They will not even be aware of the information they fail to perceive and create. Entrepreneurs will be affected in this way regardless of the level of their academic achievements and their professional, managerial qualifications.[25] In fact, Mises states:

> The entrepreneur's commercial attitude and activity arises from his *position* in the economic process and is lost with its disappearance. When a successful businessman is appointed the manager of a public enterprise, he may still bring with him certain experiences from his previous occupation, and be able to turn them to good account in a routine fashion for some time. Still, with his entry into communal activity he ceases to be a merchant and becomes as much a bureaucrat as any other placeman in the public employ. It is not a knowledge of bookkeeping, of business organization, or of the style of commercial correspondence, or even a dispensation from a commercial high-school which makes the merchant, *but his characteristic position in the production process* which allows for the identification of the firm's and his own interests.[26]

Mises develops and elaborates on this idea in his treatise on socialism, in which he arrives at the succinct conclusion that "an entrepreneur deprived of his characteristic role in economic life ceases to be a business man. However much experience and routine he may bring to his new task he will still be an official in it".[27]

Hence, to the extent that socialism forcibly prevents the free exercise of entrepreneurship in the fundamental sphere of the factors of production (capital goods and natural resources), socialism impedes both the emergence and the transmission of the practical information which would be necessary for an appropriate allocation of these factors by the central planning bureau. As this information does not emerge, it cannot be taken into account in the calculation that must accompany every rational economic decision. Thus, the people at the central regulatory agency cannot even be sure, when they make decisions and act, if they are forgoing the achievement of ends they themselves would consider more desirable. Hence, economic decisions in socialism are arbitrary and made in the most absolute obscurity.

At this point, it is very important to stress that Mises's argument is a theoretical one centered on the intellectual error which pervades all socialist ideas, since it is impossible to organize society with coercive commands, given that the supervisory agency cannot possibly obtain the information necessary to do so. Mises's theoretical argument refers to the practical impossibility of socialism.[28] To put it another way, it is the quintessential theoretical argument, since theory is merely an abstract, formal and qualitative analysis of reality, an analysis which must never lose its connection with reality, but instead must be as relevant as possible to real-world situations and processes. Therefore, it is entirely false that Mises concerned himself with the impossibility of socialism in terms of the formal equilibrium model or the "pure logic of choice", as we shall see many prestigious authors, who were incapable of distinguishing between "theory" and equilibrium analysis, mistakenly asserted. In fact, as early as 1920, Mises himself took very special care to expressly deny that his analysis could be applied to the equilibrium model. This model assumes from the beginning that all necessary information is available and thus, by definition, that the fundamental economic problem socialism poses has been resolved *ab initio* and in this way, the model leads equilibrium theorists to overlook this problem. In actuality, the problem of socialism stems from the fact that when the authorities at the regulatory agency issue an edict or command in favor of or against a certain economic proposal, they lack the information necessary for them to determine whether or not they are acting correctly, and hence they cannot make any economic calculation or estimate whatsoever. If it is assumed that the supervisory agency has at its disposal all of the necessary information and also that no changes will occur, then it is obvious that no problem of economic calculation arises, since such a problem is considered nonexistent from the start. Thus, Mises states:

> *The static state can dispense with economic calculation.* For here the same events in economic life are ever recurring; and *if we assume* that the first disposition of *the static socialist economy* follows on the basis of the final state of the competitive economy, *we might at all events conceive of a socialist production system which is rationally controlled from an economic point of view.* But this is only conceptually possible. For the moment, we leave aside the fact that *a static state is impossible in real life*, as our economic data are for ever changing,

so that the static nature of economic activity is only a theoretical assumption corresponding to no real state of affairs.[29]

Therefore, Mises's argument is a theoretical one which centers on the logical impossibility of socialism, but it is an argument that takes account of a theory and logic of human action and the real social, dynamic and spontaneous processes it sets in motion, and not a "logic" or "theory" built on mechanical action carried out in an environment of perfect equilibrium by "omniscient" beings who are as inhuman as they are removed from reality. As Mises explained even more clearly two years later in his book on socialism:

> Under stationary conditions there no longer exists a problem for economic calculation to solve. The essential function of economic calculation has *by hypothesis* already been performed. There is no need for an apparatus of calculation. To use a popular but not altogether satisfactory terminology we can say that the problem of economic calculation is of economic dynamics: it is no problem of economic statics.[30]

This statement of Mises's fits in perfectly with the most representative of the Austrian tradition, just as it was established by Carl Menger, subsequently developed by Böhm-Bawerk, and encouraged in its third generation by Mises himself. In fact, according to Mises, "what distinguishes the Austrian School and will lend it immortal fame is precisely the fact that it created a theory of economic action and not of economic equilibrium or non action".[31] Therefore, it is not surprising that, since no economic calculation is necessary in a state of equilibrium, the only people capable of discovering the theorem of the impossibility of socialist economic calculation were the cultivators of a school which, like the Austrian school, focused its scientific research program on the theoretical analysis of the real, dynamic processes which operate in the market, and not on the development of partial or general mechanistic models of equilibrium.

We have now shown that Mises, in his above-mentioned 1920 article, had already explicitly formulated the essence of the theory of the impossibility of socialism which we covered in detail in Chapters 2 and 3. Mises's paper had a powerful impact on his young disciple Hayek, who was inspired by it to abandon the "well-intentioned" socialism of his early youth and, beginning at that time, to devote considerable intellectual effort to refining and broadening the contributions of his mentor.[32] Therefore, we cannot accept the particularly erroneous view that two distinct arguments exist against the possibility of economic calculation in socialist economies. Those who hold this view claim that the first of these arguments is simply algebraic or computational, was initially presented by Mises, and shows that economic calculation is impossible wherever there are no prices to permit the accounting of gains and losses. Supposedly, the second argument is of an epistemological nature, was mainly developed by Hayek, and shows that socialism cannot work because the central planning bureau cannot possibly obtain access to the vital practical information necessary to organize society.[33] In fact, Mises considered both arguments, the computational and the epistemological, to be simply two inseparable sides of the same coin, for it is impossible to make any economic calculation, or the corresponding preliminary judgments, if the necessary information, in the form of market prices, is unavailable. Moreover, it is the free exercise of entrepreneurship which constantly results in the creation of such information. Entrepreneurs continually bear in mind the terms of trade or market prices which have applied in the past, and they try to estimate or discover the market prices which will apply in the future. They then act in accordance with their estimates, and in this way, actually bring about the establishment of future prices. Mises himself wrote, in 1922: "It is the speculative capitalists who *create the data* to which he has to adjust his business and which therefore gives direction to his trading operations".[34]

The above considerations should not prevent us from recognizing that Mises's pioneering work of 1920 was still quite far from the refined and polished contributions which he himself and Hayek would later make in the decades that followed, and which would culminate in the analysis of entrepreneurship and of the resultant processes by which information is generated, processes that were covered in Chapters 2 and 3. Also, we must take into account that in his initial contribution, Mises was heavily influenced by a preexisting Marxist environment that he meant to challenge and that led him to place special emphasis on both money and prices as necessary for economic calculation. Therefore, in order to place Mises's 1920 article in its proper context, the next section will be devoted to an examination of the Marxist environment which prevailed in the academic and intellectual circles in which Mises moved in the years immediately prior to 1920, an environment he became intimately acquainted with in the seminar led by Böhm-Bawerk up until the time the First World War broke out.

## 3  THE FUNCTIONING OF SOCIALISM, ACCORDING TO MARX

There is no doubt that when Mises wrote his pioneering work, he had in mind the Marxist conception of socialism, a view which predominated in Europe at the beginning of the 1920s. Thus, we must pause for a moment and identify the ideas which were circulating at that time on such a relevant subject.

To begin, we should ask whether or not Karl Marx had a clear idea of how the socialist system he preached should actually work. This is an important point for two reasons: first, because Mises repeatedly accused Marx and his followers of trying to inoculate themselves against any critical analysis of the socialist system by simply arguing that such an analysis was irrelevant and utopian, since socialism would inexorably evolve from capitalism; and second, because Marx himself felt that within his theoretical framework, meticulous or detailed speculation about the specific aspects of future socialism was not "scientific". Despite the above, and the fact that this Marxist approach has definitely been systematically overused in order to avoid the theoretical discussion of the realistic chances of socialism working, this author believes that in the critical analysis of capitalism which constitutes the heart of Marxist ideas, it is possible to clearly distinguish, though in an implicit and embryonic form, an analysis of how socialism should function in practice.[35] Marx was so influenced and obsessed by the Ricardian model of adjustment and equilibrium, that his entire theory is aimed at justifying a normative equilibrium, in the sense that, according to Marx, the proletariat should coercively impose from above a "coordination" which does away with the typical features of capitalism. As for the actual, detailed analysis of the economic realities of the capitalist system, it should be stressed that Marx focuses on the disequilibria and maladjustments that emerge in the market and thus, Marxist theory is mainly a disequilibrium theory. Paradoxically, it occasionally coincides on some very curious points with the analysis of market processes carried out by Austrian economists, in general, and by Hayek and Mises himself, in particular.

Therefore, curiously, Marx understood to a point how the market, as a spontaneous and impersonal order, acts as a process which creates and transmits the information that permits a certain coordination in society. In fact, in *Grundrisse* we read:

> It has been said and may be said that this is precisely the beauty and the greatness of it, this *spontaneous* interconnection, this material and *mental* metabolism which is independent of the knowing and willing of individuals, and which presupposes their reciprocal independence and indifference. And certainly, this objective connection is preferable to the lack of any connection, or to a merely local connection resting on blood ties, or on primeval, natural or master-servant relations.[36]

Moreover, Marx explicitly recognizes both the role institutions play in enabling people to acquire and transmit practical information in the market, and their importance to the knowledge of economic agents:

Together with the development of this alienation, and on the same basis, efforts are made to overcome it: *institutions* emerge whereby each individual can acquire *information* about the activity of all others and attempt to adjust his own accordingly . . . Although the total supply and demand are independent of the actions of each individual, everyone attempts to *inform* himself about them, and this *knowledge* then reacts back in practice on the total supply and demand.[37]

If Marx condemns the market, it is precisely because he contrasts it with an "ideal" economic system in which individuals are able to subordinate all of their social relationships to coercive, centralized and communal management which is supposed to make it possible for the entire social process to arise from conscious and deliberate organization, whereas in the market, the process is impersonal and not consciously designed or controlled by anyone, and thus "alienating". Furthermore, this organized management of all of society depends upon the a priori formulation of a detailed plan to enable the authorities to organize the entire society, just as an architect drafts intricate plans for a building before constructing it: "What distinguishes the worst architect from the best of bees is this, that the architect raises his structure in imagination before he erects it in reality".[38] Therefore, it is based on this sole contrast between the "anarchy" of the production characteristic of the spontaneous order of the market and the "perfect organization" which supposedly results from central planning that Marx criticizes capitalism and defends the socialist system, which he claims will inexorably replace it.

It is evident that Marx's essential error lies in both his confusion of the concepts of practical and scientific information, and in his belief that practical information is objective and can be "absorbed" by the central planning body. Marx overlooks the subjective, exclusive, dispersed, tacit and inarticulable nature of practical information, which was carefully described in Chapter 2, and he fails to realize that from a logical standpoint, not only is it impossible to centrally coordinate social maladjustments, but also, new information can only be constantly developed and created as a result of the capitalist entrepreneurial process, which cannot be reproduced in a coercive and centralized manner. In other words, new technologies, products and distribution methods, and in general, new entrepreneurial information, can logically only emerge from the spontaneous market process which Marx so criticized and which the force of entrepreneurship drives. Hence, paradoxically, from his own viewpoint, Marxist socialism is a utopian socialism, since a proper understanding of the logical nature of the information created and used in the market invariably leads one to conclude that the very forces of technological and economic development that operate there make it impossible for the market to move toward a social order based on the centralized and coercive organization of all practical information.

This and no other is Marx's fundamental error, and the rest of his mistakes on economic and social topics can be considered simply particular consequences of this initial radical error. For example, his labor theory of value is merely the natural result of the belief that information or knowledge is objective and can be unmistakably discerned by an outside observer. On the contrary, we know that value is simply a subjective, dispersed and inarticulable idea or bit of information; in other words, the human mind estimates it or projects it upon things or economic means, and the more useful the actor subjectively believes these means will be to him in achieving the objectives he pursues, the more psychologically intense will be his perception of their value.

Marx's erroneous conception of the theory of value also invalidates his entire theory of surplus value or exploitation. It is not just that Marx selfinterestedly ignored those economic means which were not commodities and thus did not incorporate any labor in their formation process; it is also that, as Böhm-Bawerk showed,[39] the Marxist analysis betrays a complete ignorance of the importance of time preference and the fact that all human action, in general, and all production processes, in particular, take time. Thus, Marx expects workers to be paid not the value of what they produce, but considerably more, since he demands they receive in payment the entire value of their contribution to the production process, an amount assessed not at the time each contribution is made, but projected for the later time when the complete production process has concluded. In addition, Marx's analysis of surplus value inevitably rests on circular reasoning, which explains nothing. Indeed, the supposedly objective value of labor is established based on the cost of reproducing it in terms of the value of the goods necessary to maintain it, which would in turn be determined by the labor incorporated in these goods, and so on, in a vicious circle of faulty reasoning that can account for nothing.

Marx believed that the ideal socialist state would organize society like an "immense factory" planned entirely from above in a "rational" manner. He thought this would be the only way to avoid the great inefficiencies and redundancies typical of the capitalist system, and that above all, it would make it possible to abolish all market relationships in general, and the circulation of money understood as a medium of exchange, in particular. Hence, Marx explicitly states:

> In the case of socialized production *the money capital is eliminated.* Society distributes labour-power and means of production to the different branches of production. The producers may, for all it matters receive paper vouchers

entitling them to withdraw from the social supplies of consumer goods a quantity corresponding to their labour-time. *These vouchers are not money. They do not circulate*.[40]

Elsewhere, also in reference to the vouchers, Marx indicates that they are "no more money than a ticket for the theatre".[41] Marx later passed on this entire notion to his disciples, and Friedrich Engels popularized the best-known version of it in his *Anti-Dühring*, where he writes:

> Society can simply calculate how many hours of labour are contained in a steam-engine, a bushel of wheat of the last harvest, or a hundred square yards of cloth of a certain quality ... *Society will not assign values to products*. It will not express the simple fact that the hundred square yards of cloth have required for their production, say, a thousand hours of labour in the oblique and meaningless way, stating that they have the *value* of a thousand hours of labour. It is true that even then it will still be necessary for society to know how much labour each article of consumption requires for its production. It will have to arrange its plan of production in accordance with its means of production, which include, in particular, its labour-powers. The useful effects of the various articles of consumption, compared with one another and with the quantities of labour required for their production, will in the end determine the plan. *People will be able to manage everything very simply, without the intervention of much-vaunted "value"*.[42]

Thus, it is in the context of these contributions by Marx[43] and his most immediate disciples that we should view the emphasis Mises placed, in his 1920 article, on the requirement of money and monetary prices for economic calculation. This and other matters will be elaborated on in the following section.

## 4 ADDITIONAL CONSIDERATIONS ON MISES'S CONTRIBUTION

### Mises's Refutation of Marx's Analysis

It is important to bear in mind that Mises's argument that socialism involves a logical impossibility is not only a theoretical case against the chances that socialism will function in the future, but also a well-aimed, full-scale attack on the very heart of Karl Marx's analysis. Actually, Mises agrees entirely with Marx that in a state of equilibrium, no money or medium of exchange would be necessary, assuming all information were objective and available to the central regulatory agency. Thus, Mises expressly states: "Money is necessarily a dynamic factor; there is no room left for money in a static system".[44] Nevertheless, as we have seen, Mises's essential argument does not refer to an equilibrium model which is as hypothetical as it is impossible, and in which no changes ever occur, and all social maladjustments have disappeared, because they have been coercively coordinated from above by a central planning bureau which possesses all of the vital information. On the contrary, in such circumstances, which cannot possibly be established in practice, Mises sees no potential problem of economic calculation whatsoever. The fundamental contribution Mises made was precisely to show that it is theoretically impossible in the real world for a central planning agency to coercively coordinate society. In this sense, Mises's contribution not only exposes the logical impossibility of socialism, but also constitutes the definitive theoretical argument against the teachings of Marx.

Clearly, only someone with Mises's keen, profound grasp of the real-life operation of market processes could come to realize that economic calculation and social coordination are impossible outside of the market. Nonetheless, it is important to note that when Mises refers to "market price" and "competition", the absence of which is precisely what precludes economic calculation outside of the market, he means something altogether different from that of the neoclassical equilibrium theorists when they refer to "price" and "competition". For Mises, price is any historical term of trade which inevitably emerges in the competitive process that the force of entrepreneurship drives; it is not a simple parameter that indicates the terms on which each alternative must be offered with respect to the rest. Even more important, the term competition conveys to Mises a meaning which is virtually the exact opposite of the one the neoclassical school attributes to the word. While the so-called "model of perfect competition" refers to a certain state of equilibrium in which all participants passively confine themselves to selling the same product at a given price, for Mises, competition denotes a dynamic process of rivalry between entrepreneurs who, rather than sell at given prices, constantly make decisions and undertake new actions and exchanges which result in new information that continually materializes in the form of new market prices.

Later, in the chapter devoted to Oskar Lange, we shall study in much greater detail the differences between the concepts of price and competition as adhered to by Mises and by neoclassical economists. At this point it should be emphasized that Mises, in his original 1920 article, focused his challenge on the view of central planning which was implicit in Marx's contributions, which has already been discussed. Since Marx specifically disputed the need for monetary prices, it was natural for Mises to particularly stress that both prices and money are necessary for economic calculation. Later, the socialist participants in the debate finally recognized that money and prices, though understood strictly in the parametric sense, are essential to economic calculation. Only then did Hayek carry to its logical conclusion the argument (which Mises, his mentor, had also originally introduced) that economic calculation requires true market prices, not merely parametric prices, and thus that neither the exercise of entrepreneurship nor the adjustments and coordination which society demands are possible in the absence of genuinely competitive markets and private ownership of the factors of production. Nevertheless, let us remember, as has already been shown, that all of the basic elements of this fundamental argument concerning the role of the practical information or knowledge dispersed throughout the market, an argument Hayek and Mises himself would later refine and perfect, were already present at least in embryonic form in the initial contribution Mises made in 1920.

**The Monetary Calculation of Profits and Losses**

In section 2, "The nature of economic calculation", of his 1920 article, Mises distinguishes between three different types of value judgments every actor or entrepreneur can make when he acts: primary valuations, valuations of consumer goods, and valuations of the means of production. While primary valuations and valuations of consumer goods are carried out by the actor directly, that is, through an *in natura* calculation which simply requires each actor to compare on his own subjective value scale the rankings of the different ends and the means of consumption necessary to achieve them, valuations of productive factors, in contrast, are a great deal more complex. This is especially true in a productive structure which, like the modern one, consists of an extremely elaborate network of different stages of production which are interconnected in a highly complicated manner and involve time periods of quite diverse lengths. Thus, as Mises rightly states, "the mind of one man alone is too weak to grasp the importance of any single one among the countlessly many goods of higher order".[45] In fact, decisions concerning the factors of production are so complicated that they require judgments which are only possible when one possesses the information that monetary prices supply, prices which arise from the market process itself. Only in this way, through entrepreneurship, can the maladjustments present in the productive structure be eliminated, and the trend toward coordination which makes life in society possible be established.

The heart of this process consists precisely of the profit-and-loss estimates entrepreneurs constantly make when they act in the market of productive factors. In fact, whenever they encounter a profit opportunity, they act to seize it by acquiring factors of production at a market price or monetary cost which they expect to be lower than the selling price they will obtain for the consumer good once it has been produced. In contrast, losses indicate that the entrepreneur committed an error when he acted and that he allocated scarce resources to the production of certain consumer goods and services when others were more important or urgently necessary (those which generate profits instead of losses). As is logical, when entrepreneurs buy or sell factors of production and undertake production processes, they do not "act" by simply adjusting to a number of chimerical, parametric "prices", but rather they actively and continuously form true market prices into which they unconsciously incorporate the information they generate or discover from moment to moment. The absence of money, private property and freedom to exercise entrepreneurship prevents the constant creation, discovery and transmission of this information, and also, as a result, the formation of the market prices which are the essential raw material for the economic calculation that makes coordination possible in society.

## The Practical Sufficiency of Economic Calculation

Mises identified three advantages of economic calculation as it is performed in a real market economy. First, economic calculation makes it possible to take into account the valuations of the economic agents who participate in the social process. Second, economic calculation provides entrepreneurs with a guide for their actions, in the sense that it indicates the types of production processes they should and should not embark on, and it does so through the indicators or "signs" represented by the profit-and-loss estimates entrepreneurs constantly make. Third, economic calculation permits many of the valuations connected with action to be reduced to the common denominator of monetary units.

Mises expressly recognizes that neither economic calculation nor money function perfectly in a market economy. Money, as a medium of exchange, is subject to constant, unpredictable and disparate changes in purchasing power. With respect to economic calculation, a number of goods and services involve no purchases or sales in the market, basically because they are *res extra commercium* and therefore do not permit estimates in terms of monetary prices. (In fact, Mises's entire argument rests on the analysis of the consequences which would inevitably ensue if all capital goods were turned into *res extra commercium*.) Furthermore, the apparent precision of (financial and cost) accounting is deceptive, since its numerical expressions disguise the fact that they all rest on subjective judgments of a strictly entrepreneurial nature concerning the direction future events will take. As an example to illustrate this idea, Mises cites the calculation of amortization quotas which, as an accounting expression of depreciation, always entail a rough entrepreneurial judgment regarding the market price which will be charged for a replacement when, in the future, the production good has been depleted physically or technologically.

Nevertheless, despite all of its inadequacies and imperfections, economic calculation provides the only social guide for discovering the maladjustments which emerge in society. It does so by directing the action of human beings toward the discovery and coordination of these maladjustments and thus makes life in society possible. Given the characteristics of practical, dispersed information or knowledge, which were analyzed in Chapter 2, there is no substitute for market economic calculation, and although it is always based on subjective estimates and on information provided by market prices, which never exist in equilibrium, it at least permits entrepreneurs to rule out innumerable possibilities, alternatives and courses of action which might be technologically possible, but would not be economically suitable. In other words, economic calculation limits the possibilities under the consideration of entrepreneurs to a very small number of alternatives which appear a priori to be potentially profitable, and in this way, it radically simplifies an actor's decision-making process. Thus, Mises concludes: "Admittedly, monetary calculation has its inconveniences and serious defects, but we have certainly nothing better to put in its place, and for the practical purposes of life monetary calculation as it exists under a sound monetary system always suffices".[46]

**Calculation as a Fundamentally Economic (and not Technical) Problem**

Mises believes that the establishment of a socialist regime implies the elimination of rational economics, since in a socialist regime, true prices and money cannot exist in the sense that they do in a real market economy. From the perspective of the initial Marxist plan, which we have already examined and according to which prices and money would be abolished, it is clear that economic calculation would disappear entirely. In fact, Mises directs much of his article toward criticizing this proposal. We shall later see that the circumstances change very little if socialists, as a second line of defense, do permit the existence of some parametric "prices" set by the regulatory authority and some "monetary units" more like units of account than anything else. In this case, we would still be faced with the impossibility of creating and transmitting new practical information in an environment in which the free exercise of entrepreneurship is prohibited. The systematic use of institutional coercion prevents this information from emerging and being transmitted, and hence it can never be concentrated in the mind of the governing body or used by it.

Therefore, socialism does not pose a technical or a technological problem, one based on the assumption that the ends and means are given, along with the rest of the information necessary to resolve a mere problem of maximization. On the contrary, the problem socialism poses is strictly economic: it arises when there are many competing ends and means and when knowledge about them is dispersed in the minds of innumerable human beings and is constantly generated *ex novo*, and hence, when it is not even possible to know about all of the possibilities and alternatives that exist or the relative intensity with which each is desired.[47] When an engineer sets about solving a maximization problem, he always assumes that there are some alternatives in the market and some equilibrium prices and that both are known. However, the economic problem is quite different and consists precisely of discovering which ends and means are possible, as well as future market prices. That is, the issue is how to obtain the information necessary to address and resolve the technical problem. Economic calculation is a judgment made possible by the information that the entrepreneurial process constantly creates, and if this process is prevented by force, the information does not emerge, and economic calculation becomes impossible.

**Business Consolidation and Economic Calculation**

Mises's argument can also be employed to analyze the theoretical limit to the growth of any "business organization" in a market economy. In fact, a company, or a "firm", can be considered simply a *voluntary* "planning" or "organizational island" within the market, one that emerges spontaneously as its promoters entrepreneurially discover that under certain circumstances such a system is the most suitable for achieving their own objectives. Every firm involves at least a minimum of organization and planning, and through each firm, certain economic, human and material resources are organized according to the plan and commands issued by the management. From the standpoint of Mises's original argument, it is clear that the size of a company invariably limits the possibility of efficiently organizing it: there will always be a certain critical size, beyond which the volume and type of information the management needs to run the company efficiently will become so large and complex that it will far exceed the managers' capabilities of interpretation and comprehension, and thus any additional growth will tend to be inefficient and superfluous.

In terms of economic calculation, the argument could be expressed as follows: in any firm, vertical integration will be limited by the fact that once all stages have been incorporated into an entrepreneurial production process, exchanges with respect to one or more of them may disappear from the market, and market prices would thus cease to emerge for some capital goods. At that point, it would no longer be possible within a firm to make vertical transfers with the guidance of economic calculation, and hence, there would be a tendency to commit systematic errors and inefficiencies which would sooner or later reveal to the entrepreneur that he should decentralize and not vertically integrate his company to such an extent if he does not wish to endanger its competitive capacity.[48] That is, in a free market it will never be possible to bring about a complete vertical integration with respect to the stages of any production process, since doing so would prevent the necessary economic calculation. Therefore, in the market there is an economic law which limits the maximum relative size of each company.[49]

In fact, as the division of knowledge becomes broader, deeper and more detailed, and social and economic processes grow more complex as a result, it becomes more difficult for a company to integrate vertically and expand, since its management has to interpret and use a larger volume of more complex information. One of the most typical consequences of the poorly named "technological revolution", which is simply the process, characteristic of modern market economies, of expansive broadening and deepening in the division of knowledge, has been to reverse, other things being equal, the trend toward the growth of so-called "economies of scale". It is increasingly evident that it is often more profitable to invest separately in different companies than to invest through holding companies or conglomerates; and many large firms are finding that the only way for them to compete with small ones is to try to encourage and favor internal entrepreneurial initiatives (intrapreneurship).[50] In fact, even the capacity of a small personal computer has rendered obsolete innumerable and often large voluntary planning organizations which up until now were considered typical of the market.

This argument also demonstrates that Marx's theory, according to which the capitalist system tends inexorably toward the consolidation of companies, is erroneous: business consolidation will not usually go beyond the point at which the requirements of the management for knowledge or information exceed the managers' own capacity for comprehension. If a firm continually expands, a time will come when it will run into increasing difficulties, in the sense that managers will have to make their decisions more and more "in the dark", without the information necessary to discover and evaluate the different production alternatives or possible courses of action. As they will lack the aid of the information provided by market prices and the entrepreneurship of their competitors, managers' behavior will become increasingly arbitrary and excessive. Therefore, central planning cannot be considered the inexorable conclusion of the future evolution of capitalism: the very course of the market limits the possible centralization of each company. This limit is established precisely by the capacity of a company's management to assimilate information and by changes in the social division of knowledge, a division which becomes increasingly profound, complex and decentralized.[51]

## 5 THE FIRST SOCIALIST PROPOSALS OF A SOLUTION TO THE PROBLEM OF ECONOMIC CALCULATION

### Economic Calculation in Kind

The notion that a socialist economy could be organized without the use of money can be traced back, as we saw in the last section, to Karl Marx. Indeed, in the nirvana or equilibrium state which Marx believes can and should be coercively imposed by the governing body, there would be no need for money, since it is assumed that all information is given and no changes ever occur. It would simply be necessary to produce the same goods and services period after period and distribute them in the same way to the same individuals. This idea was passed down from Marx to Engels, and from him to a number of theorists who, with varying degrees of explicitness, assert that there is no reason economic calculation should present any problem at all, even in the absence of money.[52]

Apart from the fact that the central coercion agency cannot possibly access the necessary information, the problem with proposals to carry out economic calculation *in natura* or in kind is simply that no calculation, neither addition nor subtraction, can be made using heterogeneous quantities. Indeed, if, in exchange for a certain machine, the governing body decides to hand over 40 pigs, 5 barrels of flour, 1 ton of butter, and 200 eggs, how can it know that it is not handing over more than it should from the standpoint of its own valuations? To put it another way, if the regulatory agency were to devote these resources to other lines of activity, would it be possible for it to achieve ends of greater value even to itself? Perhaps the socialist theorists can be excused for initially failing to grasp the insoluble problem which the subjective, dispersed and inarticulable nature of information poses for socialism, but they cannot be excused for having committed the blatant error of thinking that rational calculations could be made without using any monetary unit as a common denominator.

Moreover, the problem posed by calculation in kind affects not only production decisions, but also decisions regarding the distribution of consumer goods and services. For there are many consumer goods and services which cannot be equally divided among absolutely all citizens, and thus it is absurd to contemplate a system of allocating them that does not involve monetary units.[53] Thus, we can conclude by applying the following ironic comment, which Mises made about Carl Landauer, to the socialist theorists who considered calculation in kind possible: "Landauer cannot understand that – and why – one is not permitted to add and subtract figures of different denominations. Such a case is of course beyond help".[54]

Despite the above, we must not allow ourselves to get carried away by the false impression that the fundamental reason why economic calculation in kind is impossible is that heterogeneous quantities cannot be added, subtracted, or, in general, handled mathematically. The essential reason why economic calculation without market prices and money is impossible is the one that was described in detail in Chapter 3; it centers on the subjective, dispersed and inarticulable nature of practical human knowledge. The idea is not that even if human knowledge did not possess these characteristics, it would still be impossible to make economic calculations in kind because we cannot carry out mathematical operations using heterogeneous quantities: on the contrary, our point is that even if a hypothetical being had the capacity to make such calculations in kind, it would still be logically impossible for him to obtain all of the necessary information. Thus, the information argument is the essential one, and the argument that calculation in kind is infeasible is very powerful, but secondary.

**Economic Calculation in Labor Hours**

Marx's adoption of the objective labor theory of value explains why different socialist theorists have found it natural to try to solve the problem that concerns us via calculation in labor hours. Although this solution appears to lead us directly to the debate on the objective versus the subjective theory of value, the analysis regarding the possibility of carrying out economic calculation in labor hours is initially independent of a particular position on the issue of which theory of value (the objective or subjective) is correct.

These theorists basically proposed that the governing body keep track of the number of hours worked by each worker and that it then provide each worker with a certain number of vouchers which would correspond to the number of hours worked and entitle him to a certain quantity of the consumer goods and services produced. The social product would be distributed by establishing a statistical register of the number of labor hours necessary to produce each good and service and by allocating goods and services to those workers willing to exchange for them the corresponding vouchers. In this way, each hour of labor would give a worker the right to obtain an hour's worth of goods and services.

It is clear that such vouchers would not constitute money and that goods and services would have no market prices, or terms of trade voluntarily established by buyers and sellers, since the ratio at which goods and services are exchanged for vouchers would be explicitly established beforehand in terms of the number of labor hours necessary to produce each good.[55]

According to Mises, economic calculation in labor hours poses two specific insoluble problems. First, even within the framework of the objective labor theory of value, this proposed calculation criterion cannot be applied to any production process in which non-reproducible natural resources are used. Indeed, it is obvious that one cannot attribute any particular number of labor hours to any natural resource which, like coal, permits the achievement of ends, yet is economically scarce and cannot be manufactured using labor. In other words, because labor is not used to produce such a resource, the consideration of labor hours does not enable one to perform the economic calculation which is required if any but arbitrary decisions are to be made concerning the resource.

Second, an hour of labor is not a homogeneous, uniform quantity. In fact, there is no "labor as such," but rather there are countless different types or categories of labor which, in the absence of the common denominator of monetary market prices for each type, cannot be added or subtracted, due to their fundamentally heterogeneous nature. The issue is not simply that efficiency varies enormously from one worker to the next, and even for each worker from one moment or set of circumstances to the next, depending upon how favorable the conditions are. It is also that the types of services provided by labor are so varied and change so continuously that they are absolutely heterogeneous and pose a problem identical to the one that was discussed in the last section with respect to economic calculation in kind: it is impossible to perform calculations using heterogeneous quantities.

Traditional Marxist doctrine has offered, as a solution, the attempt to reduce the different types of work to what is called "simple, socially necessary labor". However, this reduction of the hours of different types of labor to hours of the simplest labor is only possible when there is a market process in which both are exchanged at a price determined by the different economic agents. In the absence of this market process, any comparative judgment about different types of labor will necessarily be arbitrary and imply the disappearance of rational economic calculation. For it is impossible to reduce the different types of labor to a common denominator without a prior market process. Moreover, the problem of reducing heterogeneous hours of labor to a common unit is merely a particular case of the more general problem already discussed, that which is posed by calculation in kind and consists of the impossibility of reducing heterogeneous factors of production to a common unit.

Finally, to repeat what we stated above, even if a solution to the two specific problems mentioned (economic calculation in the case of non-reproducible natural resources and the impossibility of finding a common denominator for labor hours) could be conceived, the fundamental problem would remain: it is simply impossible for the planning agency to acquire all of the crucial practical information dispersed throughout the minds of the millions of economic agents who make up society.

**Economic Calculation in Units of Utility**

Various socialist authors who, due to the arguments of Mises, grasped the impossibility of making calculations in labor hours, believed the problem could be resolved by calculating in "units of utility."[56] Nevertheless, this proposal is perhaps even more absurd than that of calculating in labor hours. Utility is a strictly subjective concept and derives from each individual's perception of each unit of means available to him in the context of each specific action in which he is involved. Utility cannot be measured; it is only possible to compare, when making a decision, the utility which arises from different courses of action. We cannot observe utility in different individuals either, since this would require us to be able to enter the minds of other people and take on their personalities, valuations and experiences. Thus, utility cannot be observed, felt or measured by any central coercion agency.

Furthermore, not even the man who acts "measures" his utility when making decisions, but instead he simply compares the utility he believes he will derive from each of the different alternatives. Moreover, market prices do not express equivalence or measure utility;[57] they are merely historical terms of trade which show only that the parties involved in the exchanges made subjective and contrasting valuations, and that such differences in valuations made the exchanges possible.

We must conclude that the attempt to use utility as a unit for economic calculation poses an insoluble problem, not only because utility cannot be observed, but also because there is no unit or common denominator of intersubjective utility which can be measured and used in the practice of economic calculation. The concept of utility is so subjective and elusive, that the argument that it is impossible to perform an economic calculation based on units of utility takes us directly back to our essential argument, that is, that it is impossible for the central coercion agency to obtain the necessary practical information which is dispersed throughout the minds of all economic agents and which at any one moment takes the form of an endless and constantly changing series of personal valuations or judgments about the utility of certain ends and means.[58]

## NOTES

1. For an overview of the trends in the history of thought on the conception of society as a spontaneous order, see Hayek (1978b).
2. The last two chapters have sought to reveal the close relationship between our conception of society and the law in its substantive sense as a set of abstract rules applied equally to all people. Only the framework created by law understood in this sense makes the exercise of entrepreneurship and human action possible, and with it the constant generation and transmission of dispersed information which characterize the advancement of civilization. Therefore, it is not by pure coincidence that the leading classical writers on Roman law have contributed to the philosophical tradition we are discussing.
3. *"Nostra autem res publica non unius esset ingenio, sed multorum, nec una hominis vita, sed aliquod constitutum saeculis et aetatibus, nam neque ullum ingenium tantum extitisse dicebat, ut, quem res nulla fugeret, quisquam aliquando fuisset, neque cuncta ingenia conlata in unum tantum posse uno tempore providere, ut omnia complecterentur sine rerum usu ac vetustate"*, Marcus Tullius Cicero, *De Re Publica*, ii, 1–2 (1961, 111–12). The English translation above is the one Bruno Leoni offers in his *Freedom and the Law* (1991). Leoni's book is exceptional, not only because it reveals the parallelism between the market and customary law, on the one hand, and positive legislation and socialism, on the other, but also because Leoni was the first jurist to realize that Mises's argument on the impossibility of socialist economic calculation is simply "a special case of a more general realization that no legislator would be able to establish by himself, without some kind of continuous collaboration on the part of all the people concerned, the rules governing the actual behavior of everybody in the endless relationships that each has with everybody else. No public opinion polls, no referenda, no consultations would really put the legislators in a position to determine these rules, *any more than a similar procedure could put the directors of a planned economy in a position to discover the total demand and supply of all commodities and services*. The actual behavior of people is continuously adapting itself to changing conditions. Moreover, actual behavior is not to be confused with the expression of opinions like those emerging from public opinion polls and similar enquiries, any more than the verbal expression of wishes and desires is to be confused with 'effective' demand in the market" (Leoni, 1991). On the work of Leoni, who founded the journal, *Il Politico*, in 1950, see Pasquale Scaramozzino (1969) and Peter H. Aranson (1988). Leoni, like Polanyi, was a multifaceted man who was very active in the fields of higher education, law, business, architecture, music and linguistics. He was tragically murdered by one of his tenants from whom he was trying to collect the rent on the night of November 21, 1967. He was fifty-four years old.
4. In fact, Montesquieu writes the following in his *Spirit of Laws* (1748): "C'est dans ces idées que Cicéron disait si bien: 'Je n'aime point qu'un même peuple soit en même temps le dominateur et le facteur de l'univers.' En effect, il faudrait supposer que chaque particulier dans cet État *et tout l'État même, eussent toujours la tête pleine de grands projects et cette même tête remplie de petits; ce qui est contradictoire*" (*De L'Esprit de Lois*, part 4, book 20, ch. 6, p. 350, in Montesquieu, 1843). A.R.J. Turgot, "Éloge de Gournay" (1759) in Turgot (1844, 275, 288).

5. Gossen (1854, 231). "Darum würde denn die von Kommunisten projectierte Zentralbehörde zur Verteilung der verschiedenen Arbeiten sehr bald die Erfahrung machen, dass sie sich eine Aufgabe gestellt habe, deren Lösung die Kräfte einzelner Menschen weit übersteigt". The above German excerpt appears in English in Blitz's translation: "Consequently, the central authority – projected by the communists – for the purpose of allocating the different types of labor and their rewards would soon find that *it has set itself a task that far exceeds the power of any individual*" (see Gossen 1854 [1983], 255, italics added). The third German edition of Gossen's book (Berlin: R.L. Praga, 1927) includes a lengthy introduction ("Einleitung") by Hayek, in which Hayek argues that Gossen was a forerunner more of the mathematical school of Walras and Jevons than of the Austrian school, strictly speaking. This introduction has recently been translated into English by Ralph Raico and published in *The Trend of Economic Thinking: Essays on Political Economists and Economic History*, Vol. 3 of *The Collected Works of F.A. Hayek* (London: Routledge, 1991), 352–71. This is the light in which we should interpret the content of the letter from Carl Menger to Léon Walras, dated January 27, 1887. In the letter, Menger states that he finds only a few points of agreement with Gossen, and none of them are essential points ("nur in einigen Punkten, nicht aber in den entscheidenden Fragen zwischen uns Übereinstimmung, bez Ähnlichkeit der Auffassung"). See William Jaffé (1965, Vol. 2, 176, letter no. 765).
6. *Die Quintessenz des Sozialismus* (1874 [1919], 51–2. Actually, Menger's succession to the economics chair hinged on Schäffle's unexpected appointment as Trade Minister in February 1871, an event which left the university position vacant. On the unquestionable influence which the least historicist sector of the German economics school prior to Menger (Wilhelm Roscher, Karl Knies and so on) exerted on some of Menger's essential contributions, see Eric W. Streissler (1990a). A detailed critique of Schäffle's book on socialism was presented by Edward Stanley Robertson (1891 [1981]).
7. Bagehot (1898, 54–8).
8. We reproduce here in its entirety section 217 of Chapter 3 of Pareto's *Manuel d'Économie Politique* (1966, 233 and 234): "Les conditions que nous avons énumérées pour l'équilibre économique nous donnent une notion générale de cet équilibre. Pour savoir ce qu'étaient certains phénomènes nous avons dû étudier leur manifestation; pour savoir ce que c'était que l'équilibre économique, nous avons dû rechercher comment il était déterminé. *Remarquons, d'ailleurs, que cette détermination n'a nullement pour but d'arriver à un calcul numérique des prix.* Faisons l'hypothèse la plus favorable à un tel calcul; supposons que nous ayons triomphé de toutes les difficultés pour arriver à connaître les données du problème, et que nous connaissions les ophélimités de toutes les marchandises pour chaque individu, toutes les circonstances de la production des marchandises, etc. *C'est là déjà une hypothèse absurde, et pourtant elle ne nous donne pas encore la possibilité pratique de résoudre ce problème.* Nous avons vu que dans le cas de 100 individus et de 700 marchandises il y aurait 70.699 conditions (en réalité un grand nombre de circonstances, que nous avons jusqu'ici négligées, augmenteraient encore ce nombre); nous aurons donc à résoudre un système de 70.699 équations. Cela dépasse pratiquement la puissance de l'analyse algébrique, et cela la dépasserait encore davantage si l'on prenait en considération le nombre fabuleux d'équations que donnerait une population de quarante millions d'individus, et quelques milliers de marchandises. Dans ces cas les rôles seraient changés: et ce ne seraient plus les mathématiques que viendraient en aide à l'économie politique, mais l'économie politique que viendrait en aide aux mathématiques. *En d'autres termes si on pouvait vraiment connaître toutes ces équations, le seul moyen accessible aux forces humaines pour les résoudre, ce serait d'observer la solution pratique que donne le marché*". There is an English translation by Ann S. Schwier, entitled *Manual of Political Economy* (New York: Augustus M. Kelley, 1971). See p. 171 of this translation for the above excerpt.
9. Barone (1908). Specifically, Barone states: "It is not impossible to solve on paper the equations of the equilibrium. It will be a tremendous – a gigantic – work: but it is not an *impossibility* . . . But it is frankly *inconceivable* that the economic determination of

the technical coefficients can be made *a priori*... This economic variability of the technical coefficients is certainly neglected by the collectivists... It is on this account that the equations of the equilibrium with the maximum collective welfare are not soluble a priori, on paper" (pp. 287–8). It is almost unimaginable that after Barone made these clear assertions, numerous economists, many even prominent, like Schumpeter, have claimed that Barone solved the problem Mises raised of the theoretical impossibility of socialism. The statements of these mistaken economists show: first, that they failed to grasp the nature of the problem Mises raised; second, that they did not give a careful reading to Barone or to Pareto; and third, that the supposition of full information which is used to formally describe equilibrium is a mirage capable of deceiving even the most brilliant minds. Barone (1859–1924) lived a curious and intense life full of vicissitudes and devoted not only to mathematical economics, but also to journalism and writing screenplays (mainly using the extensive knowledge of military history he had acquired as chief colonel of the high-staff history office), and thus participating actively in the development of the emerging Italian film industry. On Barone, see Del Vecchio (1925) and Caffè (1987).

10. Pierson (1902). Pierson (1839–1909), who was heavily influenced by the Austrian school, was Governor of the Central Bank, Finance Minister and Prime Minister of Holland. See the biography of this important Dutch economist and statesman by J.G. Van Maarseveen (1981), as well as Arnold Heertje (1987).

11. However, Mises generously affirms that Pierson "clearly and completely recognized the problem in 1902" (1922 [1981], 117). Curiously, in the same place, Mises states in reference to Barone: "Barone did not penetrate to the core of the problem".

12. Wieser (1914 [1967]).

13. Weber (1978, ch. 2, points 12, 13, 14, pp. 100 ff.). Specifically, Weber concludes: "Where a planned economy is radically carried out, it must further accept the inevitable reduction in formal, calculatory rationality which would result from the elimination of money and capital accounting. This fundamental, and in the last analysis, unavoidable element of irrationality is one of the important sources of all 'social' problems, and above all of the problems of socialism" (p. 111). Weber even cites the article of Mises (p. 107) and indicates that he came across it for the first time when his book was already written and ready for printing, and thus these two authors appear to have conceived their contributions independently of one another. Moreover, to Weber goes the indisputable credit for having been the first to show that socialism prevents population growth and development. In fact, Weber states: "The possibility must be considered that *the maintenance of a certain density of population within a given area is possible only on the basis of accurate calculation.* Insofar as this is true, a limit to the possible degree of socialization would be set by the necessity of maintaining a system of effective prices" (1964, 184–5). For, according to the analysis in Chapter 3, the division of knowledge cannot spread and deepen in a socialist regime, since the free generation and transmission of new practical information is not permitted. Thus, it becomes necessary to reproduce an enormous volume of information, and given the limitations of the human mind, this makes an economy of mere subsistence, together with a small population, the only possibility.

14. Brutzkus's contributions initially appeared in Russian, in the journal, *Economist*, in 1921 and 1922. Next, they were translated into German, in 1928, and entitled, *Die Lehren des Marxismus im Lichte der russischen Revolution* (1928); and finally, they were translated into English and compiled in Brutzkus (1935). (There is a reprint published in 1982.) Recently, the contributions of Brutzkus have been evaluated very positively, especially because he knew how to adequately combine the historical and theoretical aspects of the problem and avoid the dissociation between theory and practice which afterwards prevailed in the debate. See Peter J. Boettke (1990, 30–35, 41–2).

15. See the lecture Kautsky delivered in Delft on April 24, 1902, the text of which appeared in English in 1907 under the title, *The Social Revolution and on the Morrow of the Revolution*. A precedent for Kautsky's position can be found in Sulzer (1899).

16. Neurath (1919). There is an English translation entitled, "Through war economy to economy in kind" (1973). We must remember that for a short period, Neurath was the director of Bavaria's *Zentralwirtschaftsamt*, the agency in charge of socialization plans during the Räterepublik, or Soviet revolutionary regime in Bavaria, a regime which held power briefly in Munich in the spring of 1919. When the revolution failed and Neurath was tried, Max Weber testified in his defense. Neurath died in 1945. An idea similar to that of Neurath was conveyed by Otto Bauer in his work, *Der Weg zum Sozialismus* (1919). In this book, Bauer, like Neurath, defends the possibility of economic calculation in kind, that is, without the use of monetary units. The Spanish economist, Juan Martínez-Alier (1990, 212–18), has recently reevaluated Neurath's contributions. It is interesting to note that both Neurath and Bauer had more or less regularly attended a seminar of Böhm-Bawerk's in which Mises was one of the most active participants up until 1913. While Neurath's comments were characterized more by his fanatical Marxist fervor than by his intellectual keenness, a fellow Marxist, Otto Bauer, had no choice but to admit that the Marxist theory of value was untenable and that in his "response" to Böhm-Bawerk, Rudolph Hilferding had merely revealed his own inability to grasp even the nature of the problem. At this time, Mises decided to write a critical analysis of socialism, based on ideas which arose from his reflections and observations during his First World War military service, first as artillery captain on the eastern front (the Carpathians), and then, beginning in 1917 following a bout of typhoid, in the economic department of the Austrian Ministry of Defence. On this topic, see the compelling intellectual autobiography of Mises, *Notes and Recollections*, annotated and translated from German into English by Hans F. Senholz (1978, 11, 40–41, 65–6, 110–11) as well as Hülsmann (2007, 255–446). In any case, the ideas of Mises on socialism were the logical corollary of the impressive theoretical integration he carried out as early as 1912 (*Theorie des Geldes und der Umlaufsmittel*). The best English edition of his book is *The Theory of Money and Credit* (1980). Mises's theory integrated the subjective, internal realm of individual valuations (ordinal) and the objective, external realm of estimated market prices set in monetary units (cardinal). The two realms can be bridged whenever an act of interpersonal exchange springs from the difference in parties' subjective valuations, a difference expressed in a monetary market price or historical term of trade in monetary units. This price has a certain real, quantitative existence, and it provides the entrepreneur with valuable information for estimating the future course of events and making decisions (economic calculation). Thus, it is obvious that if free human action is prevented by force, voluntary interpersonal exchanges will not take place, and the bridge these exchanges constitute between the subjective, internal world of direct valuations (ordinal) and the objective, external world of prices (cardinal) is destroyed, and economic calculation is rendered impossible. We owe this idea on the evolution and coherence of Misesian thinking to Rothbard (1991, 64–5). However, Rothbard, in his desire to highlight the differences between Hayek and Mises, fails to realize that the severance of the connection Mises discovered between the internal sphere of subjective valuations and the external sphere of prices poses, above all, the problem of a lack of creation and transmission of the (existing and future) knowledge or information necessary for economic calculation, and hence the contributions of Mises and Hayek, with their obvious and inevitable differences in emphasis and minor points, can be considered as two essentially indistinguishable parts of the same basic argument against socialist economic calculation: Mises focuses more on *dynamic* problems, while Hayek has perhaps at times appeared to focus more on the problems presented by the dispersed nature of *existing* knowledge. See also note 43, Chapter 2.
17. Two analyses of the "prehistory" of the debate on economic calculation are: Hayek (1935b) and David Ramsay Steele (1981b). Despite the writings cited in this "prehistory" of the issue prior to the appearance of Mises, and as Rothbard correctly points out (1991, 51), the problem of socialism was always conceived as more of a political problem related to "incentives" than an economic one. Another example of this sort of naive criticism of socialism is William Hurrell Mallock (1908 [1990]).

18. Mises (1920). Two years later, in 1922, Mises reproduced the content of this article almost word for word in a book in which he systematically criticizes all aspects of socialism: *Die Gemeinwirtschaft. Untersuchungen über den Sozialismus* (1922). The English translation has been printed in several editions and in various places, though the best edition of all is the Liberty Classics edition (1981, 95–197). Recently, the English version of Mises's seminal article has been republished with a dual introduction by Yuri N. Maltsev (from the Academy of Sciences of the former Soviet Union) and Jacek Kochanowicz (Professor of Economics at the University of Warsaw) (Mises, 1990). Although Mises's article has not been translated into Spanish, Luis Montes de Oca has done an acceptable translation of *Die Gemeinwirtschaft*, published as *Socialismo: Análisis Económico y Sociológico* in Mexico (1961) and Buenos Aires (1968), reprinted for the third time in New York (1989), and for the fourth and fifth times in Madrid (2003, 2007). This work was also translated into French and published with a preface by François Perroux (Paris: Librairie de Médicis, 1952).

19. "To Ludwig von Mises really belongs the merit of having so energetically drawn the attention of socialists to this question. However little it was the intention of Mises to contribute by this criticism to the positive development of socialist theory and praxis, yet honour must be given where honour is due", *Die Wirtschaftsrechnung in der Sozialistischen Gesellschaft* (1923, 74). The English translation above appears on p. 5 of the book, *Economic Calculation in the Socialist Society*, by Trygve J.B. Hoff (1981).

20. "A statue of Professor Mises ought to occupy an honourable place in the great hall of the Ministry of Socialization or of the Central Planning Board of a socialist state . . . both as an expression of recognition for the great service rendered by him and as a memento of the prime importance of sound economic accounting" (Lange, 1936, 53). This article was reprinted in Lippincott (1938 [1964], 55–143). Recently, Lange's article was again partially republished, in Wood and Woods (1991, ch. 17, 180–201).

21. A bust of Mises already graces at least one place: the library of the Department of Economic Theory of the University of Warsaw, where Lange taught; and in fact, it occupies a spot right next to Lange's old office. The statue was placed during a brief and moving ceremony in September of 1990, thanks to the efforts of George Koetter. (See *Free Market*, **9**, no. 2, February 1991, 8; and *Journal of Economic Perspectives*, **5**, no. 3, summer 1991, 214–15.)

22. Mises (1920, [1975], 102).

23. Mises (1922 [1981] 101).

24. Mises (1985). The original edition of this work appeared in 1927 under the title, *Liberalismus* (Jena: Gustav Fischer).

25. This essential idea of Mises's can quite clearly be traced to Carl Menger, as we can see from the content of the notebook in which the Crown Prince Rudolf began in 1876 to record ideas that were practically dictated to him by Menger, who had officially been appointed as his private instructor. In fact, on pp. 50–51 of the sixth booklet we read: "A government cannot possibly know the interest of all citizens. In order to help them it would have to take account of the diverse activities of everybody . . . However carefully designed and well intentioned institutions may be, they never will suit everybody. *Only the individual himself knows exactly his interests and the means to promote them* . . . Even the most devoted civil servant is but a *blind tool* within a bit machine who treats all problems in a stereotyped manner with regulations and instructions. He can cope neither with the requirements of contemporary progress nor with the diversity of practical life. Therefore it seems impossible that all economic activities be treated in a stereotyped way, following the same rule with utter disregard for individual interests" (Archduke Rudolf, Crown Prince of Austria, *Politische Oekonomie*, January–August, 1876, manuscript written in the prince's own hand and stored in the Osterreichisches Staatsarchiv). The historian Brigitte Hamann discovered these notes, and Monika Streissler and David F. Good translated them into English. The above translation appears as Erich W. Streissler (1990b) cites it in Caldwell (1990, 107–30, esp. 120–21). It is curious to note that Mises saw the tragic death of the Archduke Rudolf as the

result of the influence of Menger, who was aware of the destructive effect which the spread of the venomous intellectual trend against liberalism would necessarily exert on the Austro-Hungarian Empire and "had transmitted this pessimism to his young student and friend, Archduke Rudolf, successor to the Austro-Hungarian throne. The Archduke committed suicide because he despaired about the future of his empire and the fate of European civilization, not because of a woman (he took a young girl along in death who, too, wished to die, but he did not commit suicide on her account)" (1978, 34).

26. Mises (1920 [1975], 120–21). See also the interesting article by Keizer (1992).
27. Mises (1922 [1981], 191). However, see Salerno ("Ludwig von Mises as social rationalist", 1990a, 45 and 55). Salerno claims that Mises saw the problem of socialism as one of economic calculation and not of dispersed knowledge, when the two are indissolubly linked. Mises himself, as we have seen from the beginning, not only emphasized the importance of the "characteristic role" of the entrepreneur in terms of providing him with information, but Mises also invariably conceived economics as a science which concerns not things but information or knowledge, understood as spiritual realities. ("Economics is not about things and tangible objects, it is about men, their *meanings* and actions", 1966, 92.)
28. "The dichotomy between 'theoretical' and 'practical' is a false one. In Economics, all arguments are theoretical. And since economics discusses the real world, these theoretical arguments are by their nature practical ones as well" (Rothbard, 1970a, 549). In fact, there is nothing more practical than a sound theory, and both Mises's argument and that of the mathematical economists who criticized him are theoretical. It is simply that the argument Mises offers is a theoretical one which is relevant to the actual functioning of a market economy and of socialism, while the argument the mathematical economists offer is a theoretical one which is irrelevant, in the sense that it refers to an equilibrium model which presupposes, by definition, that the economic problem has already been resolved, since all necessary information is considered given and available to the regulatory agency.
29. Mises (1920 [1975], 109).
30. Mises (1922 [1981], 120–21). Thus, it makes no sense to assert that Mises considered the problem of economic calculation a mere problem of Robbinsian maximization in which the ends and means are given (Salerno, 1990a, 46). From a dynamic standpoint, neither the ends nor the means are given, but instead they must be constantly created and discovered. Calculation involves looking to the future and hence, creating new information.
31. See Mises's intellectual autobiography (1978, 36).
32. "My thinking was inspired largely by Ludwig von Mises' conception of the problem of ordering a planned economy . . . But it took me a long time to develop what is basically a simple idea" (Hayek, 1986, 143).
33. Various authors have committed the error of believing that the computational argument does not imply the epistemological argument and vice versa. For example, see Rothbard (1988, 38); Chadran Kukathas (1989, 57) and the above-cited works of Salerno.
34. Mises (1922 [1981], 121).
35. Hence, we essentially agree with Lavoie, whose chapter on Marxist socialism is one of the most brilliant in his *Rivalry and Central Planning* (1985c, ch. 2, 28–47). See also N. Scott Arnold (1990).
36. Marx (1973, 161).
37. Ibid., 161.
38. Marx (1967, 178). In other writings, Marx is even more explicit in his defence of central planning as the only means of organizing economic activity: "The united cooperative societies are to regulate national production upon a *common plan*, thus taking it under their own control and putting an end to the constant anarchy and periodical convulsions which are the fatality of capitalist production" (1974a, 213).

39. To sum up, the chief arguments against the objective labor theory of value and its main corollary, the Marxist theory of exploitation, follow:
First, not all economic goods are the product of labor. Natural resources are scarce and useful for achieving human ends, and thus they constitute economic goods even though they incorporate no labor. Moreover, two goods that incorporate an identical amount of labor can clearly have very different values if they take different lengths of time to produce. Second, the value of goods is subjective, since as we explained in Chapter 2, value is merely an estimate man makes when he acts; he projects upon the means his assessment of their importance to the accomplishment of a certain end. Therefore, goods which incorporate a large quantity of labor can be worth very little, or even nothing, if the actor later realizes they are useless for the achievement of any goal. Third, labor-value theorists depend upon an insoluble contradiction and circular reasoning: the idea that labor determines the value of economic goods, and that the value of labor is in turn determined by the value of the economic goods necessary to reproduce it and maintain the productive capacity of the worker is an example of circular reasoning; the ultimate determinant of value is never specified. Finally, fourth, the defenders of the theory of exploitation flagrantly overlook the law of time preference, and hence, the logical importance of the fact that, other things being equal, present goods are always worth more than future goods. This error leads them to expect workers to receive in payment an amount in excess of the value they produce, since defenders of this theory argue that when a worker does his job, he should be paid in cash for the entire value of a good which will be completely produced only at the end of a time period of varying length. All of the above criticism of the Marxist theory of value is analyzed in great detail in Böhm-Bawerk's classic work, "The exploitation theory" (1959a, Vol. 1, ch. 12, 241–321). Also, Böhm-Bawerk wrote an article devoted to exposing the inconsistencies and contradictions which had entrapped Marx when he tried, in volume 3 of *Capital*, to resolve the errors and conflicts in his theory of exploitation as he had initially developed it in volume 1 of the same work (Böhm-Bawerk, 1896). We have used an English translation, "The unresolved contradiction in the Marxian economic system", in *Shorter Classics of Eugen von Böhm-Bawerk* (Böhm-Bawerk, 1896 [1962], ch. 4). In the Marxist camp, only Hilferding (1877–1941) tried, though unsuccessfully, to counter the arguments of Böhm-Bawerk in "Böhm-Bawerk's Marx Kritik" (1904). Regarding this article of Hilferding's, Böhm-Bawerk concludes: "Nothing in it has caused me to change my opinion in any respect" (1959a, Vol. 1, 472). Indeed, even Otto Bauer, a socialist theorist who, like Hilferding and Mises, attended Böhm-Bawerk's seminar, remarked directly to Mises that Hilferding had not so much as understood the essence of Böhm-Bawerk's criticism of Marx. See Mises (1978, 40).
40. Marx (1967, Vol. 2, 358).
41. Ibid. (Vol. 1, 94).
42. Engels (1947).
43. Moreover, Marx regarded the interventionist and syndicalist versions of socialism as "utopian". He viewed interventionism in this way because its defenders sought to maintain the anarchic nature typical of production in the market, while correcting it with isolated governmental commands aimed at achieving socialist ends. In this respect, Marx fully accepted the arguments voiced by members of the classical school of economics against interventionism, and he felt that social and labor legislation would never reach the objectives set for it, just as it will never be possible to change the law of gravity. Therefore, official decrees will not succeed in substantially raising wages, even if one assumes state or government authorities sincerely wish to raise them. Marx viewed syndicalists as utopian due to their inability to explain how the different independent industries and companies controlled by workers could come to coordinate their activities in a rational manner from the standpoint of society as a whole. What Marx failed to realize, as we have shown in the text, is that from his own perspective, the type of socialism he developed was utopian as well, since the information necessary for economic,

technological and social advancement cannot emerge in an environment of coercive central planning.

44. Mises (1966, 249). Furthermore, Mises agrees with Marx that the "money" used in a state of equilibrium would not be money at all. He does not claim, as Marx does, that it would simply consist of vouchers which would work just like tickets for the theater, but he writes: "It is merely a *numéraire*, an ethereal and undetermined unit of accounting of that vague and indefinable character which the fancy of some economists and the errors of many laymen mistakenly have attributed to money". Elsewhere (ibid., 417), Mises adds: "It is impossible to assign any function to indirect exchange, media of exchange and money within an imaginary construction the characteristic mark of which is unchangeability and rigidity of conditions. Where there is no uncertainty concerning the future there is no need for any cash holding. As money must necessarily be kept by people in their cash holdings, there cannot be any money. The use of media of exchange and the keeping of cash holdings are conditioned by the changeability of economic data. Money in itself is an element of change; its existence is incompatible with the idea of a regular flow of events in an evenly rotating economy". The best analysis of the differences between the concept of money in a market economy and in a socialist system appears in Hoff (1981, ch. 6, "Money and the formation of prices of consumer goods in a socialist society with free choice of goods and occupation", esp. pp. 101–15). Hoff makes it very clear that although the term "money" is used in both market economies and socialist economies, the word actually denotes two radically different concepts, not only because prices in socialist regimes serve merely as parameters (that is, they fulfill a retrospective or adjustment function, not a market one, in the sense of creating and incorporating new information), but also because consumer goods alone can be acquired in socialist systems, and the state owns the only store.

45. Mises (1920 [1975], 102).

46. Ibid., 109.

47. My conception of the "economic problem" does not, therefore, coincide with the more widespread Robbinsian view held by equilibrium theorists, who believe that the "economic problem" consists of the allocation of scarce but known resources to ends which are also given. This conception of "economics" is poor and of little scientific interest, and it reduces our science to a simple, limited and short-sighted amalgam of maximizing techniques. At the same time, it is not surprising that legions of pseudo-economists, who are simply maximization technicians, are unable to perceive, using the poor tools of their technique, the theoretical factors which render socialism impossible. The development of our science will remain encumbered until those who practice it recognize fully the radical differences between science and technique in the field of economics, and until they cease, under the pretext of science, to take refuge in the much easier, more comfortable, and more secure (despite appearances) area of a technique which is scientifically irrelevant, since it can only be implemented when the economic problems of true importance, generating and discovering the necessary information, are assumed resolved. Finally, because the economic problem can only be solved in a spontaneous, decentralized manner through the free exercise of human interaction or entrepreneurship, economics is, for us, a general science of human action and its implications (praxeology), and its raw material does not comprise objective things (goods, services and so on), but subjective entities of a spiritual nature (ideas, valuations, information). The Austrian conception of economics as a science not confined to maximization (in static and mathematical terms) originated with Menger himself. In fact, A.M. Endres even refers to the "Mengerian principle of non-maximization" (1991, esp. footnote 5 on p. 281).

48. As Rothbard indicates, "if there were no market for a product, and all of its exchanges were internal, there would be no way for a firm or for anyone else to determine a price for the good. A firm can estimate an implicit price when an external market exists; but when a market is absent, the good can have no price, whether implicit or explicit.

*Any figure could be only an arbitrary symbol*. Not being able to calculate a price a firm could not rationally allocate factors and resources from one stage to another" (1970a, 547–8).

49. As early as 1934, Fritz Machlup defended this argument and stated: "Whenever a firm (or concern) supplies the output of one of its departments as an input to another of its departments instead of selling it in a competitive market at a price established by supply and demand, the problem of artificial transfer prices or of jumbled cost-and-reserve figures arises. There may still be calculations, but not according to the economic principle of what Mises termed 'economic calculations'" (1976, esp. the bibliography cited on p. 116). Hayek, for his part, arrived at a very similar conclusion in another context when he asserted: "To make a monopolist charge the price that would rule under competition, or a price that is equal to the necessary cost, is impossible, because *the competitive or necessary cost cannot be known unless there is competition*. This does not mean that the manager of the monopolized industry under socialism will go on against his instructions, to make monopoly profits. But it does mean that since there is no way of testing the economic advantages of one method of production as compared with another, the place of monopoly profits will be taken by uneconomic waste" (1935c [1970], 170).

50. This reasoning is in line with Ronald H. Coase's analysis of the nature of the "firm" (understood as a voluntary internal "organization") and the determiners of its size and development, as opposed to the alternative system represented by external interrelations, which Coase mistakenly describes as relations based on the use of the market and price system. Coase states: "It is easy to see when the State takes over the directions of an industry that, in planning it, it is doing something which was previously done by the price mechanism. What is usually not realized is that any businessman, in organizing the relations among his departments, is also doing something which could be organized through the price mechanism ... In a competitive system, there is an 'optimum amount of planning'! ... The important difference between these two cases is that economic planning is imposed on industry, while firms arise *voluntarily* because they represent a more efficient method of organizing production" (1937 [1988], footnote 14 on p. 37). See also Williamson and Winter (1991, 30–31). Thus, Mises's thesis would complement Coase's, in the sense that the entrepreneurial organization would not only have decreasing profits and increasing costs, but would also entail a prohibitive cost from the moment the market for certain factors of production began to disappear. Hence, market processes are equipped with an internal safeguard against their possible elimination through voluntary vertical integration, a safeguard which consists of each entrepreneur's vital need to plan his action based on economic calculation. Nevertheless, despite the author's view that certain aspects of Coase's analysis are significant, Coase fails to cross the theoretical boundary to an explicit recognition of entrepreneurship. Throughout his theory, Coase focuses obsessively on "transaction costs", a concept which assumes the existence of the information necessary to identify and calculate such costs. However, the fundamental economic problem is not one of transaction costs, but an entrepreneurial problem; that is, an issue of the discovery and creation of the information necessary, both in terms of new ends and the new means necessary to accomplish them. In other words, Coase's theory continues to be a static or equilibrium theory which presupposes a given framework of ends and means and does not reflect the fact that the problem of transaction costs is preceded by a much more crucial issue: whether or not the entrepreneur realizes which courses of action are the most appropriate. That is, transaction costs can be absent if they are not discovered, and what is subjectively considered a transaction cost can at any time cease to be so or can change radically in the event of entrepreneurial innovations or discoveries. Thus, the problem is not that the information is given, though dispersed and very costly or difficult to obtain, but rather that the information is not given, and if entrepreneurship is exercised well, new practical information can be created or discovered constantly without any cost at all: in dynamic social processes, the economic problem is not posed by transaction costs,

but by genuine entrepreneurial error, and this can only be resolved via the creative and non-coerced exercise of entrepreneurship.
51. Thus the theoretical refutation of Marx is rounded off. Chronologically, the refutation began with Böhm-Bawerk's critical analysis of the Marxist theory of surplus value or exploitation and the objective labor theory of value, when Böhm-Bawerk revealed the inanity of the Marxist critical analysis against capitalism. Mises rounded off the argument with a devastating, definitive blow to Marx's theories, which Mises dealt by showing that the socialist alternative system is theoretically impossible, because it fails to permit economic calculation. From this argument, we can also deduce, as an important corollary or byproduct, proof that the Marxist theory concerning the process of capitalist consolidation is invalid.
52. Among the authors who believed economic calculation possible in a moneyless economy, we could mention Karl Ballod, Nicolai Bukharin, Otto Neurath, Carl Landauer and Alexander B. Tschayanoff. In general, the idea held by these authors is that the state would have to define the needs of each citizen in terms of "objective" criteria which technicians (biologists, agronomists and so on) would provide. Then, the corresponding statistics department or institute would have to plan the quantity of consumer goods (boots, pants, shirts and so on) which would have to be produced in the course of a year. These consumer goods would later be distributed among the citizens in the same way. In addition to Neurath's works (1919, 1925), the main works of the socialist authors who defended calculation in kind are the following: Tschayanoff (1923); Bukharin and Preobrazhensky (1966); Ballod (1927); and lastly, Landauer (1931). A detailed description of the proposals these authors make appears in Hoff (1981, 50–80). On the economist Karl Ballod and his influence on the origins of planning in the Soviet Union, see Seurot (1983, 12–13). Six editions of Ballod's book were published in Russian between 1903 and 1906, and Gleb Krjijanovskij closely followed the principles contained in it when Lenin entrusted him with the mission of drafting the electrification plan (the GOELRO Plan) in 1920. For more on Ballod (1864–1933), who used the pseudonym *Atlanticus*, from Francis Bacon's 1627 work *Nova Atlantis*, see Juan Martínez-Alier (1990, 199–205). Nevertheless, in his conclusions, Martínez-Alier neglects to take account of the essence of entrepreneurship as we explained it in Chapters 2 and 3, and he overlooks the fact that natural resources are particularly damaged whenever institutional obstacles are placed in the way of entrepreneurship, since the information necessary to make appropriate decisions about those resources is not generated. For more on this topic, see Huerta de Soto (1986).
53. The socialist theorist Karl Kautsky himself ridiculed Neurath's ideas on calculation in kind and concluded that "it is obvious that bookkeeping *in natura* would soon lead to inextricable chaos", quoted by Hoff (1981, 79). Furthermore, Hoff demonstrates in great detail that none of the proposals for in-kind distribution of consumer goods and services which the different socialist theorists presented (and of which eight different versions, divided into two large groups, were actually considered) is possible (also see pp. 54–70). The Russian economist Boris Brutzkus also described as absurd the proposals of Bukharin and Tschayanoff concerning the possibility of making economic calculations in kind (1935, 17.)
54. Mises (1922 [1981], footnote on p. 119).
55. The procedure described above for performing economic calculation in labor hours was outlined by Karl Marx (1974b, 1970 edn), when he wrote: "He receives a certificate from society that he has furnished such-and-such an amount of labor (after deducting his labor for the common funds); and with this certificate, he draws from the social stock of means of consumption as much as the same amount of labor cost. The same amount of labor which he has given to society in one form, he receives back in another". The author who most convincingly defended the claim that economic calculation in labor hours is possible was Otto Leichter (1923). Paradoxically, in this book, Leichter fiercely criticizes the proposals of calculation in kind. His ideas were later developed and refined by Walter Schiff (1932). Leichter's solution was specifically disputed by

Mises (1924). William Keizer (1987) wrote a piece in English in which he comments on this article of Mises's. The second article which Keizer discusses is Mises (1928), in which Mises examines the contributions of J. Marschak, Otto Neurath and Boris Brutzkus.

56. Stanislav Strumilin (1877–1974), in the three articles he published in 1920, indicated that he did not consider economic calculation in labor hours possible unless this concept were made complete by the use of units of utility. A detailed explanation of his system of economic calculation, which Lenin abandoned when he reintroduced the market and money in the NEP period, appears in M.C. Kaser's article on Strumilin (1987). Brutzkus, in his cited work, meticulously criticized the possibility of performing economic calculation in units of utility. For his part, Kautsky (1922) vehemently argued that economic calculation in labor hours is impossible unless the historical market prices which prevail prior to the establishment of a socialist economy are taken as a starting point (perhaps as an indirect way of capturing utility ratios). Mises (1924) roundly refuted Kautsky's proposal.

57. *"Todo necio / confunde valor y precio"* ("All fools confuse value with price"), Antonio Machado, "Proverbios y Cantares" 68 (1989, 1: 640, 820).

58. A good study on the different authors who in German attempted to answer Mises's challenge, the majority of whom we have cited in earlier footnotes, is Günther K. Chaloupek (1990); see especially the entire bibliography cited there. The economic-calculation debate in German, which is less well known than the subsequent debate that took place in the English-speaking world, was made complete by works which clearly supported Mises's position and which Chaloupek failed to cite. See especially Max Weber (1922); Adolf Weber (1932, 2: 369), C.A. Verrijn Stuart and Pohle and Halm (1931, 237 ff).

# 5. The unjustified shift in the debate toward statics: the arguments of formal similarity and the so-called "mathematical solution"

This chapter will show that once Mises issued his initial challenge, the socialist participants in the debate quickly centered their efforts on solving the problem that socialism would pose in a strictly static sense. These efforts were totally unnecessary, and thus this shift of the socialist theorists toward statics is described as "unjustified", given that Mises himself had already indicated that socialism did not present any problem of economic calculation at all in static terms. The chapter will attempt to explain why the socialists so completely misunderstood the nature of the problem to be discussed. Specifically, it will analyze the destructive effect exerted on the debate by both the paradigm of economic equilibrium analysis and the arguments developed to show the formal similarity which exists in strictly static terms between the market and the socialist model. Then the chapter will examine the "mathematical solution", which socialist theorists proposed in several versions, and conclude with an analysis of the response that Mises, Hayek and Robbins gave to this whole set of solution proposals.

## 1 THE ARGUMENTS OF FORMAL SIMILARITY

In the last chapter, we saw that the longest-standing school of thought within the socialist tradition naively maintained that a socialist system could dispense with the economic concepts of value and interest, which classical theorists had discovered and analyzed for capitalist economies. In response to this position, different economists hastened to show that even in an ideal socialist economic regime, with all information available and no changes (equilibrium model), the basic concepts of value and interest would have to be conserved. This argument, which was initially formulated in terms of verbal logic and later in formalized mathematical terms, sprang from a desire to make an impression upon the socialist theorists who unrealistically believed that it was possible to do away with the concept of value in their models. Thus, to demonstrate that the ideal communist system required the basic concepts of value and interest even in equilibrium, economists made the theoretical concession of considering from the beginning that the fundamental economic problem (that is, acquiring the necessary information) had already been resolved. However, it was this concession which led to the unwarranted shift in the debate toward the field of statics, where it was meaningless, and as a result, great confusion arose among the debate's participants and among those who later analyzed and evaluated its content and the main conclusions to be drawn from it. Indeed, when the assumption was made in equilibrium models, whether formalized in mathematical terms or not, that all information was available and unchanging, it became almost inevitable to consider the problem of socialist economic calculation as merely an algebraic or computational problem, which could be overcome by simply finding a practical procedure for solving the corresponding systems of mathematical equations. Hence, the argument of formal similarity, which was originally conceived to refute the claims of socialist theorists, was later used by them to evade the fundamental economic problem posed by socialism (that is, how the central planning agency can obtain the crucial, practical information it needs, data which is always created anew and dispersed throughout the minds of millions of economic agents). Thus, economists committed the error of viewing the problem as simply the practical difficulty of solving numerous and complex systems of equations, without ever perceiving that socialism presents any other problem of theoretical impossibility *per se*. As this phenomenon illustrates, the great danger of applying the mathematical method in economics is that it renders the truly important economic problems indistinguishable to even the most brilliant minds.[1]

## The Formal Similarity Arguments Advanced by Eugen von Böhm-Bawerk and Friedrich von Wieser

Eighteen eighty-nine was perhaps the most significant year with respect to formal similarity arguments. Indeed, that year saw the publication of Friedrich von Wieser's book, *Der Natürliche Wert* (Natural value). One of Wieser's primary objectives for the book was to show that even in a community or state organized economically according to communist principles, economic goods would not cease to have value. Wieser believed the essential laws of value to be independent of any institutional and social environment, and that therefore they must be taken into account in any socialist system. Wieser's is clearly an analysis of equilibrium which reveals that the characteristic logic of choice must be identical in a market system and in a socialist system, and this precisely constitutes the argument of a formal similarity between the two systems.[2]

Also in 1889, Eugen von Böhm-Bawerk, in the second volume of his magnum opus *Capital and Interest*, developed an argument quite similar to Wieser's, but in reference to the interest rate. Böhm-Bawerk views interest as an essential economic concept which must be present in any economic system, whether capitalist or communist. Hence, the fiercely criticized "surplus value" or "exploitation" typical of the capitalist system would not disappear under a socialist regime. In fact, quite the opposite is true: the state or supervisory agency would be obliged to maintain it, since the concepts of time preference and interest cannot be eliminated from any economy.[3]

Although these contributions were intended to show that the categories of value and interest must also exist in a socialist regime, when Wieser and, to a lesser extent, Böhm-Bawerk based their reasoning on equilibrium arguments which presuppose that all necessary information is given, they made it relatively easy to incorporate their viewpoint into the neoclassical paradigm. This paradigm centers on equilibrium and defines the problem of socialist economic calculation as merely one of operating technique, of solving a very large number of highly complex equations. However, it must be stated, in defense of these Austrian authors, that at least they were aware that the model they were using would be very difficult, if not impossible, to actually put into practice. Specifically, in 1914, Wieser even intuited Mises's essential argument with respect to socialist economic calculation and the impossibility of the central planning agency's obtaining the necessary practical information. In fact, Wieser stated:

> The private economic system is the only historically tried form of a large social economic combination. The experience of thousands of years furnishes proof that, by this very system, a more successful social joint action is being secured, than by *universal submission to one single command*. The one will and command which, in war and for legal unity, is essential and indispensable as the connecting tie of the common forces, detracts in economic joint action from the efficacy of the agency. In the economy, though it has become social, *work is always to be performed fractionally* . . . Part-performances of this sort will be executed far more effectively by thousands and millions of human beings, *seeing with thousands and millions of eyes*, exerting as many wills: they will be balanced, one against the others, far more accurately than if all these actions, like some complex mechanism, had to be *guided and directed by some superior control. A central prompter of this sort could never be informed of countless possibilities*, to be met in every individual case, as regards the utmost utility to be derived from given circumstances or the best steps to be taken for future advancement and progress".[4]

## Enrico Barone's Contribution as a Formal Similarity Argument

In the first section of the last chapter, we commented on certain aspects of Enrico Barone's 1908 piece, "Il Ministro della Produzione nello Stato Colletivista", which Hayek later translated into English and published in his *Collectivist Economic Planning*.[5] Of interest to us now is the way in which Barone followed Wieser's lead in terms of developing the arguments of a formal similarity between capitalism and socialism. The main novelty of Barone's position lay in his criticism of what he considered the awkward and vague nature of the formal similarity arguments employed by his predecessors (Wieser and, to a lesser degree, Böhm-Bawerk). Barone went so far as to claim he was capable of rigorously and formally presenting and proving, using mathematical analysis, what until then had been only an imperfect intuition.[6] However, we must take issue with this presumptuous statement of Barone's, since that so-called "mathematical precision" can only be achieved at the expense of nearly all of the model's remaining significance and explanatory value from the standpoint of economic analysis. Indeed, unlike Wieser, Barone does not conceive the economy as a social process consisting of a set of interrelationships between different agents who act consciously to pursue their ends; instead, he conceives it as simply a set of functional relationships and quantitative results. What was a more or less rigorous, genetic-causal economic analysis, rooted in each actor's ends and means, becomes a mechanical set of functional relationships in which human beings do not take part, time does not count, and "prices" are not the result of human interaction, but emerge from the intersection of two curves or are mere numerical solutions to a simultaneous system of equations. Thus, Barone clearly illustrates the effects of the corrupting colonization of economics by the body of engineers and technicians trained in the mechanistic tradition of P.S. Laplace. As a result, it is not surprising that Barone's analysis is necessarily and essentially static and therefore irrelevant from the standpoint of Mises's criticism of socialism. In fact, for the first 40 pages of his article, Barone assumes that the necessary information, with respect to the amount of capital as well as the technical relationships between the different factors of production and the tastes and ends of individuals, is given and known.[7] As we saw in the first section of the last chapter, it is only at the end of his article that Barone, very vaguely and in passing, indicates that the information he initially assumed to be available to enable him to formally develop his argument in mathematical terms could never be known.

Therefore, it is obvious that, contrary to the erroneous interpretation of the debate which has until now prevailed due to the clumsy and opportunistic description of it given by Oskar Lange and Joseph Schumpeter,

Barone in no way refuted Mises's argument concerning the impossibility of socialist economic calculation before Mises had even formulated it. Indeed, as we have already shown by explicitly citing Mises,[8] his argument is dynamic and refers to the impossibility of the central agency's obtaining the vital practical information it needs to plan the economy. Hence, Mises himself was the first to note that in the imaginary nirvana of equilibrium, it would not be necessary to even consider the problem he had pointed out. Thus, Barone did not refute Mises's argument, since in his formal similarity analysis, Barone begins precisely by assuming that the necessary information is given and that the economic problem Mises identified has been resolved *ab initio*. Not only did Barone not refute Mises's argument, but, on the contrary, at the end of his article, Barone explicitly stresses, though in a superficial and vague manner, the fundamental idea which would later lie at the heart of the Misesian argument, that is, that it is logically impossible to acquire, by a mechanism other than by observing the result of market processes themselves, the knowledge assumed given in order to formulate the corresponding system of mathematical equations. As we have already seen, Pareto himself had conveyed this idea with clarity before even Barone.[9]

**Other Formal Similarity Theorists: Gustav Cassel and Erik Lindahl**

The above formal-similarity arguments were brought together in 1918 by Cassel, who, with respect to both price determination and the maintenance of the interest rate, viewed the situation in a socialist economy as formally similar to that in a market economy. Cassel even stated that "the principles of price formation are valid for the whole economy, and specifically, are independent of the particular organization of production". He also considered so-called perfect competition "highly necessary as a theoretical condition for implementing the principle of setting price according to cost". All of the above led Cassel to conclude that the "socialist order can be considered theoretically simpler" even than the market itself. Cassel's ideas exerted a very negative, indirect influence on the course of the debate, because they provided the theoretical basis for Kläre Tisch's doctoral thesis, which Schumpeter supervised in 1932, and which contributed greatly to convincing him that the formal similarity theorists (Pareto, Barone and so on) had already resolved, before Mises himself, the problem of economic calculation Mises raised. Cassel's ideas survived for years among his disciples, and even in 1939, Lindahl continued to blindly defend formal similarity arguments, while overlooking all that the debate on socialist economic calculation had contributed up to that point.[10]

## 2 ANALYSIS OF THE MATHEMATICAL SOLUTION

Earlier, when we interpreted the contribution of Marx, we concluded that his ideal model of society could ultimately be considered an equilibrium model which he felt it possible and advisable to coercively impose via a central planning agency. Later, we saw that different theorists developed the formal conditions of this equilibrium model and, by assuming that the fundamental economic problem of obtaining information had been resolved *ab initio*, they led different authors to believe that socialism simply posed an algebraic problem of mathematically solving a more or less complex system of numerous equations. Thus, it gradually became common to think that the theorists who saw a formal similarity between capitalism and socialism (Wieser, Barone and so on) had proven that, contrary to what Mises indicated, socialist economic calculation was "theoretically" possible, and that if it presented a difficulty, it was only the algebraic difficulty of solving the corresponding systems of equations. However, we have shown this interpretation to be completely erroneous from beginning to end. To equate economic theory with equilibrium analysis is unacceptable and absolutely unwarranted, since, in any case, equilibrium analysis is only one part of economic theory (perhaps the least vital part). As we have already demonstrated, Mises's analysis is a *theoretical* analysis, but, in the best Austrian tradition, it concerns dynamic social processes, and consequently, the impossibility of centrally acquiring the key practical information which economic agents possess, use and constantly create. Therefore, the problem is not, as many conclude, that even if the central agency were to obtain the necessary information, calculation would still be impossible, due to the enormous practical difficulty of algebraically solving the corresponding systems of equations. On the contrary, we should approach the problem from precisely the opposite direction: even if at some point it became possible to solve the extremely complex and numerous systems of equations presented by the formal similarity theorists, the insurmountable theoretical and logical problem of acquiring the information crucial for formulating these equations would always remain. Hence, the shift the formal similarity theorists initiated toward statics in the debate concealed from many brilliant minds the nature of the fundamental economic problem Mises had raised concerning socialism, and it prompted the false belief that economic calculation could be made possible simply by improving the algebraic techniques of solving the corresponding systems of equations. We shall now examine the contents of the most important proposals of a "mathematical solution".

## The Article by Fred M. Taylor

The first serious attempt to mathematically solve the problem of central planning was undertaken by Fred M. Taylor in a lecture entitled "The guidance of production in a socialist state", delivered December 27, 1928, on the occasion of his inauguration as president of the American Economic Association.[11] Taylor's brief, ambiguous article divides the analysis of the economic calculation problem into two parts. In the first, he explicitly supposes that all necessary knowledge or information is available; and in the second, which is very short, he attempts to design a system for discovering this information.

Taylor's paper was the first return, after Mises, to static or equilibrium analyses, in which it is presumed that all necessary information is available, and therefore, that the economic calculation problem is merely an issue of computation or mathematical technique. According to Taylor, economic calculation could be performed using arithmetical tables, which he called "factor valuation tables" and which would contain, in quantitative terms, the relative valuations of all factors of production. Taylor believed socialism should be organized based on the sale of each good and service at a price which coincides with its respective cost of production, to be calculated using the above tables. Given that Taylor, throughout most of his article, explicitly supposes that the authority of the socialist state could have available to it sufficiently accurate numerical data to formulate these tables, he obviously begs the question, because he implicitly bases his reasoning on the assumption that the fundamental economic problem socialism presents can be solved. Hence, Taylor was the first to commit the distinct error which the vast array of socialist writers would commit: in an attempt to evade the truly vital dynamic concerns involved in socialist economic calculation, he centers his analysis on the strictly algebraic or mathematical concerns typical of the static equilibrium model.

As Gerald P. O'Driscoll pointed out, the chief error all of these writers commit lies not in the type of answer they give to the problem, but rather in the question they ask.[12] Indeed, the scientifically relevant question with respect to economic calculation is not, as the socialist theorists of the equilibrium model would have it, whether or not it is possible to algebraically solve the corresponding mathematical formulas in the event that all the information necessary to formulate them were available, but on the contrary, whether, from a logical and theoretical standpoint, the information necessary to formulate these equations can be obtained.

Finally, Taylor devotes the last five pages of his article to a very brief proposal of a practical procedure for acquiring, with a certain degree of precision, the information necessary to formulate his "factor valuation tables". Later, we shall closely examine the content of his famous "trial-and-error" method, though at this point we need only to emphasize that Taylor himself saw the first part of his article, on the static analysis of socialism, as the most significant and his main contribution to the topic of socialist economic calculation.

**The Contribution of H.D. Dickinson**

Unlike Taylor's article, which was discussed above and which went practically unnoticed when it was published, the detailed and explicit proposal of a "solution" to the problem of socialist economic calculation that Henry Douglas Dickinson offers in his article, "Price formation in a socialist community"[13] sparked the long and heated debate in English on socialist economic calculation, a debate in which, among others, Maurice H. Dobb and Abba P. Lerner participated.

Dickinson starts from the idea that, while in theory it would be quite difficult to formulate a Walrasian system of simultaneous equations, in practice the problem could be greatly simplified by a grouping process, by putting together the goods and services which are most closely related. In this way, Dickinson believes that it would be possible to establish a system of equations manageable enough to be mathematically solved through the traditional procedures and without turning to market processes. Curiously, Dickinson makes explicit reference to the "problem" of the dispersed nature of the knowledge involved in market processes, when he states that the ignorance of economic opportunities which is typical in a market economy would be eliminated in a socialist regime, due to the systematic publicizing of the "information" related to production, costs, sales, inventories, and in general, all statistical data which may be relevant. Specifically, Dickinson concludes that in the socialist system, all companies would operate as if made "of glass", that is, without keeping secrets of any kind, and maintaining a complete "information transparency" toward the outside.[14]

These assertions Dickinson makes are as surprising as they are difficult to uphold. Furthermore, his naivety is comparable only to his ignorance of how a market economy functions. Dickinson fails to understand that the model of general equilibrium, as it was developed by Walras and Pareto, is simply a model of formal similarity in which the only thing its authors reveal is the type of information that would be necessary to establish and maintain a state of equilibrium. However, neither Pareto nor Walras built their hopes up regarding the possibility of obtaining the necessary information by procedures other than the market itself.[15] Therefore, the problem is not one of computation; it does not consist of resolving a series of Walrasian simultaneous equations (even if the equations have been formulated in a simplified manner by grouping together the most similar goods and services, as Dickinson proposes), but rather of acquiring the subjective, practical information which is only found and created in a dispersed form and is necessary to establish the parameters and variables of such equations.

As for the argument that dispersed knowledge would present no problem in a socialist system in which the principle of "information transparency" prevailed and all statistics were widely publicized, it is purely fallacious. Information is not static, objective and always available somewhere, such that only cost problems and a deliberate restriction on publicity could keep it from reaching everyone. On the contrary, information is essentially subjective and dynamic and is constantly being created *ex novo* as a consequence of the force of entrepreneurship within the context of a market economy. Hence, if the free exercise of entrepreneurship is prohibited, and the economy is coercively organized from above via commands, as demonstrated in Chapters 2 and 3 of this book, the practical information vital for coordinating the social process will not even emerge or be generated. Therefore, it is worthless to proclaim empty general principles involving information transparency or a broader publication of data if the institutional restriction on the free exercise of entrepreneurship precludes the emergence of the necessary information. Moreover, constant change and the dynamic nature of information render existing, historical information useless and irrelevant. Though it may have been incorporated into lavish and detailed statistics and distributed free of charge with complete transparency, it retains only a historical or "archeological" value if, as occurs in all real, unfrozen economies, circumstances change, new ends and means are discovered, and new information constantly emerges or is created. As early as 1912, the Dutch economist Nicolaas Gerard Pierson advanced the argument that in a real economy, not even the most widespread and detailed publication of statistics could be of any use, given the constant changes which make statistical information obsolete even before it is published.[16]

Finally, we must conclude by pointing out that only six years later, in 1939, Dickinson himself admitted that although initially (in 1933) he had believed that his mathematical solution represented a workable procedure for carrying out economic calculation in a socialist regime, he had later radically changed his mind. He had realized his mistake because "the data themselves which would have to be fed into the equation-machine, are continuously changing".[17] As we know, this is precisely the argument Austrians have offered from the very beginning for their rejection of any sort of mathematical solution.

### The Mathematical Solution in the German Literature

Various authors in the German literature also tried to come up with a mathematical solution to the problem of economic calculation. Among them is Kläre Tisch, who has already been mentioned, and who, in her doctoral thesis, which she wrote under the supervision of Schumpeter and based on the work of Cassel and Walras, concluded that it was possible to construct a system of equations with as many equations as unknowns, a system which, once solved, could dispose of the problem of economic calculation. Herbert Zassenhaus commits the same error, though he himself explicitly recognizes that such a system could only be used if the ministry of production possessed *beforehand* all of the necessary information and this information remained constant while the equations were being solved. Thus, neither Tisch nor Zassenhaus realizes that the essential problem lies precisely in establishing a way to obtain the information the planning agency needs to formulate its system of equations.[18]

## 3 THE MATHEMATICAL SOLUTION AND ITS ADVERSE CONSEQUENCES FOR THE DEBATE

The most important adverse consequence which the mathematical solution proposed by Taylor and Dickinson had on the course of the debate on socialist economic calculation was that it shifted the attention of the participants toward the problems of static economics. Indeed, the mathematical solution answers the wrong question (whether or not economic calculation is possible under static conditions, that is, when all necessary information is available and no changes occur). In this sense, the mathematical solution definitely brought down the theoretical standard of the debate, and it distracted minds from the fundamental economic problem as Mises had initially presented it. This fundamental economic problem was basically a theoretical issue of *economic dynamics* and involved the impossibility of performing economic calculation in the absence of a market process driven by entrepreneurship, since entrepreneurship alone enables economic agents to constantly discover the practical, dispersed information which is necessary to make market estimates on costs and benefits.

Another negative consequence of the mathematical solution was that it created the erroneous impression that both Hayek and Robbins, in response to the assertions of Taylor and Dickinson, withdrew to a "second line of defense" and recognized that economic calculation was possible in theory, yet continued to hold that it was impossible in practice, strictly for reasons of algebraic workability, that is, because of the practical difficulty of solving the corresponding systems of equations. Apart from the fact that this version of the story rests on the previously described, grave methodological error of equating theory with economic equilibrium analysis, we do not believe it corresponds with reality for the following reasons.

First, for Hayek, the essential argument on the impossibility of economic calculation lies not in the practical difficulty of algebraically solving a system of countless equations, but in the insoluble, theoretical-dynamic problem of assuming that the central regulatory agency can acquire the subjective, practical information that is created in dispersed form and found scattered throughout the minds of millions of economic agents. In fact, in his article, "The present state of the debate", published in 1935, Hayek writes that the essential economic problem with the mathematical solution is that:

> the usual theoretical abstractions used in the explanation of equilibrium in a competitive system include the assumption that a certain range of technical knowledge is "given" . . . It is hardly necessary to emphasize that this is an absurd idea even in so far as that knowledge is concerned which can properly be said to "exist" at any moment of time. But much of the knowledge that is actually utilized is by no means "in existence" in this ready-made form.[19]

Hence, for Hayek, the fundamental problem economic calculation poses has nothing to do with the strictly "algebraic" difficulty of solving the corresponding system of equations.

Second, when Hayek mentions the practical problem of solving the system of equations, he refers to it as one of a very different nature or rank from the fundamental problem indicated in number one above, and in any case, he attaches only secondary importance to it and addresses it almost in passing when he states:

> Now the magnitude of this essential mathematical operation will depend on the number of unknowns to be determined. The number of these unknowns will be equal to the number of commodities which are to be produced . . . At present we can hardly say what their number is, but it is hardly an exaggeration to assume that in a fairly advanced society, the order of magnitude would be at least in the hundreds of thousands. This means that, at each successive moment, every one of the decisions would have to be based on the solution of an equal number of simultaneous differential equations, a task which, with any of the means known at present, could not be carried out in a lifetime.[20]

Furthermore, completely regardless of the reasons that computer science cannot solve the economic calculation problem, reasons that were examined in Chapter 3, if we now focus strictly on the algebraic problem posed by a system of multitudinous equations, we see that the impressive progress in computer techniques and the extraordinary development of computer capacity which have taken place have proven insignificant in terms of solving the problem. Indeed, according to Paul Samuelson and William Nordhaus, with the most modern computers and the techniques Herbert Scarf and Harold Kuhn developed in the 1960s and 1970s, it is currently possible and relatively easy to solve economic equilibrium problems composed of 50 markets and 10 or 20 different types of consumers. The most modern supercomputers could be used to solve systems of equations based on 100 different types of productive factors, 10,000 goods, and 100 different types of consumers.[21] These magnitudes still come nowhere near the number of different goods and services identifiable in an underdeveloped economy, like that of the former Soviet Union, where the number of products far exceeded 12 million. Sir Alec Nove has mentioned a comment made by the academician Nikolai Fedorenko, who stated that the economic calculation problem which the last five-year plan of the former Soviet Union posed would take 30,000 years to formulate and solve.[22] No matter how unfeasible these figures seem, we must not deceive ourselves by thinking they constitute the fundamental reason for the failure of socialism. For even if tomorrow's computers make it possible to solve systems of hundreds of millions of equations in a tenth of a second, it will always remain impossible to coercively obtain the economic information necessary to formulate such systems of equations.

Third, one possible explanation for the misunderstanding of Hayek's position lies in the order in which he presents the points in his argument.[23] Indeed, to criticize the mathematical solution, Hayek follows an order similar to the one anyone faced with a purely algebraic problem would have to follow. He begins by referring to the problem of formulating the corresponding equations. It is here that Hayek mentions the fundamental theoretical problem: the impossibility of acquiring the information necessary to formulate them. Hayek then writes that, even if we assume for the sake of argument that it has been possible to formulate the equations that describe the equilibrium system, it would be *practically* impossible to algebraically solve such a system. Clearly, Hayek focuses on the essential theoretical argument that it is impossible to obtain the information necessary to formulate the corresponding equations, and he attaches only secondary importance to the problem of algebraically solving them.[24] Nevertheless, it is perhaps because he follows the above order in his explanation that many commentators on the debate have mistakenly assumed that Hayek withdrew to a "second line of defense" and hid behind the practical difficulties of solving a system of equations, rather than centering on theoretical arguments of logical impossibility. Such an interpretation is unfounded, and Hayek himself refuted it in detail.[25]

Fourth, Mises is particularly clear in showing that the argument that it would be difficult to algebraically solve the system of equations is not only, as Hayek believed, of a secondary nature, but also totally unnecessary and theoretically irrelevant.[26] For Mises, the fundamental problem is that the knowledge necessary to formulate the equilibrium equations can never be centrally available. Furthermore, in 1940 he raised the additional argument, which Hayek had not developed beforehand, that even if a system of equations describing an equilibrium state could be formulated (an impossible feat using the knowledge typical of a state of disequilibrium, the only knowledge available in real life), it would offer no help at all to the planning or regulatory authorities who must decide what specific decisions or steps would move the economy from the current, real state of disequilibrium to the desired, ideal state of equilibrium. In the words of Mises himself:

> It was a serious mistake to believe that the state of equilibrium could be computed, by means of mathematical operations, on the basis of the knowledge of conditions in a non-equilibrium state. It was no less erroneous to believe that such a knowledge of the conditions under a hypothetical state of equilibrium could be of any use for acting man in his search for the best possible solution of the problems with which he is faced in his daily choices and activities.[27]

## 4 THE "TRIAL AND ERROR" METHOD

As far back as 1935, Hayek doubted that Taylor and Dickinson really had in mind, as a solution to the economic calculation problem, a method literally based on mathematically solving a Walrasian system of equations. Instead, Hayek believed that what Taylor and Dickinson actually, though ambiguously, proposed was the reiterative search for a solution to the Walrasian system of equations by a procedure based on the "trial and error" method.[28]

Chronologically, Taylor was the first to expressly mention the trial and error method. In fact, for him: "The method of trial and error ... consists of trying out a series of hypothetical solutions till one is found which proves a success".[29] Dickinson, for his part, was somewhat less explicit and simply referred to a "process of successive approximation" to the correct solution.[30]

Given the ambiguous and confusing quality of their writings, it is not easy to derive a clear, detailed idea of what Taylor, Willet Crosby Roper and Dickinson understood by "trial and error method", though in principle this method was proposed as a *variant* of the mathematical solution, an attempt to avoid the thorny problem of having to algebraically solve an extremely complex system of equations. In fact, these authors, as well as Lange himself (as we shall see), considered the mathematical solution the most appropriate, yet felt that, as long as practical difficulties to finding the solution to the corresponding system of equations remained, it would be possible to reach a very close approximation by a procedure of trial and error. It would only be necessary to adopt the equilibrium solutions inherited from the preceding capitalist system and then make the marginal adjustments necessary to return the system to equilibrium whenever changes occurred.

The practical way to employ this method would be to order the managers and people in charge of the different sectors, industries and companies to continually transmit to the central planning agency their knowledge regarding the different production circumstances in general, and the different combinations of productive factors in particular. Based on the information received, the central planning agency would tentatively set an entire series of provisional prices, which would have to be communicated to company managers, so that they could estimate the quantities they could produce at these prices and act accordingly. The activity of the managers would reveal errors, which would take the form of production shortages (whenever demand exceeded supply) or surpluses (whenever supply exceeded demand). A shortage or surplus in a certain line of production would indicate to the central planning agency that the price established was not correct and that, therefore, it should be appropriately lowered or raised, according to the circumstances. This process would be repeated until the new equilibrium so sought after were found. The highly praised method of trial and error consists basically of this.

**Criticism of the Trial and Error Method**

The trial and error method we have just described is not only deceptively simple, but, for the reasons that will now explained, it is also incapable of resolving the fundamental economic problem socialism poses.

First, it is theoretically absurd to think the real capitalist system could ever reach a state of equilibrium. In the capitalist system, the prices the parties set are market prices which are in constant flux, driven by the creative force of entrepreneurship; they are not equilibrium prices which the socialist system can somehow inherit as a reliable starting point. Thus, not only do the socialist theorists betray a profound lack of understanding with respect to the way the market works, but paradoxically, they also admit that from the standpoint of their (mistaken) conception, the market, as it is usually in equilibrium, works much "better" than it actually does. In contrast, we know that the market is never in equilibrium and that, far from an imperfection, this is the most intimate and typical characteristic of the market. Hence, it is especially pathetic that socialist theorists have had to refrain from criticizing the market for its lack of equilibrium in the tactical interest of presenting a trial and error method which will make socialism possible and which can only conceivably be formulated based on the equilibrium prices of the capitalist system they so revile.

Second, it is inadmissible to assume that the changes which would take place in the economic system once it moved from capitalism to socialism would be relatively insignificant. On the contrary, the changes and distortions would inevitably be so major in all economic and social areas that they would necessitate a complete and total restructuring of the entire price system. This would follow from the disappearance of the right to own factors of production and the drastic change in the distribution of income which result from any revolutionary shift from one economic system to another. However, it would also arise from the very altered perceptions of the different economic agents as to the ends they should pursue and the means available to them, in light of the different place each individual occupies on the new social scale and in light of the immense degree of institutional coercion and rigidity introduced, to the detriment of free entrepreneurship in all social areas. Thus, it is theoretically inadmissible to hold that the existing prices in the capitalist economic system just prior to the introduction of socialism could be taken as a starting point, to be followed simply by whatever minor detail adjustments are necessary to keep the system in equilibrium.[31]

Third, even if we imagine, for the sake of argument, that the change from capitalism to socialism does not significantly affect the price system, it is important to remember that only in rare cases could a product surplus or shortage reliably indicate to a central planning agency what it should do with the price. Specifically, the different economic agents must have choices and perceive them as such if a product shortage or surplus is to indicate whether or not it is necessary to raise or lower the prefixed price. In other words, wherever alternatives do not exist or are not perceived, shortages have little meaning, since they are forced by the lack of, or the lack of knowledge of, goods and services which are similar, but of different quality, or available at different prices, or even goods and services which are different, yet to some extent can be used as substitutes. Hence, a shortage is not a symptom which automatically indicates that the price should be raised, since on many occasions the most economical course of action would be to attempt to develop, introduce, and try new, alternative products.

Fourth, for a shortage to be significant and in any way assist the central planning agency in making decisions, it is also essential that the number of "vouchers" issued to convey the right to acquire factors of production and consumer goods and services not be excessive. (We do not say "monetary units", since, as explained before, the concept of money differs radically from a socialist system to a capitalist system.) Indeed, if too many monetary units are issued, there will be a generalized shortage of goods, services and productive resources, and this shortage will not provide any precise indication of how much the price of each good, service, or factor of production should be raised, nor by what amount the production of each type of these should be increased.[32]

Fifth, if, as is most common, the shortage ends up manifesting itself as a chronic or recurrent feature of the socialist system, the economic agents (consumers, managers and so on) will sooner or later learn from experience, and their own innate entrepreneurial ability will lead them to try to obtain any good obtainable in exchange for the corresponding monetary units. Thus, there is a generalized flight to real values on the part of all economic agents, who try to acquire anything, even if they do not need it immediately or at all, since they realize that scarcity is the dominant feature of the economic system and that it behooves them to acquire any type of good, even an unnecessary one, as a precaution against a future time when the good may become both useful and unavailable. This phenomenon occurs identically in the area of production. János Kornai has very clearly explained that in a socialist system, industrial managers soon discover that scarcity of the different inputs, or productive factors, is the chronic, dominant feature. Furthermore, the manager realizes that he loses nothing by maintaining a very large inventory of productive factors, since the financial cost of doing so, given the absence of rigorous budget restraints, causes him no real problem. In contrast, if the manager is unable, due to the shortage of a certain material or factor of production, to achieve an objective the planning agency has coercively imposed, the manager does face a very significant, real risk. Consequently, there emerges a widespread, continuous tendency to demand and accumulate an excessive quantity of all sorts of inputs, or factors of production, including ones which are not strictly necessary, and as a result, the widespread shortage of resources inexorably becomes the defining characteristic of the socialist economic system.[33] Therefore, it is obvious that if the economic system is absolutely, chronically and constantly riddled with shortages of most of the economic, consumer goods and productive factors in society, then a central planning agency cannot possibly find an equilibrium solution by a process of trial and error based on observing the *shortages* which occur in the economic system.[34]

Sixth, we must stress that the economic system is not a mere conglomeration of isolated goods and services, such that a shortage or surplus of any particular product automatically indicates the need for a price increase or decrease. On the contrary, the economic system continuously gives rise to a set of closely interrelated consumer goods and services and factors of production. Thus, for instance, the shortage of a good may not be evident even though it exists, because it is camouflaged by the presence or absence of other goods which are directly or indirectly related as complementary or substitute goods. It may also occur that a shortage appears to exist, yet because of the circumstances, it would be wiser to make better use of existing substitute goods than to raise the price. This means that the central planning agency could not be guided by the shortage or surplus of individual goods, but would have to be aware of and monitor the shortage or surplus of all goods as a group, and these goods are interrelated. Thus, a method which, like the trial and error method, is designed to be applied in isolation for each good or service is patently useless.[35]

Seventh, Mises argues that the trial and error method is only applicable as a means of addressing those problems in which the correct solution is recognizable by a series of indisputable signs and facts which are independent of the trial and error method itself. The circumstances are completely different when the only available sign of having found the correct solution consists precisely of the fact that it has been found by the method or process considered suitable for solving the problem. To put it another way, the trial and error method may be useful when a bit of knowledge exists as a point of reference against which to adjust the corresponding solution. If, as occurs in the socialist system, this point of reference does not exist because the corresponding entrepreneurial market process has been eliminated, the central planning agency will lack the guide necessary to approach the correct solution via the mechanism of trial and error. And let it not be said that such guides consist precisely of objective surpluses or shortages. Apart from the fact that, as we have already seen, these guides are neither objective nor do they indicate beyond all doubt what should be done, such guides emerge as an endogenous result of the application of the trial and error method itself, and therefore they do not constitute an objective guide at all. They are simply the successive, arbitrary and fortuitous manifestations of a circular process of discoordination and inefficiency, a process which leads to nothing. In an economy in which people are free to exercise entrepreneurship, in a sense it could be said that, when the different economic agents act entrepreneurially, they are following a procedure of trial and error to approach acceptable solutions; that is, to discover and coordinate the maladjustments which arise in society. This is so because the interrelated entrepreneurship of the different actors generates information which could not emerge from the isolated activity of each individual, no matter how much the trial and error method is used, and this information is the essential raw material for estimating the profits and costs of each human action. In this way, by following the guide provided by the calculation of profits and losses, economic agents tend to act in a coordinated manner. In contrast, if one coercively prevents the free exercise of entrepreneurship, one eliminates the only process which permits the coordinated adjustment of the different individual behaviors that comprise life in society. Consequently, one eliminates the only external guide that enables each actor to discover whether or not he is approaching the solution which for him is most suitable.[36]

Eighth, the crucial weakness of the trial and error method is that it involves the assumption that the community will remain static, and therefore that most social circumstances will not change while the "trial" is carried out and the possible "error" exposed. Nevertheless, if we consider that (as always occurs in real life) adjustments spark off widespread changes which to some extent affect the prices of all productive factors and consumer goods and services, then any correction that is attempted as a result of real or apparent errors will always be made too late and will therefore be profoundly distorting. In other words, as Hayek has shown,[37] the use of the trial and error method is not feasible in the real word, in which changes constantly occur. Each individual change exerts almost innumerable influences on the prices, quality and types of goods produced in society, and thus it is impossible to arrive, via the trial and error method, at a hypothetical equilibrium solution before new and subsequent changes in information render the solution totally obsolete. If the real world were unchanging and information remained constant, finding an equilibrium price system by the trial and error method might appear more feasible, if it were thought that equilibrium could constitute a somewhat clearer point of reference against which to compare the different possible, tentative solutions. However, contrary to what socialist theorists may assume, the real world is not in equilibrium, nor is it static, and hence it is impossible to find a solution to the corresponding system of equations via the trial and error method.

Ninth and last, the most powerful argument against the trial and error method is that it completely excludes entrepreneurship (see Chapter 2). The essential question is *who* will apply the trial and error method. Clearly, if the decisions regarding the adoption of tentative solutions are not made by the individual economic agents who possess the practical information, then the trial and error method will lead nowhere, for reasons we highlighted in Chapter 3. In addition, the central planning agency will lack the vital practical information which is only created and available in the minds of the people who act by exercising entrepreneurship. Moreover, the information necessary to coordinate and adjust society will not even be created if everyone is not free to exercise entrepreneurship. And if this information is not even generated, it can hardly be transmitted to a central planning agency. As we have mentioned, if the trial and error method is to make any sense, it must be applied on an individual level within the context of a market economy in which people are completely free to exercise entrepreneurship and can, without hindrance, take possession of the fruits of their own entrepreneurial creativity. Furthermore, let us recall that information is strictly subjective, and different actors will interpret the same observable real-world events in different ways and thus generate different information regarding them, according to each actor's particular circumstances and the context in which he acts. When faced with a certain shortage, it cannot be at all reassuring in economic terms for the central planning agency to automatically apply a pre-established rule (to produce more of the good X, or to raise its price by a certain percentage), because if the entrepreneurial process were left free, human creativity would certainly find radically different solutions to the same objective problem. Hence, when faced with a shortage, rather than raising the price, it might be more appropriate to devote entrepreneurial ingenuity to finding new solutions to the problem by developing substitute goods, searching for new alternatives no one has yet discovered and so on. Thus, we see that it is logically impossible to use the trial and error method to effectively adjust the solution of a hypothetical system of equations capable of making economic calculation possible in a society in which the free exercise of entrepreneurship is prohibited. Under these conditions, the central planning agency will lack the vital practical information, which the economic agents who participate in the system will not even create, and as a result, there will be no guide by which to coordinate the continual maladjustments which can arise in society. Therefore, the centralized use of the trial and error method does not lead to any equilibrium solution, nor is it capable of directing the hypothetical central coercion agency toward the decisions and measures which will allow it to coordinate the social process.[38]

## 5 THE THEORETICAL IMPOSSIBILITY OF PLANOMETRICS[39]

The above critical observations about the use of the trial and error method to solve the problem of socialist economic calculation are fully applicable to the vast literature[40] which, following the debate and more recently, has flowed from the pens of economists of the general equilibrium school, under the generic heading of "planometrics". This line of research depends upon a varied set of highly sophisticated mathematical techniques, including linear and non-linear programming, whole-number programming, a very large part of the cybernetic theory of decision, and also a number of computer procedures involving an iterative approach. The fundamental objective of these models is to determine a priori an entire configuration of equilibrium prices. In other words, ahead of what the market would spontaneously establish, an attempt is made to find a solution which would *pre-coordinate* all of the plans of economic agents and would therefore render unnecessary the market's real coordination process, which by its very nature, always operates *a posteriori*, since the force of entrepreneurship sets it in motion. In short, the purpose of planometric techniques is none other than to replace the competitive entrepreneurial process with a mechanism that would make it possible to centrally precoordinate society.

It is true that up to this point, it has been impossible to put any of the planometric models into effect, and that even socialist theorists admit it to be highly unlikely that they will be implemented. Nevertheless, some people still argue today that this situation chiefly results from limitations to computer capacity, as well as from the shortage of sufficiently qualified personnel and from technical difficulties in obtaining the necessary information. However, as the years have gone by, the notion that the market could be replaced with an all-inclusive system of computerized planning, to be applied via planometric models, has been gradually abandoned by even the very authors who carry out this program of scientific research. Furthermore, the failure which followed the introduction of planometric techniques in the countries of Eastern Europe during the 1970s gave rise not only to the abandonment of new practical attempts of this sort, but also to a profound sense of disappointment among all those who had naively pinned their hopes on these techniques.[41] Despite all of the above, two important factors remain which now justify a separate study of planometrics, precisely after having examined, in the last section, the theoretical infeasibility of the trial and error method.

First, let us note that various writers in this field continue to naively affirm that even though there have been only failures and frustrations up to now, it may be possible that in the future, successive refinements of the theory, together with foreseeable improvements in computer capacity, will permit what thus far has been impossible. Hence, for example, Richard Musgrave, in a study in which he evaluates the result of the economic calculation debate, concludes that planning, as an efficient system, could be implemented by allowing planners to simulate the competitive market and by applying the corresponding computer techniques. Kenneth Arrow, for his part, states that due to the development of mathematical programming and of high-speed computers, a system of central planning no longer appears an impossible future goal, since the functioning of a decentralized system can be simulated by simply choosing the corresponding centralized algorithm.[42] According to these and other authors, improvements in linear programming and computer technology would make it possible to solve the problem of socialist economic calculation as Mises and Hayek presented it.

Second, other planometrics theorists, led by Leonid Hurwicz, claim not only to have refuted Hayek's computational argument (which, as we know, was merely of secondary importance to him), but also to have incorporated into their planometric models the fundamental argument concerning the dispersed nature of information.[43] Thus, Hurwicz begins by assuming that each economic agent initially possesses only information which is available exclusively to him (consumers about their own preferences, producers about the technologies they could employ and so on). Hence, in his planometric models, the corresponding production functions are never considered known to the central planning bureau, but instead, only to the individual economic agents. In fact, in many models, it is supposed that not even the producers know all of their production functions, but only those with which they have had some experience. Given the nature of prices as efficient transmitters of information, the only knowledge which, according to these models, is to be transmitted between the central planning bureau and economic agents is a mere list of prices for *all* goods and services in the economy, a list which the central planning bureau is to publish in response to another, one which would reflect the quantities of each good and service produced by each economic agent. The transmission of this immense amount of information from the central planning agency to economic agents (prices) and from economic agents to the central planning agency (quantities produced) would not present any special problem, according to planometrics theorists, particularly if we take into account the latest advances in the field of telecomputing. Finally, different computer iteration procedures would make it possible to modify prices as surpluses and shortages arose, and this method would eventually give rise to that system of equilibrium equations which would offer a solution to the economic problem posed. Thus, a sort of "computer dialogue" would take place between the central authority, which would tentatively establish prices, and economic agents, who would receive instructions to produce the largest quantities they could while keeping prices equal to the corresponding marginal costs (that is, making marginal revenue equal marginal costs). These quantities would be communicated to the central authority, which would review, modify and retransmit the prices to the economic agents, and so forth, until the surpluses and shortages disappeared.

The planometric proposal we have just described does not differ greatly in fundamental content from those Oskar Lange made in the 1930s, proposals that will be very closely analyzed in the following chapter. Despite the ingeniousness of the above planometric strategy, it will now be shown that planometric models have not actually, in any way, come to incorporate Hayek's contribution regarding the problem of the dispersed quality of knowledge, and that therefore they are useless for providing a solution to the problem of socialist economic calculation. Furthermore, we shall digress a bit to consider the possible role of computers and computer science in this matter, and confirm what was demonstrated in Chapter 2, to the effect that developments in computer science, far from providing the solution to the problem of socialist economic calculation, in reality make it much more complex and difficult.

Even though the specific criticism of the mathematical trial and error method (in the last section) applies to the whole of modern planometrics theory, it is also necessary to respond to the two particular aspects that have just been highlighted. Many planometrics specialists believe that the problem has theoretically been resolved, that the dispersed nature of information has even been taken into account, and that now we must only wait for the necessary advances in computer capacity in order to put the corresponding models into effect. On the contrary, as we shall see, planometric models have not taken account of certain essential characteristics of the real world, qualities which Austrian economists had already described and which render the functioning of these models theoretically impossible, completely regardless of the future development of computer capacity, in terms of both hardware and software.

First, planometric models in general, and Hurwicz's theory in particular, have only come to incorporate the principle of the dispersed nature of information in an awkward and adulterated form. This is so because the fact that information is dispersed in the minds of all the individual economic agents is essentially inseparable from the subjective and strictly personal quality of information, as we saw in detail in Chapter 2. If information is not only dispersed, but also personal and subjective, it will convey a very different meaning to each economic agent, and therefore, it will be impossible to transmit it, with one sole meaning, to any planning center. In other words, the same price, the same external material object, the same quantity, and the same experiences will have a very different meaning or interpretation for one person than for another. The same can be said for the different options viewed as possible for carrying out a certain project, achieving a certain end, or producing a certain good or service. Also, a product surplus or shortage will communicate a very different meaning, depending upon the actor who observes it, and, according to the circumstances, it may prompt very different behaviors (an attempt to reduce demand, the creation of substitute goods, the search for new horizons, or any combination of these behaviors and so on). Thus, the subjective nature of information invalidates Hurwicz's entire model, which is based on a constant dialogue or transmission of information that is erroneously considered objective; this exchange takes place between agents (possessors of a hypothetically dispersed, yet objective, knowledge) and the central planning bureau.

Second, and intimately related to the above argument, is the fact, which was also discussed in detail in Chapter 2, that the knowledge that is vital to human action is mostly of a tacit, or inarticulable, nature. If most of the knowledge man uses when acting cannot be formally articulated, it can hardly be transmitted in an objective manner to anyone. It is not just that economic agents interpret the same prices or historical terms of trade in very different ways; it is also that these prices convey information to certain actors because, to a greater or lesser extent, these actors share a certain store of practical, inarticulable knowledge about the characteristics of the goods and services which were exchanged and gave rise to those prices, as well as about a thousand other circumstances that they subjectively consider relevant in the context of the actions in which they are involved. For example, the articulate or formalized part of the message that an actor interprets when he realizes that a pound of potatoes sells for 30 monetary units (the articulate portion would be "the price of a pound of potatoes is 30 m.u.") represents a minimal part of the total amount of information the actor knows, generates and uses in the context of his specific action (information regarding his desire to buy potatoes, the different levels of quality available in potatoes, the quality of the potatoes his supplier normally provides, the actor's excitement about cooking with potatoes, the dish he plans to prepare for his guests, the other foods he plans to prepare to accompany the potatoes, and a thousand other details).[44]

Third, from a more dynamic perspective, a price or set of prices conveys a certain meaning to an actor only because he finds himself immersed in a certain project or action; that is, he has committed himself to achieving certain ends or ideals, which he alone can truly imagine and pursue in all of their richness and complexity. An actor believes in a certain project, and imagines it and eagerly pursues it based on subjective expectations and feelings which are basically inarticulable and therefore cannot be transmitted to any planning center. The entrepreneur who believes in an idea and pursues it against all odds, and often in spite of the most adverse conditions and against the opinion of the majority, in the end may reach his goal and obtain the corresponding profits. The end he aspires to, the profit he intends to generate, or the truth he seeks is not something given which can be seen with perfect clarity, but rather something he intuits, imagines or creates. And it is precisely this *creative tension* which makes it possible to discover and create the information that sustains society and leads to its advancement. Creative tension arises from the variety present in the market; or rather, from the different opinions or interpretations that spring from the same facts, events and circumstances, which, nevertheless, are interpreted differently by different economic agents. Planometrics theorists overlook or explicitly eliminate this creative tension from their models, which, as they are intended to achieve an a priori coordination of the entire economic system, totally exclude the possibility of actors' responding creatively to the incentive discoordination provides.[45] It therefore becomes an inevitable conclusion that the dialogue or transmission of dispersed information between economic agents and the central planning agency, as Hurwicz proposes it, is theoretically impossible. This is due to two factors: first, economic agents, to a great extent, lack the knowledge which would have to be transmitted,[46] since such knowledge arises only from a process in which actors can freely exercise their entrepreneurship, and second, they could not transmit the knowledge they do possess either, because it is mostly of a tacit, inarticulable nature. The entrepreneur's knowledge is inarticulate, since it is more of a "thought technique" which can only be applied if the actor is in a context typical of a market economy, and the actor can only learn this technique intuitively, by putting it to practical use. That minds of the caliber of Arrow and Hurwicz have failed to recognize the essential characteristics of the type of knowledge economic agents use and generate, and thus, that these minds are ignorant of the most fundamental principles of the functioning of the market, justifies the remark Hayek made in 1982, when he had no choice but to call both of these authors "irresponsible", particularly for believing that practical, subjective and inarticulable knowledge can be transmitted in the form of a computer dialogue between economic agents and the central planning bureau, an idea Hayek severely termed "the crowning foolery of the whole farce" that is planometrics literature.[47]

Fourth, we must bear in mind that planometric price-adjustment models require that, once the information has been transmitted to the central planning agency, all trade or production activities be suspended while this agency resolves the corresponding optimization problem and sends economic agents the new information about equilibrium prices. Some economists, like Benjamin Ward, even arrive at the absurd conclusion that such a system is much more efficient than that of a real market economy, in which exchanges are constantly taking place at prices which do not correspond with equilibrium prices, and therefore can be considered "false". That *real* market prices are labeled "false" because they do not coincide with some unknown, hypothetical prices which exist solely in the clouded minds of equilibrium theorists is surprising at the very least. It is absurd to view as false something which exists and has actually come about as a result of free human action, but it is even more absurd when we consider that no true equilibrium price can ever be known. Furthermore, the great advantage of the market process over the planometric adjustment model lies precisely in this real-life possibility of carrying out supposedly false exchanges. In fact, in the planometric model, while all action and exchange stand still and information is transmitted to the planning agency and it resolves the corresponding system of equations, millions of economic agents are prevented from discovering and creating new information, and many human actions are thwarted, all to the detriment of society's process of adjustment, coordination and development. In contrast, in the real market process entrepreneurship drives, even though equilibrium is never reached (and thus, all real-life exchanges are, in this sense, false), new information is constantly generated, and all maladjustments or disparities tend to be revealed by the force of entrepreneurial alertness and then suitably coordinated and adjusted. The main advantage of real market processes, as opposed to the planometric models of the "Walrasian auctioneer", is that in real processes, even though exchanges are constantly taking place, and no exchange occurs at an equilibrium price (and thus the actual prices are, in this sense, false), these processes work well in both theory and practice, since any maladjustment or disparity creates the incentive necessary, and the resultant tendency, for it to be discovered and eliminated through the innate force of entrepreneurship. In this way, a huge amount of vital information is created and continually transmitted to society in general. In contrast, in order to function, planometric models not only require that human action and the creation of new information be frozen for a certain period, but they also eliminate the creative exercise of entrepreneurship, which is the key to social creativity and coordination.[48]

Fifth, the chief underlying weakness of planometric models is found in their extreme minimization and trivialization of the problem posed by the constant market changes which occur in a complex modern economy. In the real world, a modern society cannot allow itself the luxury of waiting for the solution to a programming problem with implications for the activity and lives of all its members. Furthermore, such a solution is theoretically impossible, since the problem cannot even be considered without dictatorially freezing or forcing reality, given the impossibility of transmitting and generating the necessary information. To illustrate the above, Michael Ellman states that it took six years just to compile the information necessary to formulate a linear-programming problem commissioned in the 1960s by the planning department for metal industries in the former

Soviet Union, and that the problem was formulated using over 1,000,000 unknowns and 30,000 restrictions.[49] As is logical, the solution to this problem was purely imaginary, since the relevant information changed radically (or certainly would have) within this six-year period. Thus, by the time the problem was resolved, it had changed completely, and hence the solution found was totally obsolete. Because planometrics specialists lack the necessary information, it is clear that in a dynamic, real world, they would be forced to blindly and perpetually seek a nonexistent equilibrium solution which they could never hit upon, since it would be in a process of continual change. Therefore, we can conclude with Peter Bernholz that under the real conditions of a variable economy, rational economic calculation is impossible if a planometric system of central planning is used.[50]

Sixth, planometrics theorists not only show a profound ignorance of the way in which real market processes operate, but they also lack an understanding of the fundamental elements of the theory of computer systems. Let us recall that the type of information which can be stored on a computer is totally different from that which economic agents consciously use in the market. The former is objective, articulate information, and the latter is subjective, tacit, practical information. The latter, which is the vital sort for economic problems, cannot be stored or handled using a computer. Furthermore, it is obvious that information which has not yet been generated by the economic system cannot be transmitted or handled using computer procedures either. In other words, both inarticulable, practical information and a large share of the articulate information result from a social market process, and until this process has generated the information, it cannot be transmitted or stored in any computer data-storage system. Also, and perhaps this is the most important point, if we begin by considering that even the most complex computers of each generation may be used in a decentralized manner by the economic agents themselves (different actors, entrepreneurs, agencies and institutions), it is clear that on a decentralized, individual level, these powerful machines will create a context in which it will be possible to generate practical, inarticulable knowledge which is infinitely more varied, complex and rich, and the complexity of this information will render it impossible to handle in a centralized way using computers. In other words, a computer system could possibly handle and account for control systems simpler than itself, but what it will not be able to do is account for or solve systems or processes which are more complex than itself, systems in which the computer capacity of each element is qualitatively equal in complexity to that of the central planning bureau. Lastly, it is obvious that no computer can, or will ever be able to, perform typically human, entrepreneurial activities. That is, a computer will never be capable of realizing that a certain bit of objective information has been incorrectly interpreted and that, therefore, unexploited profit opportunities remain. A computer will not be able to conceive new projects no one has yet imagined. A computer will not be able to create new ends and means, or pursue against the tide activities which are not in fashion, or courageously struggle to make a success of a company no one believes in and so on. At most, a computer can be a powerful, useful tool for handling articulate information in order to facilitate human entrepreneurial activity as described in Chapter 2, but computers will never eliminate or replace this entrepreneurial activity.[51] In fact, not only does computer science offer no help in replacing the complex processes of spontaneous coordination which operate in the economy, but on the contrary, it will in any case be the economic theory of market processes which will be able to assist in developing a more advanced computer science. Indeed, recent developments in computer science theory concerning expert systems and the utopian concept of "artificial intelligence" have revealed that only a profound analysis of the processes by which information is created and transmitted in the market has led to significant advancement in these areas.[52]

Finally, in concluding these comments on planometrics it should again stressed that the use of the mathematical method in economics can cause great confusion and harm if the scholars who use it are not extremely careful. To be specific, the mathematical method is only suitable for describing equilibrium systems, or at most, crude, repetitive, and mechanical caricatures of the real processes of change and creativity that operate in the market. Furthermore, the mathematical method does not permit the formal expression of the essence of entrepreneurship, which is the basic, key element in all of economic and social life. The mathematical economist constantly runs the risk of believing that prices and costs are determined by intersecting curves and functions, and not by a sequence of very concrete human actions and interactions. He may come to believe that the functions he works with are real and can be known. In short, he may get the idea that the information he assumes is given in order to construct his models does actually exist in objective form somewhere in the market, and thus could be compiled. In light of the effects the mathematical method has generally had in the different spheres of economics, particularly in the case of the proposals for socialist economic calculation which we have studied, one wonders if this method has not done significantly more harm than good in the development of our science.[53] The argument that Mises and Hayek advanced in favor of a market economy and against socialism differs totally from the reasoning mathematical "welfare" economists use to justify private enterprise; the latter base their reasoning on perfect competition as an expression of the Paretian ideal of efficiency. In this book, the basic argument is not that competition provides an optimum combination of resources, but that it is a dynamic process driven by flesh-and-blood people, a process which tends to adjust and coordinate society. The essential argument is not that a system of perfect competition is better than a monopoly system, but that markets and uncoerced human action provide a process of creativity and coordination. Therefore, the argument that is being defended is indeed radically different from the standard argument found in microeconomics textbooks, an approach which, for all the reasons given, we consider basically irrelevant and erroneous, whether it is viewed as a positive analysis of the real economy or as a normative analysis of how it should operate. The clearest sign that welfare theory is fallacious lies in the fact that, paradoxically, it has given rise to the idea that through its models and methods, the resource allocation mechanism could be resolved in a planned economy with no market. Economic equilibrium and welfare theory, which began as a descriptive, positive theory about the functioning of the market, has ended up being an instrument to advance, via its mathematical methods and models, a system of economic calculation which stamps out both the market process and its most intimate characteristic: entrepreneurship.[54]

## NOTES

1. Although Mises considered the mathematical method devastating, regardless of the area of economics in which it is applied, perhaps the issue of economic calculation most clearly revealed to him that the mathematical method simply fails to take account of market processes and conceals the fundamental theoretical problem of socialism, that is, how society can be coordinated when the free exercise of entrepreneurship is prevented. Thus, it is understandable that he asserted, with equal courage and severity: "The mathematical method must be rejected not only on account of its barrenness. It is an entirely vicious method, starting from false assumptions and leading to fallacious inferences. Its syllogisms are not only sterile; *they divert the mind from the study of the real problems and distort the relations between the various phenomena*" (1966, 350).
2. Wieser (1889). On page 60 of the English translation (1889 [1971], we read: "Even in a community or state whose economic affairs were ordered on communistic principles, goods would not cease to have value ... That value which arises from the social relation between amount of goods and utility, or value as it would exist in the communist state, we shall henceforth call 'Natural Value'". This author has given this book a careful reading and finds Wieser's concept of "natural value" absurd and phantasmagorical. It is a concept of value which can only be applied to a hypothetical equilibrium model which is never actually realized. As a result, Wieser commits the error of assuming that value is objective; specifically, he considers interpersonal comparisons of utility possible. Wieser would have avoided this and other grave errors in his book if, more in keeping with the true "Austrian" tradition Menger began, he had based his analysis on the study of dynamic market processes and not on the model of equilibrium. Thus, Mises strongly criticizes Wieser for abandoning and betraying the paradigm Menger initiated, which focuses on the general and interrelated study of market processes. Mises concludes that Wieser: "was not a creative thinker and in general was more harmful than useful.

He never really understood the gist of the idea of subjectivism in the Austrian School of thought, which limitation caused him to make many unfortunate mistakes. His imputation theory is untenable. His ideas on value calculation justify the conclusion that he could not be called a member of the Austrian School, but rather was a member of the Lausanne School (Leon Walras et al. and the idea of economic equilibrium)" (Mises, 1978, 36). Wieser's deviationism is overlooked by Mark Blaug in the following comment, in which he nonetheless brilliantly and concisely defines the unique Austrian perspective: "The Austrians at one and the same time rejected Marshall's partial equilibrium analysis and the kind of economics that Walras advocated, which was, in the first place, an economics explicitly formulated in mathematical terms and, in the second place, an 'end-state' rather than a 'process' economics, that is, one that focused attention on the nature of equilibrium outcomes and not on the process by which equilibria are attained. The Austrians had no sympathy for Walras' analysis of the existence and uniqueness of multimarket equilibrium in terms of the metaphor of simultaneous equations and even less for his discussions of multimarket equilibrium in terms of price adjustments to net excess demand. Indeed *all* Austrians, including Wickstead and Robbins, eschewed the very notion of a determinate theory of pricing and underlined discontinuities and indivisibilities, *being perfectly content with a general tendency toward equilibrium that is never in fact completely realized*" (Blaug, 1990, 186). Incidentally, we should note that Blaug underwent a much-talked-about conversion. He began by dismissing the Austrian school out of hand, but later came to renounce his faith in the general equilibrium model and the Walrasian neoclassical paradigm and concluded: "I have come slowly and extremely reluctantly to view that they [the Austrian school] are right and that we have all been wrong" (de Marchi and Blaug, 1991, 508). See also his less emphatic *Economics Through the Looking Glass* (1988, 37) and his book review (1993, 1571).

3. See note 39, Chapter 4, where all of Böhm-Bawerk's arguments are outlined against the Marxist theory of exploitation. Specifically, Böhm-Bawerk concludes: "Income from capital is today reviled by the socialists as an exploitational gain, a predacious deduction from the product of labor. *But it would not disappear under socialism.* On the contrary, the socialistically organized state would itself be the one to maintain it in full force as against the workers – and it would be compelled so to maintain it . . . Nothing in the world can or will change the fact that possessors of present goods, when they exchange them for future goods, obtain an agio . . . Interest is proven to be an economic category which arises from elemental economic causes and hence will appear everywhere, irrespective of the type of social or juridical organization, provided there exists an exchange of product for future goods" (1959b, section 5, "Interest under socialism", 345 and 346).
4. Wieser (1914 [1967], 396–7).
5. See note 9, Chapter 4.
6. See Hayek (1935a, 257–8).
7. Ibid., 247.
8. See Mises's own words cited in the text above notes 29 and 30 of Chapter 4.
9. See note 8 of Chapter 4.
10. Lindahl (1939 [1970]). Lindahl devotes an entire section to the "Pricing problem in a community with a centralized planning" (pp. 69–73) and concludes that "the Central Authority will have to solve a problem of exactly the same nature as the Central Bank in a community with free entrepreneurship". We must especially criticize Lindahl's "dynamic" analysis which, because it implies that the information which is at any moment crucial is given, constitutes, more than anything else, a purely static analysis, in which the variables and parameters simply refer to different points in time, understood in a deterministic or Newtonian sense, and in which, therefore, the concepts of uncertainty, a lack of information, and the creative power of human action and entrepreneurship are conspicuous by their absence. Lindahl follows the tradition of the formal similarity arguments which Cassel developed in 1918 and which we have

already discussed in the text (Cassel 1918 [1932]). See also the English translation (1918 [1967]). (Cassel's own words, where cited in the text above, have been translated from the Spanish version, 1918 [1960], 101–5, 202–5.) See also footnote 18 and the criticism George Halm levels against Cassel in Halm (1935, 184–6.)

11. This was the presidential address given at the 41st annual meeting of the American Economic Association in Chicago, Illinois on December 27, 1928. The speech was later published (Taylor, 1929). The article also appeared in Lippincott (1938 [1964], 41–54). It is curious to note that Fred Manville Taylor (1855–1932), who is no relation to Frederick Winslow Taylor – the author of *The Principles of Scientific Management* – was a great defender of *laissez faire* and the gold standard, but his methodological leaning toward equilibrium analysis (in his case partial and Marshallian) inexorably led him to assume that the problem of economic calculation could be resolved without much trouble.

12. O'Driscoll states: "Fundamental advances seldom come through providing new answers to old questions. *Fundamental advances occur when someone poses new questions.* What constitutes a lasting contribution in economics is asking a new question, setting a new direction of research . . . The basic reason most economists did not understand the theoretical argument against socialism is that *they were asking the wrong question.* Hayek's opponents kept asking whether an economic czar could efficiently allocate resources *if he had all the necessary information.* The answer to that question is, of course, 'Yes.' Hence, in the mythology of economic history the defenders of socialism are credited with having 'refuted' Mises and Hayek. The defenders did no such thing, they simply posed and answered a different and irrelevant question" (1989, 345 and 348).

13. H.D. Dickinson (1933). Dickinson (1899–1969) was a student of Edwin Cannan and a professor at Bristol until 1964. David Collard writes: "Dick, as he was universally known, was a much loved, unworldly, eccentric figure with a keen sense of fun and a most astute mind" (see the article on this likable figure in economics in Collard, 1987, 836). Hayek himself shows a certain respect and affection toward Dickinson, even in those places where he most strongly criticizes him.

14. Thus, we see that the obsession of socialists and interventionists with "information transparency" can be traced back quite a long time. This notion, which rests on an error of perception as to the type of information used in market processes, has spread and achieved great popularity even in western countries, and it is often embodied in excessive regulations that lay an almost unbearable burden on many companies which are obliged to generate a huge, unnecessary and costly volume of statistical and accounting information which has not even slightly improved the degree of coordination and efficiency of the societies in question. In this area, as in many others, the interests of socialists, who believe that fostering large companies and information transparency facilitates their task of coordinating via commands, have converged with those of equilibrium theorists, who believe that an improvement in statistical information can facilitate the achievement and maintenance of efficient markets, that is, ones that more closely resemble those of their own models. Moreover, both are supported, as is natural, by the privileged special interest groups which directly benefit from the above regulations (auditors, accountants, accounting professors, registrars of business names and so on). They are all mistaken in their concept of information, since statistics are always "water under the bridge". They can be interpreted subjectively in the most diverse manners, and not only do they not assist in the entrepreneurial processes of coordination, but they make them more difficult and distort them to the extent that entrepreneurs allow themselves to be influenced by their apparent accuracy. This is all in addition to the unnecessary cost and poor resource allocation which arise from the coercive imposition of excessive accounting and information obligations far in excess of the level business customarily requires. On this topic, see Benito Arruñada's article (1991), in which he quite rightly criticizes, for this and other reasons, the accounting and business law reform introduced since the beginning of the nineties. See also Gillespie (1990) and Huerta de Soto (2009c).

15. "It is perfectly true that Vilfredo Pareto and Enrico Barone had shown which information a socialist planning authority would have to possess in order to perform its task. But to know which kind of information would be required to solve a problem does not imply that it can be solved if the information is dispersed among millions of people" (Hayek, 1982 [1984], 58).
16. "And as regards the fixing of prices, the socialistic state would soon find that no mathematical formula was of any avail, and that the only means by which it could hope to solve the problem were exact and repeated comparisons between present and future stocks and present and future demand; it would find that prices could not be fixed once and for all, but would have to be altered frequently. Not the theory of averages but the value of things in exchange would, in most cases, have to serve as its guide in fixing prices; and why should it reject the services of that guide?" (Pierson, 1912, 2: 94).
17. Dickinson (1939, 104).
18. Tisch's proposal appears in her doctoral thesis (1932), which was supervised by Joseph A. Schumpeter. Hayek views the errors in this doctoral thesis and Schumpeter's ignorance and reverential overestimation of mathematical analysis as the causes of Schumpeter's mistakes in this area, particularly his having devised and propagated (Schumpeter, 1950) the myth that, even before Mises himself, Pareto and Barone had managed to resolve the problem of socialist economic calculation. See Hayek (1982 [1984], 59 and 60). See also Zassenhaus (1934 [1956]). The proposals of Tisch and Zassenhaus are analyzed in detail and criticized by Hoff (1981, 207–10). Also worth reading are the critical observations in Halm (1935).
19. Hayek (1935c, 210).
20. Ibid., 212. This argument parallels the one Pareto put forward in 1897 (see Chapter 4, note 8).
21. Samuelson and Nordhaus (1985). It is commendable that in this edition of their well-known textbook, Samuelson and Nordhaus admit the validity of Hayek's essential argument, when they add in a footnote: "But even if extremely fast computers – thousands of times more powerful than current ones – were produced, we would still have to face another immovable obstacle: *We do not have access to the smallest part of the data necessary to solve a complex problem of general equilibrium*" (excerpt translated from the Spanish edition 1985 [1986], 830). It is a shame that Samuelson and Nordhaus relegate this fundamental idea to the end of a footnote and exclude it from the main text of their popular treatise. Furthermore, this essential idea contradicts the content of the book itself (pp. 839 and 840 in the Spanish edition), which includes a brief and terribly confusing summary of the debate and reveals that the authors have not managed to grasp the fundamental economic problem Mises and Hayek explained concerning socialist economic calculation. On top of that, the following statement was still present in the 1989 edition of Samuelson's textbook: "The Soviet economy is proof that, contrary to what many skeptics had earlier believed, a socialist command economy can function and even thrive". This is an embarrassing assertion, at least in light of the events which began to unfold in Eastern Europe that year and the information which, for the first time, surfaced on the real functioning of those economies, information provided directly by the interested parties (Samuelson 1989, 837).
22. "This is but one of the difficulties attributable to the sheer scale of the required coordination between multimillion plan instructions. Academician Fedorenko quipped that next year's plan, if fully checked and balanced, might be ready in 30,000 years time" (see Nove 1987a, 881). Unfortunately, Alec Nove also fails to recognize the fundamental economic problem posed by socialism, and at this point he continues to believe that the problem consists merely of the algebraic difficulty of solving the corresponding system of equations. To be specific, Nove writes "by ear" and reveals that he has not read or understood Mises's essential argument when he states: "Critics, such as Barone and L. von Mises, pointed out some major weaknesses in this approach to socialist planning: *the number of calculations required would be enormous*". We know that the essential argument Mises voiced against socialist economic calculation is not this one (in fact,

*The unjustified shift in the debate toward statics* 165

Mises never even expressly stated this one), but rather that, even if it were possible to solve inordinately complicated systems of equations, under socialism the information necessary to formulate them would never be available.

23. Don Lavoie, in his outstanding book, *Rivalry and Central Planning* (1985c, 91), also adds the argument that, in his opinion, Hayek committed a strategic error when he included in his *Collectivist Economic Planning* (1935a) his English translation of the article Barone published in 1908, since this article mentioned (and only in passing) that planning based on a Walrasian system of equations was 'unfeasible', mainly due to the difficulties involved in solving the corresponding system of equations. Lavoie was quite right when he concluded: "However, to at least Mises and Hayek if not also Robbins, the problem was *formulating the equations* – not solving them. In a world of complexity and continuous change, the central planners would lack the knowledge of the coefficients that go into the equations" (1985c, 91).

24. Lionel Robbins was perhaps the least clear in terms of emphasizing the merely secondary nature of the argument concerning the practical difficulty of algebraically solving the system of Walrasian equations. It appears that Robbins was so convinced of the absurdity of considering a practical solution of this type that he did not bother to develop and refine the fundamental theoretical argument. Nonetheless, in his defense, we can point to Robbins's observations on economic calculation, which he included though gave secondary importance to, in a book devoted to an analysis of problems of another sort (identifying the causes of the Great Depression). In Robbins (1934, 151) after stating that "on paper" it is conceivable that the economic calculation problem could be resolved via a series of mathematical calculations, he concludes: "But in practice this solution is quite unworkable. It would necessitate the drawing up of millions of equations on the basis of millions of statistical tables based on many more millions of individual computations. By the time the equations were solved the information on which they were based would have become obsolete and they would need to be calculated anew. The suggestion that a practical solution of the problem of planning is possible on the basis of the Paretian equations simply indicates that those who put it forward have not begun to grasp what these equations mean".

25. "I feel I should perhaps make it clear that I have never conceded, as is often alleged, that Lange had provided the theoretical solution of the problem, and I did not thereafter withdraw to pointing out practical difficulties. What I did say (in *Individualism and Economic Order*, page 187) was merely that from the factually false hypothesis that the central planning board could command all the necessary information, it could logically follow that the problem was in principle soluble. *To deduce from this observation the 'admission' that the real problem can be solved in theory is a rather scandalous misrepresentation*. Nobody can, of course, transfer to another all the knowledge he has, and certainly not the information he could discover only if market prices told him what was worth looking for" (Hayek, 1982 [1984], 58).

26. In fact, for Mises, "there is therefore *no need* to stress the point that the fabulous number of equations which one would have to solve each day anew for a practical utilization of the method would make the whole idea absurd even if it were really a reasonable substitute for the market's economic calculation. *Therefore the construction of electronic computers does not affect our problem*" (Mises, 1966, 715 and the last line of footnote 11 on p. 715). Esteban F. Thomsen expresses a similar view in his work, *Prices and Knowledge: A Market Process Perspective* (1992, 83–6).

27. This brilliant additional argument of Mises's, which has not been refuted, appeared for the first time in German in his *Nationalökonomie: Theorie des Handelns und Wirtschaftens* (1940, 641–5), in section 4 ("Die Gleichungen der mathematischen Katallaktik") of the chapter he devoted to confuting attempts to solve the economic calculation problem. Previously, in 1938, the essential ideas in this section had been published in French under the title, "Les équations de l'économie mathématique et le problème de calcul économique en régime socialiste" (Mises, 1938). It was reprinted in the same journal 50 years later (Mises, 1987), with a commentary by Jean Bénard which

reveals that this author also fails to grasp the economic problems involved in socialist economic calculation. The argument was later expanded and further elaborated in English in *Human Action* (1966, 710–15).

28. "It is improbable that anyone who has realized the magnitude of the task involved has seriously proposed a system of planning based on comprehensive systems of equations. What has actually been in the minds of those who have mooted this kind of analysis has been the belief that, starting from a given situation, which was presumably to be that of the pre-existing capitalistic society, *the adaptation to the minor changes which occur from day to day could be gradually brought about by a method of trial and error*" (Hayek, 1935c, 213).

29. Taylor (1929 [1964], 51).

30. Dickinson (1933, 241). Between the proposals Taylor and Dickinson put forward in 1928 and 1933, respectively, in 1931 another American, Willet Crosby Roper, also suggested the trial and error method and believed that successive shortages evident in the economic system would in any case be a clear sign to the central authority that it needed to modify its instructions and would point it toward the "correct" solution. However, although Roper does not hide that he strongly sympathizes with socialism, he is clearly aware of the enormous difficulties that would arise in practice if the trial and error method, which he himself proposes, was applied. Specifically, he states: "This description of the process makes it seem rather simple and easily accomplished. It is a question, apparently, of adjusting a few mistakes at the beginning and then sitting down to watch the system work. But again, *we ignore the almost incredible complication of the economic process* . . . At the establishment of a price system with perhaps only one or two considerable errors (an almost unbelievable assumption), those one or two errors would involve changes extending through the whole structure. If the number of serious mistakes were greater, it would take a considerable time and a great deal of careful calculation to reach a position of equilibrium, where the factors would be priced exactly according to marginal productivity, where these prices would be equal for factors of equal efficiency, and where the whole theoretical system of stable equilibrium was realised. *As a matter of fact, this equilibrium could be reached only in a static economy which can never exist*. . . . It seems safe to say that the pricing apparatus necessary for an efficient centralized collectivism is, at best, only a remote possibility". He concludes: "It indicates that the best chance for success of a socialist society lies in a decentralized organization which retains, so far as possible, the strong features of capitalism" (Roper, 1931, 58, 59, 60, 62).

31. Hayek (1935c, 213). On this issue, Hayek merely follows the intuition initially developed by Mises, who, back in 1920, stated: "The transition to socialism must, as a consequence of the levelling out of the differences in income and the resultant readjustments in consumption, and therefore production, *change all economic data*, in such a way that a connecting link with the final state of affairs in the previously existing competitive economy becomes impossible" (Mises, 1920 [1975], 109–10). When we connect this reasoning with that presented in note 27, we see that the basic argument Mises introduced in 1920 was completed and perfected over a span of twenty years, and the process yielded this version: (i) it is a definite error to believe that the initial conditions correspond with those of a state of equilibrium; (ii) it is impossible to calculate the final state of equilibrium due to a lack of information; and (iii) even if one supposes, for the sake of argument, that the above two problems have been resolved, there would be absolutely no guide available to direct the innumerable actions necessary to move from the initial state of equilibrium to the final state of equilibrium (the culmination of Mises's argument; see note 27).

32. Hoff very graphically explains that "just as in tennis a score of 6–0, 6–0 gives no indication of how much better the winner is, so stocks of unsold goods do not reveal how strongly the different goods are desired" (1981, 117–18).

33. See Kornai (1980, 1982).

34. Also, Hoff points out that under these circumstances, another insoluble problem

lies in the *degree* of the price increase which the central planning agency must establish whenever a shortage occurs. According to Hoff, the fact that a shortage exists does not convey any information about how to carry out (that is, in connection with which specific goods and to what degree) the corresponding price rise (1981, 119).

35. I owe this argument to Robert Bradley, from the economics department of the University of Houston. See "Socialism and the trial and error proposal", pt. 4 of his article, "Market socialism: a subjectivist evaluation" (1981, 28–9). Bradley concludes: "It is logically possible that a good and its substitutes all have equilibrating prices, yet their prices not be indices of the scarcity. In this case, the bad prices merely camouflage each other. So we can see that monitoring individual prices is not enough; the CPB would have to be in command of all price interrelationships. Thus the 'trial and error' method becomes inadequate since it only applies to prices individually" (p. 29).

36. According to Mises: "The method of trial and error is applicable in all cases in which the correct solution is recognizable as such by unmistakable marks not dependent on the method of trial and error itself . . . Things are quite different if the only mark of the correct solution is that it has been reached by the application of a method considered appropriate for the solution of the problem. The correct result of a multiplication of two factors is recognizable only as the result of a correct application of the process indicated by arithmetic. One may try to guess the correct result by trial and error. But here the method of trial and error is no substitute for the arithmetical process. It would be quite futile if the arithmetical process did not provide a yardstick for discriminating what is incorrect from what is correct . . . If one wants to call entrepreneurial action an application of the method of trial and error, one must not forget that the correct solution is easily recognizable as such; it is the emergence of a surplus of proceeds over costs. Profit tells the entrepreneur that the consumers approve of his ventures; loss, that they disapprove. The problem of socialist economic calculation is precisely this: that in the absence of *market* prices for the factors of production, a computation of profit or loss is not feasible" (1966, 704–5).

37. In the words of Hayek: "Almost every change of any single price would make changes of hundreds of other prices necessary and most of these other changes would by no means be proportional, but would be affected by the different degrees of elasticity of demand, by the possibility of substitution and other changes in the method of production. To imagine that all this adjustment could be brought about by successive orders by central authority when the necessity is noticed, and that then every price is fixed and changed until some degree of equilibrium is obtained is certainly an absurd idea . . . To base authoritative price-fixing on the observation of a small section of the economic system is a task which cannot be rationally executed under any circumstances" (1935c, 214). Five years later, in 1940, in a response to Lange, Hayek would even more clearly assert: "It is difficult to suppress the suspicion that this particular proposal (the trial and error method) has been born out of an excessive preoccupation with problems of the pure theory of stationary equilibrium. If in the real world we have to deal with approximately constant data, that is, if the problem were to find a price system which then could be left more or less unchanged for long periods, then the proposal under consideration would not be so entirely unreasonable. With given and constant data such state of equilibrium could indeed be approached by the method of trial and error. *But this is far from being the situation of the real world, where constant change is the rule*" (1940 [1972], 188).

38. See also, in the next chapter, the criticism of the trial and error method that Oskar Lange proposed.

39. Wilczynski has popularized this word and states: "Planometrics is a branch of economics concerned with the methodology of constructing economic plans especially arising at the optimal plan, with the aid of modern mathematical methods and electronic computers" (1978, 17, 24, 46). Other terms which have at times been used to refer to this branch of economics are "computopia" and "the theory of mechanisms for resource

allocation", names we owe to Egon Neuberger (1966) and Leonid Hurwicz (1973), respectively.

40. As for "planometrics" literature, see, for example, the following works: Hardt et al. (1967); Ward (1967a, 1967b); Hurwicz (1973) and Arrow and Hurwicz (1977). In Lavoie (1985c, 94), we find an exhaustive summary of all the existing English-language works on the topic. In German, see the overview of planometrics literature in Seidl (1982). A brief but valuable review of the main contributions in this field and of the main problems associated with them appears in Bennett (1989, esp. ch. 2, 9–37). Also of interest is Bernholz (1987, 161–7). Finally, we should mention the Soviet school established under the auspices of Leonid V. Kantorovich, who was obsessively concerned with the development and perfecting of optimization techniques and was never able to grasp the economic (rather than "technical") problem socialism poses, nor, thus, to provide any solution to the gradual breakdown of the Soviet model (see Gardner, 1990, 638–48, and all references cited there).

41. On the disappointment related to the application of planometric models, Michael Ellman states: "Work on the introduction of management information and control systems in the soviet economy was widespread in the 1970's, but by the 1980's there was widespread scepticism in the USSR about their usefulness. This largely resulted from the failure to fulfill the earlier exaggerated hopes about the returns to be obtained from their introduction in the economy" (1987, 2: 31). Jan S. Prybyla makes a similar assertion (1987, 55). For his part, Martin Cave (1980), after pointing out the profound disparity and separation between two groups of researchers, those who devote their efforts to formulating abstract planometric models, and others who concentrate on studying real systems, he concludes that the increasing skepticism surrounding planometric models as possible substitutes for the market derives from the fact that "they do not, nor are they intended to, do justice to the complexities of a centrally-planned economy" (p. 38). Even Hurwicz appears to have resigned himself to the view that planometrics is useful only as a purely intellectual exercise, which would correspond to an initial theoretical step (that of "formulating" the problem) toward solving the problem of economic calculation. This step would later have to be brought into effect by letting in market forces and adjusting the plan to the realities of the market, rather than the opposite; that is, adapting the market to the parameters of the planometric model (Hurwicz, 1971, 81).

42. The error these two authors commit lies in their ignorance of the fundamental functioning of market processes, which was explained in Chapter 2. Arrow has gone so far as to assert: "Indeed, with the development of mathematical programming and high speed computers the centralized alternative no longer appears preposterous. After all, it would appear that one could mimic the workings of a decentralized system by an appropriately chosen centralized algorithm" (Arrow, 1974a, 5). It seems almost inevitable that even the most brilliant minds, like Arrow, lose the ability to perceive fundamental economic problems when they become obsessed with mathematical equilibrium analysis. In fact, Musgrave (1977) makes the very same mistake. Another writer who commits an error similar to that of Arrow and Musgrave is Wilczynski, even if it is more understandable in his case, considering his commitment to socialist ideology. Wilczynski actually states: "The feasibility of the computational optimal prices conclusively refutes any grounds for the claim that rational pricing was impossible under socialism. Even though much remains to be done on the practical level, there is a sound theoretical basis. In fact, in some respects, socialism provides the possibility of improving on capitalism" (1978, 138). Another author who has, from the general equilibrium theory, arrived at the conclusion that the essential principles for organizing a centrally planned economy can be easily drawn from the Walrasian model is the French economist Maurice Allais. Allais, who combines the natural mental confusion which results from the use of the mathematical method in economics with a very distinctive idiosyncrasy, has gone so far as to assert that in an equilibrium economy with perfect competition, interest on capital would disappear. (This is clearly an absurd idea, because even

under such circumstances, it would be necessary to deal with the applicable capital depreciation rates, and the subjective forces of time preference would continue to exert their influence.) Allais proposes that land be nationalized and that "prices" be expressed in terms of a unit of account based on a unit of "specialized labor" time (Allais, 1947 and 1948). With respect to these proposals made by Allais, Karl Pribram makes the following comment in his work, *A History of Economic Reasoning* (1983, 459): "It has been one of the strange episodes in the history of economic reasoning that radical minds, bent on overthrowing the existing economic order, nevertheless believed – or pretended to believe – that, contrary to any historical experience, the pattern for the organization of a 'planned' economy could be supplied by a model of the Walrasian type in which full reliance was placed on the automatic working of equilibrating forces". Finally, two well-known economists from Eastern Europe, Wlodzimierz Brus and Kazimierz Laski, make the same point in a recent work in which, as we shall see in detail later, they unambiguously show that Mises and Hayek were in the right in the socialist economic calculation debate, and that in no way did Oskar Lange or anyone else answer them satisfactorily. Brus and Laski blame the neoclassical model in general, and the Walrasian model in particular, because they fail to take account of the essential figure in the capitalist system: the entrepreneur. They also criticize the fact that the model of "perfect competition" does not allow for any of the typical struggle and rivalry that exists between entrepreneurs, a rivalry which results in the constant creation of new information. The authors conclude: "The Walrasian model overlooks the true central figure of the capitalist system, namely the entrepreneur *sensu stricto*. Formally there are entrepreneurs in the Walrasian model, but they behave like *robots*, minimizing costs or maximizing profits with the *data given*. Their behavior is that of pure optimizers operating in the framework of exclusively passive competition, reduced to *reactive* adjustment of positions to an exogenous change. This can scarcely be a legitimate generalization of competition, which in *reality* is a constant struggle affecting the data themselves. It is here that the static approach of the general equilibrium theory becomes particularly pronounced, contrary to the actual *dynamics* of a capitalist system" (Brus and Laski, 1989, 57). On the same topic, see Huerta de Soto (1990b, 36).

43. See Hurwicz (1973, 5). Hurwicz has boasted of incorporating the contributions of Hayek and Mises into his models: "The ideas of Hayek (whose classes at the London School of Economics I attended during the academic year 1938–39) have played a major role in influencing my thinking and have been so acknowledged. But my ideas have also been influenced by Oskar Lange (University of Chicago 1940–42) as well as by Ludwig von Mises in whose Geneva Seminar I took part during 1938–1939" (Hurwicz, 1984, 419). With the above statement, Hurwicz simply reveals that, as Lavoie has shown, Hurwicz failed to grasp the messages of both Hayek and Mises, despite having attended, as he himself affirms, their respective classes and seminars. In fact, not only do Hurwicz's writings lack a theory of entrepreneurship, but he also constantly assumes that information is *objective* and although dispersed, that it can be transmitted with the same meaning to everyone. Thus, he overlooks the essential characteristics of entrepreneurial information, which lies at the heart of market processes; basically, he neglects to consider its subjective and inarticulable nature. See Lavoie (1982). Furthermore, as Hurwicz makes clear in his response to Kirzner in the article published in the *Cato Journal* (1984), Hurwicz views the problem of dispersed knowledge as merely an issue of transmitting existing information, and he fails to even consider the problem the creation of new information poses, and this is the most important problem in a market process and is the central element in Kirzner's entire theory of entrepreneurship. The distinguished Frank Hahn makes the same errors as Hurwicz, and as late as 1988, he dared to confidently assert that sooner or later, the "market socialism" Lange and Lerner developed would provide an alternative far superior to the market economy of the capitalist system (see Hahn, 1988, esp. 114). A detailed critique of Hahn's position appears in Seldon (1990, ch. 6, 124–44).

44. "The articulate information supplied by prices is only informative because they are juxtaposed against the wide background of inarticulate knowledge gleaned from a vast experience of habitual productive activity. A price is not just a number. It is an indicator of the relative scarcity of some particular good or service of whose *unspecified qualities and attributes we are only subsidiarily aware*. Yet were these qualities of a good to change in the slightest respect this could change incremental decisions about the uses of the good just as a significantly as a change in price . . . Hayek was not contending that prices as numbers are the only pieces of information that the market transmits. *On the contrary, it is only because of the underlying inarticulate meaning attached to the priced goods and services that prices themselves communicate any knowledge at all*" (Lavoie, 1982, 32–3).

45. Lavoie, in the paper we have been discussing, draws, following Polanyi, a noteworthy analogy between the role of inarticulable knowledge in the area of scientific research and in the area of the market. He concludes: "Market participants are not and could not be 'price takers' any more than scientists could be 'theory takers.' In both cases a background of unquestioned prices or theories are subsidiarily relied upon by the entrepreneur or scientist, but also in both cases the focus of the activity is on *disagreeing* with certain market prices or scientific theories. Entrepreneurs (or scientists) actively disagree with existing prices (or theories) and commit themselves to their own projects (or ideas) by bidding prices up or down (or by criticizing existing theories). It is only through the intricate pressures being exerted by this rivalrous struggle of competition (or criticism) that new workable productive (or acceptable scientific) discoveries are made or that unworkable (or unacceptable) ones are discarded . . . Without the '*pressure*' that such personal commitments impart to science and to the market, each would lose its 'determining rationality.' It is precisely because the scientist has his reputation – and the capitalist his wealth – *at stake* that impels him to make his commitments for or against any particular direction of scientific or productive activity. Thus private property and the personal freedom of the scientist play analogous roles. When either form of personal commitment is undermined, for example when scientific reputation or economic wealth depend on loyalty to a party line rather than to a personal devotion to truth or a pursuit of subjectively perceived profit opportunities, each of these great achievements of mankind, science and our advanced economy, is sabotaged" (Lavoie, 1982, 34 and 35). Polanyi (1969b) draws the same analogy between the market and the advancement of science.

46. Machlup (1984, ch. 6, "New knowledge, disperse information and central planning"). See especially p. 200, where Machlup refers to the fact that "the knowledge of people's preferences is not only dispersed over millions of minds and not only subject to continual change but that it has too many blank spaces to be transferred in the form of price-or-quantity responses. The described planning system cannot give the people what they want, because they themselves cannot know what they want if they do not know what they could have. A steady stream of innovations in a free-enterprise system keeps altering the 'production possibilities,' including those that relate to new products and new qualities of existing products. Imaginative entrepreneurs, stimulated by anticipations of (temporary) profits, present consumers with options that have not existed hitherto but are expected to arouse responses of a kind different from those symbolized in the customary model of market equilibrium and in models of allocative equilibrium. The availability of new products makes a market system quite unlike the scheme of official indicators of quantities or prices announced by a central board and private proposals of prices or quantities submitted in response by the consuming public. *The organized feedback shuttle allowing informed decisions by a planning board does not give a place to the phenomenon of innovation*".

47. "It was probably the influence of Schumpeter's teaching more than the direct influence of Oskar Lange that has given rise to the growth of an extensive literature of mathematical studies of 'resource allocation processes' (most recently summarised in K.J. Arrow and L. Hurwicz, *Studies in Resource Allocation Processes*, Cambridge University Press,

1977). As far as I can see they deal as irresponsibly with sets of fictitious 'data' which are in no way connected with what the acting individual can learn as any of Lange's" (Hayek, 1982 [1984], 60). On p. 61 of this same work, Hayek adds that "the suggestion that the planning authority could enable the managers of particular plants to make use of their specific knowledge by fixing uniform prices for certain classes of goods that will then have to remain in force until the planning authority learns whether at these prices inventories generally increase or decrease is just the *crowning foolery of the whole farce*".

48. Ward (1967b, 32–3). In this work, Benjamin N. Ward also makes some passing remarks about the simplifications in these mathematical models (basically their static, linear nature), but he assumes that a bottleneck would never form in the communication between the different sectors and the planning agency because it "involves at each round sets of numbers that should not exceed $n^2$ for any one unit, where $n$ is the number of sectors, and is generally much less" (p. 61). Nevertheless, he adds that, in any case, if the time period necessary to complete the iteration were too long, the process could stop at a partial iteration, before it reached completion, and the result would be a plan which, although not optimum, would in practice be at least an "improvement". As Lavoie has indicated, it seems incredible that Ward has not realized that with this proposal, he abandons the most important *raison d'être* of the Walrasian *tâtonnement* process. If economic agents must stop all activity while linear-programming experts calculate the equilibrium solution to adopt later, and this solution is only an approximate and intermediate one, then why, after all, should the planometric process be initiated, if decentralized market mechanisms and the corresponding legal system constantly offer a more accurate result, without the necessity of ever halting action, or of thwarting the creation of new information, and without the additional cost entailed by the involvement of planometric theorists? See Lavoie (1985c, 99). Edmond Malinvaud commits a very similar error when, beginning with the study of the process of determining the optimum production level of public goods, he focuses on the analysis of the iterative processes of approaching the optimum equilibrium solution in a socialist system (1971; see also 1967). Frankly, it is very difficult to comprehend the obsession of all these authors with replacing the infinite variety and richness of human social life with a totally rigid, cold and mechanical model.

49. Ellman (1987).

50. "With different and changing production functions, the size of firms and the structure of industry become a problem. New goods and changing preferences also pose the problem of which firms or industries to expand, to contract, to abolish, or to create ... Under these conditions the Central Planning Board will not be able to get the information necessary for reliable *ex ante* planning because of the nature and complexity of the situation. *Rational calculation does break down if central planning is used*" ("The problem of complexity under non stationary conditions", in Bernholz, 1987, 154).

51. Lindbeck (1971; translated from p. 86 of the Spanish edition) states: "It is obvious that computers cannot take over from markets the task of generating information (about consumer preferences and productive technology) nor that of *creating* incentives to promote efficient functioning according to the preferences of consumers". Thus, he concludes: "The chances of *substituting* computers for decentralized market competition, in order to manipulate information and calculate approximations of the optimal allocation, are very limited". In light of the arguments given in the main text, I would say they are nil.

52. See especially Lavoie et al. (1990), as well as the bibliography these authors cite. We shall not busy ourselves with listing and examining other inadequacies of the planometric models from the standpoint of the methodology used in equilibrium and welfare economics itself. The corresponding criticisms are not only irrelevant in comparison with the fundamental arguments presented in the text, but they can also be found in any standard manual on the topic, for example, Bennet (1989, ch. 2). Also of interest is Bergun (1941).

53. In the words of Mises himself: "The mathematical economist, blinded by the prepossession that economics must be constructed according to the pattern of Newtonian mechanics and is open to treatment by mathematical methods, misconstrues entirely the subject matter of his investigations. *He no longer deals with human action but with a soulless mechanism mysteriously actuated by forces not open to further analysis.* In the imaginary construction of the evenly rotating economy there is, of course, no room for entrepreneurial function. *Thus the mathematical economist eliminates the entrepreneur from his thought.* He has no need for this mover and shaker whose never ceasing intervention prevents the imaginary system from reaching the state of perfect equilibrium and static conditions. *He hates the entrepreneur* as a disturbing element. The prices of the factors of production, as the mathematical economist sees it, *are determined by the intersection of two curves, not by human action*" (1966, 702).
54. Perhaps the first equilibrium theorist to recognize the radically different nature of the argument Mises and Hayek put forward in favor of the market was Richard R. Nelson (1981). I agree with Nelson when he states that "orthodox" welfare theory lacks relevance, but do not share his idea that the theories of Hayek in particular, and of the Austrian school in general, though relevant, are in a very primitive stage of development. Such an assertion makes sense only if one considers any theory constructed with a high degree of formalism to be developed, even if it is untenable and irrelevant, while also overlooking the important contributions the Austrian school has been making in all areas of economic science. As we saw at the end of note 2, even Mark Blaug has come to understand the fundamental differences between the Austrian and the neoclassical paradigms, as well as the irrelevance of the latter. See also Huerta de Soto (2009a).

# 6. Oskar Lange and the "competitive solution"

In this chapter and the next, we shall examine the different attempts of socialist economists at formulating a "competitive solution" to the problem that socialist economic calculation poses. With this in mind, we shall accomplish two goals in this chapter: first, we shall present a series of introductory considerations which place the most significant implications of this new proposal in their proper context, and we shall analyze the most important historical precedents for the proposal; second, we shall carefully study the "solution" Oskar Lange developed. Although our focus on Lange may at times appear too meticulous and extensive, his contribution – the best known and most often cited of those made by socialist theorists – has been so incorrectly interpreted that it is necessary to make a close and thorough examination of it. The analysis of the competitive solution will be concluded in the next chapter, which will be devoted to a study of (among other matters) the contributions made by Henry D. Dickinson, Evan F.M. Durbin and Abba P. Lerner in this area.

## 1 INTRODUCTORY CONSIDERATIONS

One feature shared by all versions of the so-called "competitive solution" is an attempt to introduce a sort of "quasi-market" (in the words of Mises), in which the behavior of the different economic agents resembles as closely as possible that of their counterparts in a capitalist system. When we examine the different contributions, we shall see that they are generally characterized by their ambiguity and contradictory nature, and to the extent that the proposed systems are intended to remain socialist, that is, to systematically and coercively restrict the free exercise of entrepreneurship, they provide no answer to the problem Mises and Hayek initially raised concerning the impossibility of economic calculation wherever the necessary information is not created.

Also, we shall see that there are two major types of competitive solution. The first is conceived as a simple, secondary solution to make practicable the algebraic calculation of equilibrium prices as prescribed by the mathematical solution that was analyzed in the last chapter. The second is conceived as a completely autonomous solution aimed at achieving the best of both worlds, socialism and capitalism, through a "market socialism" which, in its most watered-down form, would be difficult to distinguish from democratic socialism or social democracy, and in its most original form, is an attempt to "square the circle", to solve all of society's problems.

At this time, in any case, it must be emphasized that the widespread acceptance, among socialist theorists, of competitive solution proposals quite clearly amounts to an implicit acknowledgment on their part of the soundness of Mises's original contribution, published in 1920, regarding the impossibility of economic calculation in socialist economies. In other words, the Austrian attack which Mises and Hayek launched against socialism was so devastating that in practice, socialist theorists were forced to withdraw to a weak second line of defense, one built on precisely the essential elements of that economic system they so hated and wished to destroy. Fritz Machlup has shown that Mises's success has in fact been so complete that today no one doubts that in theory and in practice, planning is impossible without a decentralized price system. Nevertheless, most theorists are still, to say the least, inexplicably grudging about recognizing the merit of Mises's achievement. Furthermore, they have not yet fully understood or answered the fundamental elements of his challenge, which was simply to demonstrate theoretically that in a system without private ownership of the means of production or freedom to exercise entrepreneurship, the practical, dispersed, subjective information which is essential to the coordination of society cannot be created.[1]

Therefore, it is not surprising that the chief Austrian participants in the debate also persisted in highlighting the significance of the fact that their socialist opponents abandoned their traditional notion that a system of central planning managed by a government agency is the only rational method of organizing society, that they did an about-face and began to recommend, with differing levels of intensity, the reintroduction of competition.[2] Thus, for Mises,[3] the demonstration of the fact that economic calculation is impossible in a socialist regime prevailed at a speed unprecedented in the history of economic thought, such that socialists have been unable to avoid admitting their final defeat and have ceased to preach the traditional Marxist doctrine that socialism is superior to capitalism precisely because socialism permits the elimination of the market, prices and competition. In contrast, they now strive, with comic insistence, to justify socialism with the argument that it permits the preservation of the market, and they even try to show that the market and capitalism are distinct historical categories which are not necessarily connected.[4]

Hayek, in his customary genteel tone, could not resist making some sarcastic comments, both in the 1935 article in which he sums up the state of the debate[5] and in his 1940 work expressly devoted to criticizing the "competitive solution".[6] Hayek draws attention to the great significance of the fact that the young socialists who have most diligently and seriously studied the economic problems that socialism poses have abandoned the idea that a centrally planned economy could work, and they have instead tended to argue that competition could be maintained even when private ownership of the means of production were abolished. Thus, they have abandoned the traditional Marxist notion that planning is not only the exact opposite of competition, but that its main purpose is to eliminate competition, and in this way to permit the realization of the true socialist ideal.

## 2  HISTORICAL PRECEDENTS FOR THE COMPETITIVE SOLUTION

Before Lange, Dickinson, Durbin and Lerner made their polished contributions on the competitive solution, theorists had been developing it, albeit in an awkward and incomplete fashion, in writings both in German and English. In German, theoretical development began in this field in the 1920s as a reaction against Mises's seminal article, and Eduard Heimann and Karl Polanyi were principally responsible. Their common denominator was to defend a solution based on a certain degree of "competition" among a number of monopolies or "trusts" which, with union or government supervision, would constitute the backbone of the economic organization of socialism. In English, with the exception of some brief observations from Roper on the topic, there were initially very few writings on the competitive solution, and the fact that Mises and Hayek commented on it and critiqued it before Lange, Dickinson, Durbin and Lerner published their sophisticated works shows that the concept was probably forming in seminars through oral tradition as the implications of the debate grew more serious. This also explains the fact that many of the ideas these authors later included in their works were already "floating around" in the academic world several years earlier.

**The Contributions of Eduard Heimann and Karl Polanyi**

Eduard Heimann was one of the first theorists to write about the competitive solution in German and did so in his 1922 work, *Mehrwert und Gemeinwirtschaft: Kritische und Positive Beiträge zur Theorie des*

*Sozialismus* (Surplus and collective economics: critical and positive contributions to the theory of socialism].[7] Heimann realizes the essential importance of prices and the market, but he wishes at all costs to establish a socialist system. He tries to resolve this obvious dilemma by proposing what he calls *freundlichen Wettbewerb* (peaceful or friendly competition). This type of competition would exist, in an ordered and controlled manner, between the managers of the different entrepreneurial and sectoral organizations into which, according to Heimann, the economic system should be divided. In any case, Heimann, a socialist with Christian roots, still expresses serious doubts about whether competition and socialism are ultimately compatible. Furthermore, his scientific honesty is unmistakable, since he explicitly recognizes the great advantages of capitalistic competition, and he was one of the first theorists who, shortly after Mises himself, acknowledged the grave problem of economic calculation which would necessarily afflict any socialist system. Nevertheless, Heimann maintains that if the managers of the different sectoral monopolies simply had different ends, ideals and interests, then the result of their activity would be as competitive as that which is constantly produced in a real market economy. In this way, he believes that economic calculation problems would be avoided and that most of the advantages of the competitive system would remain, even without private ownership of the means of production and with an egalitarian distribution of income. Moreover, Heimann proposes the abolition of rents, interest and dividends, which would go directly to the central coercion agency. Finally, the managers of the sectoral monopolies would be instructed to fix their prices at the level of their costs, and they would never be able to use the monopolistic power their situation granted them.

George Halm has stated,[8] in a detailed critique of Heimann's proposals, that the "competition" between the managers of the sectoral monopolies would only be competition in quotation marks. It is impossible to fathom how the managers of the sectoral monopolies could come to know their costs, not only because free competition and entrepreneurship would be prohibited within each sector, but also because depreciation rates are an essential factor in determining cost, and they are calculated based on the interest rate, which would not be the result of a competitive process, but would be set by the central authorities, and thus would be completely arbitrary. Furthermore, Heimann does not understand that the essence of market functioning is the exercise of entrepreneurship, which alone makes it possible to constantly discover and create the practical information necessary for economic calculation in each specific context. In Heimann's model, the free exercise of entrepreneurship is prevented in extremely broad spheres of economic life, and thus the model does not permit the generation of this information, nor does it resolve the economic calculation problem. Indeed, it is unclear how the managers of the different monopolies could act entrepreneurially, not only because they would be unable to obtain the corresponding entrepreneurial profits (which would be eliminated by definition, and hence would not act as an entrepreneurial incentive for the discovery and creation of the information necessary for economic calculation), but also because they would not have the chance to foster entrepreneurship even within their own sectors.

More than a decade before Halm, Mises himself had already pointed out[9] that Heimann's proposal is extremely vague, mainly because it does not explain the nature of the relationship which would exist between the different industrial groups and the state or central planning agency. For if the different monopolized sectors would act as true owners of their respective means of production, then we are looking at a syndicalist type of system, one similar to that tested in the former Yugoslavia, with all of the perverse results and lack of coordination characteristic of such a system. At the same time, if the corresponding union organizations would play merely a managing role, and the responsibility for overall economic coordination would ultimately fall on a state planning center, then the typical economic-calculation problems Mises described in detail would emerge in all of their strength. In short, it is theoretically impossible to conceive of a sort of controlled and peaceful competition other than liberal competition. Competition either exists or it does not, depending upon whether the exercise of entrepreneurship is free or not (and, as we saw in Chapter 2, always subject to the traditional principles of private law), and Heimann's proposals would only make sense in a static, unreal world, in which no changes ever took place and all information necessary for economic calculation were already available. Finally, and this critical argument of Mises's is highly significant and has been systematically and blatantly ignored by the market socialism theorists who followed, it is absurd to believe, as Heimann proposes, that prices can be established in terms of costs. According to Mises, this proposal is nonsensical not only because costs are subjective and can only be judged tacitly and entrepreneurially in the context of each concrete action (and therefore cannot be objectively transmitted to the planning bureau or generated directly by it), but also because the monetary costs which are considered in personal economic calculation are simply estimates of productive-factor prices, and hence, any suggestion that we turn to costs in order to set prices is invariably an example of circular reasoning which leaves the economic-calculation problem unsolved.

Karl Polanyi,[10] in his 1922 article on socialist economic calculation,[11] after explicitly affirming that economic calculation is impossible in a central planning system, also makes a nebulous proposal for "guild socialism" in which the "ownership" of the means of production would be assigned to a central planning bureau, while the right to use production and consumer goods and services would be assigned to the corresponding guild production associations. Polanyi's is an ambiguous solution similar to the one Heimann offered, and it also fails to reveal who would ultimately possess the final decision-making power: the central coercion agency or the guild associations. If the central planning agency wields the ultimate decision-making power, then we again face the problem of how to acquire dispersed knowledge, which prevents economic calculation in centralized systems. If, in contrast, it is the professional, syndicalist associations which ultimately and systematically coerce their members and make the decisions, then we are looking at a sort of syndical socialism which lacks any coordinating capacity.[12]

## Early Criticism Leveled by Mises, Hayek and Robbins against the Competitive Solution

Let us now focus on the scientific English-speaking world. Before Lange, Dickinson, Durbin and Lerner made their contributions, except for some brief comments W.C. Roper made on the topic,[13] little had been written in English on the competitive solution. Nevertheless, as indicated previously, a relatively developed doctrine existed in academic circles and allowed both Mises and Hayek to make a series of early critical observations about this type of proposal.

The first observations about the competitive solution in general came from Mises and appear in the "artificial market" section of his work, *Socialism* (*Die Gemeinwirtschaft*), which was published in 1922 and expanded and translated into English in 1936. Mises holds that the market is the "focal point" and essence of the capitalist system, that it can flourish only under capitalism, and that the market and competition can never be "artificially" imitated under socialism. The support Mises provides for this assertion is in complete harmony with the explanations, in Chapter 2, of the coordinating nature of entrepreneurship, and it reveals that between 1920, when he published his initial article, and the writing of his 1922 book on socialism (revised and expanded when published in English in 1936), though Mises defended the same ideas, his ability to articulate them in writing improved quite substantially.

In fact, as we have already seen, Mises explicitly affirms that it is the entrepreneur who creates the practical information necessary for economic calculation. In the words of Mises: "It is the speculative capitalists [that is, entrepreneurs] who create the data to which he has to adjust his business and which therefore gives direction to his trading operations."[14] However, information is only created, discovered, or "seen" if the entrepreneur is pursuing an end which acts as an incentive for him to grasp this information. Thus, the incentive is the end or profit the entrepreneur strives to achieve with his action, and if property rights are not recognized, and therefore the entrepreneur cannot achieve his objective, profit, or end, he will not even generate the information necessary for economic calculation, and the entire coordinating process typical of a market economy will not be triggered. Mises states: "Without the striving of the entrepreneurs for profit . . . the successful functioning of the whole mechanism is not to be thought of . . . The motive force of the whole process which gives rise to market process for the factors of production is the ceaseless search on the part of the capitalists and the entrepreneurs to maximize their profits".[15] Hence, it is impossible to divorce the market and its typical functions – in terms of price formation and the coordinating capacity of the individual actions of its participants – from the institution of private ownership of the means of production. In other words, the moment private ownership of the means of production is eliminated, it becomes useless to instruct company managers to act as if they were entrepreneurs, since they are left "in the dark" when they lose the possibility of achieving what they subjectively estimate their potential profits to be.[16]

Furthermore, according to Mises, it is futile for a hypothetical "state bank" to auction its resources among those managers who offer the chance to obtain a higher rate of profit. "Such a state of affairs would simply mean that those managers who were less cautious and more optimistic would receive capital to enlarge their undertakings, while more cautious and more skeptical managers would go away empty-handed. Under capitalism, the capitalist decides to whom he will entrust his own capital".[17] Therefore, the process is not based on offering the highest rate of profit, but on the practical information generated in a capitalist market when entrepreneurs act in accordance with their speculations about the future and are driven by the psychological tension they feel between the desire to obtain profits and their subjective estimate of their chances of incurring losses. A manager who finds himself in conditions different from those of an entrepreneur in a free market will never have access to the same practical information as the entrepreneur, and therefore, in a socialist system, the final entrepreneurial decision will ultimately be made by the central planning agency in charge of deciding who will receive the corresponding funds and resources. As we already know, this central agency will never succeed in acquiring the practical information it would need to avoid acting arbitrarily. Mises concludes that "the alternative is still *either* socialism or a market economy", but that it is unrealistic to conceive of market socialism as a possible intermediate solution.[18]

In the last five sections (which cover 25 pages) of his 1935 article in which he sums up the "state of the debate", and under the heading "pseudo-competition", Hayek criticizes both the models which had been developed in the German literature, and which were presented in detail when we discussed Heimann and Polanyi, as well as the other proposals for market socialism which the youngest generation of socialist economists were formulating verbally in London's economic circles (proposals which had not yet appeared in writing).

Concerning the German tradition model of competition among sectoral monopolies, each of which would follow the rule of matching prices with costs, specifically, of producing a volume at which marginal prices and costs coincide, Hayek repeats and expands on the arguments we offered against Heimann's and Polanyi's proposals, arguments which Mises, Halm and Weil initially raised. Hayek points out that if intrasectoral competition is prohibited, then it becomes impossible within each sector for the price and cost information necessary for economic calculation to emerge. In addition, he criticizes the proposal that costs be used as a guide for setting prices or determining a certain volume of production. For it is not only that costs are subjective and can only be established in a market context in which all of the possible opportunities given up when one acts can be properly estimated; it is also that costs invariably depend on expectations of the future. In the words of Hayek: "The competitive or necessary cost cannot be known unless there is competition",[19] and this means not only true competition among the different sectors, but also, and especially, competition among the different companies at an intrasectoral level. Hence, costs are not something which can be objectively known by a planning bureau or by sectoral monopoly managers, but rather are subjective valuations which are estimated according to the entrepreneurial capacity of each economic agent who makes decisions in the market.

Furthermore, the marginal-cost criterion involves, as Mises has already shown, a sort of circular reasoning that makes it impossible to apply. Not only are costs subjective, opportunity costs, but when they are assessed, the numerical calculations taken into account are precisely the estimated prices of the factors of production. Thus, prices can hardly be determined based on costs if the latter are also simply prices. This is particularly clear when one reflects on the role capital depreciation plays as a component of cost. Indeed, capital is simply the present value of a future series of rents or prices which correspond to the services of a capital good, and these rents or prices must be estimated prior to calculating the present value of such a good, and thus, its depreciation rate as a component of the cost. Therefore, it is impossible to determine price in terms of cost, since the depreciation component of the latter requires that future prices be estimated first. In the words of Hayek himself: "Much of what is usually termed cost of production is not really a cost element that is given independently of the price of the product but a quasi-rent, or a depreciation quota which has to be allowed on the capitalized value of expected quasi-rents, and is therefore dependent on the prices which are expected to prevail".[20]

Moreover, Hayek emphasizes the impossibility of establishing, in any manner other than a purely arbitrary one, which monopolized sector or industry would constitute the basis for the socialist model we are discussing. Would each sector comprise all of the intermediate industries or stages which give rise to a certain final consumer good or service? Or, in contrast, would each sector include all of the industries or companies which produce the same intermediate good? Or would a combination of these systems be used? Furthermore, it is clear that because each final consumer service and good has a different subjective meaning for each decision-making individual or agency, the concept of sector or industry, regardless of the criterion adopted, would be completely arbitrary. Besides, such sectors could not remain unaltered with the passage of time, since changes in the goods and services produced or in the technologies or capital goods used, assuming that the criterion did not change, would result in constant variations in the companies to be included in each sector. Therefore, the concept of industry or sector is theoretically absurd: it cannot be objectively established and can have different forms, and it would only make sense in a static world in which all information were given and no changes ever occurred.[21]

The second model Hayek analyzes and criticizes is that in which pseudo-competition is considered desirable, not only on an intersectoral level, but on an intrasectoral level as well; that is, among the different companies in each sector. In this second model, the central planning bureau appears as a sort of "superbank" which appropriates the profits earned in all companies and sectors and distributes the corresponding investment funds among them. The means of production are publicly owned, but the different companies are intended to operate competitively on an individual level; in other words, to seek profits and avoid losses.

Hayek's critical observations about this second group of competitive-socialism proposals, in which competition is meant to extend to the broadest sphere compatible with public ownership of the means of production, and in which the central planning agency only intervenes to appropriate profits and distribute the corresponding investment funds, are of a certain interest, mainly due to their implications as a precedent for the modern economic theory of property rights and for the analysis of the public-choice school concerning the behavior of bureaucrats and civil servants.[22]

Nevertheless, they do not incorporate the essential theoretical arguments that Mises had already voiced. Indeed, Hayek points out that even if competition is permitted at all levels, if there is no private ownership of the means of production, it will be necessary to develop or discover an alternative system for confirming that the corresponding managers are acting correctly. Hayek lists and analyzes a series of possible systems which could be devised as alternatives to the private ownership of the means of production.[23] The past successes or failures of future managers is worthless as a criterion, since it is not the past that is of interest, but the future behavior of the corresponding manager. Furthermore, it is not possible to objectively discern whether a manager is acting foolishly when he appears to be incurring losses, because he may actually be investing properly from a longer-term perspective, with the expectation that in the future those losses will turn into large profits. The establishment of a system of bonuses or "monetary incentives" in favor of managers would present the same difficulty: the distribution of the bonuses would require prior, objective and unequivocal knowledge of whether a course of action had succeeded or failed, and this is not possible, given the dispersed and inarticulable quality of the information involved in the process, as well as the uncertain nature of all future events. Moreover, a system of "bonuses" would only provoke excessively optimistic and reckless behavior if these were not counterbalanced by "negative bonuses" in the case of losses or errors. However, the establishment of monetary or other penalties depending on the seriousness of the losses entails the risk of making entrepreneurial behavior too conservative. Hayek concludes that there is no alternative system which would make it possible to reproduce or simulate, in a socialist system, the typically competitive behaviors that derive from private ownership of the means of production.[24]

None of the above possible solutions, or any of the corresponding criticisms, penetrates the heart of the problem, which does not arise solely from a lack of the incentives necessary for the system to function just as market processes function in a capitalist system. Indeed, the problem is also one of *dispersed knowledge*, and it cannot be eradicated, as we have been following in Mises's footsteps to explain. In fact, if production goods are publicly owned and the community, through the central coercion agency, appropriates the corresponding profits, dividends and interest, it is clear that no individual agent can acquire those same profits, since this would contradict the proposed model of socialism and would mean the reintroduction of the capitalist system and of private ownership of the means of production. If each economic agent is forcibly prevented from pursuing his own goal or profit, he will not discover the large quantity of practical information crucial to economic calculation and to the coordination of social processes. Moreover, even if the economic agent deceives himself and believes his situation is "identical" to what it would be in a capitalist society, and even if he believes he has his goal or profit in view (because he does not mind that once he has obtained it, he will have to hand it over to the community, or simply because of chance, or any other reason), it is obvious that to pursue that goal and undertake the corresponding course of action, given that by definition he does not possess his own resources, he will have to resort to requesting them from the corresponding central planning agency that represents the community. It will inevitably be this planning agency that will ultimately decide whether or not to provide the corresponding resources, yet as we know, this agency lacks the vital, practical (and essentially subjective and tacit) information dispersed in the minds of economic agents, and therefore the state agency will invariably tend to act in an arbitrary, rather than a coordinating, manner. In other words, in the absence of private ownership of production goods (that is, if one is not free to enjoy the profits or fruits of one's own creativity, to build a capital base, and to draw from it the resources necessary to pursue new actions), a forced dislocation occurs between the individual agents who potentially possess dispersed knowledge ("potentially" because knowledge is not creatively generated when individual agents are prevented from acquiring the profits they earn) and the central planning bureau. Despite any good intentions, this agency will never be able to access the dispersed knowledge that citizens could potentially generate, and hence, it will have no choice but to decide in an arbitrary, and not a coordinating, manner to whom it will supply the resources at its disposal.

Finally, we cannot overlook the fact that when Lionel Robbins was writing his 1934 book, *The Great Depression*, he took the opportunity, a year before Hayek wrote on the subject, to make some brief critical comments on the proposals for competitive socialism. According to Robbins, it is not enough for managers in the socialist system to try to "play" at competition and "compete" with each other when buying and selling their products, as if they were acting in a capitalist system. He feels that such proposals involve a simplistic conception of the economic system, as if it were a static system in which prices and all other information were generated *ipso facto*, in an objective manner, by the force of consumer demand. In contrast, Robbins stresses that in the real world, tastes, technology, resources, and in general, all knowledge is in a process of continual change, and therefore, "the entrepreneur must be at liberty to withdraw his capital altogether from one line of production, sell his plant and his stocks and go into other lines. He must be at liberty to break up the administrative unit".[25] In short, one must be free to sell property if the information necessary for the market to operate is to be created, and this is clearly incompatible with public ownership of the means of production and the centralized control of the economic system which it ultimately entails. Hence, we see that along with the arguments against the computational, or purely algebraic, solution discussed earlier, Robbins offers a series of comments on "artificial competition", and though they are brief, they are not altogether off-base.[26]

This concludes the analysis of the first early criticisms that Mises, Hayek and Robbins leveled against the so-called "competitive solution", assessments based on the fact that the dispersed nature of knowledge renders economic calculation impossible wherever the means of production are not privately owned. We shall now closely examine Oskar Lange's proposal for a "competitive solution".

## 3 THE CONTRIBUTION OF OSKAR LANGE: INTRODUCTORY CONSIDERATIONS

The reason why we shall carefully study the contribution of the Polish economist, Oskar Lange, lies, apart from this author's importance to the history of the debate about socialist economic calculation, in the need to evaluate the soundness of the most widespread version of it printed in the textbooks which circulate as secondary sources on the debate and the authors of most of which have until now taken for granted that Lange effectively refuted the theoretical challenge Mises and Hayek had issued concerning socialism. We shall see that this interpretation, which had become a true *myth* of economic science,[27] does not correspond with reality. In fact, an increasing number of professional economists are beginning to realize that the myth that "Lange was able to refute Mises" is completely unfounded.

In the scientific life of Oskar Ryszard Lange (1904–65), it is possible to identify four very distinct stages in terms of his conception of the socialist system. The first stage was characterized by his defense of a socialist model which was influenced, in general, by the model the Austrian Marxists developed, and in particular, by Eduard Heimann and Karl Polanyi, whose contributions have already been analyzed. In the second stage, Lange developed his "classic model", which was firmly rooted in neoclassical welfare theory, in the "trial and error solution", and in the introduction of decentralized mechanisms of "competition" in order to find the corresponding equilibrium solutions. The third stage was an ambiguous one in which Lange, who was profoundly affected by Hayek's criticism of his system, criticism he never managed to answer, reached the highest level of liberalism in his proposals, though he never explicitly and satisfactorily reconciled them with his socialist ideal. The fourth and last stage, which began with his entry into the Polish communist party and ended with his death, was characterized by a frank withdrawal from his earlier proposals, in the sense that he ended up explicitly praising the theory and practice of the Stalinist system, and he even eventually recanted his competitive solutions (which were simply leading him to an implicit abandonment of the socialist system) and proposed a rigid, Stalinist sort of central-planning system in which, given dramatic advances in computer science, he believed no competitive solution was necessary. We shall study each of these stages in detail.

**The Lange–Breit Model**

Lange's first proposal concerning the manner in which a socialist system should function was written jointly with Marek Breit in 1934 in the form of a chapter entitled, "The road to the socialist planned economy", which formed part of a collective work, *Political Economy and Tactics for Socialist Organization*, which was printed in Warsaw that same year.[28] The 1934 Lange–Breit model is practically a copy of the model of "competitive" sectoral monopolies that Heimann and Polanyi had attempted to develop in the 1920s. Indeed, Lange and Breit conceive the economy as a set of highly autonomous "sectoral trusts", the management of which would be strongly influenced by union representatives. In any case, the trusts would be coordinated by a central bank which, apart from controlling and monitoring their functioning, would take care of providing them with the necessary financial resources. Each of these sectoral monopolies would be ordered to keep rigorous accounting records and to establish prices in terms of production costs. Of course, all means of production would be publicly owned, and the corresponding profits and dividends would have to be transferred to the central bank. Lange and Breit felt it important to separate economic organizations from political authority as far as possible, and to ensure that the corresponding sectors did not end up as consumer-exploiting monopolies, they believed it would be necessary to establish a legal obligation to require the sectors to offer a job to any worker who requested one in any sector.

Clearly, as stated, the proposals of Lange and Breit coincide almost exactly with those that Heimann and Polanyi developed in the 1920s, and therefore, all the criticisms we studied in earlier sections, which were mainly formulated by Mises and Hayek, apply to the proposals of Lange and Breit as well. Though all of the arguments against this sort of model will not be repeated here, its naive, ambiguous nature is obvious, especially because it takes no account of the fact that the lack of real competition on an intrasectoral level renders economic calculation utterly impossible. The same is true regarding the insurmountable problem of objectively defining the monopolistic industrial sectors in a manner other than a purely arbitrary one. Moreover, the managers responsible for the corresponding sectors would lack the entrepreneurial freedom necessary to discover and create the information essential for economic calculation. This fact is particularly grave. It makes the order to "produce at prices which cover costs" completely unrealistic, given that costs are not objective and are ultimately simply prices rendered intangible by the rule itself, which involves inescapable circular reasoning (especially considering the impossibility of calculating the component of the costs represented by depreciation rates). Last, the central bank authority responsible for supplying funds to companies and sectors would, due to the insoluble problem posed by the dispersed, subjective nature of knowledge, lack the information necessary to carry out its duties in a coordinating, and not purely arbitrary, manner.

In short, neither Lange nor Breit either took into account or answered any of the criticisms that Mises had expressed over 10 years earlier regarding Heimann's and Polanyi's models of "competitive" monopolies. Clearly, Lange and Breit had not read the works Mises published between 1920 and 1928, and as a result, they were unaware of the problems which beset their proposal due to their ideological blindness and the fact that they had not given their ideas the necessary careful reflection. It is also possible that they conveniently concealed Mises's criticisms, which they neglected to mention and left unanswered, for ideological or political reasons.

## 4  OSKAR LANGE AND HIS CLASSIC MODEL OF "MARKET SOCIALISM"

We shall follow Tadeusz Kowalik's example[29] and refer to the second stage in Lange's scientific life as that of his *classic* model of "market socialism". This stage began when, in October 1936 and February 1937, he published the two-part article, "On the economic theory of socialism". The article was republished in 1938 in the book with the same title, in which Fred M. Taylor's paper on socialism also appeared. Benjamin Lippincott wrote the introduction to the book.[30] After receiving a scholarship from the Rockefeller Foundation, Lange studied at the London School of Economics, and also at Chicago, Berkeley, and especially, Harvard, where he completed two academic years and was heavily influenced by Schumpeter, with whom he exchanged ideas at length. In addition, Lange had the opportunity to talk and work with the socialist economists and brothers, Alan and Paul Sweezy, as well as with Wassily Leontief. One outcome of this intellectual atmosphere was the paper, "On the economic theory of socialism", in which Lange sought to express his conviction that neoclassical equilibrium theory, and specifically "welfare economics", provided, without a doubt, the strongest theoretical foundation for the socialist system. Lange also intended his paper to refute, based on this idea, Mises's argument on the theoretical and practical impossibility of rational economic calculation in a socialist system. Let us consider how Lange developed his arguments and whether or not he successfully refuted Mises.

**Market Prices versus "Parametric Prices"**

Lange's big dream was that it would be possible to simulate the final state toward which the market process and competitive economics tend, but without a capitalist market; that is, without private ownership of the means of production or the free exercise of entrepreneurship. This hope was based on the belief that it would be possible to arrive at a list of "parametric prices", which, although not determined in a free market, would nevertheless permit rational economic calculation by incorporating the vital information essential for it, and would thus enable society's different economic agents to act in a coordinated manner. We shall see that Lange's contribution is built on a mistaken conception of how market processes work (or more accurately, on his ignorance of such processes, since Lange focuses solely on the neoclassical paradigm of equilibrium, on economic welfare theory, and on the model of "perfect competition"). Moreover, we shall be able to confirm that the procedure he proposes does not in any way resolve the problem of coordination nor that of rational economic calculation in a socialist economy, just as Mises had discovered and asserted 15 years earlier.

By "parametric prices" we should understand the various terms on which different goods and services are offered, terms which prompt purely passive or adaptive behavior in economic agents. In fact, Lange considers the essential function of prices to be merely parametric; in other words, each economic agent "separately regards the actual prices as given data to which he has to adjust himself".[31] Hence, parametric prices are ratios of a sort, or abstract "terms of trade" which, in principle, can be arrived at by any procedure, arbitrary or not. Moreover, with parametric prices it is possible to keep "accounting" records, though only in the simplest formal or instrumental sense. Nevertheless, as is logical, parametric prices alone do not guarantee one the ability to make a "rational" economic calculation; that is, one which serves a coordinating function with respect to the behavior of the different economic agents. This will only be feasible if the above prices incorporate the information or knowledge necessary for the coordinating function or economic calculation to be performed.

Mises's fundamental argument had nothing to do with this parametric concept of prices, but instead was based on the concept of *market prices*, that is, those established through the free exercise of entrepreneurship, and without which the information necessary to coordinate the behavior of economic agents and make their economic calculation rational is not generated. In contrast, Lange holds that Mises's market prices are not necessary for economic calculation, and that via merely parametric prices, which are not determined in a competitive market where the means of production are privately owned and entrepreneurship is freely exercised, rational calculation would nonetheless be possible. That is, he believes the information necessary to perform it would be available, and that this calculation would properly coordinate the behavior of the different agents. Let us now analyze Lange's argument paragraph by paragraph.

**Lange's First Paragraph**

Lange begins his theoretical argument against Mises's ideas in this way:

> Professor Mises' contention that a socialist economy cannot solve the problem of rational allocation of its resources is based on a confusion concerning the nature of prices. As [Philip] Wicksteed has pointed out, the term, "price" has two meanings. It may mean either price in the ordinary sense, i.e. the exchange ratio of two commodities on a market, or it may have the generalized meaning of "terms on which alternatives are offered." Wicksteed says, "Price, then, in the narrower sense of 'the money for which a material thing, a service, or a privilege can be obtained,' is simply a special case of 'price' in the wider sense of the terms on which alternatives are offered to us." [Wicksteed, 1933, 28.] It is only prices in the generalized sense which are indispensable to solving the problem of allocation of resources.[32]

Let us take a close look at this paragraph. To begin with, the fact that Wicksteed informs us that for the purposes of his specific analysis, basically at the point of equilibrium, it is helpful to use the term "price" in a broad sense, that is, that of a simple ratio or term on which alternatives are offered, in no way means that Wicksteed believed such parametric prices could serve as true substitutes for market prices where the latter do not exist or are not known. On the contrary, as acting human beings, we are constantly obliged to make decisions and assess different alternatives, and according to Mises, we cannot make these decisions rationally if we do not take account of "true market prices" that incorporate the necessary information. To assert that Mises is mistaken in his reasoning concerning the impossibility of socialist economic calculation because his concept of price (market price) is too narrow or limited is tantamount to asserting that the problem Mises raised was simply that of the impossibility of doing any sort of "computations" or "algebraic calculations" due to the lack of a numerical accounting system, regardless of the real content of the data used in it, and not, as was the case, the problem of the impossibility of performing a coordinating, rational economic calculation in the absence of prices which incorporate the information necessary to do so. As Hayek has stated, for Lange to declare that Mises is mistaken because he needlessly makes economic calculation contingent on the use of market prices, in the strict and limited sense of the term, when any system of parametric prices enables one to perform calculations, is so naive that it seems "an inexcusable legerdemain of which a thinker not prejudiced by political preconceptions should be incapable".[33]

Therefore, what is essential is to establish whether the parametric prices which are not market prices can come to incorporate the information necessary for one to calculate rationally and coordinate the maladjusted behaviors of social agents, a problem which, as we shall see, Lange was unable to satisfactorily resolve.

Karen I. Vaughn has pointed out that Lange, in the paragraph in question, shows that he completely misunderstood Wicksteed's meaning with respect to prices.[34] Indeed, according to Wicksteed, anyone who wishes to make an economic decision will confront the fundamentally *subjective* problem of estimating the opportunity cost involved in the action he is considering. So when a person contemplates, for example, making a purchase, he undoubtedly finds out, among other particulars, the price of the good in question, or the ratio at which it is exchanged for the money paid in the market. The "terms on which alternatives are offered" to the actor are subjectively assessed by him and include not only the terms of trade indicated by the price, but also all of the other subjective factors the actor ponders, some more and some less, when he makes his decision. Hence (and we could expect no less of Wicksteed, one of the most prominent subjectivist theorists), it is impossible to distinguish the parametric function from the non-parametric functions of prices, because the two aspects are indissolubly united in the concept of market price, and actors always judge them subjectively and together.[35]

**Lange's Second Paragraph**

Let us now consider Lange's explanation of how prices in a generalized sense (parametric prices) could come to be known by industry managers and the central planning agency in a socialist system, and how such prices could satisfactorily replace the monetary market prices which exist in the capitalist system. In the words of Lange himself: "The economic problem is a problem of choice between alternatives. To solve the problem three *data* are needed: (1) a preference scale which guides the acts of choice; (2) *knowledge* of the 'terms on which alternatives are offered;' and (3) *knowledge* of the amount of resources available. Those three *data* being *given*, the problem of choice is soluble".[36]

The first observation we should make is that Lange's last sentence above contains a blatant pleonasm. Indeed, as any moderately educated person knows, the English word "data" derives from the Latin *datum-data*, which refers precisely to knowledge or information which is "given". "Given", in turn, is the past participle of the verb "to give". In short, what Lange literally asserts in his last sentence is that if the information which is given, is given, then the problem of economic calculation is soluble. Hayek indicates that unscholarly expressions (such as "given data") or "semantic redundancies" (to use Don Lavoie's gentler terminology) of this sort appear constantly in Lange's writing. In general, such phrases are irresistibly attractive and are frequently uttered by mathematical economists, specifically by those who frame their science in terms of equilibrium, within the neoclassical–Walrasian paradigm, because in some way (semantically, at least), these expressions ease their consciences by assuring them that they know something which, in reality, they do not know, or will ever be able to know.[37] As a matter of fact, the confusion which arises from the above pleonasm forms the very basis for the entire content of Lange's much-trumpeted "refutation" of Mises's argument concerning the impossibility of economic calculation in a socialist economy. Indeed, for Mises, the essential economic problem is how to acquire the necessary information in the absence of a market, market prices, and the free exercise of entrepreneurship. However, if we assume *ab initio* that this information is given, then logically, no economic calculation problem exists, since we begin by supposing it has already been resolved. Thus, what Lange ultimately tells us in the last sentence of the paragraph we are discussing is this: "If we assume that the economic calculation problem has been solved at the outset, then the economic calculation problem is solved".

Lange belabors the aforementioned pleonasm in the first sentence of the next paragraph when he writes: "It is obvious that a socialist economy *may regard the data under 1 and 3 as given*, at least in as great a degree as they are given in a market economy".[38]

We may well wonder: how? Contrary to what Lange asserts with absolutely no reasoning, it is not at all obvious that in a socialist economy, information (not even the information under 1 and 3) can come to be given (or rather, "known", since we suppose this is the meaning Lange attaches to the expression "given") in the same way and to the same degree as it is given (or rather, "seen", "discovered" or "created") in a market economy. The key issue is this: by whom, through whom, and how is this information acquired? For, as showed in detail in Chapter 2, in a market economy, information is not "given" at all. Quite the reverse: it is constantly created, discovered and noticed by thousands and thousands of economic agents who interactively exercise their entrepreneurship within a market context, including ownership rights to the factors of production. It is inadmissible to suppose from the beginning, as Lange does, that this process by which new information is constantly created and discovered can be emulated or replicated in a socialist system in which, by definition, the free exercise of entrepreneurship is prohibited and property rights have been abolished. Moreover, if, under such circumstances, the agents themselves cannot even create or discover this information, then we can hardly expect a hypothetical central planning bureau to be able to obtain it. Information cannot be considered "given" at the central level, not only because it is of a subjective, practical, dispersed and inarticulable nature, but also because it is not even generated at the level of individual economic agents when they are unable to freely exercise their entrepreneurship. We need not develop this key argument even further here, since it has repeatedly been explained in detail from diverse perspectives at other points in this book.

**Lange's Third Paragraph**

Lange continues his reasoning as follows: "The *data* under 1 may be either *given* by the demand schedules of the individuals or be established by the judgement of the authorities administering the economic system. The question remains whether the data under 2 are accessible to the administrators of a socialist economy. Professor Mises denies this. However, a careful study of *price theory* and of the *theory of production* convinces us that the data under 1 and under 3 *being given*, the 'terms on which alternatives are offered' are determined ultimately by the technical possibilities of transformation of one commodity into another, i.e., by the *production functions*."[39]

Initially most striking in this paragraph is the reference (in italics) to "price theory" and the "theory of production", the "careful" study of which leads Lange to assert that, if the necessary information (that under headings 1 and 3) is "given", no economic calculation problem exists, because the terms on which different alternatives are exchanged or offered will be given by the technical possibilities of transformation incorporated in the corresponding production functions. The fact that Lange explicitly bases his assertion on the neoclassical–Walrasian "price theory" and "theory of production" not only reveals the "scientific imperialism" of this paradigm (which overlooks another price theory, one that does not rest on the absurd assumption that all necessary information is given from the start), but it also shows the inadequacies and dangers which beset the methodology rooted in the obsessive use of mathematics, equilibrium analysis, and the presumption that the fundamental economic problem is merely one of maximizing known functions subject to known restrictions. It is not simply that, as Mises indicates, "economic equilibrium theory" is an irrelevant intellectual game, but also (and this is much more serious) that it corrupts even brilliant scientific minds by obliging them to start from unrealistic assumptions and leading them inexorably to erroneous conclusions, and all in a manner that goes virtually unnoticed, except by the sharpest and most profound theorists. The economic theory of equilibrium and the neoclassical–Walrasian model are the "opium of the economic scientist", and they separate him from the reality he should study, infuse him with absolute complacence, and immunize him against most of his potential opportunities to detect his errors. Lange attempted to show that economic welfare theory, developed within the neoclassical–Walrasian paradigm, was the most important theoretical foundation possible for the socialist system. The fact that most equilibrium theorists have agreed that his analytical model can be applied to both a capitalist and a socialist system, and the fact that this model can serve as a basis for justifying the possibility of economic calculation in the latter, in my opinion robs most of neoclassical price theory of scientific credibility. One of the most important theses of this book is precisely that the theoretical–critical analysis of socialism which it contains, and which is embodied in actual, historically significant events in the countries of the former Eastern bloc, implies the collapse and total loss of prestige, in theoretical and practical terms, of both socialism as an economic and social system, as well as much of neoclassical economic theory as a serious scientific paradigm worthy of consideration.

Moreover, it is not surprising that Lange, and most of the authors of neoclassical economics, fail to understand how Mises can affirm that economic calculation is "theoretically impossible" in a socialist economy. This is so, because to the above authors, "theory" means simply their own, and as we have seen, they base it on assumptions which from the beginning eliminate precisely the need for any economic calculation. That is, from the neoclassical perspective, socialist economic calculation is always, by definition, theoretically possible. These authors cannot conceive of any theory but the one they themselves have built on the concepts of equilibrium and maximization. Specifically, they completely overlook the paradigm developed by Austrian theorists in general, and Mises and Hayek in particular, a paradigm based from the start on a *theoretical* study of the real institutions that emerge in society and of the market processes which the force of entrepreneurship drives. In the Austrian paradigm, information is never assumed given, since it is constantly generated within a certain institutional context which permits the coordination of the maladjusted behaviors of human beings.[40]

In regard to this matter, Lavoie has pointed out that because neoclassical theorists assume in their market-economy models that all vital information is available to participating economic agents, and that under certain static conditions the market reaches a particular equilibrium, it is virtually inevitable for these theorists, almost without realizing it, to end up taking the tiny step involved in making similar presumptions with a socialist model, and hence to arrive at the parallel conclusion that in a socialist system a certain equilibrium is attainable.[41] Kirzner adds that Lange failed to recognize the true challenge Mises posed against socialism because Lange's knowledge of economics was confined, in general, to neoclassical price theory, and in particular, to the model of "perfect competition". This model, which even today most introductory textbooks portray as one of the most important for comprehending the real economic system, totally eliminates the role of entrepreneurship in the discovery and use of profit opportunities in a dynamic process of constant change which coordinates the economy. Since Mises's argument rests on a concept of entrepreneurship which is altogether absent from the neoclassical paradigm, it is not surprising that Lange, who lacked the necessary analytical tools, ended up believing that the market behaves just as the textbooks indicate, and that therefore, it is possible to simulate, in a socialist economy, the equilibrium model so elegantly presented in them.[42]

As has already been shown, even though Lange sees no obstacle to compiling information of types 1 and 3, it is theoretically impossible to do so in the absence of free entrepreneurship, since in this case, the corresponding information will not be generated or discovered (nor will its tacit, subjective nature permit its transmission to a central authority). It is the information under heading 2, that is, the knowledge of terms of trade and production functions, which appears to pose a problem in Lange's opinion, however he immediately asserts that this problem could be solved very easily, as long as the information under 1 and 3 were given (which, we repeat, we know is impossible). In an extraordinary manner, Lange solves this problem by affirming at the stroke of a pen, and without proof or justification, that "the administrator of the socialist economy will have exactly the same knowledge or lack of knowledge, of the production functions as the capitalist entrepreneurs have".[43]

The crux of Lange's entire refutation of Mises lies in this dogmatic (that is, without any theoretical or empirical proof or justification) assertion. As we know, Mises's reasoning essentially shows that the information generated through the free exercise of entrepreneurship cannot be reproduced by a system devoid of entrepreneurship, and that thus, it is theoretically impossible for the "administrator of the socialist economy" to possess "exactly" the same information as that available to entrepreneurs in a capitalist economy. We know that information is subjective and dynamic, and that it is constantly created as those who are free to grasp profit opportunities through entrepreneurship come to perceive these opportunities. Because entrepreneurship is, by definition, eliminated when private ownership of the means of production is abolished, and as a result, individuals lose the possibility of freely perceiving goals and striving to achieve them, such goals cease to act as an incentive, and the information vital to reaching them is not generated. Consequently, by definition, wherever free entrepreneurship does not exist, one can never assume that the information which arises only from the process entrepreneurship drives will be generated. Hence, it is not surprising that in 1982, Hayek made the following statement regarding Lange's startling assertion:

> This *brazen* assertion is crucial for Lange's refutation of Mises' argument, but he offers no evidence or justification for it, even in this limited form confined to production functions. Yet it has been expanded by Lange's pupils into the even more *fantastic assertion* that a central planning board "would receive exactly the same information from a socialist economic system as did the entrepreneurs under the market system" (Thus Robert L. Heilbroner, *Between Capitalism and Socialism*, New York 1980, p. 88) . . . I am afraid this is a blatant untruth, an assertion so absurd that it is difficult to understand how an intelligent person could ever honestly make it. It asserts a sheer impossibility which only a miracle could realize.[44]

Moreover, we must bear in mind that so-called "production functions" do not exist in reality. In real life, there is a flow of new, constantly generated information regarding the different possibilities of combining productive factors to achieve a certain good or service. The economic agents involved in production discover this information little by little as they exercise entrepreneurship and test different ideas. These agents constantly recognize what they believe to be new profit opportunities, which entail not only modifying goods and services (with respect to the way they are presented and defined, as well as to price and quality), but also making commercial and technological innovations. The same occurs with an even higher degree of complexity in the case of the means of production in which the continual discovery of slight, previously unnoticed changes yields large profits. We can hardly consider that certain, hypothetical "production functions" exist, when the information necessary to define them does not exist. That is, the actual economic agents involved in the production process do not possess this information (nor does any planning board, much less experts or economists, no matter how specialized in the theory of production), unless they create it bit by bit in a tacit, subjective and *dispersed* manner. The problem of production is not a technical problem of functions that can be objectively solved. On the contrary, it is a purely entrepreneurial human problem: in the context of different actions, entrepreneurs continually try out new and extremely diverse combinations and alternatives, which in the framework of a market economy, together with the expected market prices and the enormous variety of other subjective information that affects the actor, constantly make him *see* possibilities of obtaining subjective (that is, monetary, *ceteris paribus*) profits that he deems worth pursuing.

Therefore, it is clear that Lange fails to recognize the fundamental distinction between two radically different types of knowledge: "scientific" and "practical". In fact, he appears to so utterly confuse the practical knowledge which the economic agents who act in society generate daily and possess in dispersed form with the scientific knowledge that economists believe permits them to theorize about social processes, that he ends up naively convinced that both the scientist and the planning board could easily acquire this practical knowledge in real life. Nevertheless, the two types of knowledge (practical and scientific) differ sharply in nature. For even when scientific knowledge is transformed into a theory about practical knowledge, as occurs in economic science, this theory is at most a *formal* one concerning the processes by which knowledge is created and transmitted. Furthermore, the theory must always rest on the idea that theorizing on practical knowledge does not in any way permit an outside observer to overcome the theoretical impossibility of accessing the specific content, whether the observer is a scientist or a planning agency. Precisely for this reason (that is, the fact that the theorist cannot possibly obtain the "material" content of the practical knowledge on which he theorizes, as well as his failure to distinguish between practical and scientific knowledge), economic calculation is impossible in a socialist system, and most of the economic theory formulated thus far within the neoclassical paradigm is irrelevant.

**Lange's Fourth Paragraph**

Lange extends this confusion between the two types of knowledge to the two concepts of price which apply to them. Indeed, within the realm of practical knowledge lie market prices, which incorporate much of this knowledge and are continually created and modified by the force of entrepreneurship. Within the realm of scientific knowledge (though only in the poor, limited, and narrow scientific version of equilibrium), we could place "parametric prices", which, assuming all relevant information is given, reflect the terms on which the different alternatives are offered, and to which each actor must passively adjust his behavior. Lange's great mistake stems from his belief that parametric prices can incorporate the information market prices contain. Yet, Lange has the incredible audacity to claim Mises commits the error Lange himself is guilty of when he states:

> Professor Mises seems to have confused prices in the narrower sense, i.e. the exchange ratio of commodities on a market, with prices in the wider sense of "terms on which alternatives are offered." As, in consequence of public ownership of the means of production, there is in a socialist economy no market on which capital goods are actually exchanged, there are obviously no prices of capital goods in the sense of exchange ratios on a market. And hence Professor Mises argues, there is no index of alternatives available in the sphere of capital goods. But this confusion is based on a confusion of 'price' in the narrower sense with 'price' in the wider sense of an index of alternatives. It is only in the latter sense that 'prices' are indispensable for allocation of resources, *and on the basis of the technical possibilities of transformation of one commodity into another*, they are also *given* in a socialist economy.[45]

Lange's confusion is evident, for he believes parametric prices in a socialist economy would (due to the corresponding technical possibilities of transformation, that is, "known" production functions) incorporate information identical to that which would emerge in a market economy. In other words, Lange confuses parametric prices with market prices. With his usual perspicacity, Israel M. Kirzner has expanded on this point even further and has drawn attention to Lange's cardinal error: his assumption that the market tends toward equilibrium by a process throughout which prices perform an unchanging parametric function, such that during the entire process, all economic agents view market prices as given, simply adapt passively to them, and stand no chance of changing them. Hence, Lange is sadly mistaken in his interpretive model of the market, since in the real market, it is not the parametric function of prices which gives them their key role, but instead their *nonparametric* function, which is embodied in the fact that entrepreneurs constantly discover disparities in prices and act to seize the resulting profit opportunities by buying and selling, and therefore continually modifying and creating these prices *ex novo*.[46] Therefore, market prices are "nonparametric", in the sense that they provide information about existing disparities, create an incentive to buy and sell, and ultimately, undergo continual modifications as a consequence of the exercise and force of entrepreneurship. Economic agents do not behave in a passive or reactive manner, but rather in a typically entrepreneurial, that is, proactive, manner: they remain constantly alert in order to discover, generate and take advantage of all new profit opportunities. Prices are not a given to which people adapt. On the contrary, it is people who are constantly acting, creating prices and modifying them. Furthermore, only this entrepreneurial (and nonparametric) function of prices leads to the discovery of existing maladjustments in the behavior of those in society and triggers a general process or tendency toward social coordination. Hence, it is clearly absurd to hold, as Lange does, that the nonparametric function of prices in a market economy, a role which necessarily depends upon the free exercise of entrepreneurship and alone sparks the coordinating tendencies of the social process, can be simulated in a system in which, by definition, free entrepreneurship has been totally eliminated and prices are viewed only from a parametric standpoint.[47]

## 5 CRITICAL ANALYSIS OF LANGE'S CLASSIC MODEL

### A Preliminary Clarification of Terminology

We shall now describe and then critically analyze Lange's "competitive solution" model. Nevertheless, we must first make a terminological clarification. Indeed, as we saw in the last section, it makes sense to describe Lange's "solution" as "competitive" only if one is referring to the awkward and narrow meaning "competition" conveys in the paradoxically named "perfect competition" model. In other words, Lange's solution is only competitive in the sense that it involves no competition, since competition is conceived only in terms of the static situation which the neoclassical model of general equilibrium describes. The same can be said for Lange's and his followers' use of the expression "market socialism". Here the word "market" does not refer to a real market, that is, a social process which the force of entrepreneurship drives and which has the general features that were explained in detail in Chapter 2 of this book. On the contrary, the term alludes to an entire series of passive behaviors displayed by economic agents. All creative exercise of entrepreneurship is ruled out, and all information is assumed available to the agents. In short, the classic model of "market" or "competitive" socialism which Lange and his followers developed incorporates these terms precisely because this model rests on neoclassical–Walrasian economic theory, in which the concepts of "market" and "competition" are emptied of their meaning and are unconnected with the real-life essence and nature of these institutions. Now that we have made this brief terminological clarification, let us take a detailed look at Lange's classic model as he developed it in the original version of his article, "On the economic theory of socialism".[48]

## A Description of the Model

Lange views the neoclassical theory of prices and perfect competition as the ideal theoretical foundation for the socialist system, and hence he begins his proposal with a detailed review of the typical elements of economic equilibrium theory as textbooks usually explain them. According to the neoclassical paradigm, in the model of "perfect" competition, equilibrium is reached whenever the three following conditions are met: first, "subjectively" speaking, all individuals who participate in the economic system must achieve their "maximum" at market prices; second, "objectively" speaking, the supply and demand for each good and service must be identical at equilibrium prices; and third, the income of all consumers must be equal to the income derived from the services of their productive factors.

As is well known, the first condition is satisfied whenever consumers maximize their utility and producers their profits, which in turn requires that consumers equalize weighted marginal utility, with respect to prices, for all consumer goods and services, and that producers make weighted marginal productivity ratios equal to prices for all factors of production and produce a volume at which a product's marginal cost is equal to its price (or marginal revenue). Moreover, at the industry or sector level, if we assume there is complete freedom of entry and exit, the price of a product will be equal to the average costs of production. If we take into account that consumers' income will be determined by the prices of productive-factor services and that supply and demand must always remain equal, it is possible to determine, via a typically Walrasian process of *tâtonnement* (or trial and error), the set of prices necessary to clear the market. In this process, if the quantities supplied differ from those demanded, competition among buyers and sellers will modify prices until the equilibrium point is attained.[49] After furnishing this explanation of the manner in which equilibrium is "theoretically" and "practically" reached in a "capitalist system", Lange tries to show that it could be reached in a socialist community by a similar procedure.

According to Lange, the first condition, which we have labeled "subjective", would be met in the case of consumers by permitting them to maximize their utility in a fully competitive market of consumer goods and services, just as was explained for the capitalist system. Nevertheless, producers would no longer be allowed to act to maximize profits, but instead they would be subject to two rules; the central planning bureau would coercively impose these rules and monitor producers' compliance with them. The two rules are designed to simulate the results of producers' maximizing behavior in the market, and thus, they involve replacing the principle of profit maximization with each of the results this principle yields within the perfect competition model.

The first rule requires producers to choose the combination of factors which minimizes the average costs of production. The second rule, which also applies to the managers of the different factories, requires them to produce the volume at which marginal costs equal prices. Overall production at the sectoral level would also be determined by the second rule, but instead of the managers of each company, it would be the managers of each sector who would be required to comply, and hence to increase or decrease the overall production of each industry accordingly. Therefore, Lange maintains, compliance with the second rule at the level of each sector would perform the same function that the principle of free entry and exit performs in a competitive market.

In Lange's model, both the prices of consumer goods and services and wages are determined by the market, and the central planning agency sets only the prices of the factors of production. In this sense, all the central planning agency needs to do initially is to establish some prices for the factors of production, and it can choose these prices intuitively or arbitrarily. Company and sector managers, as well as consumers and workers, make all of their decisions passively, that is, they key them to the above prices and apply the above rules, and in this way the quantity of each good and service to be demanded and supplied is determined. If, with respect to some production goods, the quantities demanded and supplied do not coincide, the central planning agency has to review and modify the prices by a process of "trial and error" which comes to a halt at the moment the final equilibrium price is reached, in other words, supply and demand have been equalized. Hence, the prices the central planning bureau establishes for productive factors are of a merely parametric nature: they determine the passive behavior of economic agents, who must simply adapt to that data, and they objectively generate certain indicators (product surpluses or shortages), which unequivocally lead the central coercion agency to modify prices to the extent and in the direction necessary to achieve equilibrium. In short, the central planning agency takes the place of the market with respect to the allocation of capital goods, and the socialist system can formally reach the equilibrium of the perfect competition model via the same trial and error procedure Walras devised for the competitive system, the procedure Taylor had already proposed as a solution for the socialist system eight years earlier.

**Two Interpretations of Lange's Model**

At this point, we could make two different interpretations of Lange's model: both a narrow and a broad interpretation. We could view the model as an attempt at a solution to the secondary problem (which we described as "computational" or merely of algebraic calculation) of solving the Walrasian system of equilibrium equations, which was discussed when we studied the mathematical solution. According to this interpretation, the chief virtue of Lange's model is that it avoids the need of solving such a system, either by hand or with the help of computer procedures. However, because it assumes that all the information necessary to formulate and compute the problem or system of equations has already been generated and given (that is, already exists somewhere in the market), Lange's model would not solve the fundamental problem raised by Mises (that is, that it is impossible for the information necessary for economic calculation to be created and transmitted in the absence of private ownership of the means of production and the free exercise of entrepreneurship).

We could also view Lange's model as an attempt to solve the basic problem voiced by Mises, in which case we see that since the free exercise of entrepreneurship is prevented in highly significant areas of the market, the information essential to economic calculation is not generated, and the model fails to answer the Misesian challenge. As we shall see later,[50] certain almost irrefutable evidence indicates that Lange considered his model a mere computational device (which was inevitable, since he never really comprehended Mises's challenge, mainly due to the distorted view of the economic world he had obtained from the neoclassical–Walrasian tools that had so hypnotized him). Nevertheless, because others who have interpreted the work of Lange and his disciples have deemed the model an attempt to resolve the fundamental problem Mises raised concerning the creation and transmission of information, we shall now develop our critical analysis of Lange's model from the broadest possible perspective; that is, we shall view it as an attempt to solve the true problem Mises expressed.

**Critical Analysis of the Broadest Interpretation of Lange's Model**

Before we proceed further, it should be noted that Lange's contribution incorporates and combines a series of elements (the trial and error method, the setting of prices in terms of marginal costs, instructions from the central planning bureau to managers and so on), almost all of which, as we have seen, socialist theorists had already proposed, though in an isolated manner. Thus, Lange's main innovation was simply to have linked them more logically with the neoclassical–Walrasian model as the common denominator. In this sense, we could repeat here all of the comments and critical observations that have already been made concerning the various components of the different solutions to the problem of socialist economic calculation, components that have already been analyzed and which Lange incorporates into his model to a greater or lesser extent. Moreover, the reader should now have no trouble realizing that because Lange's model entails the prevention of the free exercise of entrepreneurship in essential spheres of the market and at different levels, this model cannot possibly constitute a solution to the problem of economic calculation in a socialist system. If the free exercise of entrepreneurship is prohibited in a fundamental area (for instance, that of capital goods), entrepreneurship is not permitted to create, uncover and transmit the basic (practical, subjective, dispersed and inarticulable) information necessary for individuals to calculate rationally and adapt their behavior in a coordinated manner. Nonetheless, it is important that some particularly significant critical comments are made in light of Lange's model, comments that will illustrate in different instances the application of our essential argument to this specific model.

**The impossibility of assembling the list of capital goods**
First, we should ask: How can the central planning agency parametrically set prices for capital goods, the type, number, quantity, quality and characteristics of which are unknown to the very agents involved in the process of production? A capital good is any *intermediate stage* in a process of production, as subjectively viewed by the actor involved. In other words, anything the actor deems useful for achieving a goal (unless it consists merely of services provided by labor) is a capital good. That is, what constitutes a capital good will be recognizable only to the actor involved in the process, who will discover this information gradually and entrepreneurially, and thus its subjective, practical, dispersed and inarticulable nature will render it impossible for the central planning agency to possess. Furthermore, let it not be said that experience, that is, whatever appears to have constituted a capital good in the past, will assist one in assembling the corresponding lists. For the concept of capital good is subjective and also strictly *prospective*; that is, the actor determines it depending upon how he believes events will unfold in the future. Hence, the fact that something seems to have worked in the past does not guarantee that it will accomplish the same goal in the future. On the contrary, only those goods which the actor subjectively considers potentially useful, in light of their specific features (their particular level of quality, their availability at a proper time and in a suitable location and so on), for achieving a certain end or completing a certain project will be capital goods.

However, the issue is not simply that the central coercion agency cannot possibly acquire the dispersed information necessary to identify existing capital goods. It is also that this information will not even be effectively discovered or created, to the extent that ordinary economic agents themselves are unable to freely exercise their entrepreneurship. Indeed, if economic agents cannot act entrepreneurially, that is, if they cannot think up new ends, pursue new profit opportunities, and make the most of them, then profit will not act as an incentive, and consequently, vital practical information about ends and means, information which would emerge in a free market economy, will not even be created.

This first argument alone renders Lange's model theoretically and practically impossible, and therefore the model cannot in any way represent a solution to the economic calculation problem raised by Mises. In practice, as Hayek indicates in the extensive reply to Lange he published in 1940, the fixing of parametric prices by the central planning board will be purely arbitrary not only in terms of the figures chosen, but also (and this is much worse) in terms of the type and number of goods to which a figure will be set. Also, the fixing of such prices will yield a series of crude, uniform categories of poorly named "capital goods" believed to have been considered as such in the past, and these categories cannot incorporate the necessary distinctions between different, specific circumstances of time, place, quality and so on. These are precisely the distinctions which, when perceived subjectively and entrepreneurially, make the goods we observe in the outside world capital goods, and thus bestow upon them their most intimate, subtle, and essential characteristic.[51]

### The complete arbitrariness of the time period for which parametric prices are fixed

Second, not only will the "parametric prices" established and the list of "capital goods" drawn up be arbitrary, but the time period during which the planning agency considers that "prices" should remain constant will be totally arbitrary as well. This is one of the points on which Lange's ambiguity is most evident, since in one place he states that price readjustment will always take place "at the end of the accounting period", and in another place he indicates in passing that prices will be readjusted "constantly".[52] In both cases, the period will be totally arbitrary, because the planning bureau will lack the information entrepreneurs possess in a truly competitive economy, information which permits them to modify prices at the juncture and for the period they consider most appropriate and conducive to the achievement of their ends. The central planning agency will never have access to this information, so if the authorities choose the accounting period, it will undoubtedly prove too long, and if the decisions are *ad hoc*, according to an appraisal of the course of events, they will still be made on a purely arbitrary basis, given that the central agency cannot possess the first-hand knowledge economic agents possess concerning these events.

### The lack of a true market for labor and consumer goods and services
Third, even though Lange states that a completely free and competitive market would necessarily exist for consumer goods and services, as well as for labor, one is left with the impression that this "market" would only be nominally "free" and "competitive".⁵³ Indeed, a truly competitive market for consumer goods and services requires, not only on the side of demand, but also on that of supply, the totally unfettered presence of true entrepreneurs or free actors. If coercion crops up on either side, the market ceases to be competitive. Thus, one cannot fathom how the managers of the socialist system, who are not true entrepreneurs, since they cannot freely seek the profit or benefit (defined in subjective terms) they deem most fitting, could generate the information which is constantly created in a capitalist system concerning the continual launching of new consumer goods and services, the improvement of existing goods, changes in quality, in commercial distribution, and in physical location, advertising systems and so on. Therefore, consumers would be obliged to choose from the restricted "menu" of consumer goods and services the socialist managers offered them. Without a doubt, market socialists, and Lange in particular, speak excessively of a "competitive market for consumer goods" (and even overuse the term "consumer sovereignty" as applied to a socialist system), because in a socialist system, there is no more sovereignty or freedom than, for instance, that enjoyed by a prisoner who considers himself free whenever he restricts his actions to the sphere permitted by the four walls of his cell.⁵⁴

### The inanity of the "rules" proposed by Lange
Fourth, Lange's rules of adopting the combination of factors which minimizes average costs and producing the volume at which prices equal marginal costs are impossible to apply. The fact that Lange considered his "rules" obvious and feasible is another sign of the damaging effect exerted on his education by neoclassical cost theory, and in particular by the very widespread belief that costs are objective and determined by functions that involve "given" information. Nevertheless, as was firmly established in Chapter 2 of this book, costs are merely subjective assessments of the value an actor attaches to those ends he forgoes when he chooses, undertakes, or commits to a certain course of action. Costs are subjective valuations of lost alternatives, and hence, they constitute typical entrepreneurial information which each actor continually estimates or creates whenever he is able to freely exercise his entrepreneurial function and alertness. Moreover, this information shares all the characteristics that we have already analyzed with respect to entrepreneurial information, especially a subjective, practical, dispersed and inarticulable nature. It is clear that if

costs are not given (that is, if cost functions do not exist), but instead are subjectively estimated through constant trial and error in each course of action, then industry managers can hardly be instructed to comply with the above rules, and still less can the central planning bureau objectively monitor such compliance.

Lange's proposal simply reveals that, in practice, neoclassical cost theory has failed to successfully incorporate the subjectivist revolution, except in purely nominal terms, and in fact continues rooted in the old, outdated objectivism of David Ricardo and Alfred Marshall.[55] Therefore, it should not surprise us that James Buchanan, though perhaps he exaggerates slightly, has asserted that the entire controversy surrounding the possibility of economic calculation in socialist economies stems from a lack of understanding on the part of socialist theorists regarding the true, subjective nature of costs.[56] The late Jack Wiseman, in a noteworthy article published in 1959, in which he deals with the problem costs pose in socialist economic planning, stresses their subjective nature and defines them as the valuation of opportunities lost when choosing a certain course of action over other potential plans and projects. Only the person who undertakes the corresponding projects can make this subjective appraisal, which is embodied in an often implicit decision whether or not to go ahead with a certain plan. This process never yields information which makes it possible to objectively set prices by making them equal to cost data established objectively beforehand. Hence, Wiseman concludes that Lange's rules cannot serve as any guide for the managers of socialist industries, and thus, that any similar rule will be arbitrary, in terms of both specific content and the efforts of the central planning bureau to practically and effectively monitor compliance.[57]

Therefore, it is of very little use to instruct the managers of the corresponding factories and companies to employ that combination of factors for which average costs are lowest. Given the subjective nature of costs, this rule is devoid of content and is tantamount to ordering managers to "do the best they can", but without allowing them to simultaneously perform those entrepreneurial actions which alone can guarantee the desired result of reducing costs.[58] In fact, in a market economy in which entrepreneurship can be freely exercised, entrepreneurs constantly get new ideas, intuitions and so on, regarding the creation of new combinations of capital goods and new, cheaper and more efficient characteristics which can be entrepreneurially tested, and if successful, give rise to the corresponding entrepreneurial profits and the gradual elimination of competitors. If they want to survive, these competitors are forced to introduce the improvements and innovations which have already been discovered and successfully tested. In the system Lange proposes, this entire process is absent: there is no possibility of freely exercising entrepreneurship, and thus information on procedures for reducing the costs of capital goods is not even generated. Moreover, even if it were generated by accident, it would be irrelevant, since the central planning bureau establishes parametric prices for these goods beforehand, and the only potential solution available to a manager who, by a fluke, had an entrepreneurial idea would be to attempt to convince the central planning authorities that the good in question could be produced more economically and effectively in another way, and thus that its price should be lowered. Naturally, this would be an impossible task, not only due to the difficulties involved in transmitting practical, dispersed, subjective, and inarticulable knowledge, an obstacle that has already been considered repeatedly, but also because, by definition and according to Lange's model, the central planning agency only reduces prices when it has become clear, *a posteriori*, that excess production exists, but not when a more or less "bright" or "original" manager believes it would be better to do things differently in the future.[59]

All of these arguments apply to Lange's second rule as well, as does the argument Mises and Hayek had already developed to counter the attempted use of "marginal cost criteria" by the German theorists Heimann and Polanyi, who proposed a model of socialist organization based on a set of "competitive monopolies or trusts". Let us recall that the marginal cost rule is pointless, because it is not costs which determine prices, but in any case, prices which determine costs. Therefore, the rule is ambiguous, as is all circular reasoning. Furthermore, one of the most important components of cost is the rate of depreciation on a capital good, so to calculate cost, one must know the future replacement value of the capital good. It would be impossible to obtain this information in the system Lange proposes, since this value would depend upon either the arbitrarily chosen parametric price to be established in the future, or the future result of the arbitrary process of adjustment based on the trial and error method suggested by Lange.

In addition, Lange writes of "marginal costs" as if they were independent of the time period considered by the manager of the industry or company in question. Indeed, the literature of market socialist theorists contains a radical distinction between the short-term rule (though the short term is not defined) of equating prices with marginal costs and a theory of long-term investment in which increases and decreases in equipment are explicitly taken into account. However, if the goal is to establish a practical, effective rule, and a planning board is to monitor compliance, then it will be necessary to expressly indicate the time period to be taken into account in each specific case, so that it becomes possible to know, with respect to this period, which factors will be fixed and which will be variable, and thus, the corresponding marginal costs can be calculated. Obviously, there is no objective, rational criterion for deciding which time period should be chosen, and this constitutes one more sign that the rule of Lange's which we are discussing cannot feasibly be imposed.[60]

In short, with respect to costs, Lange's entire proposal exudes a static conception of the economy, in which it is presumed that no changes occur and that all information necessary to calculate costs is already available. If these two conditions were present, then Lange's rules could be applied, if we could assume no future changes would affect the given costs. Nevertheless, in the real world, in which information is not given and costs are subjective and change constantly, neither of the two rules formulated by Lange can be used to make socialism possible.[61]

### The theoretical impossibility of the trial and error method

Fifth, Lange attaches so much importance in his model to the application of the trial and error method that we have no choice but to return to this topic. Though the arguments we have already offered are certainly sufficient to show that Lange's solution is unfeasible, we are obliged to again voice each and every one of the nine criticisms of the trial and error method which were expressed in detail in the last chapter.

Specifically, let us recall that the rule of observing the state of inventories or stock to identify any surplus or shortage and to modify prices accordingly is deceptively simplistic, because there is no objective reference point to guide such an observation, nor is it possible to generate or transmit the information which would be necessary to modify prices in the appropriate direction. In fact, neither a shortage nor a surplus of a product can be objectively discerned by merely consulting certain statistical figures concerning stock. Instead, regardless of the calculation or figure reflected by statistics, a shortage or surplus exists when, depending upon the specific circumstances of a case, the actor subjectively judges that one exists. A product surplus may not be such, if one subjectively considers a longer time period or expects an increase in demand to occur during that period. Under these circumstances, it would be a grave error for the central planning agency to reduce parametric prices, with the idea that doing so would bring them closer to the hypothetical equilibrium prices which would form in the market. Likewise, an apparent shortage may not be such, if one anticipates a drop in demand or, even if mistaken, one believes it advisable to cope by focusing on innovation or the use of substitutes, rather than by increasing the price. As the concepts of "surplus" and "shortage" are purely subjective, they can only emerge within the context of an entrepreneurial action which is freely performed, and they constitute a bit of subjective, practical, dispersed and inarticulable information which therefore cannot be transmitted to the central planning agency. Furthermore, as we already know, if managers are unable to exercise their entrepreneurship with complete freedom, the information crucial to rational economic calculation will not even be generated at their level. Hence, the decisions of the central planning board to raise prices when product shortages are "observed" and to lower prices when product surpluses are "perceived" are purely arbitrary and in no way permit rational economic calculation.

In the real economic world, there are no supply and demand functions which mysteriously and objectively indicate the quantities supplied and demanded at each price and which permit any outside observer to determine, by simply observing the level of stock, how to modify the price in order to reach the equilibrium price. Prices do not result from the intersection of supply and demand curves or functions, but instead they spring from a series of human interactions driven by the force of entrepreneurship, by which actors constantly try to forecast future conditions and direct their actions toward making the most of these conditions.

Moreover, in the equipment or capital-goods sector, Lange's proposed method is, in many cases, theoretically inapplicable at its root, as is invariably true for the typical equipment good, which is specially contracted for and produced in small quantities, as opposed to a standardized capital good produced on a massive scale. We do not understand how Lange could believe it conceivable, even hypothetically, that in the case of equipment goods such as large industrial premises, sizable real estate properties, blast furnaces, shipyards, special vessels and so on, one could objectively identify any surplus or shortage of the good in question simply by observing changes in inventories. If the decision to modify the price is postponed for the number of years necessary to accurately assess the degree and duration of the observed scarcity or surplus, then by the time the appropriate decisions are made, it will undoubtedly be too late. However, if they are made hastily, based on the partial intuitions of the central planning authorities, grave and irreversible errors will most probably be committed.[62]

Finally, Lange's model allows for two possibilities: either all transactions are brought to a halt while the central planning board determines whether surpluses or shortages exist, which prices should be modified, and the direction and amount of the modifications, or transactions are permitted at "false prices". In the first instance, which we analyzed when we studied planometric models, all economic activity stops, and during this period, the system loses all its flexibility and potential for calculation. Lange does not appear to have thought of this possibility, but what he did not realize is that if transactions are allowed at false prices, a series of distorted signals will be sent to the whole system and will prevent the achievement of the equilibrium Lange so desires. This problem does not arise in a real market economy, in which discoordinated transactions actually provide an incentive for entrepreneurs, always desirous of obtaining profits, to continuously discover and expose this discoordination. Without freedom for all economic agents to exercise entrepreneurship and unconstrainedly pursue profits, there is no guarantee that a general, coordinating process which adjusts the behavior of all participants in the system will be established. This appears to be something that Lange never understood.

**The arbitrary fixing of the interest rate**
Sixth, it is important to point out that the fixing of the interest rate (understood as the price of present goods with respect to future goods, or the ratio between the value given to present consumption and that attached to future consumption) in Lange's socialist model will be purely arbitrary. Savers or suppliers of present goods will be prevented from making a rational economic decision about the allocation of their resources between present and future consumption, due to both the restricted "menu" of present goods the system offers them and the impossibility of having at their future disposal consumer goods and services as plentiful and diverse as those generated by a system in which entrepreneurship can be freely exercised to discover and satisfy an increasing number of needs. Moreover, we are assuming the central coercion agency does not insist on implementing "forced saving" policies, as it usually does, to the widespread detriment of current consumers.

The problem is even more serious, if that is possible, from the perspective of demanders of present goods. It is the managers of the different socialist companies who must request present goods to carry out their investment plans. They must employ labor and obtain the natural resources and capital goods necessary to manufacture the different stages of capital goods with which the consumer goods and services that will be available in the future will be produced. Here, again, we clearly see the double problem which lies at the theoretical heart of our thesis. As these managers cannot freely exercise their entrepreneurship, they will not even create the practical information they need to rationally allocate their resources. In other words, because they cannot reap the profits of their respective entrepreneurial projects, they will not even generate the necessary ideas. Furthermore, it will be up to the central planning body, specifically the state bank in charge of distributing the corresponding funds, to decide which manager will ultimately be loaned the funds, along with the amount and conditions of the loan. This means the final decision will be in the hands of people who will lack the practical, first-hand information necessary to make it (not only because this information is not even generated at the managers' level, but also because its basically subjective, practical, dispersed and inarticulable nature would prevent its transmission to the central coercion agency even if it were generated). The economic calculation performed at the time the decisions are made about how the central planning agency will distribute the funds will therefore be purely arbitrary. In short, Lange's model prevents the existence of a true capital market, and particularly a market for securities which represent the ownership of the companies. As Ludwig Lachmann has indicated,[63] this undoubtedly constitutes one of the most serious defects of Lange's entire model.

**Ignorance of the typical behavior of bureaucratic agencies**
Seventh and last, Lange's model cannot work because it does not allow for the real future behavior of the different economic agents, especially of the managers of the nationalized companies and of the bureaucrats in charge of the central planning body, within the institutional framework established in the model itself. In Lange's model, economic calculation is theoretically impossible, since the model does not permit the existence of true entrepreneurs as we defined them in Chapter 2, and we have now examined this problem from several angles. Nevertheless, we have not yet given any consideration to the type of specific behaviors which Lange's model would foster among the different economic and social agents it envisages. Thus, the task before us is to incorporate into our analysis the viewpoint of the "public choice" school, which has undergone extensive development and focuses particularly on the analysis of the processes of human interaction in political and bureaucratic contexts in which, by definition, coercive institutional relationships predominate. With this in mind, we should take into account the following criticism that James Buchanan leveled against Lange for not having examined one of the most important facets of the problem, that is, how economic agents would behave within the institutional framework he had designed:

> By the third decade of this century, economic theory had shifted to a discipline of applied mathematics, not catallaxy. Even markets came to be viewed as "computing devices" and "mechanisms," that may or may not secure idealized allocative results. Markets were not, at base, viewed as exchange institutions, out of which results emerge from complex exchange interaction. Only in this modern paradigm of economic theory could the *total absurdity* of the idealized socialist structure of Lange–Lerner have been taken at all seriously, as indeed it was (and, sadly, still is) by practicing economists. We may well ask why economists did not stop to ask the questions about why socialist managers would behave in terms of the idealized rules. *Where are the economic eunuchs to be found to operate the system?*[64]

The foundations of the public choice school were undoubtedly laid by Mises himself, when he conceived of economics as a very broad science concerned with theoretically studying all processes related to human action. In this way, Mises led researchers to begin applying economic analysis to human actions which take place outside the market, understood in the strict, traditional sense, in political and bureaucratic spheres, for instance. Within this context, we must consider Mises's key, pioneering work on bureaucracy, which was published in 1944, and in which he shows, for the first time, that bureaucracy must invariably emerge in all social spheres in which the free entrepreneurial pursuit of profit is prohibited.[65] In this work, Mises also explores many of the points which were later researched in greater depth by, among others, the Hungarian economist János Kornai, in his economic analysis of the real functioning of former Eastern bloc economies. It is enlightening to read Kornai's own wording of the conclusions he draws about Lange's model from the standpoint of the public choice school, conclusions which involve the behavior of both the central planning body and the managers of the corresponding companies. Kornai writes:

> *Lange's model is based on erroneous assumptions concerning the nature of the "planners."* The people at his Central Planning Board are reincarnations of Plato's philosophers, embodiments of unity, unselfishness, and wisdom. They are satisfied with doing nothing else but strictly enforcing the "Rule," adjusting prices to excess demand. *Such an unworldly bureaucracy never existed in the past and will never exist in the future.* Political bureaucracies have inner conflicts reflecting the divisions of society and the diverse pressures of various social groups. They pursue their own individual and group interests, including the interests of the particular specialized agency to which they belong. Power creates an irresistible temptation to make use of it. *A bureaucrat must be interventionist because that is his role in society; it is dictated by his situation* . . . Lange's model is based on an equally erroneous assumption concerning the behaviour of the firm. He expects the firm to follow the Rule designed by the system engineers. But society is not a parlor game where the inventor of the game can arbitrarily invent rules. Organizations and leaders who identify themselves with their organizations have deeply ingrained drives: survival, growth, expansion of the organization, internal peace within the organization, power and prestige, the creation of circumstances that make the achievement of all these goals easier. An artificial incentive scheme, supported by rewards and penalties, can be super-imposed. A scheme may support some of the unavowed motives just mentioned. But if it gets into conflict with them, vacillation and ambiguity may follow. The organization's leaders will try to influence those who imposed the incentive scheme or will try to evade the rules . . . What emerges from this procedure *is not a successfully simulated market, but the usual conflict between the regulator and the firms regulated by the bureaucracy.*[66]

Hayek had also identified these problems in his 1940 response to Lange. In fact, Hayek showed that Lange's model would invariably lead to the worst form of bureaucracy, since the central planning agency would be obliged to monitor managers' compliance with rules for which compliance could not be objectively monitored. Everywhere the system would be rife with arbitrary decisions from the coercion agency and "perverse" behaviors from managers intent on demonstrating, at least on paper, their compliance with the established rules, and also on assuring themselves of all sorts of corrupt practices, connections and support within the planning body.[67]

Furthermore, Lange himself acknowledged these problems at least partially and even came to assert that "the real danger of socialism is that of a bureaucratization of economic life".[68] However, Lange reveals that he does not understand the real extent of this danger when, in the next line, he adds that in any case, the danger would be no greater than the one bureaucratization poses in a capitalist system, in which the entrepreneurial managers who make the decisions are practically civil servants, since they are not usually the owners of the capital and answer to virtually no one. It would be difficult to come up with a narrower and more erroneous conception of capitalism. All real market economies are characterized by a complete freedom to exercise entrepreneurship, regardless of who exercises it in the position of leader at any specific time or under any specific conditions (stockholders, managers and so on), a matter which is as dependent on historical circumstances as it is theoretically irrelevant. In contrast, in a socialist regime, everyone is forcibly banned from exercising entrepreneurship at least in the area of capital goods, and the making of fundamental decisions is separated from the only people who, in a context of entrepreneurial freedom, could create or discover the information necessary to make them correctly.

In any case, Lange passed down his preoccupation with the bureaucratization of socialism to his disciples, who produced an entire body of literature on the design and establishment of "bonus and incentive systems". Their efforts have not resolved the problems raised, and in practice, such systems have resulted in nothing but utter failure, despite the great hopes they inspired at the time, hopes practically no one remembers today.[69] The bonus and incentive system designed to make socialism workable is itself unworkable from a theoretical standpoint, since it would require that the central planning agency in charge of providing the incentives and awarding the bonuses have a priori access to knowledge which it cannot possibly come to possess. Indeed, the idea that a third party can furnish incentives and bonuses involves the implicit assumption that this party will know, before issuing the reward or fine, whether the new production system has been successfully introduced, the new good or service successfully produced, or the rule successfully followed. Nevertheless, the central planning board cannot possibly acquire this knowledge, for the reasons we have already repeatedly mentioned in this book. The coordination of maladjusted behaviors in society cannot be objectively and directly observed from the outside, but constitutes a process about which one can only formally theorize, by indicating that the emergence of an entrepreneurial profit will reveal that such coordination, which is not directly observable, has occurred. Moreover, if the coordinating effects in each specific situation are not directly discernible and only, given the case, manifest themselves to outside observers after very lengthy time lags, and only in general terms and in a very vague, partial and imperfect manner, it is obvious that the entire system of bonuses and incentives which presupposes objective knowledge of the events which give rise to them can be neither theoretically nor practically useful for simulating the functioning of the entrepreneurial process, which is driven by the desire for profit, an aspiration which arises in all truly competitive market economies. Furthermore, it is theoretically absurd to award a bonus based on the assumption that a bit of particularly valuable information has already been created, since it was known that the information was acquired *before* the granting of the bonus.[70] In other words, the point is not to reward "services rendered", but to provide powerful motivation for people to create and discover, in the future, necessary information which today has not yet been acquired (and since it is not yet known, no one even imagines that it could exist, nor the value it would have, and thus a related bonus system cannot possibly be devised). Therefore, we need a system of incentives and bonuses that are to be granted in the future in all cases in which actions exert a coordinating effect, even though the objective result of this adjustment or coordination may never be clearly evident to a third party, or may only be known very partially and following a very prolonged period of time. This is something which can only be provided by a competitive economy, with private ownership of the means of production, and in which people enjoy complete freedom to exercise entrepreneurship. Under these conditions, as we already know, the subjective end of each action constitutes the *motive*, or the *profit* the action is expected to yield, and this end justifies the action, gives rise to the creation of the necessary information, and if achieved, becomes real profit for the actor, and the subjective effect of this profit cannot be equaled by any artificial system of bonuses, regardless of how well-designed or perfect it is.

**Other Comments on Lange's Classic Model**

Our critical examination of Lange's classic model would be incomplete without a review of the statements he makes on pages 89 and 106 of the article that concerns us.

On page 89, Lange maintains that the knowledge of central planners concerning the economic system would invariably be far superior to that of any individual, private entrepreneur, and thus that the process of adjustment by the state trial and error method would be much faster and more effective than the adjustment process in the capitalist system. It would be difficult to find a poorer understanding of the workings of the capitalist system than that which Lange betrays when he expresses this idea in all seriousness in his article. Though the central planning agency may perhaps have an overview of the economy which is more accurate than that of any individual entrepreneur, the problem is actually a very different one, that is, that the central planning body will never have access to the total volume of dispersed information which the entire network of thousands and thousands of entrepreneurs constantly and spontaneously generate, use, and transmit in the capitalist economic system. Therefore, the issue is not to compare the knowledge of the central planning agency with that of an isolated, individual entrepreneur, but with that generated and used by the entire network of individual entrepreneurs who freely exercise entrepreneurship in a free society. Hence, not only will the adjustment process not be shorter in the socialist system, but it will never be successful, since the planning board cannot possibly acquire the information necessary to move prices toward the hypothetical equilibrium. In any case, we cannot fathom how Lange could come to believe that his adjustment method would necessarily be shorter and more effective than that of a market economy, because according to his model, managers would just passively adapt to the parametric prices of capital goods, and no price could be modified except by the decision of the central agency. In other words, until the necessary information had been received and processed, and the determination had been made of what should be done, managers could not modify their behavior with respect to prices in any way, something which entrepreneurs can do (and do constantly) in a capitalist system, by immediately seizing the profit opportunities they encounter and constantly triggering the adjustment process without any unnecessary time lag.

On page 106, Lange asserts that economic cycles are eliminated in his model. He argues that the "superior information" of the supervisory agency would enable it to react in time to entrepreneurial errors, and thus to prevent the cyclical economic crises which affect market economies. However, if Lange believes the supervisory agency has access to enough information to allow it to opportunely adopt the measures necessary to avert a crisis, then why does he wish to entrust managers with decentralized decision making in very important areas of society (consumer goods, labor, adjustment to parametric prices and so on)? Furthermore, Lange lacks an adequate theory of economic depression, which Mises and

Hayek[71] view as simply the stage in which a productive structure readjusts after being distorted by state interventionism (fiscal, monetary, or of any other type) in the market. From this perspective, depression would be the inevitable reaction of the market to any coercive imposition of an allocation of resources and productive factors that does not correspond with the one consumers freely wish to maintain. This only occurs in a controlled economy in which government aggression (monetary, fiscal, or of another sort) forces widespread malinvestment of resources. From this standpoint, Lange's model would not only fail to prevent the emergence of economic depressions, but it would also invariably cause intense, chronic and widespread malinvestment of society's productive factors and capital goods. Consequently, society would be plunged into a "chronic depression", or a constant malinvestment of productive resources, a phenomenon which has been manifesting itself in the real world, including signs of cyclical deterioration, and has been studied[72] in some detail by theorists from the economies of the former Eastern bloc.[73]

## 6 THE THIRD AND FOURTH STAGES IN LANGE'S SCIENTIFIC LIFE

### The Third Stage: The 1940s

Lange was profoundly stunned by the 1940 article in which Hayek analyzed and criticized, in great detail and point by point, the different elements and implications of Lange's model. As a result, according to Gabriel Temkin,[74] Lange began to experience increasingly serious doubts about his "competitive solution" model, a fact corroborated by the following: first, in his correspondence with Hayek, Lange expressly acknowledged that Hayek had successfully raised a series of essential errors and problems which the model, being purely static, could not solve, and hence, Lange promised that in the months that followed, he would write an article to answer Hayek;[75] second, despite his promise, Lange never wrote the article which in his letter he claimed would answer Hayek's criticism of his model; and third, years later, in 1944, Lange refused to revise his original 1936–37 essay on socialism so it could be published again, and argued that his ideas had changed so substantially in the interim that they required a completely new article, and that he planned to include his new conception of socialism in a special chapter of the economic treatise he had begun writing.[76] Part of the treatise was published, but the eagerly awaited chapter did not appear in it, nor in any of the numerous other works and papers Lange published before his death, with the sole exception of the disappointing 1967 article on "The computer and the market", which will be commented on in detail later.

Thus, it seems clear (and perhaps the most characteristic feature of Lange's thinking in the 1940s) that he, himself, finally realized that his "solution" was no solution at all, since it was purely static. However, Lange did not have the scientific honesty to publicly acknowledge that his model therefore provided no answer to the challenge Mises and Hayek had issued, which had always been "dynamic" in nature. To make matters worse, in the aforementioned letter to Hayek, Lange even refers to a "third line of defense" concerning dynamic problems, a defense Hayek supposedly introduced *ex novo* in his 1940 article. Lange refuses to see that from the very beginning, from Mises's first formulation of it in 1920, the problem had always been exclusively dynamic.

At any rate, what seems plain is that Lange largely abandoned his classic model, and in the very letter to Hayek which we cited above, he recognizes the need to allow free-market processes to operate whenever possible. Nonetheless, he reveals that his obsession with the neoclassical model of perfect competition remains intact when he establishes, as a criterion for permitting market behavior (and thus the abandonment of the parametric price system and the trial and error method employed by the regulatory agency), the requirement that a sufficiently large number of companies operate in each sector (since supposedly, and according to the traditional model of perfect competition, such a circumstance would indicate a close approximation to the "real" competition which exists in the market). From this new perspective on socialism, public ownership of the means of production would have to extend only to the most glaring cases of monopoly, oligopoly, oligopsony and other similar situations.[77]

Even more enlightening, if possible, are the two lectures Lange gave in Chicago in 1942 on "The economic operation of a socialist society"[78]: there he not only attempted to reconcile an extremely broad definition of the market principle with public ownership of the means of production, but he also excluded virtually all mention of perhaps the most characteristic feature of his model of the 1930s, that is, the establishment of parametric prices by the central planning board and the introduction of a trial-and-error method to permit, based on the observation of inventory shortages and surpluses, the modification of these prices, so as to move them toward their "point of equilibrium". Lange continued to base his reasoning exclusively on neoclassical welfare and equilibrium theory, and thus he lacked the theoretical tools necessary to confront the "interesting dynamic problems" which, as he himself admitted, Hayek had raised. Moreover, in these lectures, Lange maintained that the essential principle for establishing prices in the socialist market should be to fix them in terms of the costs incurred, including not only private costs, but also the "social costs" each company incurs, and that both types of costs are "objective" in nature. The fact that Lange failed to realize that this principle is theoretically and practically inadmissible and that therefore, he derived no benefit from the criticisms he had received from Hayek on the issue is also disheartening.

However, perhaps the most fundamental shift in Lange's focus during this period is reflected in his 1943 article, "Economic foundations of democracy in Poland", in which he expressly defends the socialization of only the most important and strategic industries (including the banking and transportation sectors). Furthermore, Lange is on his guard against the special privileges which would be granted to these state monopolies, and he considers such privileges very dangerous to the Polish democratic system. Private ownership of the means of production should in any case be maintained for farms, craft businesses, and small and medium-sized industries, since "this would make it possible to sustain the flexibility and capacity for adaptation which only exclusively private enterprise allows".[79]

### The Fourth Stage: From the Second World War until His Death. The Abandonment of the Market, and Praise and Justification of the Stalinist System

Hayek's healthy influence on Lange would not last long. Beginning with the Second World War, Lange's admission to the Polish Communist Party, and his greater involvement in the politics of his country, Lange progressively abandoned the market as part of his conception of socialism, and this gradual change in his views culminated in his theoretical and practical justification of the Stalinist economic model, which was being applied in the Soviet Union, and which this country had decided to impose on its recently acquired "satellites" as well.[80]

Lange's abandonment of the competitive solution and of the market socialism model reached its peak in the 1953 work in which he praises Stalin's economic system, in terms of both theory and practice.[81]

As Kowalik explains, Lange's change of opinion may have been heavily influenced by the idea that the "war economy" model Stalin dictatorially imposed from above would make it easier to force a rapid "industrialization" of the economic system and an "efficient" mobilization of all resources toward the socialist ideal (all of which constitutes a definite betrayal of the democratic, "liberal" spirit Lange had flaunted earlier). Nevertheless, the views that Lange held in the final decades of his life were simply the natural result of the theoretical equilibrium model, upon which he had based his entire conception of socialism. Indeed, as already explained, the Marxist ideal could be reinterpreted as the conscious desire to forcibly impose the nirvana of equilibrium on all social spheres and at all levels, thus forcing a utopia while destroying the real mechanisms which, driven by entrepreneurship, make the processes of social coordination possible. Lange had two options: he could accept *in toto* the challenge of Mises and Hayek and give up his arsenal of theoretical equilibrium arguments, comprehend the true functioning of the market, and hence, abandon his socialist ideal built on public ownership of the means of production; or, he could maintain the ideal of equilibrium at any cost, back down on the introduction of competitive criteria (which were inexorably leading him toward the abandonment of socialism), and take refuge in a utopian equilibrium model which could be most effectively implemented via the systematic exercise of Stalinist coercion. In 1956–57, Lange refused permission for the publication of a Polish translation of his classic 1936–37 work because, as Kowalik states, "he did not want to lend his support to the 'socialist freemarketers'".[82] Lange's abandonment of the competitive solution and the 180-degree turn in his model of socialism were complete.

In light of these considerations, it should come as no surprise that in the last paper in which Lange deals with socialist economic calculation, an article published posthumously in 1967 (Lange had passed away in 1965 during a surgical operation in London), he, himself, wrote the following:

> Not quite thirty years ago I published an essay "On the Economic Theory of Socialism." Pareto and Barone had shown that the conditions of economic equilibrium in a socialist economy could be expressed by a system of simultaneous equations. The prices resulting from these equations furnish a basis for rational economic accounting under socialism (only the static equilibrium aspect of the accounting problem was under consideration at the time). At a later date Hayek and Robbins maintained that the Pareto–Barone equations were of no practical consequence. The solution of a system of thousands or more simultaneous equations was, in practice, impossible, and consequently the practical problem of economic accounting under socialism remained unsolvable . . . In my essay I refuted the Hayek–Robbins argument by showing how a market mechanism could be established in a socialist economy which would lead to the solution of the simultaneous equations by means of an empirical procedure of trial and error . . . Today my answer to Hayek and Robbins would be: so what's the trouble? Let us put the simultaneous equations in an electronic computer and we shall obtain the solution in less than a second. *The market process may be considered as a computing device of the pre-electronic age.*[83]

These words of Lange's are thoroughly disappointing. They show the culmination of a huge step backwards in his conception of the problem socialist economic calculation poses: Lange reverts to viewing the problem as a purely static one (in contrast with what even he, himself, had recognized in his private correspondence with Hayek in 1940). Moreover, Lange offers a partial, biased description of the debate (as if it had been about matters of statics, and not dynamics and the entrepreneurial process), and in short, ends up denying that there is any need to bring in the market, which he depicts as an archaic mechanism for calculating equilibrium prices, a mechanism peculiar to the stages that precede the introduction of computer systems. There is no need to repeat here all of the arguments that have been expressed thus far to demonstrate the theoretical impossibility, now and under any future circumstances, of organizing society and performing economic calculation via central planning assisted by the most powerful computer systems.[84] Hence, what any historian of economic thought can confirm, and I reflect here with sadness and disappointment, is that at the time of his death, Lange had clung to statics and believed the ideal model of equilibrium could be realized in society through a planning system based on computer calculation . . . and imposed through the brute force of Stalinism.[85]

**Langian Epilogue**

The tension between the two possibilities that Lange faced (either abandoning his socialist ideal and replacing it with a complete market economy, or taking refuge in the trenches of equilibrium and Stalinism) persisted among the leading socialist theorists in general, and among Lange's closest Polish disciples in particular. Still, it was not until 25 years later that two of his most brilliant students, Wlodzimierz Brus and Kazimierz Laski, explicitly acknowledged that Lange had failed to confront the challenge of the Austrian school regarding socialism. These authors asserted that all of the "naïve reformers" (among whose ranks they, themselves, were numbered during a stage in their lives) had been similarly unsuccessful, since they believed that a certain combination of the market and coercive planning could make the socialist system possible. This theoretical error went uncorrected until recently, when, as a result of the traumatic events which took place in the countries of the former Eastern bloc, economic theorists in those countries at last came to fully grasp the accuracy and true content of the writings of Mises. For an economist from the western world, in which the contributions of the Austrian school within the field of the economic analysis of socialism remain, for the most part, sadly hidden in the absurd tangle of the neoclassical–Walrasian paradigm, this confession from two of Lange's most brilliant pupils is so moving and chilling that their exact words bear repeating here:

> [A]s the article "The Computer and the Market" written shortly before his death seems to witness, *he [Lange] never succeeded in confronting the Austrian*

*challenge* ... Other contributions to the theory of market socialism made by Polish economists – and by economists of other socialist countries as well – *failed to do this either*: those of non-Marxist provenance followed mainly the Walrasian approach, while Marxist pro-marketeers – *including the present authors* – formed the ranks of Kornai's "naïve reformers," viewing the prospect of the market-plan combination with excessive optimism. To some degree these *theoretical failures* might have been caused by politicoideological constraints, but even in countries and periods when such constraints were at their lowest (for example, Poland 1956–1957, and Czechoslovakia before the 1968 Soviet invasion), *the full extent of the problems arising from the Mises–Hayek strictures was not brought into the open*. It was only – or mainly, to be cautious – under the impact of the mostly frustrated experience of market oriented reforms that the issues in question came to the forefront.[86]

# NOTES

1. See Machlup (1984, 191): "At the present juncture of the discussion, writers on the theory or practice of central economic planning no longer doubt that a price mechanism is an indispensable tool of the planner's task. The Mises challenge has definitely prevailed on this point, as it has also on a second: 'decentralized procedures' are manifestly accepted by the present protagonists of planning". On page 190, we read: "these discussions did not address the essence of the Mises challenge. The issue is not whether calculations are possible and practicable with all available 'data' but whether the relevant data could become available to the central planning agency. The Mises challenge was that the information necessary for rational central planning could not be obtained and that market prices of privately owned means of production as well as products are required for a rational allocation of resources".
2. Hoff (1981, 238). Hoff even states that some "competitive solution" proposals would actually fall outside the strict definition of socialism, and that therefore, they should not even be answered. Hoff's assertion is unjustified from the perspective of our definition of socialism (any system of institutional aggression on the free exercise of entrepreneurship), which is both broad and precise, and therefore allows us to apply the above criticism of the socialist system whenever any degree of this sort of aggression is committed in any social sphere, no matter how small.
3. "It is therefore nothing short of a full acknowledgement of the correctness and irrefutability of the economists' analysis and devastating critique of the socialists' plans that the intellectual leaders of socialism are now busy designing schemes for a socialist system in which the market, market prices for the factors of production, and catallactic competition are to be preserved. The overwhelming rapid triumph of the demonstration that no economic calculation is possible under a socialist system is without precedent indeed in the history of human thought. The socialists cannot help admitting their crushing final defeat. They no longer claim that socialism is matchlessly superior to capitalism because it brushes away market, market prices and competition. On the contrary. They are now eager to justify socialism by pointing out that it is possible to preserve these institutions even under socialism. They are drafting outlines for a socialism in which there are prices and competition" (Mises, 1966, 706). Incidentally, this assertion of Mises's, like many others he made, may have appeared bold when it was written, in 1949, but it has turned out to be prophetic, and forty years later, history has proven him absolutely right, as Robert Heilbroner, a socialist and well-known pupil of Oskar Lange, has acknowledged. Heilbroner states: "Less than 75 years after it officially began, the contest between capitalism and socialism is over: *Capitalism has won*. The

Soviet Union, China and Eastern Europe have given us the *clearest possible proof that capitalism organizes the material affairs of humankind more satisfactorily than socialism* ... Indeed, it is difficult to observe the changes taking place in the world today and not conclude that the nose of the capitalism camel has been pushed so far under the socialist tent that the great question now seems how rapid will be the transformation of socialism into capitalism, and not the other way around, as things looked only half a century ago" (1989). See also Heilbroner (1990, esp. 1097 and 1110–11). Heilbroner concludes that "socialism has been a great tragedy in this century" and that "Mises was right". See also the fascinating interview Robert Heilbroner gave Mark Skousen (1991).

4. It is in the writings of Oskar Lange that we first encounter the tragicomic efforts of "market socialism" theorists to convince both their socialist fellow travelers and the general public that "the market" is an institution which has nothing to do with capitalism and that it can also be successfully used as a tool in socialism. Indeed, this author even stated that the market is a "rather old institution, an institution which is so characteristic of capitalism that it is frequently confused with capitalism but which actually is historically much older than capitalism" and that "prices and money are not only characteristic of modern capitalism, but are an institution that has to be preserved in the socialist society" (1942 [1987], 13). Modern market socialists repeat this idea ad nauseam. See, for example, Legrand and Estrin (1989). In his brilliant critical analysis of market socialism Anthony de Jasay (1990, 35) ironically describes the position of "market socialists" on this point as follows: "Apologists for capitalism usurp the market, appropriating it as if the market – an efficient institution – depended for its functioning on capitalism – repugnant and alienating system. However, the suggestion that market and capitalism go together is but a 'sleight of hand.' Traditional socialists fall for this trick, and think they dislike and mistrust markets when in fact it is capitalism they reject. This is a confusion, a failure to see that the market can be trained to serve socialist goals just as it now serves capitalist ones. Indeed, though the authors do not say so, they tacitly treat the market as a neutral tool in the hands of its political master who can use it in fashioning the kind of society he wants".

5. "So many of those of the younger socialists who have seriously studied the economic problems involved in socialism have abandoned the belief in a centrally planned economic system and pinned their faith on the hope that competition may be maintained even if private property is abolished" (Hayek, 1935c, 238).

6. "The first and most general point can be dealt with fairly briefly, although it is not unimportant if one wants to see these new proposals in their proper light. It is merely a reminder of how much of the original claim for the superiority of planning over competition is abandoned if the planned society is now to rely for the direction of its industries to a large extent on competition. Until quite recently, at least, planning and competition used to be regarded as opposites, and this is unquestionably still true of nearly all planners except a few economists among them" (Hayek 1940 [1972], 186).

7. Heimann (1922).

8. Halm's critique of Heimann's proposal is contained in "Further considerations on the possibility of adequate calculation in a socialist community" (Hayek, 1935a, 189–200). Section 25 of Halm's article was included because Hayek wanted Halm to summarize the state of the matter, in light of the debate in the German academic world before 1935.

9. Mises's criticism of Heimann first appeared in Mises (1924). An expanded version of this article appears in the appendix of Mises (1922 [1981], 475–8).

10. Karl Polanyi (1886–1964) should not be confused with his brother, Michael, who, as we have seen, was one of the chief creators of the theory that tacit, dispersed knowledge makes economic calculation impossible in any system in which people are not free to exercise human action or entrepreneurship. It seems paradoxical that the two brothers held such strikingly opposing theoretical positions, yet the same was true for Ludwig von Mises and his brother Richard, who developed a positivist concept of probability and defended the application of mathematics and statistics to research in the social

11. See Polanyi (1922). He later tried to answer the criticism he had received, mainly from Mises and Felix Weil, in another article, which he published in the same journal (1924).
12. The main criticisms of Polanyi's proposal come from Mises and appear in the same places he criticizes Heimann's contribution (see note 9). In, *Socialism* (1922 [1981], 473–5) Mises criticizes Polanyi. See also Weil's critical article (1924). Hoff (1981, 243) points out that Weil called Polanyi's proposal "impossible and even meaningless".
13. Roper (1931, 60, 62) dwells on the necessity of maintaining competition, and he explicitly states that the degree of efficiency which can be expected of a socialist system will depend on the degree to which such a system can simulate the competition which normally develops under a capitalist regime. See also note 30, Chapter 5.
14. Mises (1922 [1981], 121).
15. Ibid., 119.
16. "If the prospect of profit disappears the mechanism of the market loses its mainspring, for it is only this prospect which sets it in motion and maintains it in operation" Mises (ibid., 119).
17. Ibid., 121.
18. Ibid., 123.
19. Hayek (1935c, 227).
20. Ibid., 227.
21. Ibid., 231.
22. The connection with the modern public-choice school is clear in the following remark Hayek makes regarding the problem bureaucracy poses: "It will at best be a system of quasi-competition where the person really responsible will not be the entrepreneur but *the official who approves his decision* and where in consequence all the difficulties will arise in connection with freedom of initiative and the assessment of responsibility which are usually associated with *bureaucracy*" (ibid., 237). At this point we could repeat all of the arguments more recently developed by the school of public choice with respect to the economic analysis of the perverse effects of political and bureaucratic behavior, arguments we have cited elsewhere (Chapter 3, note 27).
23. Hayek views these different proposals for incentives or systems for monitoring managers' success in a "socialist market economy" as a problem of great theoretical interest, since "in their pure form they raise the question of the rationale of private property in its most general and fundamental aspect" (1935c, 219). With this statement, Hayek appears to catch a glimpse of the scientific research program of the modern economic theory of property rights, a program which, though it is heavily restricted by the defects of the neoclassical paradigm of complete information and equilibrium, has reached a remarkable degree of development. In the following chapter, we will conclude our critical analysis of the proposals for establishing systems of bonuses and incentives designed to make a socialist regime possible.
24. See ibid., 238. Nevertheless, we believe Hayek is excessively gracious here with his opponents, and we cannot agree with him when he also states that although it is "illegitimate to say that these proposals are impossible in any absolute sense, it remains not the less true that these very serious obstacles to the achievement of the desired end exist and that there seems to be no way in which they can be overcome". On the contrary, for reasons given in the text, we believe that it is impossible to resolve the economic calculation problem in a system in which competition is as extensive as possible, yet production goods are publicly owned. With the above statement, Hayek may give the impression that such proposals are not logically impossible, and that the problem is actually a practical one – that of finding appropriate incentives to replace those that exist in the capitalist market. However, the problem is not finding proper substitute incentives, but

the fact that it is theoretically impossible, in the absence of private property, for the economic calculation problem to be resolved, since agents do not generate the necessary information, nor does the central agency in charge of distributing the corresponding funds have access to the practical information necessary to do so in a way that is not completely arbitrary.

25. Robbins (1934, 154).
26. Lavoie (1985c, 159, footnote 10) points out that in this brief analysis, Robbins paradoxically appears to stray from his own "Robbinsian" conception, in which the economic subject is a mere maximizer. Though Lavoie seems inclined to believe Robbins was, in practice, much more Austrian than Kirzner and other authors portray him, this author feels that Robbins's dynamic, Austrian interpretation of market processes was usually very poor and confusing, since he was unable to clearly distinguish between the two interpretations, much less guard against the static conception's nearly always being deduced from his work.
27. "Lange concocted what could only be called the Mythology of the Socialist Calculation Debate, a mythology which, aided and abetted by Joseph Schumpeter, was accepted by virtually all economists of whatever ideological stripe" (Rothbard, 1991, 53).
28. Lange and Breit (1934).
29. See Kowalik (1987b, 126).
30. See Lange (1936, 1937, 1938 [1964]).
31. See Lange in Lippincott (1938 [1964], 70).
32. Ibid., 59–60.
33. "That the 'alternatives which are offered to us' become known to us in most instances only as money prices is Mises' chief argument. To turn this against him is an inexcusable legerdemain of which a thinker not prejudiced by political preconceptions should be incapable." See Hayek (1982 [1984] 58). This article, "Two pages of fiction", is essential to our critique of Lange in this section, and thus, we shall follow it very closely. Incidentally, Arthur Seldon writes about how this article came about. He explains that in 1982 Hayek sent him a copy of the article along with a letter in which he indicated, among other things, that he was "particularly indignant about the steadily repeated silly talk of Oskar Lange having refuted Mises". The article originally appeared in *Economic Affairs* (1982). The "Two pages of fiction" the intriguing title mentions refer precisely to pages 60 and 61 of Lange's article as reprinted in the book which Lippincott edited and we are now discussing. These two pages have been used time and again (without further scientific discussion) as a basis for the unjustified myth that Lange refuted Mises. See Seldon (1984, 26, 27).
34. See Wicksteed (1933, 28).
35. Perhaps it is worthwhile to reproduce here the words of Karen I. Vaughn on this matter: "It is instructive that Lange decided to quote Wicksteed's formulation of the meaning of price in the beginning of his article; instructive primarily because it reveals Lange's complete lack of understanding of exactly what Wicksteed was trying to show. In the *Common Sense of Political Economy* [London: Routledge and Kegan Paul, 1933], Wicksteed described the essentially subjective nature of the opportunity costs that faced anyone attempting to make a rational economic decision. That is, when one considers making a purchase, the price represents the market exchange value, but the 'terms on which alternatives are offered' includes not only the market price, but all the subjective elements that must be calculated in one's choice, *the subjective value of all the foregone alternatives* [p. 28]. Obviously, this has nothing to do with the distinction Lange was trying to make between market prices and centrally planned prices. The prices which Lange's planning board would set, far from providing a more encompassing kind of price, would figure in an individual's subjective calculus in exactly the same way as market prices more conventionally do. Individuals would still have to personally evaluate the whole range of alternatives, the 'terms on which alternatives are offered' to them, but the administered price would substitute for the market price. *The real problem, then, of how legislated prices would be made to represent actual relative scarcities of the*

*commodities available for exchange, could not be exorcised with an impressive incantation.* Lange has still to show that the tâtonnement he prescribed could be made to yield measures of relative scarcity as well as market exchanges. *This, he did not accomplish*" (Vaughn, 1981, xxii–xxiii). Perhaps the greatest defect in Vaughn's otherwise interesting introduction is that she fails to mention the contributions Mises made in his 1949 work, *Human Action*, which in another place she even erroneously and unfairly underrates when she states that "Mises' so-called final refutation in *Human Action* is mostly polemic and glosses over the real problems" (Vaughn, 1976, 107). Finally, see also Vaughn (1980).

36. Lange in Lippincott (1938 [1964], 60).
37. Hayek (1982 [1984], 54).
38. Lange in Lippincott (1938 [1964], 60).
39. Ibid., 60–61.
40. Thus, neoclassical theorists do not understand that economic calculation depends on the existence of certain historically contingent institutions (such as money, markets and free exchanges), historical categories which are "special features of a certain state of society's economic organization which did not exist in primitive civilizations and could possibly disappear in the further course of historical change" (Mises, 1966, 201, main text and footnote 1, in which Mises adds that "the German historical school expressed this by asserting that private ownership of the means of production, market exchange, and money are 'historical categories'"). Hence, it is now clear that the ideas of Mises do not contain the spectacular contradiction Lange attributes to him simply because Lange sees him as an "institutionalist" who, at the same time, defends the universal validity of economic theory. Lange cannot understand why the Austrian school, from the time Carl Menger founded it, has centered its scientific research program on the theoretical (general, abstract, and historically independent) analysis of the institutions (patterns of behavior or human action, such as money, the market, law and so on) and processes which evolve in society. In fact, Menger dedicated his *Grundsätze* to Wilhelm Roscher, since he believed his subjectivist contribution and his work on the evolutionary emergence of institutions provided the initial, necessary theoretical foundation for the historicist school (Friedrich Karl von Savigny, Edmund Burke) as opposed to the Cartesian rationalism which was beginning to flood all scientific thought. The theoretical spectacles of the neoclassical paradigm are so poorly adjusted that they prevent Lange from distinguishing even the most obvious circumstances of the scientific environment in which he lives, which he perceives only in a distorted monochrome (see Lange in Lippincott, 1938 [1964], footnote, p. 6). Also, it is interesting to note that Langlois's book, *Economics as a Process* (1986), which shows a clear "Austrian" influence, is subtitled "Essays in the New *Institutional* Economics", and plainly constitutes, like the works of Mises, a book of economic (and thus not "institutionalist" or historicist) *theory* on institutions. Despite Lange, the economic theory of social processes and institutions is one thing, and "institutionalism" is quite another. Also of great interest is Boettke (1988). Finally, see again note 2, Chapter 5, especially Mark Blaug's critical comments about the neoclassical–Walrasian paradigm, and his shift toward the tenets of the Austrian school.
41. "To the neoclassical participants in the debate, the relevant knowledge is assumed to be given to market participants, and the main analytic conclusion is that under certain static assumptions the capitalist equilibrium is determinate. *It is a small step from this analysis to the adoption of similar assumptions and the arrival at similar conclusions for socialism*" (Lavoie, 1985c, 115).
42. In the words of Kirzner himself: "That Lange did not understand this nonparametric function of prices must certainly be attributed to a perception of the market system's operation primarily in terms of *perfectly competitive equilibrium*. (Indeed, it is this textbook approach to price theory that Lange explicitly presents as his model for socialist pricing.) Within this paradigm, as is now well recognized, the role of the entrepreneurial quest for pure profit, as the key element in bringing about price adjustment, is

completely ignored. It is not difficult to see how Lange could conclude that such a (non entrepreneurial) system might be simulated under socialism" (1985, 128–9). On the economic theory of market processes, which centers on the concept of entrepreneurship (and is unrelated to, and especially critical of, the neoclassical–Walrasian paradigm), see not only the works of Mises and Hayek cited in this book, but also, particularly, all works written by Kirzner, and in general, the rest of the Austrian theorists. For a critique of the concept of equilibrium in economic analysis, written by a prestigious economist of the former Eastern bloc, see Kornai (1971).

43. Lange in Lippincott (1938 [1964], 61).
44. Hayek (1982, 55, 56). The reference to Heilbroner was necessary; for when he assumes that the information would be available not only to company managers, as Lange asserts, but also to the central planning bureau, he claims an even greater logical impossibility, so to speak. To the impossibility that managers who are not entrepreneurs could generate entrepreneurial information, he adds the even more serious problem of the transmission and centralized comprehension of an infinite volume of subjective, tacit, inarticulable and dispersed information in constant change. Let us recall, in partial defense of Heilbroner, his retraction and his recognition of capitalism's absolute triumph over socialism (see note 3 of this chapter), though we still do not know whether Heilbroner considers this triumph an unexpected empirical event which lacks a theoretical explanation, or on the contrary, he has begun to detect the blatant errors he committed throughout his entire past intellectual life.
45. Lange in Lippincott (1938 [1964], 61).
46. In the words of Kirzner himself: "Lange failed to recognize that the distinctive aspect of the market is the manner in which prices *change*, that is, that market prices are in fact treated nonparametrically. It is one thing to imagine that socialist managers can be motivated to obey rules on the basis of centrally promulgated 'prices;' it is quite another to take it for granted that the *nonparametric* function of price (in which, that is, price is not being treated as a datum but is subject to change by individual market participants), a function which depends entirely on entrepreneurial discovery of new opportunities for pure profit, can be simulated in a system from which the private entrepreneurial function is completely absent" (Kirzner 1985, 31; see also 126–9).
47. This error has also been committed by all of the commentators who, following Schumpeter, have maintained that, even before Mises made his contribution, Vilfredo Pareto and Enrico Barone had "demonstrated" that socialist economic calculation is possible. As we saw when we discussed these authors, they established only an argument of formal similarity. In other words, they formally identified the type of information a socialist authority would have to be able to access in order for economic calculation to be possible under static conditions. Nevertheless, as is obvious, it is one thing to establish the type and quantity of information necessary to the achievement of this objective, and it is quite another to resolve the theoretical problem of how to acquire this information, a task which Mises and Hayek maintain is impossible under socialism, due to the typical characteristics of such a system. Furthermore, we have seen (see notes 8 and 9 of Chapter 4) that Pareto himself, and to a lesser extent, Barone, expressly established that the knowledge or information which concerns us could never be obtained in the absence of the market. Finally, as we already know, the authors of modern planometrics theory, beginning with Arrow and Hurwicz, commit the same error. (See Section 5, Chapter 5 for a detailed analysis of this theory.) The economists of Eastern Europe, whom John Gray (1989, 174) identifies as among the most educated economic scientists with respect to the history of economic thought, have begun on a broad scale to acknowledge Mises and Hayek's argument that the abolition of capitalist-market institutions renders economic calculation impossible, in contrast with most of their colleagues in western countries, who remain lost in the fallacies of the neoclassical–Walrasian paradigm. Among these economists, Wlodzimierz Brus and Kazimierz Laski, for example, deserve special attention, mainly because they were once pupils of Oskar Lange and even collaborated with him on a book. (See *Problems of Political Economy of Socialism*,

1962.) Laski contributed an article on the conditions for general equilibrium between production and consumption, pp. 108–51; Brus provided an article on the problems of marginal accounting in a socialist economy, pp. 175–94 (see Laski, 1974; Brus, 1974). It is moving to read the more recent affirmations of these economists in which they indicate that the neoclassical–Walrasian model is useless as a theoretical foundation for a socialist economy, because the model does not allow for entrepreneurship, and that therefore, the hitherto widely accepted belief that Lange refuted Mises is completely unfounded. In fact, in their own words, "The technological knowledge necessary to fill the elements of the Walrasian equations is not a datum but rather information which can only be discovered in the process of competitive struggle. Thus what matters is the peculiar entrepreneurial 'thinking technique,' a kind of intuition, which is generated by actually finding oneself in a competitive situation . . . All these aspects are absent in Lange's model of market socialism, *which seems to corroborate the assertion that its claim to a convincing refutation of the Mises/Hayek challenge has been unjustified*" (Brus and Laski, 1989, 58). See also the Hungarian author János Kornai, who in his article, "The Hungarian reform process" (1986), explicitly states that Lange "lived in the *sterile* world of Walrasian pure theory" (p. 1727) and criticizes the role of the neo-classical school in the debate because the "emphasis shifted one-sidedly to the issue of computing the correct price signals. What got lost was the crucial Mises–Hayek idea regarding *rivalry*. In a genuine market process actors participate who want to make use and can make use, of their *specific knowledge* and opportunities. They are rivals. In that sense the market is always in a state of dynamic disequilibrium. Some win and some lose. Victory brings rewards: survival, growth, more profit, more income. Defeat brings penalties: losses, less income, and in the ultimate case exit. Using the vocabulary of the present paper, the Mises–Hayek market implies a *hard budget constraint* and a buyer's market. As long as the system and the policy do not assure the prevalence of these two conditions, there is no genuine market. *The great shortcoming of the Lange model is that it does not even contemplate these conditions and many of Lange's followers committed the same error*" (pp. 1727–8). Finally, the Russian economist Gabriel Temkin asserts along the same lines as above that "the Lange model lacks any trace of entrepreneurship, whether in purely theoretical or in practical terms. Being wedded strongly to the General Equilibrium framework, entrepreneurship is just defined away because, within that framework, there is no room for a theory of entrepreneurial choice . . . And, since neither the entrepreneur nor the market can be adequately simulated in a socialist economy based on public ownership, it is only the routine task of a manager that can be, at best, reproduced. But here, again, the imitation would be far from exact or even close." Temkin concludes, in honor of Mises, that "perhaps the honorary statue of Mises, about which Lange quipped half a century ago, should after all be erected, if not on Red Square then in Budapest, closer to his native Austria" (1989, 53). We would personally add that in light of the historical events which have occurred in the other countries of Eastern Europe, that this statue should be put up in the capitals of all of the states which have ceased to be socialist, and particularly in Berlin, Warsaw, Prague, Budapest and also Moscow. (As we pointed out in note 21, Chapter 4, the statue of Mises has at least been set up in the library of the Economics Department at the University of Warsaw, right next to what was once Lange's official office.)

48. See Lange in Lippincott (1938 [1964], 65–89).
49. Negishi (1987).
50. See particularly the excerpt from Lange's "The computer and the market" (1967), which appears at the end of this chapter, in the section devoted to the "fourth stage" in Lange's intellectual life. See also the observations made on those and the following pages.
51. In the words of Hayek himself: "That the price fixing process will be confined to establishing uniform prices for classes of goods and that therefore distinctions based on the special circumstances of time, place, and quality will find no expression in prices is probably obvious. Without some such simplification, the number of different commodities

for which separate prices would have to be fixed would be practically *infinite*. This means, however, that the managers of production will have no inducement, and even no real possibility, to make use of special opportunities, special bargains, and all the little advantages offered by their special local conditions, since all these things could not enter into their calculations" (1940, 193). Nevertheless, in this article, Hayek fails to present, with all of its implications, the fundamental argument that has been offered in the text.

52. Lange advocates the first solution on p. 82 of his article, "On the economic theory of socialism" (1938 [1964]) when he states: "Any price different from the equilibrium price will show at the end of the accounting period a surplus or a shortage of the commodities questioned". He favors the second solution four pages later (p. 86) when he mentions in passing: "Adjustments of those prices would be constantly made". Despite appearances, Lange's ideas are muddled. Once we look beneath the surface, the confusion and ambiguity in his thinking could not be more obvious.

53. Henry D. Dickinson, who, shortly after Lange, became one of the leading defenders of the "competitive solution", explicitly recognizes that the existence of a free and competitive market for consumer goods would be more a fiction than a reality in market socialism, and he shamelessly indicates that the state machinery of propaganda and advertising would create among the citizens the false impression of free choice of consumer goods and services. In his own words: "The powerful engine of propaganda and advertisement, employed by public organs of education and enlightenment . . . could divert demand into socialist desirable directions *while preserving the subjective impression of free choice*" (1939, 32). Lange himself soon showed his true colors and devoted the entire fourth section of "On the economic theory of socialism" to the thesis that his model would apply even if the central coercion agency decided to prevent the free choice of jobs and consumer goods and services, and instead imposed authorities' particular preferences on all of society. Hence, it is not surprising that during the last part of his academic life, Lange praised and justified the Stalinist system, as we shall see.

54. We owe this analogy to Bradley (1981, 39, footnote 86). The same can be said of the supposedly competitive "labor market". A competitive labor market requires the constant emergence of new job opportunities, as the result of new investment projects, the creation of new companies, the appearance of new entrepreneurial ideas and so on. All of the above is inconceivable in Lange's model, in which there are no entrepreneurs, but only managers who confine themselves to following, like robots, a series of rules established beforehand from above.

55. Unfortunately, modern textbooks continue to offer a completely uncritical view of the neoclassical–Walrasian paradigm and the conditions of optimum outlined by the "perfect competition" model within the parameters of economic welfare theory. Furthermore, many of the most prestigious textbooks even refer to "Lange's rules" and explicitly state that they would permit the achievement of the same optimum in a socialist economy. In making this assertion, the textbook writers neglect to make any clarification whatsoever and overlook all the problems that are discussed in this book, which are not even mentioned in passing. The resulting damage to the education of economics students may take years to mend and could even become irreversible. As an example, see the well-known book by Gould and Ferguson, *Microeconomic Theory* (1980, 445), where we read the following conclusion, which is expressed without any clarification or comment: "*Proposition (Lange–Lerner Rule)*: To attain maximum social welfare in a *decentralized socialist society*, the state planning agency should solve the constrained maximization problem and obtain the *shadow prices* of all inputs and outputs; publish this *price-list* and distribute it to all members of the society; and *instruct* all consumers and all plant managers to behave as though they were *satisfaction or profit-maximizers* operating in *perfectly competitive markets*" (italics added). Thus, we find the most ridiculous absurdity presented categorically and raised to the level of a "scientific conclusion" in a "prestigious" textbook.

56. See Buchanan's introduction in Buchanan and Thirlby (1981, 3–10) and Buchanan (1969, 21–6, 34–5, 41, 96). It is maintained above that Buchanan exaggerates somewhat,

because the assessment of costs, though essential to rational economic calculation, accounts for only one part of all the information created and transmitted entrepreneurially (which also includes the valuation of the ends to be accomplished). At the heart of the controversy, there is no incomprehension about the true, subjective nature of costs as much as a fundamental lack of understanding about the true nature of human action and entrepreneurship, as defined in Chapter 2. Buchanan concludes: "Modern economic theorists measure their own confusion by the degree to which they accept the Lange victory over Mises, quite apart from the empirical record since established" (Buchanan and Thirlby, 1981, 5).

57. In the words of Wiseman himself: "It is no longer possible, once uncertainty is admitted, to interpret the opportunity-cost problem as one of scarcity alone, to be solved by a choice between alternative factor inputs and product outputs with all prices known. That is, opportunity cost is no longer a simple question of summation and comparison of known data. Prices and other variables have to be estimated: opportunity cost decisions involve uncertainty (and therefore judgement) as well as scarcity. The cost problem now arises as a *choice between alternative plans of action* . . . Since opportunity costs cannot be treated simply as known money costs, but must be considered as estimates of *foregone alternative revenues*, it is no longer useful in conditions of uncertainty to speak of equality of marginal money cost and price as a property of an efficient resource distribution". Wiseman concludes that in a socialist system "the marginal-cost rule, as normally framed, gives no clear guidance to those responsible for the organization of production in such an economy. Attempts to reinterpret the rule in such a way as to take account of uncertainty preclude the possibility of a direct check on the efficiency of collectivist managers in obeying that rule. Any indirect, objective, check used as a supplement to the marginal rule will in fact supplant that rule as the directive for managerial effort, and *in any case no completely objective check is possible*. Further, whatever rule or check is adopted, imperfectly competitive behaviour is to be expected" (Wiseman, 1953 [1981], 229, 234–5.) Thirlby had arrived at the same conclusions earlier, and in his notable article, "The ruler" (1946 [1981]), he states that any rule which establishes the existence of an objective and discernible relationship between revenue and costs (whether it be that marginal revenue is equal to marginal cost, or price is equal to marginal cost, or total revenue is equal to total cost and so on) "has not the objectivity that is by implication attributed to it; consequently that the application of the rule is *impracticable*". Incidentally, this entire theory reveals that a large part of both the so-called "theory of public utility pricing" (see Wiseman, 1957) and the "economic analysis of law" with respect to antitrust legislation lacks a theoretical foundation.

58. Paul Craig Roberts, in his "Oskar Lange's theory of socialist planning: an obscurant of socialist aspirations" (Roberts, 1990, ch. 5, esp. 96–8), also reaches the conclusion that Lange's "rules" cannot be applied in practice. Although I am indebted to Roberts for some significant contributions, such as his demonstration of both the incompatibility between Marxism and "market socialism", and the mere *ad hoc* and *a posteriori* rationalization involved in the consequently misnamed Soviet "central planning", I find Roberts's analysis of socialism faulty, because it is not subjectivist enough, that is, it does not rest on a study of the repercussions which the systematic use of coercion causes for people and social processes. Moreover, simply revealing the existing contradictions between Marxism and Lange's model is not sufficient to discredit the latter: if Lange's model becomes a "hope" for many people, it will be necessary to refute it with more forceful arguments than those Roberts employs. Furthermore, Roberts fails to include the concept of entrepreneurship anywhere; his idea of the initial challenge and the contributions of Mises and Hayek to the debate is poor and confused; and he centers his work more on Polanyi's not altogether satisfactory (due to its overly "objectivist" nature) analysis of "polycentric and hierarchical" structures in society than on Polanyi's theory of the tacit, inarticulable nature of practical knowledge, a theory we know to be much more relevant to the theoretical study of socialism. Finally, Roberts does not realize that the imposition from above of a "nirvana-like" social equilibrium model

which involves no changes or adjustments is entirely consistent with Marx's aspirations (the elimination of alienation, since the origin and progress of any social process would be identifiable to those involved, and the conscious direction of the economy). Hence, we should not be surprised by the "fatal attraction" socialism (and interventionism) usually hold among equilibrium theorists, though I agree with Roberts that the link with Marx is severed the moment an attempt is made, as with the model of "competitive socialism", to introduce certain market institutions to facilitate the achievement of this equilibrium. This incompatibility between the allocation criteria characteristic of the market and traditional socialist ideology has also been explained by Dembinski (1991, esp. 68–9).

59. "In the discussion of this sort of problem, as in the discussion of so much of economic theory at the present time, the question is frequently treated *as if the cost-curves were objectively given facts*. What is forgotten is that the method which under given conditions is the cheapest *is a thing which has to be discovered anew*, sometimes almost from day to day, by the entrepreneur, and that, in spite of the strong inducement, it is by no means regularly the established entrepreneur, the man in charge of the existing plant, who will discover what is the best method. The force which in a competitive society brings about the reduction of price to the lowest cost at which the quantity salable at that cost can be produced is the opportunity for anybody who knows a cheaper method to come in at his own risk and to attract customers by underbidding the other producers. *But, if prices are fixed by the authority, this method is excluded.* Any improvement, any adjustment of the technique of production to changed conditions will be dependent on somebody's capacity of convincing the S.E.C. (Supreme Economic Council) that the commodity in question can be produced cheaper and that therefore the price ought to be lowered. Since the man with the new idea will have no possibility of establishing himself by undercutting, the new idea cannot be proved by experiment until he has convinced the S.E.C. that his way of producing the thing is cheaper. Or, in other words, every calculation by an outsider who believes that he can do better will have to be examined and approved by the authority, which in this connection will have to take over all the functions of the entrepreneur" (Hayek, 1940 [1972], 196–7). In his article, "Role of planning in socialistic economy" (in Lange, 1962), Lange reveals that he never understood this fundamental argument of Hayek's, and though Lange recognizes the practical difficulty entailed in setting prices based on marginal costs, he indicates that the variable average costs of the companies with the highest cost in each sector could provide a good, realistic approach to this objective (pp. 32–4). Lange fails to understand that the practical approach he suggests involves using a purely arbitrary figure which is extracted from an interpretation of past events and has nothing to do with the concept of cost which is essential to rational economic calculation. Thus, the rule he proposes would only serve to equate prices with nominal "cost" figures which are exaggerated, as they include and conceal all sorts of inefficiency and superfluity.

60. On this issue, Abram Bergson has stated: "In practice, what we have to reckon with is not a unique marginal cost for a given level of output, but a complex of marginal costs, each of which is pertinent to a particular period of time. As a longer period of time is considered, more of the 'fixed factors' become variable" (1948, 427).

61. Perhaps Lavoie has provided the simplest explanation of this point: "The MC = P rule will optimize allocation within a given framework of means and ends as long as future costs are expected to be the same as current costs. This is a world of static expectations, which are reasonable in a static world. In a world of continuous change, however, an entrepreneur must try to anticipate demand, to form expectations, and to act on them. He should view his costs on the basis of the specific alternatives that appear available to him at the time of his choice. Both his estimate of revenue and his estimate of costs depend on his expectations at the time of decision" (1985c, 141).

62. As Hayek states: "I believe that preoccupation with concepts of pure economic theory has seriously misled both our authors [Lange and Lerner]. In this case it is the concept of perfect competition which apparently has made them overlook a very important field

to which their method appears to be simply inapplicable. Wherever we have a market for a fairly standardized commodity, it is at least conceivable that all prices should be decreed in advance from above for a certain period. The situation is, however, very different with respect to commodities which cannot be standardized, and particularly for those which today are produced on individual orders, perhaps after invitation for tenders. A large part of the product of the 'heavy industries' which, of course, would be the first to be socialized, belongs to this category. Much machinery, most buildings and ships, and many parts of other products are hardly ever produced for a market, but only on special contracts. This does not mean that there may not be intense competition in the market for the products of these industries, although it may not be 'perfect competition' in the sense of pure theory; the fact is simply that in those industries identical products are rarely produced twice in short intervals; and the circle of producers who will compete as alternative suppliers in each instance will be different in almost every individual case, just as the circle of potential customers who will compete for the services of a particular plant will differ from week to week. What basis is there in all these cases for fixing prices of the product so as 'to equalize supply and demand'?" (1940 [1972], 188–9).

63. "The stock exchange is perhaps the most characteristic of all the institutions of the market economy ... What really distinguishes capitalism from a socialist economy is not the size of the 'private' sector of the economy, but the ability of the individual freely to buy and sell shares in the material resources of production. Their inability to exercise their ingenuity in this respect is perhaps the most important disability suffered by the citizens of socialist societies" (Lachmann, 1977, 161).
64. See Buchanan (1986, 25). See also Levy (1990).
65. See Mises (1969).
66. Kornai (1986, 1726–7).
67. Hayek (1940 [1972], 198–9).
68. Lange (1938).
69. It might be helpful to recall the following works: Rosenberg (1977); Snowberger (1977); and Weitzman (1976).
70. We owe this significant idea about the irrelevance of the system of bonuses and incentives in a socialist system to Israel M. Kirzner, who states: "To reward managers for meeting or exceeding target output quantities presupposes that *it is already known* that more of these outputs is urgently required by society ... But if they are assumed already known, *we are simply assuming away the need for entrepreneurial discovery*". Kirzner arrives at the conclusion that therefore, "incentives to socialist managers deny the essential role of entrepreneurial discovery" (1985, 34–5). On the failure when trying to establish a bonus system for central and private bankers see Huerta de Soto (2009c, 647–71). We shall return to the topic of establishing bonuses and incentives when, in the next chapter, we analyze the related proposals offered by Dickinson and give consideration to a series of additional factors which also fully apply here.
71. Mises and Hayek developed the "Austrian theory of economic cycles" in parallel with their analysis of socialist economic calculation, which explains why the common denominator of these consists of the discoordinating effects provoked by artificial credit expansion and state aggression on the market. For a summary of the most significant works on the "Austrian theory of economic cycles", see Huerta de Soto (1980, 2009c).
72. See, for example, Stankiewicz (1989).
73. In the main text, we have passed over four additional observations Lange makes about the capitalist system, since either they are not directly related to the problem of economic calculation, or the answers to them can be considered already implicit in our analysis. Moreover, Lange (1938) offers rather unoriginal arguments which form part of the traditional verbiage of socialist ideology and have already been sufficiently refuted elsewhere. Thus, he states: (i) that socialism would redistribute income and thereby make the "maximization of social welfare" possible (as if it could be measured, individual utility functions existed and could be known, and all this information could

reach the regulatory agency); (ii) that in its decision making, the planning agency could consider the "true" social and external costs (same errors as above, to which we should add that "market imperfections" arise precisely because an absence or poor state definition of property rights prevents entrepreneurship and economic calculation in important spheres of the market); (iii) that entrepreneurs in a capitalist system are bogus (then how could we describe those "poor devils" – managers and public officials – of the socialist system?); and, most striking of all, (iv) that capitalism has ceased to be compatible with the economic and technological advancement of society. We need not repeat that there is no greater obstacle to progress than institutional coercion against the free, creative exercise of entrepreneurship, and fortunately, a generation after Lange's death, the problem as socialists themselves perceive it has made a 180-degree turn, and today it has become quite clear, and no one doubts anymore, that it is the socialist system, and not the capitalist one, which is incompatible with technological innovation and systematically thwarts economic progress.

74. Temkin (1989, 55, footnote 6).
75. See the letter that Lange wrote to Hayek on August 31, 1940, upon receiving Hayek's article entitled, "Socialist calculation: the competitive solution." This letter appears in volume 2 of the *Complete Works* of Oskar Lange (1973; *Dziela* in Polish), and in the letter we read: "There is no question that you have succeeded in raising essential problems and in showing gaps in the *pure static solution given by me*. I intend to work on this subject and give an answer to your paper . . . sometime in the fall" (p. 567). Lange finally catches on and promises to tackle the crucial scientific problems: Mises made it clear in 1920 that socialism poses no problem in static terms, so Lange's recognition that his is a "pure static solution" is tantamount to an admission that it is no solution at all. (Unfortunately, Lange did not fulfill his promise, and he never addressed the true, dynamic problem socialist economic calculation poses.)
76. "The essay is so far removed from what I ought to write on the subject today that I am afraid that any revision would produce a very poor compromise, unrepresentative of my thoughts. Thus, I am becoming inclined to let the essay go out of print and express my present views in entirely new form. I am writing a book on economic theory in which a chapter will be devoted to this subject. This may be better than trying to rehash old stuff". Lange made this comment in writing in 1944, and it appears in his *Dziela* of 1975 (Vol. 3), and Kowalik also cites it (1987b, 127 and 129).
77. "Practically, I should, of course, recommend the determination of prices by a thorough market process whenever this is feasible, i.e., whenever the number of selling and purchasing units is sufficiently large. Only where the number of these units is so small that a situation of oligopoly, oligopsony, or bilateral monopoly would obtain, would I advocate price fixing by public agency" (from the letter to Hayek dated August 31, 1940 and reprinted by Kowalik, 1987b, 127).
78. See Kowalik (1986, 11–24), where he reproduces these two lectures of Lange's in their entirety. For the reasons supplied in the text, Kowalik considers that in the 1940s, Oskar Lange moved "away from the advocacy of an integral socialism toward a mixed public (public and private) economy, operating through a fully-fledged market mechanism" (ibid., 1–2).
79. Lange (1943); cited by Kowalik (1987b, 127).
80. Karl Pribram has pointed out that the shift in Lange's theoretical position coincided with his entrance into the Polish Communist Party (1983, 708, footnote 32). Kowalik, for his part (1987b, 127), appears to try to justify this Copernican turn of Lange's by arguing that for tactical reasons, given the political and academic circumstances in Poland at the time, it would have been extremely unwise to oppose the Stalinist trend, and that social scientists were afforded very limited freedom of speech. Kowalik's defense of Lange appears to be more a charitable remark than anything else, especially in light of the numerous writings Lange published in prestigious international journals, in which he explained and justified his change of opinion, and defended and praised the Stalinist system. (Noteworthy among these writings is "The practice of economic

planning and the optimum allocation of resources", 1949). Thus, in the end, Lange's position came to agree almost completely with that of Maurice Dobb, whose views will be analyzed in the next chapter. Dobb saw no greater hypocrisy than that of "market socialists", and he felt socialism would not triumph unless it were presented in all its crude reality, that is, without "masks" or any "competitive" make-up.

81. Lange (1953); cited by Kowalik (1987b, 129).
82. Kowalik (1987b, 128).
83. Lange (1967 [1972], 401–2). Lange's naive, misplaced trust in the power of computers to make socialist economic calculation possible is also evident in his lecture, "The role of science in the development of socialist society", which he delivered before the General Assembly of members of the Polish Academy of Sciences on May 19, 1962 (see Lange, 1970, 143–66, esp. 156–7 and 162–3).
84. On the impossibility of using computers to solve the problem of socialist economic calculation, see the arguments expressed in Chapter 3 of this book. Also of interest are the observations by Norman Barry (1984), in which he emphasizes that Lange's confidence in computers rests on ignorance of the essential distinction between scientific information and the practical, subjective, and inarticulable information economic agents use in society (see particularly page 588). On this issue, Rothbard has pointed out the uselessness of computers and computer programs, regardless of how advanced they are, if the basic information entered into them is erroneous because entrepreneurship is coercively prevented. He concludes: "Lange's naïve enthusiasm for the magical planning qualities of the computer in its early days can only be considered a grisly joke to the economists and the people in the socialist countries who have seen their economies go inexorably from bad to far worse despite the use of computers. *Lange apparently never became familiar with the computer adage, GIGO ('garbage in, garbage out')*" (Rothbard, 1991, 72).
85. In short, what Lange discovered was the huge similarity between the normative conclusions of equilibrium theory and the traditional Marxist model (the objective of which is to impose this equilibrium on society), and thus, Lange sought to complete his life's scientific work by constructing a synthesis of the neoclassical equilibrium model and Marxist theory, a project he even partially carried out (see Lange, 1963, 1968). Paradoxically, in this work, Lange paid a final tribute to his old opponent, Ludwig von Mises, when Lange recognized that the synthesis of all economic science should eventually take the form of a "praxeology" or "general theory of human action" (1963). Nevertheless, by conceiving human action as mere reaction of passive subjects in an environment in which all information is available, Lange reduces the general economic problem to one of mere allocation or static efficiency, and consequently, he fails in his attempt to construct a praxeological science, a goal Mises had already achieved with his magnum opus, *Human Action*, in which he examines all the implications of the general theory of human and entrepreneurial action as it is pursued by human beings in real life. On this topic, see Rothbard (1971). Bruna Ingrao and Giorgio Israel, in their historical study of the formation of the neoclassical–Walrasian paradigm (1987 [1990], 253), describe Lange's viewpoint as a "normative" approach to general equilibrium, as opposed to John Hicks and Paul Samuelson's view, which the authors consider more "descriptive". However, we feel the distinction between the two perspectives should not be exaggerated, for if Lange proposed, in "normative" terms, the use of the general equilibrium model as a basis for socialism, it was precisely because he believed this model provided, in "positive" terms, an acceptable "description" of the market. Likewise, if Mises and Hayek refuted this idea of Lange's, it was because they considered the general equilibrium model fundamentally erroneous in a descriptive sense. The Austrian theory of market processes rests on premises which are much less restrictive and more realistic than those of the general equilibrium model, and thus, as an explanatory tool, it is much more powerful and widely useful in positive terms, and from a normative standpoint, it constitutes a different and much stronger and more effective defence of the market economy and the "invisible hand" than that proposed

by the equilibrium model. For Austrians, the problems of the existence, uniqueness and stability of general equilibrium constitute an irrelevant intellectual game, since the real world is much more accurately described in terms of entrepreneurship, and all that is necessary to construct the entire economic analysis is an understanding of the creative and coordinating force of the pure entrepreneurial act. Not only do these problems constitute an irrelevant intellectual game, but it is a very dangerous game as well, as we see from the fact that the general equilibrium model is used constantly in a normative sense, even, as Lange attempted, as a basis for the failed socialist system. See also Huerta de Soto (2009a).

86. Brus and Laski (1989, 60).

# 7. Final considerations

This final chapter will begin with an analysis of the contributions of three theorists – Durbin, Dickinson and Lerner – who, in line with the approach Lange defined with his "classic model", also attempted to formulate a "competitive" solution to the problem of socialist economic calculation. We shall particularly focus on the innovations these authors sought to introduce, with respect to Lange's model, and whether or not they were able to comprehend and answer the challenge originally issued by Mises. We shall conclude that "market socialism" amounts to an essentially contradictory and hopeless attempt to achieve an absurd goal, to "square the circle". This view is also held by a group of socialist theorists who, led by Maurice Dobb, have always pointed to the conflict between traditional socialism and the competitive model, and in fact, a secondary debate emerged, strictly in the socialist camp, between supporters and critics of market socialism. The chapter will conclude with a few final thoughts on the true meaning of the impossibility of socialism and the contributions of Austrian theorists.

## 1 OTHER MARKET SOCIALISM THEORISTS

A large portion of the last chapter was devoted to a careful analysis of Oskar Lange's proposals. Generally speaking, they are the most commonly cited and considered by the secondary sources which, thus far nearly always in a biased, erroneous manner, have described and commented on the controversy over socialist economic calculation. At the same time, the other market socialism theorists, more often than not, simply repeat Lange's original arguments, though they modify the details slightly. From this group, we shall study Durbin, Dickinson and Lerner in some depth. Specifically, we shall concentrate on determining whether any of them came to understand the true essence of Mises and Hayek's challenge and were able to offer a theoretical solution to it, and conclude that, apart from the fact that their theoretical analyses merely involve small variations in detail with respect to Lange's "classic model", these market socialists failed in their attempt to solve the economic problem socialism poses.

### Evan Frank Mottram Durbin

Durbin may have raised certain hopes initially, since he was in contact with the theoretical contributions of the Austrian school of his day, and he was able to clearly distinguish between the Austrian and the neoclassical–Walrasian paradigms. In addition, he wrote a treatise on economic cycles which was profoundly influenced by the ideas that Hayek had presented on the subject.[1] Nevertheless, we shall see that despite this healthy "Austrian" influence, Durbin failed to grasp the heart of the socialism problem Mises and Hayek raised, and in fact, his "solution" was formulated in such strictly static terms as Lange's.

Durbin's contribution appears mainly in an article entitled, "Economic calculus in a planned economy", which was published in December of 1936.[2] Durbin claims to be "almost certain" that the problem of economic calculation in a socialist economy could be resolved if the central planning board were to order the different production units to act in accordance with the following two rules: first, to calculate the marginal productivity of all movable factors of production; and second, to allocate productive factors for those uses for which marginal productivity is highest. Companies would be instructed to produce the highest volume compatible with "normal" profits ("average cost rule"). To minimize the possibilities of error involved in calculations of marginal productivity, Durbin deems it necessary to calculate the corresponding demand curves. Furthermore, he maintains that the interest rate should be established by the "free" new capital market, yet at no point does he clarify how such a market would function in a system in which private ownership of the means of production is prohibited. Finally, Durbin believes the economy should be organized in terms of large sectors, "trusts", or monopolies which would be ordered to "compete" with each other.

There is no need to repeat here the arguments that have already been expressed concerning the proposal of competitive "trusts" (originally defended by Heimann and Polanyi) and the possibilities of organizing a true capital market, based on the services of a monopolistic state bank, where there is no private ownership of the means of production. These issues have already been closely analyzed in earlier chapters. At this point, it should be emphasized that Durbin's proposal contains exactly the same error Lange and others had committed before, that is, the presumption of a context of equilibrium in which no changes occur and all information necessary to calculate the marginal productivity of productive factors is given and easily attainable.

Indeed, the rules designed by Durbin could serve as a rational guide for economic calculation if the information necessary to calculate the marginal productivity of each factor of production could be obtained in an environment in which there is no private ownership of the means of production or freedom to exercise entrepreneurship without hindrance. Let us bear in mind that to calculate marginal productivity, one must make a purely entrepreneurial estimate concerning the following: first, which goods or services consumers will demand in the future and in what quantities; second, what specifications, characteristics, technological innovations and so on must be included; third, what maximum prices can be charged in the market for these consumer goods and services once they have been produced; and fourth, what will be each good's average period of production and what interest rate must be used to determine the present value of the corresponding future marginal-productivity values. Logically, the above information can only be generated in a competitive market, by the different economic agents who participate, and it is generated as they exercise their entrepreneurship without any institutional encumbrance. For this to occur, there must be true competition, but not among mysterious trusts or monopolies (it is unclear whether they would be organized horizontally or vertically), but at all inter- and intrasectoral levels of society. Moreover, it is essential that any person be able to freely use his own entrepreneurial creativity to discover and generate, in an attempt to earn entrepreneurial profits and avoid losses as far as possible, the (always practical, subjective, dispersed and inarticulable) information necessary to perform the actions most conducive to his goals.

We should also remember that in the real world, the type and quantity of productive factors are not given, and not all can be divided into homogeneous units, but instead, depending on the imagination, desires and ends of each entrepreneur, as well as the specific information he generates in accordance with his particular circumstances of time and place, what constitutes a "movable" factor of production and a relevant unit of this factor will vary from case to case, that is, it will depend on the subjective perception of the entrepreneur in question. Moreover, the implicit assumption that the corresponding future demand curves are known or can somehow be calculated reveals Durbin's profound ignorance of the manner in which market processes truly function in real life.

In fact, in a competitive market, there are no supply, demand, or any other sorts of curves or functions. For the information necessary to draw or describe them does not exist, and therefore it is not available anywhere (not to a company or industry manager, or much less to a scientist or central planning agency), not only because the information which would make up the demand curve is dispersed, but also because this information is not even forming constantly in the minds of the individual participants in the market. In other words, supply and demand curves can never be discovered in the market, simply because they do not exist. At most, they have a merely interpretive value within economics, and any person, whether an expert in economics or not, who, almost without realizing it, begins to think of such functions or curves as real will commit serious errors. This is because information about the quantities that will be bought or sold at each price is not abstractly considered by each economic agent, nor is it stored in each person's memory for all future circumstances. On the contrary, such information is strictly subjective and dispersed and only emerges at the specific moment an economic agent decides to make a purchase or a sale, as a result of the entrepreneurial process itself, along with numerous particular influences and circumstances which the agent involved in the transaction subjectively perceives. Hence, this information is created *ex novo* at that moment; it did not exist before, and it will never be replicated. Therefore, at most, entrepreneurs in a real market economy try to estimate what could be viewed as certain isolated points along hypothetical future supply and demand curves. Still, this approach is not necessary for the formulation of price theory, nor do we find it appropriate, since it could somehow imply a recognition that such curves or functions exist or could exist in the future. If the entrepreneur acts correctly, he makes pure entrepreneurial profits; if he acts in error, he incurs losses. It is precisely the incentive of achieving the former and avoiding the latter which encourages the tendency of entrepreneurship to continuously create and discover the appropriate information. Without these incentives, the free exercise of entrepreneurship is impossible, and therefore, so is the creation of the information necessary to make coordinating decisions and rational calculations. Economic and social life, in all of its manifestations, including prices, arises from a combination of multiple human actions, and not from the intersection of mysterious functions or curves, which do not exist in real life and have been surreptitiously introduced in our science by a whole horde of "scientistic" thinkers who have come from the world of polytechnics and applied mathematics and have not yet managed to grasp the very harmful effects the use of their methods exerts on the science of economics.[3]

Hence, Durbin, like Lange and other socialist theorists, assumes that economic agents have access, in objective form, to information the very creation of which is a theoretical impossibility in the absence of private ownership of the means of production and the free exercise of entrepreneurship. Without these institutions, the information will not be generated, the managers of the corresponding sectors will not be able to objectively follow Durbin's rules, and the central planning agency will most certainly not be capable of monitoring and verifying whether or not these sectors are acting correctly, according to these rules. Thus, Durbin commits his gravest error when he explicitly asserts: "The ability to discover marginal products is not dependent upon the existence of any particular set of social institutions".[4] Furthermore, if Durbin believes the information necessary to calculate marginal productivity will always be available, regardless of which social institutions are present (whether capitalist, socialist, or any combination of the two), then it is unclear why he rejects the Walrasian procedure proposed by Lange and based on the same assumption that Durbin makes, that is, that the necessary information is available in objective, unequivocal form. Moreover, Durbin holds that the "technical" difficulties in calculating the marginal productivity of the different factors are the same in a capitalist system as in a planned economy, and he refuses to recognize that the problem is not technical but economic, and to discuss any "practical" aspect beyond his own "theoretical" observations.[5]

Therefore, we see that, like Lange, Durbin views as "theory" only the marginalist model of equilibrium (though in his case, rather than the general Walrasian equilibrium, it is more the partial Marshallian equilibrium and the theory of marginal productivity), in which the information necessary for calculating the corresponding marginal productivities is presumed "given". He fails to see that this theory rests on suppositions which are so restrictive that they render the theory practically irrelevant. Durbin is unfamiliar not only with the formal theory of the social coordination processes entrepreneurship drives, but also with the role certain social institutions play by encouraging or restricting entrepreneurship, the economic analysis of property rights, and the theoretical problem posed, in the absence of entrepreneurial competition, by the dispersed, subjective nature of knowledge. It is not surprising that Durbin's attempt to solve the socialist economic calculation problem was unsuccessful, since his theoretical tools were unsuitable, both for understanding the problem Mises originally raised and for finding a feasible solution for it. Thus, we can conclude, as Hoff does in his critical analysis of Durbin's contribution,[6] that "in his anxiety not 'to dogmatize on practical questions' he has overlooked the crux of the whole problem, namely, how the data on which the socialist trusts are to base their calculations are to be obtained".[7]

## Henry Douglas Dickinson's Book, *The Economics of Socialism*

The publication in 1939 of Dickinson's book also augured well for the author's finally understanding, fully addressing, and attempting to answer Mises and Hayek's original challenge.[8] The fact that in this book, Dickinson explicitly abandons the contentions he made in his 1933 article on price formation in a socialist system, and that he does so for precisely the essential reason his Austrian opponents had stressed to him (that is, the information necessary to implement his proposal of a mathematical solution would never be available) seemed a hopeful sign that Dickinson was capable of grasping all the implications of his new "intuition".[9] Moreover, Dickinson had a very attractive personality. Collard tells us he was "a much loved, unworldly, eccentric figure with a keen sense of fun and a most astute mind";[10] and Hayek, in his 1940 article, praises not only the comprehensive nature, but also the length, organization, conciseness, and clarity of Dickinson's work, and adds that to read it and discuss its content was a true intellectual pleasure.[11] Finally, Dickinson's openness and scientific honesty manifest themselves quite plainly in the highly favorable review he published in 1940 of the original Norwegian version of Trygve J.B. Hoff's book.[12] Nevertheless, unfortunately, we could point out that many of Dickinson's proposals coincide entirely with those Oskar Lange made earlier, and even so, Dickinson expressly cites Lange only in the bibliography of his book. For this reason, most of our criticisms of Lange in the last chapter also apply here, in Dickinson's case.

As Don Lavoie has quite astutely shown,[13] despite everything, Dickinson's book basically maintains the former, static position of this author, and thus Dickinson remains unable to solve the economic calculation problem as Mises and Hayek had formulated it. This is particularly evident in the role which, according to Dickinson, both uncertainty and the entrepreneurial function would necessarily play in a socialist system. In fact, Dickinson believes that one of the advantages of the socialist system would be to reduce the uncertainty which typically emerges in the capitalist system as a result of the interaction between many separate decision-making entities. This supposed "reduction" in uncertainty would be achieved through the intervention of the central planning agency, which by imposing a series of conscious, direct production ratios via commands, would necessarily reduce the high levels of uncertainty normally present in the market. Dickinson again refers to the openness which would exist in a socialist system, as opposed to the typical behavior of companies in a capitalist system, which he asserts is characterized by excessive "secrecy" and a lack of "information transparency".

In making these assertions, it is clear that Dickinson implicitly considers the central planning bureau capable of accessing information which would permit it to coordinate society from above, and thus to reduce the degree of uncertainty and the errors entrepreneurs normally commit. However, Dickinson never explains how this would be possible, especially in light of the fact that the information the planning agency needs to lessen uncertainty is not generated from above, but "from below", that is, at the level of the economic agents themselves. Also, as we know, such information is subjective, practical, dispersed and inarticulable, and hence it cannot possibly be transmitted to a central planning body, or even created, in the absence of complete freedom for the exercise of entrepreneurship. Furthermore, when Dickinson advocates total "information transparency" and the publicizing of all the "commercial secrets" which are guarded in the capitalist system, he is implicitly assuming the information is objective and that once all of the data and secrets of the different economic agents were spread throughout the social framework, the level of uncertainty would drop significantly. However, we must consider that any economic agent can literally flood his competitors or colleagues with all the information concerning his plans without necessarily reducing the level of uncertainty. This is because it is only possible to flood others with information which can be articulated or transmitted in a formalized manner. Moreover, the data must be interpreted; all interpretations are subjective; and in countless situations, the economic agents and their competitors may not subjectively interpret the same data in exactly the same way, and thus the data could not take on the same subjective meaning it conveyed to the entrepreneur who originally "issued" the information. The limit could conceivably lie in a set of circumstances in which the entrepreneur would not only transmit the information, but would also indicate how, in his subjective opinion, future events would unfold, and what the best course of action would be. If economic agents decided to follow the "intuitions" of the issuer, they would simply be giving up the chance to interpret the data themselves, and thus to personally exercise their entrepreneurship, and they would be limiting themselves to merely following the entrepreneurial leadership of another. The socialist system can only eliminate uncertainty via the "ostrich method", that is, people must bury their heads in the sand and refuse to see uncertainty or recognize that it is not a "problem" (except in the absurd mental constructions of befuddled equilibrium theorists), but a social reality which is inherent in human nature and which man constantly faces through the exercise of his entrepreneurship.

We find another indication that Dickinson's model remains essentially static in the way he attempts to deal with the level of uncertainty central planning could not eliminate. Dickinson proposes the establishment of an uncertainty surcharge which would enter into the total cost of production along with the other elements that "normally" comprise it. Although Dickinson admits it would be complicated to calculate this uncertainty surcharge, he believes it could be done by calculating the frequency of changes in the sales and prices of each good and service. With this proposal, Dickinson reveals that he has not yet grasped the essential difference between risk and uncertainty, a difference that was covered in Chapter 2.[14] It involves unique events, with regard to which a possible frequency distribution cannot even be conceived to exist. The information economic agents create and test concerning what they believe may happen in the future is typically entrepreneurial, inarticulable, creative and suited to possible alternatives, and thus it can never be compiled in a centralized manner in such a way as to permit the formulation of a frequency distribution.

Dickinson's approach to the role "entrepreneurship" would have to play in the socialist system is, if possible, even less satisfactory. For in Dickinson's model, entrepreneurship is a fundamentally ambiguous, crude caricature. Logically, private ownership of the means of production is prohibited, and the central planning body is invested with vast powers, both to establish guidelines for the coordination of individual plans, and to distribute the corresponding financial funds, intervene in the labor market, monopolize advertising and propaganda, entirely control and direct international trade and so on. Furthermore, Dickinson views this coercive agency, which he calls the "Supreme Economic Council", as not only "omnipresent and omniscient", but also "omnipotent" in terms of its capacity to introduce changes whenever its members perceive the need for them.[15] Nonetheless, the fact that the managers of the different companies in the socialist system are subjected to the planning bureau does not mean that Dickinson believes they would have no chance to freely make certain choices.[16] In fact, Dickinson holds that each of the companies in the socialist system must have its corresponding capital, keep its own profit and loss account, and be "managed" by a method as similar as possible to that used for managing companies in the capitalist system.

Dickinson clearly realizes that it is necessary for managers to be financially responsible for the performance of their companies, and to share in both the losses and the profits. What our author neglects to explain is how this financial responsibility can be achieved in a system in which private ownership of the means of production is prevented by force. As we learned in Chapter 2, wherever the means of production cannot be privately owned and man cannot freely obtain the benefit of his action, the coordinating entrepreneurship of social processes does not emerge. Furthermore, Dickinson maintains that even though the acquiring of profits is not necessarily a sign of entrepreneurial success, the incurring of losses is always a sign of a managerial failure or error.[17] Logically, if this "intuition" of Dickinson's is raised to the rank of principle, it is clear that managers will tend to be conservative officials who are invariably fearful about undertaking new activities, introducing technological and commercial innovations, modifying the production process and so on, since losses will always be viewed as an error and unfavorable for the professional career of the official, and possible profits may not be recognized as successes.

Dickinson seeks to solve the problem of motivating and rewarding managers by establishing a system of "bonuses" or financial payments which would be keyed to the results obtained by the company an official manages. Of course, such bonuses would not be identical to entrepreneurial profits, not only because that would mean, in practice, a reintroduction of the detested capitalist system, but also because, as just mentioned, Dickinson does not deem profits a sign of efficiency in all cases. With this proposal, Dickinson again falls into the trap of the static model. In fact, as we already know,[18] the bonus system implicitly presupposes that the agency entrusted with awarding the bonuses has access to information which, due to its subjective, dispersed, and inarticulable nature, could never be accessible to the agency. To award bonuses based on results implies that it is possible to know whether these results are favorable or unfavorable. And if it is possible for a planning body to know whether results are favorable or unfavorable, clearly the exercise of entrepreneurship is not necessary to generate this information. However, if the free exercise of entrepreneurship must be permitted in order for the information to emerge, it makes no sense to establish a bonus system, because until this information has emerged, one cannot know if the exercise of entrepreneurship will be successful or not. This is precisely the essential argument that Kirzner discovered and formulated against the different attempts (at this point, all failures) to establish incentive systems in socialist countries.[19] Entrepreneurial success can only be judged subjectively, by the person who is exercising entrepreneurship. The actor measures it from an overall perspective and considers not only the corresponding financial profits, but also all of the other circumstances which he subjectively values as profit. Moreover, this profit arises continually, varies with respect to its amount and nature, and constantly guides the actions of the entrepreneur by providing him with information about the direction he should take. In contrast, the bonus system may, at most, be useful at a managerial level, but not at an entrepreneurial level. Bonuses are awarded *a posteriori*, based on objective information and according to a plan which has been established or agreed upon beforehand and articulated in a totally unequivocal fashion. Bonuses do not guide action, since they are awarded in a rigid and objective manner after the fact. Most of all, the granting of bonuses involves an interpretive judgment about events, a judgment which is only meaningful if made entrepreneurially, but not if it arises from the commands of a central planning agency (which lacks the information necessary to award bonuses in anything but an arbitrary manner), or if bonuses have been established beforehand for all cases and depend on the meeting of certain, more or less measurable criteria.

In brief, what Dickinson fails to understand is that the term "incentive" has two very different meanings. One can conceive of a strict, limited, and practically irrelevant meaning, which would refer to the design of mechanisms for motivating economic agents to make good use (according to the pre-established rule) of the objective information already available to them. It is not this meaning which has been attached to the term from the beginning of this book, but a much broader meaning, one which is also more precise and relevant to economics: incentives comprise all of the ends which can possibly be imagined and created *ex novo*, and with respect to which people not only transmit the objective information they already possess, but (and this is much more important) they bring about the constant creation and discovery of the subjective information they do not yet possess, information essential to the achievement of the proposed ends. In a socialist system, although a clumsy attempt can be made to establish incentives in the first sense, each person is forcibly and systematically prevented from freely reaping the full benefits of his entrepreneurial activity, and thus it is impossible by definition to establish incentives in the second, broad, and true sense.

In addition, Dickinson recommends that bonuses or incentives be provided for technological experimentation and innovation, as if the central planning board could possess the quantity and quality of information necessary to enable its members to determine which projects are worth financing and which are not, as well as which results of experimentation indicate success and which do not. However, as Lavoie states:

> The idea of specified incentives as a deliberate planning device is contradictory to the idea of experimentation as a genuinely decentralized discovery procedure. If the central planning board does not have the knowledge necessary to differentiate bold initiative from reckless gambling, it could not allocate incentives among managers to encourage the one and discourage the other.[20]

This very problem inevitably confronts those western governments which strive to encourage both scientific research and cultural and artistic development via subsidies and other state incentives. In all such cases, the corresponding government agencies end up granting the incentives and subsidies in a purely arbitrary manner, one which coincides with the predictions of the public choice school. In the absence of other, superior criteria, agencies provide incentives based on contacts and political influence and so on, and fail miserably to encourage valuable technological innovation or true cultural or artistic development.

In his approach to entrepreneurship, Dickinson explicitly and implicitly assumes that full information is available, that society is static, and that change never occurs. These assumptions transform all economic problems into mere technical issues simple managers can resolve. Throughout this book, such suppositions have been strongly criticized, and they reveal

Dickinson's inability to confront the problem of calculation in socialist economies. As Mises puts it, "the capitalist system is not a managerial system; it is an entrepreneurial system",[21] and Dickinson is among those who confuse the entrepreneurial function with the managerial function, and who therefore inevitably close their eyes to the true economic problem.

Finally, it is curious to note Dickinson's naivety in believing that his system would make it possible to establish, for the first time in the history of humanity, real "individualism" and "freedom", in other words, a sort of "libertarian socialism" with great intellectual appeal.[22] Nevertheless, given the enormous power that the central planning agency would invariably have in Dickinson's model, together with his characteristic arbitrariness, propaganda manipulation, and incapacity to perform economic calculation, his socialist system would be, at the very least, a very authoritarian system in which individual freedom would suffer dreadfully and there would be no chance of a truly democratic system functioning. In fact, Dickinson himself admits (and these are his exact words) that "in a socialist society the distinction, always artificial, between economics and politics will break down; the economic and the political machinery of society will fuse into one".[23] As Hayek has shown,[24] this assertion of Dickinson's sums up one of those doctrines most energetically espoused by Nazis and fascists. If we cannot distinguish politics from economics, it will be imperative that a sole, prevailing value scale regarding every matter of human life be imposed on all agents and members of society, which, as is logical, could only be achieved through the widespread use of force and coercion. Indeed "politics" always refers to systematic and institutional coercion, force, and commands (that is, to *socialism* as it has been defined throughout this book), while "economics" refers to voluntary contracts, the free exercise of entrepreneurship, and the peaceful pursuit by all individuals of the most varied ends, within a legal context of voluntary exchange and cooperation. The great marvel of life in a capitalist society driven by the force of entrepreneurship lies in the fact that each person or economic agent in such a society learns to voluntarily discipline and modify his behavior in terms of the needs and desires of others, all in an environment in which each person pursues the richest and most varied and unpredictable ends. Clearly, this is something Dickinson never desired nor was able to understand.

**The Contribution of Abba Ptachya Lerner to the Debate**

The contributions of Lerner to the debate did not take the form of explicit replies to the books and articles of Mises or Hayek, but instead they simply appeared in a series of articles Lerner published in the 1930s, in which he commented on and criticized the proposals of the other socialist theorists who participated in the debate, particularly Lange, Durbin, Dickinson and Dobb.[25] In addition, Lerner later made a number of observations relevant to our topic in his book, *The Economics of Control*, which was published in 1944.[26]

In his articles, Lerner attempts to tackle not only the problems of statics, but also the "dynamic" problems which the socialist economy poses. Moreover, in *The Economics of Control*, he expressly mentions[27] that total planning would require a centralized knowledge of what goes on at each factory, of daily variations in supply and demand, and of changes in technical knowledge within all branches of production. Lerner also explains that because a central planning agency cannot conceivably acquire such knowledge, the only option is to rely on the "mechanism" of prices. However, despite these observations, Lerner's contribution, like those of the other market socialists, is still explicitly and implicitly based on the assumption that all of the information necessary to implement his proposal would necessarily be available, and thus Lerner manages neither to answer the challenge of Mises and Hayek nor in turn to solve the socialist economic calculation problem. Furthermore, we could even point out that Lerner was the most extreme in terms of defending the equilibrium model as a "theoretical" foundation for socialism and ignoring and denying the need to study the truly interesting problems entrepreneurship raises. Let us consider three concrete examples which very clearly illustrate this characteristic position of Lerner's.

First, mention must be made to Lerner's critical analysis of the cost rules formulated earlier by different market socialists, in general, and by Taylor, Lange and Durbin, in particular. In fact, Lerner criticizes Taylor's use of the principle of equating price with total average costs. He also criticizes the focus of Lange's rules, for their aim of simulating the market "mechanism" more than the final state toward which the market tends; and he is especially critical of the application of Durbin's rules, which, according to Lerner, signify a return to the practical principle of establishing prices in terms of average costs, since managers are required to produce the highest volume compatible with obtaining a "normal" level of profits.[28]

According to Lerner, it is not so important to find a practical rule as to directly pursue the final objective of the socialist system, which can only be done by ensuring that no factor or resource is used to produce a good or service while the production of others more highly valued is neglected. The only way to ensure this is to order managers to make prices equal to marginal costs in all cases ($MC = P$), a principle which, though it coincides with Lange's second rule, must be followed exclusively and without the obsession Lerner believes Lange had with simulating the functioning of a competitive market. According to Lerner, it is unnecessary to insist, as Durbin does, that managers obtain "normal" profits, since such profits are simply a sign of static equilibrium, and what the socialist system really needs is a guide for the allocation of productive resources in a "dynamic" world. Therefore, we see that Lerner's so-called "dynamic analysis" is limited to an attempt to find a rule applicable, in his opinion, to all of the circumstances which arise on a daily basis in a socialist economy. Paradoxically, Lerner's solution is as static as those proposed by Durbin, Lange and Dickinson, and hence, we could repeat here all of the detailed criticism we expressed earlier concerning the rule of establishing prices based on marginal costs. At this point, it is enough to repeat that marginal costs are not "objective" in the sense that they are given and can be unequivocally observed by a third party. On the contrary, they are a typical example of entrepreneurial information, that is, information gradually generated in a subjective, dispersed, tacit, practical and inarticulable manner in the minds of those who freely exercise their human action or entrepreneurship, and therefore it cannot be supposed that information about costs is created or discovered by managers who cannot freely exercise their entrepreneurship, due to the elimination of private ownership of the means of production. It is even more absurd to assume that such information can be transmitted to the central planning body and that this body is somehow capable of monitoring the compliance of the different industry managers with the rule ($MC = P$).

Second, curiously, Lerner himself realizes that the relevant prices which must be taken into account in his rule ($MC = P$) are not "present" prices (which have already emerged in the market, even in the recent past), but future prices as economic agents foresee them ("expected future prices").[29] Therefore, Lerner's fundamental rule must be established in such a way that each manager equates prices to marginal costs according to his own expectations. Nonetheless, not only is it impossible for these expectations to arise if managers cannot freely exercise their entrepreneurship (due to the absence of private ownership of the means of production), but it is also theoretically impossible for a bureaucratic inspector and member of the central planning bureau to objectively monitor whether or not the rule is being followed (that is, whether or not each manager is acting correctly "in accordance with his own expectations"). Hence, Lerner intuits an idea that is basically correct, but he fails to realize that it demolishes his entire proposal and reduces it to utter nonsense.

Third, Lerner views the issue of whether the central planning agency will be able to estimate future marginal costs more or less accurately than the entrepreneurs who act in a competitive society as a "sociological" or "practical" issue and one that therefore does not belong to the field of "economic theory".[30] Moreover, Lerner expressly criticizes Durbin's attempt to analyze the practical effects socialism would have on incentives and the behavior of managers in the socialist system. Lerner remarks jokingly that with this endeavor, Durbin was attempting to solve a problem which was completely unrelated to the theoretical possibility of economic calculation in socialist economies.[31] It is obvious that the one answering the wrong question, and with analytical tools and "theoretical" conclusions unsuitable for tackling the problem Hayek and Mises raised as to the impossibility of rational economic calculation in a socialist system is Lerner himself. Indeed, when he hides behind a hypothetical system in which economic agents are instructed to act in a certain way, yet he neglects to consider whether or not they will be able to act in this way based on the information they can create and the incentives which motivate them, Lerner deliberately alienates himself from the relevant theoretical problems and takes refuge in the aseptic nirvana of general equilibrium and welfare economics.

Lerner's obsession with equilibrium and statics is especially evident in his criticism of Lange, whom he sees as unnecessarily trying to reproduce or simulate the mechanisms of competition, when in Lerner's opinion the truly important matter is to articulate the conditions necessary to define the "socialist ideal" from the perspective of "welfare economics", regardless of the method used to achieve this ideal. In fact, the goal is no longer even to establish a model of "perfect" competition (though such a model of "competition" has nothing to do with the competition which emerges between entrepreneurs in real life), but to define as clearly as possible the nirvana or "paradise" described by "welfare economics", while the discovery of the practical systems most appropriate for reaching this paradise via coercion is left to sociology, psychology and politics.[32] Hence, Lerner insists that rather than simulating a system of "perfect competition in equilibrium" by trial and error or any other method, it is important to try to achieve the social optimum *directly* by instructing managers to equate prices to marginal costs.

Of all the theorists that have been analyzed up to this point, Lerner was perhaps the most mesmerized by the neoclassical model of general equilibrium and welfare economics, even to the point that he deemed any analysis which did not refer to the assumptions, implications and formal exposition of welfare economics to fall outside the scope of "theory". This explains his sole, insistent recommendation that company managers be instructed to follow the dictates of welfare economics, and with precisely this objective, he wrote his 1944 work, *Economics of Control*, as a practical manual for interventionism, a recipe book for neoclassical equilibrium and welfare economics, to be used directly in the practice of social engineering by the bureaucrats of the central intervention or planning agency, to aid them and facilitate their "arduous task" of systematically coercing the rest of the citizenry in the area of economics.[33]

Lerner fails to realize that by reasoning in this manner, he falls into a trap he built himself. Indeed, the marvelous ivory tower of welfare economics keeps him isolated in perfect stagnancy from the real economic problems posed by socialism and offers him complete "immunity" (or at least he believes so) to the theoretical criticisms Mises and Hayek formulated. Nevertheless, the view from the ivory tower is not clear, but opaque, and Lerner thus lacks the analytical tools necessary not only to solve the crucial economic problems, but also to perceive them. His isolation in the paradigm of welfare economics is so profound that Lerner even considers the differences which separate the real world from the equilibrium model of "perfect competition" to be a clear "defect" or "failure" of the capitalist system (which socialism is at least potentially capable of forcibly correcting), rather than a defect of the very analytical tools of the model. In other words, if the world does not behave as the theory of nirvana predicts, let us destroy the world and construct nirvana, but let us never try to amend the theory in an attempt to understand and explain how the real world works and what happens in it.[34] Hence, a criticism Tadeusz Kowalik levels at Lange applies fully to Lerner as well:[35] Kowalik asserts that Lange lacked the analytical tools necessary not only to solve the problem of socialist economic calculation, but also to understand and examine the truly significant economic problems.[36]

## 2   MARKET SOCIALISM: THE IMPOSSIBLE SQUARING OF THE CIRCLE

In view of our analysis of the proposals of Lange and the rest of the market socialists of his school,[37] it can be concluded that theoretically and practically, only two alternatives exist: either people enjoy complete freedom to exercise entrepreneurship (in a context in which private ownership of the means of production is recognized and defended, and there are no restrictions beyond the minimum of traditional rules of criminal and private law necessary to avoid both the asystematic assault on human action and breaches of contract); or there is systematic, widespread coercion of entrepreneurship in more or less broad areas of the market and society, and specifically, private ownership of the means of production is prevented. In the latter case, it is impossible to freely exercise entrepreneurship in the affected social areas, particularly that of the means of production, and the inexorable result is that the rational economic calculation we have already described in detail in our analysis becomes unachievable in any of them. It has been shown that the second type of system renders impossible both social coordination and economic calculation, both of which can only take place in a system of complete freedom for the exercise of human action. What market socialists have attempted, with phantasmagorical results, is to formulate a "theoretical synthesis" in which a socialist system is established (one characterized by systematic aggression against human action and by public ownership of the means of production), yet the existence of a market is maintained. For ideological, romantic, ethical or political reasons, they stubbornly refuse to abandon socialism, and because Mises's and Hayek's criticisms have made a strong impact on them, they seek to reintroduce the market into their models, in the vain hope of attaining "the best of both worlds", and of making their ideal more popular and attractive.

Nevertheless, what socialists do not wish to understand is that the mere, violent restriction of free human action in any social area, especially that of the factors or means of production, is enough to keep the market, which is the quintessential social institution, from functioning in a coordinated manner and from generating the practical information necessary for economic calculation. In short, what market socialists fail to comprehend is that systematic violence cannot be employed with impunity against the very essence of our humanness: our capacity to act freely in any particular set of circumstances, at any time and in any place.

At least market socialists have not comprehended this until recently, for Brus and Laski (who have described themselves as "ex-naïve reformers" and who for many years defended market socialism), following Temkin, have endorsed these words written by Mises:

> What these neosocialists suggest is really paradoxical. They want to abolish private control of the means of production, market exchange, market prices and competition. But at the same time they want to organize the socialist utopia in such a way that people could act as if these things were still present. They want people to play market as children play war, railroad, or school. They do not comprehend how such childish play differs from the real thing it tries to imitate ... *A socialist system with a market and market prices is as self-contradictory as is the notion of a triangular square.*

More recently, following Mises's example, Anthony de Jasay has more graphically concluded that "market socialism" is "an open contradiction in terms, much like hot snow, wanton virgin, fat skeleton, round square".[38]

One can only fathom why this obsession with "squaring the circle" (which all market socialism entails) has been the object of scientific interest and effort if one considers the three following factors: first, the strong, stubborn, political–ideological motivation to avoid abandoning the socialist ideal, for emotional, romantic, ethical, or political reasons; second, the use of the neoclassical equilibrium model, which describes the real functioning of the capitalist market in only a very limited, poor, and confusing manner, and which involves the assumption that all necessary information is available, and thus suggests that a socialist system could operate on the same theoretical premises as the static model; and third, the express renunciation and even condemnation of the theoretical analysis of how human action really functions in environments that lack private ownership of the means of production, under the pretext that considerations about incentives and motivations are "foreign" to the field of economic "theory".

Some socialist authors, at most, propose the introduction of bonuses or incentives which clumsily simulate the entrepreneurial profits of the market, yet these authors fail to understand why the managers in a socialist system would not act like the entrepreneurs in a market economy, if these managers receive the generic order to do just that, or to "act in a coordinated manner", or "for the common good" and so on. (And if economists themselves make this mistake, what can we expect of non-specialists?) These theorists do not understand that general directives, no matter how well-intentioned, are useless when concrete decisions must be made in the face of specific problems which arise at a particular time and in a particular place. They do not comprehend that if all people simply devoted themselves to acting under coercive instructions (both "obvious" and empty) to "work for the common good", or to "coordinate social processes", or even to "love thy neighbor", we would necessarily end up acting in a discoordinated manner, against the common good, and to the grave detriment of neighbors near and far. This is because it would be impossible to creatively perceive the different profit opportunities in each set of concrete circumstances and to assess and compare them in light of potential subjective costs.

In contrast, members of the Austrian school have been tirelessly devising and perfecting an alternative paradigm in the field of economic science; they have been developing, in formal, abstract (though non-mathematical) terms, an entire general theory on the behavior of (real, non-mechanical) human action in society and its different implications. A key element in this theory is the very exercise of human action or entrepreneurship, which constantly uncovers new ends and means and generates information which permits rational, decentralized decision making, and thus, coordination among all human beings, and in turn, the emergence of an extremely complex social network. Theorists from the countries of the former Eastern bloc, in particular, are increasingly studying, commenting on, and popularizing this paradigm, and they view the theoretical works of Mises and Hayek as more relevant, and cite them more, than those of the great western neoclassical theorists, like Samuelson, or even members of the Chicago school, like Friedman. To the extent that this is occurring, it is not surprising that a great number of former market socialists have abandoned their old positions.[39] Market socialism has failed as a proposed solution to the problem of socialist economic calculation, both in theory and in repeated attempts at practical reform in the socialist systems of Eastern Europe, and consequently, the very theorists who until recently had defended it are abandoning it in all directions as a model to follow.[40]

## 3  MAURICE H. DOBB AND THE COMPLETE SUPPRESSION OF INDIVIDUAL FREEDOM

We have waited until the end to analyze a position of certain theoretical interest, which from the beginning has had its main proponent in Maurice Dobb. Dobb begins by more or less explicitly recognizing the impossibility of socialist economic calculation, but then he concludes that both this impossibility and the inefficiency it involves are irrelevant. In other words, he decides that they constitute a "cost" which must not be taken into account, given that the socialist ideal must be pursued *per se*, for ethical, ideological and political reasons, regardless of the results. Hence, supporters of this position label as "hypocritical" or "naive" those market socialists who strive to introduce as many capitalist mechanisms as possible into the socialist system. Defenders of this view wish to call things by their name and avoid deceiving anyone: socialism either means the complete suppression of autonomy and individual freedom, or it is not socialism.[41]

What these theorists desire, in the purest socialist tradition, is to forcibly impose upon all people their own particular view of the way the world should be. Furthermore, these theorists have realized that the clumsy, partial imitation in a socialist system of elements characteristic of a market economy, far from alleviating the economic calculation problem, makes it much more obvious and difficult. In fact, if decentralized decision making is permitted at a certain level, the problem posed by the impossibility of centralizing dispersed knowledge manifests itself much more clearly and intensely, and thus, gives the impression that the problems of social coordination have worsened (if this is not actually the case). In contrast, if all freedoms (including consumers' freedom of choice and workers' freedom of choice regarding jobs) are suppressed, and economic agents are forcibly prevented from making any other type of autonomous decision, and a unified plan for all social spheres is imposed from above, then although the problem of socialist economic calculation, as we know, cannot be solved, it becomes largely hidden, and the degree of social "coordination" and "adjustment" appears to be much greater.[42]

Let us imagine a society which functions at mere subsistence level and rests on simple economic relationships imposed completely from above by force and by the actual elimination of those who oppose the regime. We can even suppose that the brutal dictator would be assisted by the strongest computer in his task of supervising compliance with his instructions. Under these circumstances, economic calculation appears considerably more straightforward: people would do what the dictator ordered; he would choose the production combinations; and everyone else would simply obey, like slaves, and follow the instructions received from above. As Mises has plainly shown,[43] even under these extreme conditions, which are the most favorable conceivable in terms of the feasibility of socialist economic calculation, it is clear that the problem calculation poses in such a system could not be resolved, since the dictator would still lack a rational guide for making decisions. In other words, he would never know if his pre-established ends could be achieved in a more suitable, expedient manner via different combinations of factors and products or different decisions. However, if the dictator does not care – that is, if this type of socialism not only eliminates consumers' freedom to choose between consumer goods and services, workers' freedom to choose between jobs, and private ownership of the means of production, but it also (implicitly or explicitly) is meant to have no economic purpose, or efficiency is viewed as an irrelevant concession to the conservation of the system itself – then the economic calculation problem could be deemed solved, though not by making calculation possible, but instead by the contrived alternative of defining "calculation" as precisely no calculation at all, and as the constant imposition of the dictator's capricious desires on everyone else.

It is not surprising that the theorists of this school, who view competition and socialist central planning as radically incompatible, have been particularly critical when judging so-called "market socialism". Thus, the curious debate which arose between Maurice Dobb and the market socialists, especially Abba P. Lerner.[44] Curiously, Dobb agrees on this point with the theorists of the Austrian school, and he even ironically criticizes market socialists' use of the general equilibrium model and, within the neoclassical paradigm, their assumption that so many "similarities" exist between the capitalist and socialist systems that no formal difference exists between them. Dobb does not see the problem in terms of neoclassical equilibrium analysis; for him, it hinges on the radical differences between the institutions of the socialist system and those of the capitalist system, and specifically, on the fact that socialism involves the forcible abolition of all the institutions characteristic of the capitalist system.[45] Dobb even highlights the fundamental ambiguity of the solutions proposed by market socialists, who seek to reconcile the irreconcilable, and, depending upon their best interest, their current environment, and the type of argument they are considering, emphasize in their models either the characteristics typical of the market or the advantages of socialist planning. Thus, during their debate, Dobb labeled Lerner an "invisible opponent", since whenever possible, and with great ability, Lerner used the simple and curious dialectical device just described to avoid the issues raised.[46]

In short, Dobb argues that the central authority should fix all prices, that these prices should be forcibly imposed at all levels, and that consumer sovereignty and freedom of choice in the workplace should be prevented. If we take into account that this central authority pursues no goal other than to remain in power, the question of whether or not "economic calculation" is possible may seem irrelevant. In this sense, Dobb's proposal is both less contradictory and more realistic and honest than that of many market socialists. It is less contradictory and more realistic in the sense that it rests not on the formal analysis of equilibrium, but on the true institutions of socialism, which as we know, are based on systematic and all-encompassing coercion, which corresponds exactly with the political design of the model from the time of its revolutionary beginnings. Dobb's proposal is more honest than that of the market socialists in the sense that he does not strive to conceal the true face of socialism, but bases this system plainly and simply on the brutal repression and restriction of free human action.[47]

Hoff, in the context of his critical analysis of Dobb's position, offers the following helpful example of it.[48] He writes that the use of molybdenum in the production of toy swords, or of high quality lenses in elementary-school microscopes would undoubtedly be considered a poor allocation of resources in a society in which the satisfaction of the desires of consumers (or of the dictator himself) mattered, and in which, therefore, such metal and lenses could produce much greater satisfaction (to consumers or to the dictator himself) if they were devoted to other ends. Nevertheless, such an allocation would not be viewed as "inefficient" or "uneconomic" if the goal were, for example, to provide children with the best technical equipment possible, or to favor at any cost the workers who produce the lenses. Hence, we see that illogical and inefficient choices do not appear so if objectives are arbitrarily set in each case, or indeed, if no objectives exist at all. Moreover, as we know, the differences between real and democratic socialism are inevitably just a matter of degree, not of kind, and therefore, this arbitrary behavior is not exclusive to the most extreme socialist societies, but recurs constantly in the interventionist regulations which are constantly implemented in western countries.[49]

Hayek, for his part, devoted an entire section[50] of his 1935 article on the state of the debate to a detailed analysis of Dobb's position, in which he praises Dobb's courage and honesty in explaining the true implications of socialism.[51] However, Hayek wishes to stress that for socialist economic calculation to be possible in Dobb's model, not only would consumers' and workers' free choice have to be thwarted, but we would also have to assume that the socialist dictator lacks any scale of goals for his action. This is so, because once we suppose that the dictator has a set aim, then we can assert that even in Dobb's model, rational economic calculation would be impossible for the dictator, since he would lack an objective guide to tell him whether or not, when pursuing a certain end with his decisions, he is overlooking other set objectives of greater value to him. In this sense, Hayek once more agrees fully with Mises, who expressly states that the problem of economic calculation requires the dictator to at least have decided what his ends are and their relative importance on his value scale.[52] If we assume this to be the case, economic calculation becomes impossible, since the dictator would lack a rational guide to indicate whether or not he, by making certain decisions, is neglecting the achievement of ends he values more.[53]

Whether economic calculation is impossible because the dictator first decides what his objectives are and rates them in importance, or we artificially maintain that no problem of economic calculation exists, since no end of a certain importance with respect to others is pursued, clearly the allocation of resources in Dobb's model would be purely arbitrary, and the inefficiencies would be of such magnitude that the model amounts to no more than a model of, to use Mises's term, "destructionism", that is, the total destruction or annihilation of civilization and the reduction of humanity to a state of almost unimaginable poverty, slavery and terror.[54]

It is true that from a strictly economic standpoint,[55] one cannot judge the determination of an individual to whom the cost of the socialist system does not matter as long as socialism is achieved, and in fact, as we have seen, at the end of his seminal 1920 article, Mises asserts that in this case, his argument against socialist economic calculation will not be taken into account. Nevertheless, one wonders how many followers of the socialist ideal at the grass-roots or the political level would still be willing to support it if they were aware of its true implications.[56] We must also ask how far the socialist model can be maintained by the use of force at each specific historical stage and what the possibilities are of keeping a certain country or geographic area isolated from the rest of the world, so that its people do not discover what they are really giving up by allowing themselves to be tricked or deceived by their government's official propaganda. All of these questions are of great interest and relevance, particularly with respect to the estimation, in each historical case, of the possibilities of a democratic or revolutionary conquest of power and of a socialist regime's retaining power. Still, none of the questions detracts at all from the soundness of Mises and Hayek's theoretical challenge, which has completely exposed the fact that socialism necessarily involves widespread impoverishment of the masses, because it does not permit calculation in terms of economic efficiency, and also the fact that ultimately, socialism is an impossible system incapable of achieving the glorious ends which, with the purpose of tricking the public, have usually been associated with it.

## 4  IN WHAT SENSE IS SOCIALISM IMPOSSIBLE?

Chapter 3 showed that socialism is an intellectual error because it is theoretically impossible to adjust social behaviors via a system of institutional coercion against free human interaction. In other words, the thesis of this book is that without freedom to exercise entrepreneurship, the information necessary for rational economic calculation (that is, decision making which is not arbitrary, since the information relevant in each case is subjectively considered) is not created, nor is it possible for economic agents to learn to discipline their behavior in terms of the needs and circumstances of others (social coordination). This thesis coincides with that of Mises, beginning with his 1920 article. Indeed, for Mises, "rational" indicates decision making based on the necessary, relevant information, concerning both the ends to be pursued, as well as the means and the expected opportunity costs. Mises demonstrates that only in a competitive environment in which freedom of enterprise and private ownership of the means of production exist is this information gradually and entrepreneurially generated and transmitted. Hence, in the absence of free markets, private ownership of the means of production, and the free exercise of entrepreneurship, information is not generated, and totally arbitrary decisions are made (on either a centralized or a decentralized basis). It is precisely in this way that we should interpret these words of Mises: "As soon as one gives up the conception of the freely established monetary price for goods of a higher order, *rational production becomes completely impossible.* Every step that takes us away from private ownership of the means of production and from the use of money also takes us away from rational economics".[57] He also writes, for the reasons noted, that "*socialism is the abolition of rational economy*".[58] However, what Mises never asserts, contrary to the partial and opportunistic interpretations some of his opponents have placed on his work, is that it is impossible to attempt to realize any utopia, in general, and the socialist system, in particular, through the use of force. Quite the opposite is true: Mises maintains that the theoretical knowledge that it is impossible to perform economic calculation in the socialist system will only make an impression on those who mistakenly believe that this system can achieve a higher degree of efficiency, economic development and civilization than the capitalist system, but it will not affect those who defend socialism out of envy or for emotional, "ethical", or "ascetic" reasons. In fact, in 1920, Mises wrote the following:

> The knowledge of the fact that rational economic activity is *impossible* in a socialist commonwealth cannot, of course, be used as an argument either for or against socialism. Whoever is prepared himself to enter upon socialism on *ethical* grounds on the supposition that the provision of goods of a lower order for human beings under a system of a common ownership of the means of production is diminished, or whoever is guided by *ascetic* ideals in his desire for socialism, will not allow himself to be influenced in his endeavours by what we have said ... *But he who expects a rational economic system from socialism will be forced to re-examine his views.*[59]

Hayek maintains, in full agreement with Mises, that it is, in a sense, "possible" to undertake any course of action, no matter how crazy or absurd, and that from this point of view, an attempt may even be made to bring a socialist system into practice, but that from a theoretical perspective, the question of the "impossibility of socialism" focuses merely on whether the socialist course of action is consistent with the objectives it is designed to achieve: specifically, social and economic development which is as coordinated and harmonious as that achieved through the capitalist system, and if possible, more so. Nevertheless, if the goal is to end "market anarchy" by overcoming the "inefficiencies" of the market through coercion and a centralized, rational economic plan, clearly socialism, as it cannot achieve this objective, is, in the above terms, an impossibility. To put it another way, because the socialist system renders impossible both rational economic calculation and adjusted behavior among social agents, such a system cannot possibly accomplish the goal of surpassing the capitalist system in creativity, coordination and efficiency. Finally, Hayek recognizes that the impossibility of achieving economic efficiency and the general decline in development which inevitably go hand-in-hand with the impossibility of socialist economic calculation may not change the desires of those who continue to support socialism for other (religious, emotional, ethical or political) reasons, though in this case economic science provides helpful knowledge and a very valuable service even to this second group of people, since it shows them the true *costs* of their political, ethical, or ideological choices and can help them to revise or strengthen them, as the case may be.[60]

At any rate, there is no question that Mises and Hayek's analysis was a real bombshell for all who, both experts and non-experts in economics, eagerly and naively supported socialism with the idea that it would be a panacea for all social problems and would permit a degree of economic efficiency and development unheard of under capitalism. There is also no question that for most people, the fact that socialism involves widespread impoverishment and a loss of efficiency is a powerful, and in many cases definitive, argument for abandoning socialism as an ideal. Nonetheless, we cannot ignore the fact that as an ideal, socialism has an important ethical, and even "religious", component, and therefore, we must approach it from the perspective of social ethics. For this reason, more and more research efforts are being dedicated to the analysis of whether or not socialism is an ethically admissible system, regardless of the theoretical problems of economic efficiency that have already been described. In fact, from the standpoint of at least one of the areas of social ethics which have been analyzed (that of natural law), there are potent reasons to believe that the socialist ideal is radically contrary to the nature of man (and this appears inevitable, since socialism is based on the exercise of violence and systematic coercion against the most intimate and essential characteristic of human beings: their capacity to freely act). Based on this argument, the socialist system would be not only theoretically unsound, but also ethically inadmissible (that is, immoral and unjust), and hence, "in the long run", it would be impossible to implement consistently and would be inexorably condemned to failure because it contradicts human nature. From this perspective, science and ethics are simply two sides of the same coin, and a consistent order exists in the world, in which the conclusions reached in different fields, scientific, historical-evolutionary and ethical, invariably tend to converge.[61]

If economic science shows that rational economic calculation is impossible in the socialist system, and if the theoretical analysis of social ethics shows that socialism is also impossible because it contradicts human nature, then what conclusions can be drawn from a historical–interpretive study of socialist experiences up to this point? The task is to clarify whether or not the historical events which have taken place in socialist countries fit in with Mises and Hayek's theoretical analysis of socialism. According to this analysis, what we can expect from the introduction of a socialist system, in which people are not free to exercise entrepreneurship, and precisely to the extent that this freedom is restricted, is a widespread poor allocation of resources and productive factors, in the sense that certain lines of production will be expanded excessively, to the detriment of others which provide goods and services the population may need more. Also, there will be an excessive focus on certain projects, and the only justification offered will be strictly of a technical or technological nature, and such projects will be launched without consideration for the costs they involve. Paradoxically, this uncontrolled tendency to implement projects for strictly "technical" reasons will preclude the generalized introduction of new and economically more advantageous technologies and production methods which could be discovered and actually tried in the presence of complete freedom to exercise entrepreneurship.[62] In short, the arbitrary low interest rate will lead to excessive investment in the most capital-intensive industries, to the detriment of consumer goods and services. In general, irrationality and social discoordination will extend to all levels, and therefore, other things being equal, the same amount of effort and social support will result in a much lower standard of living and in far fewer and lower quality consumer goods and services in a socialist system than in a capitalist system. In other words, other things being equal, the socialist system can only approach the capitalist system by incurring much higher, and even unnecessary and completely disproportionate, costs to people, the environment, and, in general, all of the productive factors.

Though this is not the place to carry out an in-depth analysis of the historical experiences provided by socialist systems, at this point it can be mentioned that the historical interpretation of such events illustrates and agrees fully with the a priori conclusions of the economic theory of socialism as Mises and Hayek developed it. In fact, socialist governments have proven incapable of rationally coordinating their economic and social decisions, of maintaining a minimum degree of adjustment and efficiency,[63] of satisfying citizens' desire for consumer goods and services, and of fostering the economic, technological and cultural development of their societies. Indeed, the distortions and contradictions of the socialist systems of the former Eastern bloc became so obvious to most of the population that the popular clamor for the abandonment of socialism and the reintroduction of capitalism was unbearable for the former regimes, which collapsed one after the other. In this sense, the fall of socialism in Eastern bloc countries must indeed be viewed as a great scientific triumph and an illustration, without precedent in the history of social science, of the theoretical analysis of socialism which members of the Austrian school of economics have been developing since the 1920s. Nevertheless, now that the credit which the above historical events brought to the arguments of Mises and the satisfaction they offered Hayek, the other Austrian economists, and few others, has been pointed out, it must be added that because the Austrian theoretical analysis showed a priori that socialism could not work, since it rests on an intellectual error, and that socialism would necessarily cause all sorts of social maladjustments and distortions, it is a terrible tragedy that millions of people had to endure so many years of unspeakable suffering to demonstrate historically something which from the beginning, the theoretical contributions of the Austrian school indicated would inevitably occur. Particular responsibility for this human suffering belongs not only to most members of the scientific community itself, who negligently overlooked and even fraudulently concealed the content of the Austrian analysis of socialism, but also to a clumsy and antiquated, though still predominant, positivism, according to which, experience alone, regardless of any theory, would be capable of revealing the survival possibilities of any social system.[64] With the glorious exception of Mises, Hayek, the rest of their school, and a few others, the near entirety of the social science community betrayed humanity, as its members failed, at the very least, to fulfill their vital scientific duty to notify and warn citizens about the dangers which derive from the socialist ideal. Therefore, it is essential that we make a very healthy and educational acknowledgment of scientific accountability, which, before the citizenry and in view of the future of the history of economic thought, situates each theorist in his rightful place, regardless of the fame, name, or popularity he may have acquired at other times and in other contexts.

Some words of caution are necessary regarding my comments on the historical interpretation of socialist experiences. This is because, unlike many "positivist" theorists, I do not assume or believe empirical evidence alone suffices to confirm or refute a scientific theory in the field of economics. I have deliberately asserted that historical studies "illustrate" and "agree" with the theoretical conclusions, but not that they "confirm" or "demonstrate the validity" of such conclusions.[65] Actually, though the analysis of the logical inadequacies of "positivist methodology"[66] will not be reproduced here, it is clear that experience in the social world is always historical, that is, it is always associated with highly complex events in which innumerable "variables" operate and cannot be directly observed, but only interpreted in light of a prior theory. Also, the interpretation of historical events will vary depending upon the theory, so it becomes crucial to establish beforehand, by methodological procedures other than positivist ones, theories which permit an accurate interpretation of reality. Hence, indisputable historical evidence does not exist, much less evidence which proves or disproves a theory. Furthermore, the theoretical discussion in general, and the discussion about socialism in particular, lead to extremely valuable conclusions, which, had they been taken into account in time, would have avoided, as already mentioned, not only decades and decades of unsuccessful efforts, but also numerous conflicts of all sorts and an unspeakable amount of human suffering. Therefore, to wait for history to confirm whether or not an economic system is feasible is not only a logical impracticality, since history cannot confirm or refute any theory, but it also involves the absurdity of forgoing a priori the teachings of accurate theories developed outside of experience, and furthermore, it invites the trial of any absurdity or utopia, with disproportionate human costs,[67] on the pretext of permitting the analysis of the corresponding "experimental results".

The above comments were necessary, because although at the time of the first writing of this book (1990–91), the collapse of the socialist systems in Eastern European countries and the trends reflected there over recent decades do, in general, fully confirm the "predictions" which could be inferred from Mises's and Hayek's teachings on socialism, this has not always been the case,[68] and in certain historical periods, there has even been a widespread belief to the contrary, that is, that the course of events in Eastern European countries clearly refuted the theory of the impossibility of socialism as formulated by the Austrians. Moreover, occasionally it has been written that even Hayek[69] and Robbins,[70] in view of the practical functioning of socialism in the Soviet Union, abandoned Mises's extreme position and took refuge in a "second line of defense" which consisted of the assertion that although socialism could "work" (that is, that it was not "impossible"), in practice it would necessarily pose severe problems of inefficiency. As we already know, this interpretation is completely erroneous, since neither Mises nor Hayek withdrew at any time to a "second line of defense". On the contrary, they always believed that events in the Soviet Union fully confirmed the Misesian theory of socialism, even in those historical periods in which the failures and inadequacies of the socialist system were better concealed and less obvious.[71]

## 5 FINAL CONCLUSION

In light of all that has been said about the debate on socialist economic calculation, we can conclude that none of the socialist theorists was capable of satisfactorily answering the challenge posed by Mises and Hayek. In most instances, they did not even manage to grasp the true meaning of this challenge. They moved in the context of the neoclassical–Walrasian paradigm, and they used analytical tools which greatly hindered their understanding of the true problems which arise in a system in which private ownership of the means of production is absent, as is freedom to exercise entrepreneurship. Also, the shift (which sprang, in turn, from the above situation) toward problems of statics kept them from perceiving and examining the true problems involved, and it produced the false sense that these problems had been "theoretically resolved". Consequently, the true theoretical challenge issued by Mises and Hayek went unanswered, and it has yet to be satisfactorily answered even today, as socialist theorists themselves have increasingly begun to acknowledge. Moreover, the unfolding of social, economic and political events throughout the twentieth century has fully confirmed the theoretical contributions of Mises and Hayek on the theory of socialism, although most economists from western countries still hold that the debate was concluded and settled in the early 1940s. From that time on, different lines of research have been pursued, both in "comparative systems", and in the theory of the "reform of socialist systems" and the development of planometrics. Nevertheless, this research has been marred by a near total ignorance of the theoretical problems analyzed by Mises and Hayek in the course of the debate, and this ignorance has largely contributed to the fruitlessness and failure of these lines of research.

On the Austrian side, not only the theorists originally involved in the debate (mainly Mises and Hayek), but also a growing number of young economists, have continued to develop a highly productive set of theories the scientific origin of which can be traced to the debate. In this sense, a multitude of scientific consequences have followed from the debate, which has proved highly fruitful for economic science, and thus it is particularly important to analyze the different areas of economics which have already been enriched by contributions originally intuited or developed as a result of the debate on socialist economic calculation. Most of these young authors have already been cited at different points in this book, whenever their contributions have been relevant, though a more profound and detailed study of their work will have to be left for another time.

The current situation, which has undoubtedly emerged from the historical events witnessed by the world with the collapse of the socialist regimes in the countries of Eastern Europe, is giving rise to a generalized rethinking of the "traditional" version of the debate, along the main lines of argument presented in this book. A highly significant role in this rethinking process is being played not only by an increasing number of western economists, but also by most of the scholars who until recently were considered the top theorists in socialist countries. It is hoped that if this research trend in the field of the history of economic thought continues, a widespread consensus will soon be culminated concerning the need to modify the assessment and conclusions which until now have prevailed regarding the "socialist economic calculation debate". If so, I shall consider it a great honor and source of satisfaction to have contributed my own small grain of sand to the destruction of what has simply been another pernicious, unjustified myth of economic science.

# NOTES

1. Durbin (1933).
2. Durbin (1936). See also Durbin (1937).
3. Thus, it is necessary to abandon the "functional theory" of price determination, which from the time of Marshall has always pervaded economics textbooks. Carl Menger first warned against this theory in his February 1884 letter to Leon Walras, in which he concluded that "la méthode mathématique est fausse" (see Antonelli, 1953, 282), and Emil Kauder's comments, 1957 [1990], esp. 10–11). Böhm-Bawerk later cautioned against the theory in volume 2 of *Capital and Interest* (1959b, 233–5), where he criticizes the mechanical conception of supply and demand as mere "quantities" which depend on an independent variable (price), when in real life, supply and demand are the result of actual, concrete human decisions and actions. The functional, scientistic theory of price must therefore be replaced with a "genetic-causal", or to be more precise, praxeological, theory of price, one in which prices derive from a sequence of entrepreneurial human actions. Such a theory would maintain and enhance the valid conclusions of the "functional" model while guarding against the serious risks and errors which normally result from this model. See Mayer (1932). See also Kirzner's related comments (1987, 148). Mises's similar ideas appear particularly in his *Human Action* (1966, 327–33). In addition, see the quotation in note 53, Chapter 5, along with our remarks. In Spain, a relatively recent example of harmful scientistic methodology based on "social engineering" and the use of mathematics in the field of economics is provided by socialist José Borrell Fontelles (1992).
4. Durbin (1936 [1968], 145).
5. "It may be very difficult to calculate marginal products. But the technical difficulties are the same for capitalist and planned economies alike. All difficulties that are not accountancy difficulties are not susceptible to theoretical dogmatism" (ibid., 143).
6. Durbin, who was still a young man when he tragically drowned in Cornwall in 1948, participated, along with J.E. Meade, Hugh Gaitskell, and to a lesser extent, Dickinson and Lerner, in building the ideological foundations for the English Labour Party following the Second World War (mostly through the so-called Fabian Society), and Durbin's daughter, Elisabeth Durbin, has analyzed his role (Durbin, 1985). Most of these "ideologists" ended up defending a model based on interventionism and Keynesian-type macroeconomic planning within a social democratic context. Elisabeth Durbin also authored the brief article about her father in Volume 1 of *The New Palgrave: A Dictionary of Economics* (1987, 945). See also Durbin (1984). Incidentally, we should mention that Elisabeth Durbin sat on the examination board (with Israel Kirzner, Fritz Machlup, James Becker and Gerald P. O'Driscoll) for Don Lavoie's doctoral thesis on the socialist economic calculation debate, which he read at New York University and which forms the basis of his brilliant *Rivalry and Central Planning* (1985c).
7. Hoff (1981, 224–9, esp. the heading on p. 227).
8. Dickinson (1939).
9. Ibid., 104, where Dickinson indicates that the mathematical solution he proposed in 1933 was unfeasible, not because the corresponding system of equations could not possibly have been solved, but because he realized that "the data themselves which would have to be fed into the equation machine, are continually changing".
10. See Collard's article about Dickinson (Collard, 1987, 836).
11. Hayek (1940 [1972], 185).
12. This review (*Economic Journal*, **50** (June/September 1940): 270–74), dealt with Hoff's book, published in Norwegian (1938). Dickinson concludes: "The author has produced a critical review, at a very high level of theoretical competence of practically everything that has been written on the subject in German and English".
13. Lavoie (1985c, 135–9). Incidentally, the static conception of economics and the ensuing incapacity to understand the role and nature of uncertainty in a market economy, which are characteristic of Dickinson, are shared today by authors as prestigious as, for

example, Kenneth J. Arrow, who, as we shall see in note 55, considers uncertainty an obvious "failure" of the market and its price system.
14. See "Creativity, Surprise, and Uncertainty" and in Chapter 2, Section 1, notes 12 and 13. The same confusion between risk and uncertainty pervades the new international accounting rules, as well as the new paradigms of Basel II (for banks) and Solvency II (for insurers). See Huerta de Soto (2009d).
15. See Dickinson (1933, 103, 113, and 191). As to these adjectives (omniscient and omnipresent), which Dickinson assigns to the planning bureau, Mises makes the following ironic comment: "It is vain to comfort oneself with the hope that the organs of the collective economy will be 'omnipresent' and 'omniscient.' We do not deal in praxeology with the acts of omnipresent and omniscient Deity, but with the actions of men endowed with a human mind only. Such a mind cannot plan without economic calculation" (Mises, 1966, 710). Fourteen pages earlier, on page 696, we read that "we may admit that the director or the board of directors are people of superior ability, wise and full of good intentions. But it would be nothing short of idiocy to assume that they are omniscient and infallible".
16. "Because the managers of socialist industry will be governed in some choice by the direction laid down by the planning authority, it does not follow that they will have no choice at all" (Dickinson, 1933, 217).
17. For Dickinson, the essential principle would be that "although the making of profits is not necessarily a sign of success, the making of losses is a sign of failure" (ibid., 219).
18. See all of the critical arguments we presented concerning the bonus and incentive system at the end of the seventh criticism of Lange's classic model in Chapter 6.
19. In the words of Kirzner himself (see also note 70, Chapter 6): "Incentives to socialist managers deny the essential role of entrepreneurial discovery" (1985, 34–7). Lavoie, for his part, sums up the Austrian arguments against the socialist system of bonuses and incentives in the following manner: "This implies that the planning board that examines the individual profit and loss accounts must be in a position to distinguish genuine profit from monopoly gain in the standard sense. However, this evades the question under consideration, since the calculation argument contends that the planning board would lack the knowledge that decentralized initiative generates and that this knowledge is revealed only in profit and loss accounts. *There is no superior store of knowledge against which profit figures can be compared, so that the managers' remuneration can be correspondingly altered*" (1985c, 138–9).
20. Ibid., 139.
21. Mises (1966, 708). On p. 709, Mises adds: "One cannot play speculation and investment. The speculators and investors expose their own wealth, their own destiny . . . If one relieves them of this responsibility, one deprives them of their very character. They are no longer businessmen, but just a group of men to whom the director has handed over his main task, the supreme direction of economic affairs. Then they – and not the nominal director – become the true directors and have to face the same problem the nominal director could not solve: the problem of calculation".
22. Dickinson (1939, 26).
23. Ibid., 235.
24. See Hayek (1940 [1972], 206–7).
25. For articles that are most relevant to the socialist economic calculation debate, see Lerner (1934a, 1935, 1936, 1937, 1938).
26. Lerner (1944).
27. Ibid., 119.
28. Scitovsky (1984, esp. p. 1552). Tibor Scitovsky provides a summary of the socialist economic calculation debate and Lerner's participation in it (p. 1551) which reveals not only Scitovsky's lack of understanding as to the content of the debate, but also the fact that he used only certain secondary sources that give accounts which do not correspond with the actual unfolding of events. That certain distinguished economists continue to write such things at this stage of the game is altogether disappointing. On Lerner, see

also Karen Vaughn's introduction to Hoff's book (Vaugh, 1981, 24–6) and in the same book, see Hoff (1981, ch. 12, 224–36).
29. Lerner (1937, 253, 269, 270).
30. In Lerner's own words: "The question is then the sociological one, whether the socialist trust is able to estimate this future value more accurately or less accurately than the competitive owner of the hired instrument, and here we leave pure economic theory" (ibid., 269).
31. In fact, Lerner facetiously compared Durbin to the "schoolboy in the examination room who wrote 'I do not know the social effects of the French Revolution, but the following were the kings of England'" (1935, 75).
32. Lerner writes: "Methodologically my objection is that Dr. Lange takes the state of competitive equilibrium as his *end*, while in reality it is only a *means* to the end. He fails to go behind perfect competitive equilibrium and to aim at what is really wanted. Even though it be true that if the state of classical static perfectly competitive equilibrium were reached and maintained in its entirety the social optimum which is the *real* end would thereby be attained, *it does not follow that it is by aiming at this equilibrium that one can approach most nearly the social optimum that is desired*" (1936, 74).
33. Another sign of the static nature of Lerner's analysis, in the sense that he assumes the intervention or planning agency has access to all of the information necessary to act, lies in his development of the theory of the "productive speculator", who would perform a beneficial function, to be preserved in a "controlled" economy, and who must be distinguished from the "monopolistic or aggressive" speculator, whose function must be neutralized by the mechanism Lerner calls "counterspeculation" (1944, 69, 70). What Lerner neglects to mention is that, because the difference he attempts to establish rests entirely on the subjective reasons for the speculative activity, there is no possibility whatsoever of objectively distinguishing between the two types of speculation, since there is no objective, unequivocal criterion that permits us to identify and interpret subjective human motivations. As Rothbard shows in his analysis of monopoly in *Man, Economy, and State* (1970a, Vol. 2, ch. 10, 586–620), the distinction between "competition" prices and "monopoly" prices is theoretically absurd. Because the second are defined based on the first, and the equilibrium prices which, hypothetically, would have prevailed in a perfectly competitive market are unknown in real life, there is no objective, theoretical criterion for determining whether a monopoly exists. Furthermore, as Kirzner has revealed (1973, ch. 3, 88–134), the problem of competition versus monopoly, both understood in the static sense as states or models of equilibrium, is irrelevant, since what is theoretically important is to analyze whether or not there exists a real process driven by the competitive force of entrepreneurship and unhindered by government restrictions, regardless of whether the result of entrepreneurial creativity appears at times to take the form of a "monopoly" or an "oligopoly".
34. See Lavoie (1985c, 129, footnote 8), where he refers to Lerner (1934b). See also Huerta de Soto (1990b, 2009a).
35. Indeed, Kowalik states that near the end of Lange's life, he received a letter from him (dated August 14, 1964), in which Lange wrote: "What is called optimal allocation is a second-rate matter, what is really of prime importance is that of *incentives for the growth of productive forces* (accumulation and progress in technology); this is the true meaning of so to say 'rationality'". Kowalik concludes: "It seems that he must have lacked the indispensable tools to solve this question or even to present it in detail" (Kowalik, 1987a, 131). Also, Kowalik indicates that at some points in Lange's life, he appears to have shared Lerner's conclusions. In "The economist's case for socialism," (in Lange, 1937) Lange wrote: "The really important point in discussing the economic merits of socialism is not that of comparing the equilibrium position of a socialist and of a capitalist economy with respect to social welfare. Interesting as such a comparison is for the economic theorist, it is not the real issue in the discussion of socialism. The real issue is *whether the further maintenance of the capitalist system is compatible with economic progress*". In reality, Lange did not believe the capitalist system could maintain

the pace of economic growth and technological innovation it had boasted from the Industrial Revolution to the Great Depression. He would hardly have believed that a little over a generation after his death, the essential economic problem would take a 180-degree turn, as it would become clear that it is the socialist system, not capitalism, which is incompatible with both economic progress and technological innovation (and obviously with freedom and democracy).

36. The case of Milton Friedman is interesting, because he is an author who uses the analytical tools typical of an equilibrium economist of the modern neoclassical paradigm, and yet, he is an ardent defender of capitalism as opposed to socialist systems. As a result, in the theoretical studies in which Friedman criticizes socialism, he is able neither to grasp the core of the theoretical challenge Mises issued (which Friedman almost never cites and often scorns), nor to explain the theoretical essence of the impossibility of socialist economic calculation. In fact, Friedman lacks a developed theory of entrepreneurship, and hence, of the functioning of the dynamic processes which operate in the market and are always driven by entrepreneurship. Therefore, his "critical analyses" of socialism are simply an amalgam of empirical anecdotes and interpretations regarding what goes on in the real socialist world, or vague observations about the problem the absence of "incentives" (understood in the strict sense we so criticized when discussing Dickinson) poses in socialist economies. For a clear sign of Friedman's analytical inadequacies in this area, see *Market or Plan?* (1984). In this brief pamphlet, Friedman even praises Lange's writings and calls Lerner's book, *The Economics of Control*, "an admirable book that has much to teach about the operation of a free market; indeed, much more, I believe, than about their actual objective, how to run a socialist state" (p. 12). Friedman does not realize that if the writings of Lerner and Lange are irrelevant to the building of theoretical foundations for a socialist system, it is precisely due to their profound lack of understanding about how the capitalist system really works. To put it another way, Mises and Hayek were able to construct an entire theory surrounding the impossibility of socialism precisely because they had profound theoretical knowledge about how the capitalist system really works. Hence, we strongly suspect that Friedman's praise of Lerner's book reveals Friedman's own theoretical poverty with respect to his conception of the dynamic market processes entrepreneurship drives. Moreover, Friedman unnecessarily objectifies the price system and considers it a marvelous "transmitter" of (apparently objective) information, along with the "incentive" necessary to use this information properly. He has not comprehended that the problem is a different one, that prices neither "create" nor "transmit" information, and that the human mind alone can perform these functions, within the context of an entrepreneurial action. He has not understood that the marvel of the market is not that the price system acts "efficiently" in transmitting information (ibid., 9–10), but that the market is a process which, driven by the innate entrepreneurial force of every human being, constantly creates new information in light of the new goals each person sets, and gives rise to a coordinating process among people as they interact with each other, a process through which we all unconsciously learn to adapt our behavior to the ends, desires and circumstances of others. In other words, rather than transmit information, prices create profit opportunities which are seized through entrepreneurship, the force that creates and transmits new information, and thus coordinates the entire social process. Finally, Friedman indicates (p. 14) that the fundamental problem in a socialist system is that of monitoring whether or not economic agents comply with the pre-established "rules". This is not the problem. The basic problem, as we know, is that the absence of freedom to exercise entrepreneurship prevents the generation of the information necessary for rational economic calculation and the above coordinating process to play a role in decision making. In just two places, and quite in passing, Friedman refers to the essential economic problem we are explaining, but he gives it secondary importance and does not analyze it in detail or study all of its implications. In one place, he mentions that it would be difficult for the central planning bureau to obtain the information necessary for it to supervise managers (p. 14), though he fails to realize that this sort of information would not be

created even at the level of management. In his review of Lerner's book, *The Economics of Control* (1947), when Milton Friedman studies the "institutional mechanisms" for attaining an optimum, he vaguely criticizes Lerner for not taking into account that profits are a guideline for action, and they serve to determine an entrepreneur's capacity to command resources. Nevertheless, neither in these instances nor in any other has Friedman been able to explain the reason behind the theoretical impossibility that the system Lange and Lerner propose could work. This explains Friedman's tendency to take refuge in the non-economic implications (political and ethical implications, or those regarding personal freedom) of the institutional reforms proposed by socialists; it also explains the marked weakness of his theoretical criticism of socialism. This lengthy set of observations was necessary, because Friedman is often identified with Hayek and Mises and considered a member of the same school, and the result has been great confusion among economists from the West and the former Eastern bloc who have not yet studied the problem in depth, and thus have not yet perceived the profound, radical differences between Friedman's theoretical paradigm and that of Hayek and Mises. The criticism of Friedman can in general be extended to the rest of the Chicago theorists, who are obsessed with empiricism and focused on a phantasmagorical, objectivist equilibrium (of Ricardian and Marshallian origin), and hence do not imagine there to be any problem of information in the market beyond the high "transaction costs" of acquiring it. This is an error, because it involves the implicit assumption that the actor is able to assess a priori the expected costs and benefits of his process of seeking information. That is, it absurdly implies that the actor knows a priori the future worth of information he does not yet possess, and consequently, it renders an understanding of entrepreneurship and its theoretical implications for the economy wholly impossible. The errors of the Chicago school go back to Frank H. Knight, who stated: "Socialism is a political problem, to be discussed in terms of social and political psychology, and economic theory has relatively little to say about it" (1938). Rothbard has brilliantly explained that at the root of this conceptual error lies not only the above obsession with equilibrium, but also the absence of a true theory of capital, since, following J.B. Clark, the Chicago school has always viewed capital as a mythical fund which lacks a temporal structure and reproduces itself automatically, regardless of any sort of human entrepreneurial decisions. See Rothbard (1991, 60–62). On the difference between the Austrian and the Chicago approaches to economics, see also Huerta de Soto (2008).

37. In 1948, soon after Lange and Lerner made their contributions, James E. Meade published *Planning and the Price Mechanism: The Liberal–Socialist Solution* (1948), in which he presents an analysis and proposals which are very similar to those of Lange and Lerner, and hence we must view Meade as a member of the group that has been analyzed in the main text.
38. Brus and Laski (1989, 167–8). The quotation is taken from Mises (1966, 706–7, 710). See also de Jasay (1990, 35).
39. We must agree with Arthur Seldon that it is surprising that the best-known "market socialists" continue to be socialists at all. In fact, Seldon states: "I cannot therefore see why Nove remains a socialist. That revelation also applies to other market socialists – Ota Sik of Czechoslovakia (now teaching in Switzerland), Brus, the Polish economist (now at Oxford), Kornai of Hungary (now in Budapest), Kolakowski (also at Oxford) and others" (see Crozier and Seldon, "After a hundred years: time to bury socialism", 1984, 61). However, in defence of the eminent economists Seldon mentions, we must admit that, from 1984 to the present, practically all of them, with the possible exception of Alec Nove, have ceased to be socialists. Nove may make the definitive transition once he no longer conceives the market in the perfect competition terms characteristic of the neoclassical paradigm and, like the other theorists, absorbs more and more of the Austrian theory of market processes. Nove's best-known book is perhaps *The Economics of Feasible Socialism* (1983). This book is particularly admirable due to its classification of the inefficiencies of socialist systems. Its main defect lies in Nove's poorly grounded critical analysis of capitalist systems (concerning which he points out

problems of income inequality, inflation, a lack of "democracy", and failure in the area of "externalities"), a result of interpretation errors rooted in the inadequate analytical tools (of neoclassical slant, and focused on equilibrium) Nove uses to interpret the situation in capitalist systems. Hence, we indicated above that as Nove becomes more familiar with the dynamic Austrian theory of entrepreneurial processes, his ideas will most likely take the same direction those of other very distinguished authors, like Kornai and Brus, have already taken. As to the type of socialism Nove proposes (a "feasible" sort, in the sense that he believes it could be established in one human lifetime), he offers nothing new, besides a confused amalgam composed of the nationalization of basic sectors, the focusing of planning on areas where "externalities" exist, the promotion of cooperatives in small and medium-sized industries, and the boosting of "competition" whenever possible. In Nove's model, markets are permitted to operate, but within a framework of all sorts of controls. In any case, today Nove's book is quite outdated, not only because he considered the ideal road toward socialism to be that Hungary embarked on in 1968, but also because he was unable to foresee the significant events which unfolded between 1989 and 1991, and he neglected to answer any of the detailed criticisms of market socialism covered in the text. Finally, we should mention that very hopeful signs exist regarding Nove's "conversion". In an article he wrote in March 1988 and devoted to examining and commenting on his book, *The Economics of Feasible Socialism* ("'Feasible socialism' revisited", 1990, ch. 16), Nove explicitly recognizes the validity of "some" of the "Austrian" criticisms of "market socialism" and the neoclassical paradigm and concludes: "So, there is no harm in admitting that the Kirzner type of criticism hits the target" (p. 237). Nine months later, in December 1988, in his article, "Soviet reforms and Western neoclassical economics" (1990, ch. 17), Nove admits without reservation that "the Austrians are surely more relevant to Soviet reforms than is the neoclassical paradigm", and concludes with the following cryptic assertion: "One need not to accept their [the Austrians'] conclusions, but one must take their arguments seriously" (!) (p. 250).

40. The extent to which the thinking of Mises and Hayek pervaded even that of former Marxists is clear in articles like Geoff Mulgen's "The power of the weak" (1988), which appeared in *Marxism Today* (perhaps the most prestigious journal of British socialists). In this article, Mulgen states that the institutions socialists have traditionally held most dear (the state, unions, political parties and so on) are management systems which are rigid, inflexible, centralized, hierarchical, and thus, profoundly *antihuman*. Therefore, following Hayek's teachings, he leans toward what he calls "weak power systems", because they waste much less "human energy", make use of cooperation and competition, are decentralized, can be connected together in a complex system or network, and transmit information efficiently. He believes that in the future, the English Labour Movement should be oriented to these decentralized structures and the market, and the institutions socialists have traditionally defended should be abandoned. Moreover, Mulgen even intuits our fundamental argument against the possibility of using present or future computer capacity to make socialist economic calculation possible (since the decentralized use of any computer capacity would give rise to such a volume and variety of information that the same capacity could not take account of it all in a centralized manner) when he asserts that "Lange was wrong because technology runs up against the context in which information is produced". Mulgen adds that centralized computer systems distort information, while in contrast, decentralized systems offer incentives to create and transmit information accurately, apart from the fact that entrepreneurs are constantly revolutionizing computer processing and monitoring techniques, while central planners, in the best of cases, invariably lag behind entrepreneurs in this field. In view of this sign of the theoretical dismantling of socialism, it is disheartening that authors like David Miller (1989) are still determined to construct the utopian ideal of "market socialism". It would be difficult to find anything original in Miller's contribution, which is based on the coercive establishment of a competitive system of cooperatives which the workers would manage democratically. Miller is not an economist, nor

has he studied the economic calculation debate, and he misses the reasons such a system could not work (people are not free to exercise entrepreneurship, because the means of production are not privately owned, and the information necessary to calculate efficiently and to coordinate the entire system is not generated). Nonetheless, Miller is honest enough to declare his skepticism about the possibility that such a system would be at least as efficient as competitive capitalism, and he indicates that therefore, the crucial arguments in favor of his "market socialism" must be of another sort: the greater "justice", "freedom" and "democracy" it would provide in the workplace (p. 14). In light of the above, it would be better to debate with such authors in the field of political philosophy or ethical theory, rather than in that of economic science. For a critique of this and other attempts to revive market socialism, see de Jasay (1990). See also note 4, Chapter 6 of this book. Also of interest, in German, is Martin Feucht (1983).

41. In the words of Maurice H. Dobb himself: "Either planning means overriding the autonomy of separate decisions, or it apparently means nothing at all" (1937, 279).
42. Paul M. Sweezy holds that to attempt to introduce decentralization into a socialist system would only serve to replicate there "some of the worst features of capitalism and fail to take advantage of the constructive possibilities of economic planning" (1949, 233). Thus, what Sweezy has in mind is a system of total planning, including concrete directives to the managers of the different industries regarding how they should carry out the corresponding sectoral and entrepreneurial plans. To Sweezy, all planning theory is based on political decisions (that is, on the forcible imposition of the dictator's criteria). He fails to grasp the problem (of arbitrary decision making) economic calculation poses in a socialist system, and in practice, it makes no difference to him, since he believes that once the objectives of the plan have been established, the quantity and quality of the corresponding factors of production will be "automatically" determined by the planners and will be forcibly imposed on the different sectors and companies. See the comments by Elisabeth M. Tamedly on Sweezy's position in "The theory of planning according to Sweezy" (1969, 143–5).
43. Mises, (1966, 695–701).
44. The main articles by Dobb concerning this debate are Dobb (1933 and 1935a). These articles and other relevant contributions were reprinted in *On Economic Theory and Socialism: Collected Papers* (1955).
45. In the words of Dobb: "Naturally, if matters are formulated in a sufficiently formal way, the 'similarities' between one economic system and another will be paramount and the contrasting 'differences' will disappear. It is the fashion in economic theory today for propositions to be cast in such a formal mould, and so devoid of realistic content, that essential differences disappear. The distinctive qualities of the laws of a socialist economy and of a capitalist economy... are not, of course, given in the rules of algebra, but in assumptions depending on differences existing in the real world" (1935a, 144–5). Moreover, it is interesting to note that Dobb himself admits that he initially believed the problem of economic calculation in a socialist system could be resolved through a procedure similar to that Dickinson proposes, but that later, upon perceiving the consequences which would result for the socialist system, he abandoned his initial position. Indeed, in his 1933 article, he criticizes Dickinson's model as "static" in words Hayek himself could have written. In fact, Dobb asserts that to attempt to apply the postulates of static equilibrium to a world in constant flux is a "barren feat of abstraction"; and that economics is much more than "a formal technique . . . a system of functional equations, a branch of applied mathematics, postulating a formal relationship between certain quantities" (1933, 589).
46. To be specific, Dobb remarked that he was "embarrassed by a sense of battling with an invisible opponent" (1935a, 144). Several of Lerner's comments on the establishment of the price system in a socialist system provide examples of his evasive strategy. In his 1934 article, he states: "The competitive price system has to be *adapted* to a socialist society. If it is applied *in toto* we have not a socialist but a competitive society" (p. 55).

Nevertheless, shortly afterward, in his "A rejoinder" (1935, 152), Lerner contradicts himself when he asserts: "And by a price system I do mean a price system. Not a mere *a posteriori* juggling with figures by auditors, but prices which will have to be taken into consideration by managers of factories in organizing production".

47. Years later, Dobb modified his position somewhat when he ambiguously introduced a certain level of decentralization and even competition in decision making. However, he did not formally specify what this slight decentralization would consist of, and from a theoretical standpoint, the position we believe to be of true interest is the one he held in the 1930s, which is the one we have been commenting on and will refer to in the future as "Dobb's classic model".

48. Hoff (1981, ch. 14). The example of the molybdenum swords appears on pp. 278–9.

49. Amartya Sen interprets Dobb's true mindset as follows: Dobb deemed equality of the results to be much more important than efficiency (and thus he left issues of efficiency in the background). Sen also mentions that Dobb viewed the coercive planning of investment as much more important than a supposedly perfect microeconomic adjustment. The argument that issues of "efficiency" must be subordinated to those of equality has become common currency among members of the leftist intelligentsia, who have now resigned themselves to the fact that socialism cannot compete with capitalism in terms of the creation of wealth. Nonetheless, the intellectuals who adopt this position forget: (i) that efficiency and ethics are two sides of the same coin, that is, what is inefficient cannot be just, and nothing is more efficient than morality; (ii) that the cost of the egalitarianism they propose is not only widespread poverty, but the most brutal repression of human action; (iii) that historical experience teaches that far from reducing inequality, coercion often increases and aggravates it; and (iv) that nothing is more unjust, immoral, and unethical than to impose equality by force, since man has a natural, inalienable right to think up new ends and to reap the fruits of his own entrepreneurial creativity. Sen (1987) and Huerta de Soto (2009a).

50. "Abrogation of the Sovereignty of Consumers" in Hayek (1935c, section 4, 214–17).

51. "Dr. Maurice Dobb has recently followed this to its logical conclusion by asserting that it would be worth the price of abandoning the freedom of the consumer if by the sacrifice socialism could be made possible. This is undoubtedly a very *courageous* step. In the past, socialists have consistently protested against any suggestion that life under socialism would be like life in a barracks, subject to *regimentation of every detail*. Now Dr. Dobb considers these views as obsolete" (ibid., 215).

52. "We assume that the director has made up his mind with regard to the valuation of ultimate ends" (Mises, 1966, 696).

53. In Hayek's own words: "The dictator, who himself ranges in order the different needs of the members of the society according to his views about their merits, has saved himself the trouble of finding out what people really prefer and avoided the *impossible task of combining the individual scales into an agreed common scale which expresses the general ideas of justice. But if he wants to follow this norm with any degree of rationality or consistency, if he wants to realize what he considers to be the ends of the community, he will have to solve all the problems which we have discussed already*" (1935c, 216–17). Thus, incidentally, we see here that as early as 1935, Hayek appears to have made precursory mention of "Arrow's impossibility theorem" when he wrote of the impossible task of combining individual value scales into a common scale which would express general ideals of justice, a scale all would agree on. However, it is certain that Hayek did not attribute this impossibility to reasons of pure logic within a static context in which all necessary information is considered given and subject to predetermined conditions (as in Arrow's theorem), but rather to a much more general and profound cause: individual preferences cannot possibly be formed and transmitted in a non-entrepreneurial context (and this, the essential problem which dispersed, subjective, and inarticulable information poses, lies at the heart of the Austrian criticism of socialist economic calculation). Therefore, the following alternatives exist: first, the socialist dictator could constantly impose his arbitrary wishes on society, without yielding to any pre-established end (as

in the arbitrary, dictatorial destructionism of Dobb's classic model); second, the dictator might first have established his own value scale with its corresponding hierarchy (rational economic calculation would be impossible for the dictator himself); third, the dictator could try to discover the general objectives pursued by the citizenry, according to a scale accepted by all (this is theoretically impossible, given the dispersed nature of knowledge and the strictly subjective and entrepreneurial manner in which it is generated, and Arrow's impossibility theorem would apply as well under static conditions); or fourth, the dictator could establish public ownership of the means of production, yet as far as possible, encourage economic agents to make their decisions in a decentralized way (this would be the solution of market socialists, and it is theoretically impossible also, because the practical information necessary for rational economic calculation would not be generated, as entrepreneurship would not be completely free, and profit could not act as an incentive like in a capitalist system).
54. Mises sees *destructionism* as the essence of socialism: "Socialism is not the pioneer of a better and finer world, but the spoiler of what thousands of years of civilization have created. It does not build; it destroys. For destruction is the essence of it" (Mises, 1922 [1981], 44). Hence, any attempt at systematic, institutional coercion of free entrepreneurial interaction is truly a crime against humanity, in view of the terrible consequences which invariably follow from such social experiments in the long term. Indeed, all of the great human tragedies of the last century which were not due to natural causes (and even many of these, to the extent that their effects could have been more easily mitigated in some other way) originated directly or indirectly from the often well-intentioned desire to realize the socialist utopia. Obviously, significant *differences of degree* exist with respect to the intensity with which such an ideal may be pursued, but we must never forget that the differences between, for example, the genocide committed by the Soviet state, national socialism, communist China, or Pol Pot against their people, and the destructive consequences (which led to constant conflict, social violence and moral corruption) characteristic of "democratic socialism" and the paradoxically named "welfare state", though quite substantial, are differences merely of degree, but not of kind. For the intellectual error and destructionism which lie at the core of "real" socialism and those which constitute the essence of "democratic" or "interventionary" socialism are basically the same. See Huerta de Soto (1991).
55. In addition, Dobb states: "The advantage of the planned economy *per se* consists in removing the uncertainties inherent in a market with diffused and autonomous decisions, or it consists in nothing at all" (1935, 535). This statement of Dobb's fits in perfectly with his dictatorial model of socialism, in which he attempts to dodge the problem of economic calculation by the simple, forcible imposition of the dictator's arbitrary wishes. Indeed, as we saw in Chapter 2, one of the essential features of human action is the creative nature of its results, and thus, the future is always uncertain and open to the creative imagination of entrepreneurs. Hence, the only way to get rid of the uncertainty of the future is to forcibly crush people's capacity to freely act. The "advantage" Dobb associates with central planning is based on "eliminating" uncertainty by suppressing free human action, and thus, freezing the future. It is a case of "curing" the supposed sickness by killing the patient. Curiously, Dobb's approach to uncertainty is very similar to that of neoclassical equilibrium economists, who consider it a bothersome "defect" of the market because it does not easily fit into their "models". For example, Kenneth J. Arrow states: "There is one particular *failure* of the price system which I want to stress. I refer to the presence of uncertainty" (1974b, 33.)
56. Let us remember that Lange, in his *On the Economic Theory of Socialism*, also mentions the possibility of eliminating the "free" market for consumer goods and services, and he asserts that under such circumstances, his system of trial and error and parametric prices would still function perfectly, providing parametric prices were extended not only to production goods and factors, but also to consumer goods and services. In this case, the planning body should also modify prices whenever surpluses or shortages of consumer goods occur in the absence of rationing. (Plainly, this system would

not permit economic calculation, for all of the reasons we explained in our analysis of Lange's proposal.) Though in this article Lange indicates that the fact that he discusses the theoretical possibility of eliminating the freedom of consumers does not mean he defends it (as he considers it undemocratic), we already know that at the end of his life he gradually leaned more and more toward the Stalinist solution, in which the desires of consumers are disregarded almost entirely, and the problem of economic calculation is fictitiously reduced to a coercive imposition of the plan at all levels. In German, Herbert Zassenhaus, in "Über die Ökonomische Theorie der Planwirtschaft" (1934), also defends a system of socialist economic calculation based fundamentally on eliminating consumers' freedom of choice and on a mathematical sort of solution in which decentralized competition is maintained at a certain level. Zassenhaus's writings are characterized by a lack of clarity and especially by a lack of realism, since in his view, communities remain constantly static.
57. Mises (1920 [1975], 104).
58. Ibid., 110. We must admit that Mises presents his thesis in slightly more "extreme" terms in the German edition of his book, *Socialism*. Thus, on p. 197 of the second German edition, published in 1932 and reprinted in 1981, we read: "Der Kapitalismus ist die einzig denkbare und mögliche Gestalt arbeitsteilenden gesellschaftlichen Wirtschaft". This assertion that "capitalism is the only conceivable form of social economy" is slightly softened in the English translation (1922 [1981]), where the literal rendering of the above is followed by a phrase we italicize here: "Capitalism is the only conceivable form of social economy *which is appropriate to the fulfilment of the demands which society makes of any economic organization*" (p. 194 of the English edition). The English formulation is a bit more precise than the German, though we find that the German version agrees perfectly with what Mises had written earlier in his article on economic calculation, since for Mises, "social economy" means "rational economy". On p. 117 of the German version, there appears another sentence which is slightly softened in the English translation. In German, we read: "Der Versuch, die Welt sozialistisch zu gestalten, könnte die Zivilisation zertrümmern, er wird aber nie zur Aufrichtung eines sozialistischen Gemeinwesens führen können". Then, on p. 118 of the English translation, we read: "It would never set up a *successful* socialist community". The adjective "successful" has been added. Despite these slight variations which appear in the English version as compared to the German version of *Socialism*, Mises's idea seems to be perfectly reflected in his 1920 article and it does not change substantially in his subsequent writings.
59. Mises (1920 [1975], 130).
60. Hayek reproaches Mises for sometimes using the expression "socialism is impossible" when what he really means is that rational economic calculation is impossible in a socialist system. This reproach is not wholly justified, in light of certain explicit assertions Mises makes, which have been included in the text. (It is only in *Socialism* that Mises uses some expressions similar to the one Hayek mentions, but if one considers their general context, no doubt exists as to their meaning.) "Many of the objections made at first were really more a quibbling about words caused by the fact that Mises had occasionally used the somewhat loose statement that socialism was impossible, while what he meant was that socialism made rational calculations impossible. Of course any proposed course of action, if the proposal has any meaning at all, is possible in the strict sense of the word, i.e. it may be tried. The question can only be whether it will lead to the expected results, that is whether the proposed course of action is consistent with the aims which it is intended to serve" (Hayek, 1935b, 36). Curiously, nowadays, after revolutionary changes in the countries of the former Eastern bloc have done away with socialism, the general expression "socialism is impossible" has gained widespread colloquial usage.
61. On this topic, see Huerta de Soto (2009a, 1–30, 61–2) and, particularly, the contributions made in the field of social ethics by Kirzner (1989) and Hoppe (1989). Both authors (to whose works we should perhaps add Robert Nozick's slightly outdated,

though still notable book, *Anarchy, State and Utopia* (1974) reveal that socialism is not only theoretically impossible, but also ethically inadmissible. Kirzner bases this conclusion on the stimulating theory that every person has a natural right to reap the fruits of his own entrepreneurial creativity, and Hoppe bases it on the Habermasian axiom that argumentation with another human being always means the acceptance and implicit recognition of the individuality of "the other I" and of his ownership rights to his being, thoughts, and accomplishments, and from this axiom, Hoppe logically deduces an entire theory of property rights and capitalism. For a theory of the three different but complementary levels on which to study social reality (theoretical, historical–evolutionary and ethical), see Huerta de Soto (1990c, 23–4; 2009a, 61–2). The immorality of socialism can be understood in different ways, depending upon the level considered. In other words, socialism is immoral in at least three different senses. First, from a theoretical standpoint, socialism is immoral, since, as a social system, it prevents the generation of information the system itself needs in order to achieve its chosen ends. Second, from an evolutionary perspective, there is nothing more immoral than socialism, as it consists of a constructivist utopia which disregards the value of traditional laws and customs (*mos-moris*, custom). Third, from an ethical viewpoint, socialism is an assault on the most essential principle of human nature: man's capacity to act freely and creatively, and to reap the fruits of his entrepreneurial creativity.

62. Hoff has stressed that any tendency away from entrepreneurship and toward socialism gives greater prominence at all social levels, both explicitly and implicitly, to the technical mentality characteristic of an engineer. Once we eliminate considerations of entrepreneurial profit and cost, it is almost inevitable to attach disproportionate importance to "technical" considerations. This phenomenon occurs not only at the level of the different industries and sectors, but also at the general level of society as a whole (for instance, nowadays with the global warming movement). Indeed, socialist politicians and officials inexorably end up believing they are extraordinary "social engineers" capable of adjusting society at will and introducing the "change" necessary to reach increasing levels of economic and social development. Hoff concludes: "A product which is technically perfect is ex-hypothesi ideal for its purpose from the technical point of view: it gives joy to the engineers and technical experts and can even give laymen aesthetic pleasure, but it must be insisted that the production of a technically perfect article is economically irrational and an economic misuse of labour and material, if this would have satisfied more needs had they been used for another purpose" (1981, last sentence of footnote 8). Paradoxically, the attempt to introduce the latest technological innovations in each sector of production without giving the necessary consideration to cost will eventually delay the technological development of society, since the technological innovations which would be truly advantageous to it (those which would be discovered and introduced entrepreneurially) are not discovered and cannot be applied at the appropriate time and place. For his part, D.T. Armentano (1969) insists that the socialist planner cannot possibly know which project is more economical and efficient, and thus, his decisions will tend to be discoordinated, both intra- and intertemporally, whether or not he tries to justify or "dress up" his decision with technical considerations. Referring to Mises's famous example of the socialist manager who must choose between the construction of a power plant which uses oil and another which uses nuclear energy, he concludes that "if and when the power plant is built at a particular point with particular resources, it will represent an 'arbitrary' and not an economic decision", since the information about prices and costs which in a free, entrepreneurially driven market would be spontaneously generated is not available. See Snavely (1969, 133–4).

63. Logically, "efficiency" is not conceived of in Paretian maximization terms, but as an attribute of entrepreneurial coordination within creative environments where uncertainty is present. See Huerta de Soto (2009a).

64. For example, this clumsy "positivist scientism" amounts to an obsession and pervades the American educational system and academic world in general, and the contributions

of the Chicago school, in particular, including those of one of its most prominent members, George Stigler, who feels that both parties to the debate failed to perceive the "empirical" consequences of their respective positions and that only "empirical evidence" can resolve the existing differences between the defenders of capitalism and socialism. See Stigler (1975, 1–13.) See the excellent criticism of Stigler's position voiced by Barry (1984).

65. See the observations Fritz Machlup makes in "Testing versus illustrating", in Machlup (1984, 231–2).

66. A summary of the critical analysis of positivist methodology and of the most relevant writings appears in Huerta de Soto (1982). The methodological ideas of the Austrian school were refined as the debate on socialist economic calculation progressed, and the complete formulation of the criticism of positivist methodology can be considered one of the most valuable byproducts of this debate, since for precisely the same reasons that socialism is an intellectual error (the impossibility of acquiring the necessary practical information in a centralized manner), in economics it is not possible to directly observe empirical events, or to empirically verify any theory, nor, in short, to make specific predictions, as to time and place, concerning future events. This is because the object of research in economics comprises the ideas and knowledge human beings have and create about what they do, and this information is in constant flux, is highly complex, and cannot be measured, observed, or acquired by a scientist (or a central planning bureau). If it were possible to measure social events and empirically confirm economic theories, socialism would be possible, and vice versa: socialism is impossible for the same reasons positivist methodology is inapplicable. Thus, given their "spiritual" nature, the "events" of social reality can only be interpreted historically, which always requires a prior theory. On these points, see the 33 bibliographical references in Huerta de Soto (ibid.), and especially, Mises (1957), and Hayek "The facts of the social sciences", in Hayek (1972, 57–76) and Hayek (1952). A helpful, dispassionate explanation of the Austrian methodological paradigm appears in Caldwell (1982, esp. pp. 117–38).

67. Mises stresses that the teachings of Soviet experience do not suffice to establish any theoretical argument regarding socialism, and he concludes that "the fallacies implied in a system of abstract reasoning – such as socialism is – cannot be smashed otherwise than by abstract reasoning"(1922 [1981], 535).

68. The popular interpretation of historical events has, on occasion, been comparatively "easier". Such was the case, for example, with the obvious failures of the poorly named "war communism", failures which obliged Lenin to adopt the "New Political Economy" in 1921. The historical events of recent years, which culminated in the collapse of all of the communist regimes in the countries of the former Eastern bloc, also suggest an obvious interpretation. Perhaps the task of interpreting historical events is more complicated in other periods, however, even in such instances, careful study invariably confirms the theses of the theory on the impossibility of socialist economic calculation. On this point, see, for example, the section entitled, "Does Russia refute Mises?", in Steele (1981, 105–6).

69. To Hayek, this version is nothing but a "scandalous misrepresentation" of the facts (see note 25, Chapter 5), and a particularly clear one if we consider that the comments his critics use to justify the above "withdrawal" are comments Hayek made not only in passing, but also with the obvious aim of maintaining the traditional academic courtesy he has always demonstrated, by allowing his opponents, at least on paper, to avoid total defeat. It is in this sense that we must interpret not only the observations which appear on p. 187 of *Individualism and Economic Order* (1972), but also those on pp. 238 and 242 of "The present state of the debate" (1935c), in which we read: "But while this makes it illegitimate to say that these proposals are impossible in any absolute sense, it remains not the less true that these very serious obstacles to the achievement of the desired end exist and that there seems to be no way in which they can be overcome" (p. 238). "No one would want to exclude every possibility that a solution may yet be found. But in our present state of knowledge serious doubt must remain whether such a solution can be

found" (p. 242). Hence, it is not surprising that over 40 years after the most significant part of the economic calculation debate, Hayek, in his 1982 article, was not capable of maintaining his typical patience and courtesy with his intellectual opponents, who continued to place gross misinterpretations on his supposed "withdrawal" to a "second line of defense". Hayek himself expressly recognized that his expressions of courtesy and gentlemanlike behavior were used by opponents with little scientific honesty, and that he would not have repeated the error of risking misunderstandings for the sake of good academic manners: "I might, perhaps, also add that J.A. Schumpeter then accused me with respect to that book of 'politeness to a fault' because I 'hardly ever attributed to opponents anything beyond intellectual error.' I mention this as an apology in the case that, on encountering the same empty phrases more than 30 years later, I should not be able to command quite the same patience and forbearance" (1978c, 235).

70. There is no legitimate basis for a belief that Robbins, in any sense, withdrew to a "second line of defense" when faced with the practical evidence. On the contrary, not only does Robbins explicitly recognize (footnote 1, p. 148 of *The Great Depression*) that his argument very closely follows the one Mises develops in *Socialism* (to the English translation of which Robbins actually made a large contribution, as he prepared an initial draft of some of the most important parts and then handed his draft over to his friend, J. Kahane, for the definitive writing), but also, nearly 40 years later, when the then Lord Robbins wrote his autobiography, he explicitly stuck to his opinion and recognized the validity of Mises's argument on the impossibility of socialist economic calculation, as originally formulated in 1920. In the words of Robbins himself: "Mises' main contentions that without a price system of some sort, a complex collectivist society is without the necessary guidance and that, within the general framework of such a society, attempts to institute price systems which have meaning and incentive in a dynamic context are liable to conflict with the main intention of collectivism – these still seem to me to be true and to be borne out by the whole history of totalitarian societies since they were propounded" (Robbins 1971, 107; see also 1976, 135–50).

71. Such considerable fluctuations in the level of difficulty involved in interpreting events from experience also occur, and even more dramatically, in the case of the effects which the interventionism and social democracy of western countries exert, and therefore, in these contexts, the assistance of theory is, if possible, even more essential than in the case of so-called "real" socialism.

# Bibliography

Alchian, A.A. (1969), "Corporate management and property rights", in *Economic Policy and the Regulation of Corporate Securities*, Washington, DC: American Enterprise Institute, pp. 342ff.

Alchian, A.A. and W.R. Allen (1971), *University Economics: Elements of Inquiry*, 3rd edn, Belmont, CA: Wadsworth.

Allais, M. (1947 and 1948), "Le problème de la planification dans une économie collectiviste", *Kyklos*, **1**, no. 3 (1947): 254–80; **2**, no. 1 (1948): 48–71.

Álvarez, V.A. (1945), "'El Camino hacia la Servidumbre' del Profesor Hayek", *Moneda y Crédito*, **13** (June). Reprinted as ch. 2 of *Libertad Económica y Responsabilidad Social*, 10 essays in an edition which commemorates the centenary of the birth of D. Valentín Andrés Álvarez, Madrid: Centro de Publicaciones del Ministerio de Trabajo y Seguridad Social, 1991, pp. 69–86.

Anderson, T.L. and D.R. Leal (1991), *Free Market Environmentalism*, San Francisco, CA: Pacific Research Institute for Public Policy.

Antonelli, E. (1953), "Léon Walras et Carl Menger à travers leur correspondance", *Économie Appliquée*, **6** (April–September).

Aquinas, St Thomas (1948 and 1954), *Suma Teológica* [*Summa Theologiae*], Vol. 2 (1948), Vol. 4 (1954), Madrid: B.A.C.

Aranson, P.H. (1988), "Bruno Leoni in retrospect", *Harvard Journal of Law and Public Policy* (summer).

Armentano, D.T. (1969), "Resource allocation problems under socialism", in Snavely (ed.), pp. 133ff.

Arnold, N.S. (1990), *Marx's Radical Critique of Capitalist Society: A Reconstruction and Critical Evaluation*, Oxford: Oxford University Press.

Arrow, K.J. (1974a), "Limited knowledge and economic analysis", *American Economic Review*, **64** (March): 1–10.

Arrow, K.J. (1974b), *The Limits of Organization*, New York: Norton.

Arrow, K.J. and L. Hurwicz (1977), *Studies in Resource Allocation Processes*, Cambridge: Cambridge University Press.

Arruñada, B. (1991), "El Coste de la Información Contable", *España Económica* (May): 8–11.

Bagehot, W. (1898), *Economic Studies*, London: Longmans Green. Reprinted by Clifton, NJ: Kelley, 1973.

Bailey, S. (1840), *A Defense of Joint-Stock Banks and Country Issues*, London: James Ridgeway.
Ballesteros Beretta, A. (1984), *Alfonso X El Sabio*, Barcelona: Ediciones "El Albir".
Ballod, K. (1927), *Der Zukunftsstaat, Wirtschaftstechnisches Ideal und Volkswirtschaftliche Wirklichkeit*, 4th edn, Berlin: E. Laubsche. 1st edn published in Stuttgart, 1919.
Barone, E. (1908), "Il Ministro della Produzione nello Stato Colletivista", *Giornale degli Economisti*, **37** (Sept.), English trans. F.A. Hayek, "The Ministry of Production in the Collectivist State", App. A of *Collectivist Economic Planning*, ed. F.A. Hayek, Clifton: Augustus M. Kelley, 1975, pp. 245–90.
Barrow, J.D. and F.J. Tipler (1986), *The Anthropic Cosmological Principle*, Oxford: Oxford University Press.
Barry, N.P. (1984), "The economics and philosophy of socialism", *Il Politico*, **49**, no. 4: 573–92.
Barry, N.P. (1988), *The Invisible Hand in Economics and Politics. A Study in the Two Conflicting Explanations of Society: End-States and Processes*, London: Institute of Economic Affairs.
Bauer, O. (1919), *Der Weg Zum Sozialismus* (The road to socialism), Vienna: Ignaz Brand.
Bennett, J. (1989), *The Economic Theory of Central Planning*, Oxford: Basil Blackwell.
Bergson, A. (1948), "Socialist economics", in *A Survey of Contemporary Economics*, ed., Howard S. Ellis, Homewood, IL: Richard D. Irwin.
Bergson, H. (1959), *Oeuvres*, Paris: Presses Universitaires de France.
Bergun, D.F. (1941), "Economic planning and the science of economics", *American Economic Review* (June).
Bernholz, P. (1987), "Information, motivation, and the problem of rational economic calculations in socialism", ch. 7 in *Socialism: Institutional, Philosophical and Economic Issues*, ed., Svetozar Pejovich, Dordrecht: Kluwer Academic Publishers.
Blaug, M. (1988), *Economics Through the Looking Glass*, Occasional Paper, 78, London: Institute of Economic Affairs.
Blaug, M. (1990), "Comment on O'Brien's 'Lionel Robbins and the Austrian Connection'", in *Carl Menger and His Legacy in Economics*, ed. Bruce J. Caldwell, Annual supplement to Vol. 22, *History of Political Economy*, Durham, NC: Duke University Press.
Blaug, M. (1993), "Book Review", *Economic Journal*, **103**, no. 421 (November): 1570ff.
Block, W. and I. Hexham (eds) (1989), *Religion, Economics and Social Thoughts*, Vancouver: Fraser Institute.

Boettke, P.J. (1988), "Evolution and economics: Austrians as institutionalists", *Research in the History of Economic Thought and Methodology*, **6**.

Boettke, P.J. (1990), *The Political Economy of Soviet Socialism: The Formative Years 1918–1928*, Dordrecht: Kluwer Academic Publishers.

Böhm-Bawerk, E. von (1896), "Zum Abschluss des Marxchen Systems", in *Staatswissenschaftliche Arbeiten-Festgaben für Karl Knies zur Fünfundsiebzigsten Wiederkehr*, Berlin: Haering, pp. 85–205. English trans. "The unresolved contradiction in the Marxian economic system", ch. 4 in *Shorter Classics of Eugen von Böhm-Bawerk*, Vol. 1, South Holland, IL: Libertarian Press, 1962, pp. 201–302. Spanish trans. "Una Contradicción no resuelta en el Sistema Económico Marxista", *Libertas* (Buenos Aires), **7**, no. 12 (May 1990): 165–296.

Böhm-Bawerk, E. von (1914), "Macht oder Ökonomisches Gesetz?", *Zeitschrift für Volkswirtschaft, Sozialpolitik und Verwaltung* (Vienna), **23** (December): 205–71. English trans. 1931 by J.R. Mez, "Control or economic law?", in *Shorter Classics of Eugen von Böhm-Bawerk*, Vol. 1, South Holland, IL: Libertarian Press, 1962, pp. 139–99.

Böhm-Bawerk, E. von (1959a), "The exploitation theory", ch. 12 in *History and Critique of Interest Theories*, Vol. 1 of *Capital and Interest*, South Holland, IL: Libertarian Press, pp. 241–321. English trans. of *Geschichte und Kritik der Kapitalzins-Theorien* (1884, 1900, 1914 and 1921). Vol. 1 of *Kapital und Kapitalzins*. Spanish trans. *La Teoría de la Explotación*, to which J. Reig wrote a foreword, Madrid: Unión Editorial, 1976.

Böhm-Bawerk, E. von (1959b), *Capital and Interest*, Vol. 2, *The Positive Theory of Capital*, South Holland, IL: Libertarian Press.

Borrell Fontelles, J. (1992), *La República de Taxonia*, Madrid: Ediciones Pirámide.

Bradley, R. (1981), "Market socialism: a subjectivist evaluation", *Journal of Libertarian Studies*, **5**, no. 1 (winter): 23–39.

Brus, W. (1974), "Observaciones sobre los problemas de contabilidad marginal en la economía socialista", in *Problemas de Economía Política del Socialismo*, ed. Oskar Lange, Mexico: Fondo de Cultura Económica, pp. 175–94. In English, *Problems of Political Economy of Socialism*, New Delhi: People's Publishing House, 1962.

Brus, W. and K. Laski (1989), *From Marx to the Market: Socialism in Search of an Economic System*, Oxford: Clarendon Press.

Brutzkus, B. (1935), *Economic Planning in Soviet Russia*, London: Routledge. Reissue, Westport, CI: Hyperion Press, 1982. English trans. of *Die Lehren des Marxismus im Lichte der Russischen Revolution*, Berlin: H. Sack, 1928.

Buchanan, J.M. (1969), *Cost and Choice*, Chicago, IL: Markham.

Buchanan, J.M. (1986), "The public choice perspective", ch. 3 in *Liberty, Market and State*, Brighton: Harvester Press.

Buchanan, J.M. and G.F. Thirlby (eds) (1981), *L.S.E. Essays on Cost*, New York: New York University Press.

Bukharin, N.I. and E. Preobrazhensky (1966), *The ABC of Communism: A Popular Explanation of the Program of the Communist Party of Russia*, Ann Arbor, MI: University of Michigan Press.

Burzak, T.A. (2006), *Socialism after Hayek*, Ann Arbor, MI: University of Michigan Press.

Caffé, F. (1987), "Barone", in Eatwell et al. (eds), Vol. 1, pp. 195–6.

Caldwell, B. (1982), *Beyond Positivism: Economic Methodology in the Twentieth Century*, London: Allen & Unwin.

Caldwell, B. (ed.) (1990), *Carl Menger and His Legacy in Economics*, Annual supplement to Vol. 22, *History of Political Economy*, Durham, NC and London: Duke University Press.

Campos, J.G. and A. Barella (1975), *Diccionario de Refranes*, Appendix 30 to the *Boletín de la Real Academia Española*, Madrid.

Cassel, G. (1918 [1932]), *Teoristiche Sozialökonomie*, 5th edn, Leipzig. Spanish trans. Miguel Paredes, *Economía Social Teórica*, Madrid: Aguilar, 1960. English trans. S.L. Barron, *The Theory of Social Economy*, New York: Augustus M. Kelley, 1967.

Cave, M. (1980), *Computers and Economic Planning: The Soviet Experience*, Cambridge: Cambridge University Press.

Cela, C.J. (1990), "El Dragón de Leviatán", Lecture delivered to UNESCO, July 1990, in "Los Intelectuales y el Poder," *ABC* (Madrid), 10 July, pp. 4, 5.

Cervantes, M. (1885), *Don Quixote*, trans. John Ormsby, London, 1885, available at: http://www.csdl.tamu.edu/cervantes/english/ctxt/DQ_Ormsby/part1_DQ_Ormsby.html, 3 December 2003.

Chaloupek, G.K. (1990), "The Austrian debate on economic calculation in a socialist economy", *History of Political Economy*, **22**, no. 4 (winter): 659–75.

Charemza, W. and M. Gronicki (1988), *Plans and Disequilibria in Centrally Planned Economies*, Amsterdam: North-Holland.

Cicero, M.T. (1961), *De Re Publica*, Cambridge, MA: The Loeb Classical Library. Spanish trans. Antonio Fontán, *Sobre la República*, Madrid: Gredos, 1974.

Coase, R.H. (1937), "The nature of the firm", *Economica*, in *The Firm, the Market and the Law*, **4** (November): 386–405. Reprinted Chicago, IL: University of Chicago Press, 1988, pp. 33–55.

Collard, D. (1987), "Henry Douglas Dickinson", in *The New Palgrave: A Dictionary of Economics*, Vol. 1, London: Macmillan, p. 836.

Crozier, B. and A. Seldon (1984), *Socialism Explained*, London: Sherwood Press.
de Jasay, A. (1990), *Market Socialism: A Scrutiny, This Square Circle*, Occasional Paper 84, London: Institute of Economic Affairs.
de Marchi, N. and M. Blaug (1991), *Appraising Economic Theories: Studies in the Methodology of Research Programs*, Aldershot, UK and Brookwood, VT, USA: Edward Elgar.
del Vecchio, G. (1925), "L'opera scientifica di Enrico Barone", *Giornale degli Economisti* (November).
Dembinski, P.H. (1991), *The Logic of the Planned Economy: The Seeds of the Collapse*, Oxford: Clarendon Press.
Di Lorenzo, T.J. (1988), "Competition and political entrepreneurship; Austrian insights into public choice theory", in *Review of Austrian Economics*, ed. Murray N. Rothbard and Walter Block, Vol. 2, Lexington, MA: Lexington Books, pp. 59–71.
Dickinson, H.D. (1933), "Price formation in a socialist economy", *Economic Journal*, **43**, 237–50.
Dickinson, H.D. (1939), *The Economics of Socialism*, Oxford: Oxford University Press.
Dobb, M.H. (1933), "Economic theory and the problems of a socialist economy", *Economic Journal*, **43**: 588–98.
Dobb, M.H. (1935a), "Economic theory and socialist economy: a reply", *Review of Economic Studies*, **2**: 144–51.
Dobb, M.H. (1935b), "Review of Brutzkus and Hayek", *Economic Journal*, **45**: 535.
Dobb, M.H. (1937), "Economic law in the socialist economy", in *Political Economy and Capitalism: Some Essays in Economic Tradition*, London: Routledge & Kegan Paul. Spanish trans. Emigdio Martínez Adame, "La Ley Económica en una Economía Socialista", in *Economía Política y Capitalismo*, Mexico: Fondo de Cultura Económica, 1974.
Dobb, M.H. (1955), *On Economic Theory and Socialism: Collected Papers*, London: Routledge and Kegan Paul.
Dolan, E.G. (ed.) (1976), *The Foundations of Modern Austrian Economics*, Kansas City, KS: Sheed & Ward.
Durbin, E. (1984), *The Fabians, Mr. Keynes and the Economics of Democratic Socialism*, New York: Routledge & Kegan Paul.
Durbin, E. (1985), *New Jerusalems: The Labour Party and the Economics of Democratic Socialism*, London: Routledge & Kegan Paul.
Durbin, E.F.M. (1933), *Purchasing Power and Trade Depression*, London: Chapman & Hall.
Durbin, E.F.M. (1936), "Economic calculus in a planned economy",

*Economic Journal* (December). Reprinted in *Problems of Economic Planning*, London: Routledge & Kegan Paul, 1968, pp. 140–55.

Durbin, E.F.M. (1937), "A note on Mr. Lerner's 'Dynamical' Propositions", *Economic Journal*, **47** (September): 577–81.

Eatwell, J., M. Milgate and P. Newman (eds) (1987), *The New Palgrave: A Dictionary of Economics*, 4 vols. London: Macmillan.

Eckstein, A. (ed.) (1971), *Comparison of Economic Systems: Theoretical and Methodological Approaches*, Berkeley, CA: University of California Press.

Elliott, J.H. (1986), *The Count-Duke of Olivares, The Statesman in an Age of Decline*, New Haven, CT: Yale University Press. Spanish trans. *El Conde-Duque de Olivares*, Barcelona: Crítica, 1990.

Ellman, M. (1983), "Changing views on central economic planning 1958/1983", *The ACES Bulletin*, **25**: 11–29.

Ellman, M. (1987), "Economic calculation in socialist economies", in Eatwell et al. (eds), Vol. 2, p. 31.

Ellman, M. (1989), *Socialist Planning*, 2nd edn, Cambridge: Cambridge University Press. Spanish trans. Carlos Cruz Arjona, *La Planificación Socialista*, Mexico: Fondo de Cultura Económica, 1983.

Endres, A.M. (1991), "Menger, Wieser, Böhm-Bawerk and the analysis of economic behaviour", *History of Political Economy*, **23**, no. 2 (summer): 279–99.

Engels, F. (1947), *Anti-Dühring: Herr Eugen Dühring's Revolution in Science*, trans. Emile Burns, Moscow: Progress Publishers, available at: http://www.marxists.org/archive/marx/works/1877/anti-duhring/ch26.htm, 28 September 2004. (Burns translated the above from the 1894 edition of the book, published in Stuttgart by Verlag von J.H.W. Dietz.)

Felipe, L. (1963), *Obras Completas*, Buenos Aires: Losada.

Ferguson, A. (1767), *An Essay on the History of Civil Society*, London: T. Caddel in the Strand and Edinburgh: A. Kincaid, W. Creech & J. Beel. 3rd English edn of 1773 trans. into Spanish, revised by Juan Rincón Jurado, and published in Madrid: Instituto de Estudios Políticos, 1974.

Feucht, M. (1983), *Theorie des Konkurrenzsozialismus*, Stuttgart: G. Fischer.

Friedman, D. (1989), *The Machinery of Freedom*, 2nd edn, La Salle, IL: Open Court.

Friedman, M. (1947), "Lerner on the economics of control", *Journal of Political Economy* (October): 405–16. Spanish trans. Raimundo Ortega Fernández, "Lerner y la Economía de Control", ch. 11 in *Ensayos sobre Economía Positiva*, Madrid: Gredos, 1967.

Friedman, M. (1984), *Market or Plan?*, London: Centre for Research into Communist Economies.

Furubotn, E. and S. Pejovich (1973), "Property rights, economic decentralization and the evolution of the Yugoslav firm", *Journal of Law and Economics*, **16**: 275–302.

García Villarejo, A. and J. Salinas Sánchez (1985), *Manual de Hacienda Pública, General y de España*, Madrid: Tecnos.

Gardner, R. (1990), "L.V. Kantorovich: the price implications of optimal planning", *Journal of Political Literature*, **28** (June): 638–48.

Garello, J. (1984), "Cultural protectionism", Mont Pèlerin Regional Meeting (Paris).

Gillespie, S. (1990), "Are economic statistics overproduced?", *Public Choice*, **67**, no. 3 (December): 227–42.

Gödel, K. (1931), "Über formal unentscheidbare Sätze der 'Principia Mathematica' und verwandter Systeme I", *Monatshefte für Mathematik und Physik*, no. 38, pp. 173–98. English trans. in the *Collected Works of Kurt Gödel*, Vol. 1, Oxford: Oxford University Press, 1986, pp. 145–96. (Spanish trans. Jesús Mosterín, Alianza Universidad, no. 286, Madrid, 1989.)

Gossen, H.H. (1854), *Entwicklung der Gesetze des Menschlichen Verkehrs und der daraus fliessenden Regeln für menschliches Handeln*, Braunschweig: Friedrich Vieweg & Sohn. English trans. Rudolph C. Blitz, *The Laws of Human Relations and the Rules of Human Action Derived Therefrom*, Cambridge, MA: MIT Press, 1983.

Gould, J.P. and C.E. Ferguson (1980), *Microeconomic Theory*, 5th edn, Homewood, IL: Richard D. Irwin. Spanish trans. Eduardo L. Suárez, *Teoría Macroeconómica*, Mexico: Fondo de Cultura Económica, 1983.

Granick, D. (1984), "Central physical planning incentives and job rights", in *Comparative Economic Systems: Present Views*, ed. A. Zimbalist, Boston, MA: Kluwer-Nijhoff.

Gray, J. (1989), *Liberalisms: Essays in Political Philosophy*, London: Routledge.

Hahn, F. (1988), "On market economics", in *Thatcherism*, ed. Robert Skidelsky, London: Chatto & Windus.

Halm, G. (1935), "Further considerations on the possibility of adequate calculation in a socialist community", trans. H.E. Batson, in *Collectivist Economic Planning*, ed. F.A. Hayek, pp. 131–200.

Hardin, G. (1977), "An operational analysis of responsibility", in *Managing the Commons*, ed. Garret Hardin and John Baden, San Francisco, CA: W.H. Freeman.

Hardt, J.P. et al. (eds) (1967), *Mathematics and Computers in Soviet Economic Planning*, New Haven, CT: Yale University Press.

Hayek, F.A. (ed.) (1935a), *Collectivist Economic Planning*, London: Routledge & Sons. Reprinted by Augustus M. Kelley, Clifton, 1975.

Hayek, F.A. (1935b), "Nature and history of the problem", in Hayek (ed.) (1935a), pp. 1–40.

Hayek, F.A. (1935c), "The present state of the debate", in Hayek (ed.) (1935a), pp. 201–43. Reprinted as "Socialist calculation II: the state of the debate (1935)", in Hayek (1972).

Hayek, F.A. (1937), "Economics and knowledge", *Economica*, **4**: 33–54. Reprinted in Hayek (1972), pp. 35–56.

Hayek, F.A. (1940), "Socialist calculation III: the competitive 'Solution'", *Economica*, **3**, no. 26 (May). Reprinted in Hayek (1972), pp. 181–208.

Hayek, F.A. (1944 [1972]), *The Road to Serfdom*, Chicago, IL: University of Chicago Press. Spanish trans. José Vergara, *Camino de Servidumbre*, Libros de Bolsillo, no. 676, Madrid: Alianza Editorial, 1978.

Hayek, F.A. (1945), "The use of knowledge in society", *American Economic Review*, **35**, no. 4 (September): 519–30. Reprinted in Hayek (1972), pp. 77–91.

Hayek, F.A. (1952), *The Counter-Revolution of Science*, New York: Free Press of Glencoe. There is an excellent reprint by Liberty Press, Indianapolis, 1979. Spanish translation, Madrid: Unión Editorial, 2003.

Hayek, F.A. (1952 [1976]), *The Sensory Order*, Midway Reprint, Chicago, IL: University of Chicago Press.

Hayek, F.A. (1959), *The Constitution of Liberty*, Chicago, IL: University of Chicago Press. Spanish trans. José Vicente Torrente, *Los Fundamentos de la Libertad*, Madrid: Unión Editorial. Eight editions were published between 1975 and 2008.

Hayek, F.A. (1969), *Studies in Philosophy, Politics and Economics*, New York: Simon & Schuster.

Hayek, F.A. (1972), *Individualism and Economic Order*, Gateway Edition, Chicago, IL: Henry Regnery.

Hayek, F.A. (1973, 1976 and 1979), *Law, Legislation and Liberty*. Vol. 1, *Rules and Order*. Vol. 2, *The Mirage of Social Justice*. Vol. 3, *The Political Order of a Free People*, Chicago, IL: University of Chicago Press. Spanish trans. Luis Reig Albiol, *Derecho, Legislación, y Libertad*, 3 vols, Madrid: Unión Editorial, 1976, 1985, 2006.

Hayek, F.A. (1978a), "Competition as a discovery procedure" (1968), in *New Studies in Philosophy, Politics, Economics and the History of Ideas*, London: Routledge & Kegan Paul, pp. 179–90.

Hayek, F.A. (1978b), "Dr. Bernard Mandeville", in *New Studies in Philosophy, Politics, Economics and the History of Ideas*, London: Routledge & Kegan Paul, 249–66.

Hayek, F.A. (1978c), "The new confusion about planning", ch. 14 in *New Studies in Philosophy, Politics, Economics and the History of Ideas*, London: Routledge & Kegan Paul, pp. 232–46.

Hayek, F.A. (1978d), "Socialism and science", in *New Studies in Philosophy, Politics, Economics and the History of Ideas*, London: Routledge & Kegan Paul, pp. 295–308.

Hayek, F.A. (1982), "Two pages of fiction: the impossibility of socialist calculation", *Economic Affairs* (April). Reprinted in Nishiyama and Leube (eds), pp. 53–61.

Hayek, F.A. (1986), "The moral imperative of the market", in *The Unfinished Agenda: Essays on the Political Economy of Government Policy in Honour of Arthur Seldon*, London: Institute of Economic Affairs.

Hayek, F.A. (1988), *The Fatal Conceit: The Errors of Socialism*, Chicago, IL: University of Chicago Press. Vol. 1 of *The Collected Works of F.A. Hayek*, London: Routledge, 1989. Spanish trans. Luis Reig Albiol, *La Fatal Arrogancia. Los Errores del Socialismo*, with a preface by Jesús Huerta de Soto, Madrid: Unión Editorial, 1990. (Reprinted in *Obras Completas de F.A. Hayek*, Vol. 1, Madrid: Unión Editorial, 1997.)

Hayek, F.A. (1991), *The Trend of Economic Thinking: Essays on Political Economists and Economic History*. Vol. 3 of *The Collected Works of F.A. Hayek*, London: Routledge.

Hayek, F.A. (1998), *Socialismo y guerra*. Vol. 10 of *Obras Completas de F.A. Hayek*, Madrid: Unión Editorial.

Heertje, A. (1987), "Nicolaas Gerard Pierson", in Eatwell et al. (eds), Vol. 3, p. 876.

Heilbroner, R. (1989), "The triumph of capitalism", *The New Yorker* (January 23).

Heilbroner, R. (1990), "Analysis and vision in the history of modern economic thought", *Journal of Economic Literature*, **28** (September): 1097–114.

Heimann, E. (1922), *Mehrwert und Gemeinwirtschaft. Kritische und Positive Beiträge zur Theorie des Sozialismus*, Berlin: Robert Engelmann.

Hilferding, R. (1904), "Böhm-Bawerks Marx-Kritik", in *Marx-Studien*, Vol. 1, Vienna: I. Brand.

Hoff, T.J.B. (1938), *Okonomisk Kalkulanjon i Socialistiske Samfund*, Oslo: H. Ashekovg. English trans. M.A. Michael, *Economic Calculation in the Socialist Society*, London: William Hodge, 1949, and Indianapolis, IN: Liberty Press, 1981.

Hoff, T.J.B. (1981), *Economic Calculation in the Socialist Society*, Indianapolis, IN: Liberty Press.

Hoppe, H.H. (1989), *A Theory of Socialism and Capitalism*, Amsterdam and London: Kluwer Academic Publishers.

Hoselitz, B.F. (1956), "The early history of entrepreneurial theory", *Explorations in Entrepreneurial History*, **3**, no. 4 (April): 193–220.

Huberman, B.A. (ed.) (1988), *The Ecology of Computation*, Amsterdam: North-Holland.

Huerta de Soto, J. (1980), "La Teoría Austriaca del Ciclo Económico", *Moneda y Crédito*, no. 152 (March). Reprinted in Huerta de Soto (ed.) 1986, Vol. 1, pp. 241–56.

Huerta de Soto, J. (1982), "Método y Crisis en la Ciencia Económica", *Hacienda Pública Española*, **74**, 33–48; reprinted in Huerta de Soto (ed.) (1986), Vol. 1, pp. 11–33.

Huerta de Soto, J. (1986), "Derechos de propiedad y gestión privada de los recursos de la naturaliza", *Cuadernos del Pensamiento Liberal* (Madrid: Unión Editorial), no. 2 (March): 13–30. Reprinted in Huerta de Soto (ed.) (1987), Vol. 3, pp. 25–45, and in *Estudios de Economía Política*, Madrid: Unión Editorial, 1994, pp. 229–49.

Huerta de Soto, J. (ed.) (1986, 1987), *Lecturas de Economía Política*, 3 vols, Madrid: Unión Editorial, 2nd edn 2005, 2008.

Huerta de Soto, J. (1988–89), "Conjectural history and beyond", in "'The Fatal Conceit' by F.A. Hayek, A Special Symposium", *Humane Studies Review*, **6**, no. 2 (winter): 10. Spanish trans. "Historia, Ciencia Económica y Ética Social", *Cuadernos del Pensamiento Liberal*, Madrid: Unión Editorial, no. 12 (April 1991): 78–80.

Huerta de Soto, J. (1990a), "Prólogo" to *Hayek: Su contribución al pensamiento político y económico de nuestro tiempo*, by Eamonn Butler, Madrid: Unión Editorial, pp. 9–15.

Huerta de Soto, J. (1990b), "La Crisis del Paradigma Walrasiano", *El País* (Madrid), 17 December, p. 36.

Huerta de Soto, J. (1990c), "Prólogo" to *La Fatal Arrogancia: Los Errores del Socialismo*, Vol. 1 of *Obras Completas de F.A. Hayek*, Madrid: Unión Editorial, pp. 13–27.

Huerta de Soto, J. (1991), "El Fracaso del Estado 'Social'", *ABC* (Madrid), 8 April, pp. 102–3.

Huerta de Soto, J. (1992), "F.A. Hayek: Los Fundamentos de la Economía Liberal", *Revista de Economía* (Madrid: Consejo General de Colegios de Economistas de España), no. 12: 121–5.

Huerta de Soto, J. (1995), "The economic analysis of socialism", ch. 14 in *New Perspectives on Austrian Economics*, ed. Gerrit Meijer, London and New York: Routledge.

Huerta de Soto (2006), *Money, Bank Credit, and Economic Cycles*, Auburn, AL: Ludwig von Mises Institute, 2nd edn 2009.

Huerta de Soto (2008), *The Austrian School: Market Order and Entrepreneurial Creativity*, Cheltenham, UK and Northampton, MA, USA: Edward Elgar.

Huerta de Soto (2009a), *The Theory of Dynamic Efficiency*, London and New York: Routledge.

Huerta de Soto (2009b), "Classical liberalism versus Anarcho-capitalism",

in *Property, Freedom, Society: Essays in Honor of Hans-Hermann Hoppe*, ed. Jörg Guido Hülsmann and Stephan Kinsella, Auburn, AL: Ludwig von Mises Institute, pp. 161–78.
Huerta de Soto (2009c), "Preface to the second English edition", in *Money, Bank Credit, and Economic Cycles*, Auburn, AL: Ludwig von Mises Institute, pp. xxii–xxv.
Huerta de Soto (2009d), "The fatal error of Solvency II", *Economic Affairs*, **29**, no. 2: 74–7.
Hülsmann, J.G. (2007), *Mises: The Last Knight of Liberalism*, Auburn, AL: Ludwig von Mises Institute.
Hume, D. (1981), *A Treatise of Human Nature*, Oxford: Oxford University Press.
Hurwicz, L. (1971), "Centralization and decentralization in economic processes", in Eckstein (ed.), pp. 81ff.
Hurwicz, L. (1973), "The design of mechanisms for resource allocation", *American Economic Review*, **2**, no. 63 (May).
Hurwicz, L. (1984), "Economic planning and the knowledge problem: a comment", *Cato Journal*, **4**, no. 2 (autumn).
Ingrao, B. and G. Israel (1987), *La Mano Invisibile*, Roma-Bari: Laterza & Figli. English trans. Ian McGilvray, *The Invisible Hand: Economic Equilibrium in the History of Science*, Cambridge, MA: MIT Press, 1990.
Jaffé, W. (1965), *Correspondence of Léon Walras and Related Papers*, Amsterdam: North-Holland.
John Paul, II (1981), *Laborem Exercens*, available at: http://www.vatican.va/holy_father/john_paul_ii/encyclicals/documents/hf_jp-ii_enc_14091981_laborem-exercens_en.html, 10 December 2003.
John Paul, II (1991), *Centesimus Annus*, available at: intratext.com/IXT/ENG0214/_P6.HTM, December 9, 2003, and http://www.newadvent.org/docs/jp02ca.htm, 6 May 2004.
Kaser, M.C. (1987), "Strumilin", in Eatwell et al. (eds), Vol. 4, p. 534.
Kauder, E. (1957), "Intellectual and political roots of the older Austrian school", *Zeitschrift für Nationalökonomie*, **17**: 411–25. Reprinted in *Austrian Economics*, ed. Stephen Littlechild, Vol. 1, Aldershot, UK and Brookfield, VT, USA: Edward Elgar.
Kautsky, K. (1907), *The Social Revolution and on the Morrow of the Social Revolution*, London: Twentieth Century Press.
Kautsky, K. (1922), *Die Proletarische Revolution und ihr Programm*, Berlin: Dietz Nachfolger.
Keizer, W. (1987), "Two forgotten articles by Ludwig von Mises on the rationality of socialist economic calculation", *Review of Austrian Economics*, **1**, no. 1: 109–22.

Keizer, W. (1989), "Recent reinterpretations of the socialist calculation debate", in *Austrian Economics: Roots and Ramifications Reconsidered*, ed. J.J. Krabbe, A. Wentjes and H. Visser, Bradford: MCB University Press.
Keizer, W. (1992), "The property rights basis of von Mises' critique of socialism", Manuscript awaiting publication, presented at the First European Conference on Austrian Economics, Maastricht, 9–10 April.
Keynes, J.M. (1949), *Two Memoirs*, London: Rupert Hart-Davies.
Kirzner, I.M. (1973), *Competition and Entrepreneurship*, Chicago, IL: University of Chicago Press. Spanish trans. *Competencia y Empresarialidad*, 2nd edn, Madrid: Unión Editorial, 1998.
Kirzner, I.M. (1979), *Perception, Opportunity and Profit*, Chicago, IL: University of Chicago Press.
Kirzner, I.M. (1984), "Prices, the communication of knowledge and the discovery process", in *The Political Economy of Freedom: Essays in Honor of F A. Hayek*, Munich: Philosophia Verlag, pp. 202–3.
Kirzner, I.M. (1985), *Discovery and the Capitalist Process*, Chicago, IL: University of Chicago Press.
Kirzner, I.M. (1987), "Austrian school of economics", in Eatwell et al. (eds), Vol. 1, pp. 145–51.
Kirzner, I.M. (1988), "The economic calculation debate: lessons for the Austrians", *Review of Austrian Economics*, **2**: 1–18.
Kirzner, I.M. (1989), *Discovery, Capitalism and Distributive Justice*, Oxford: Basil Blackwell.
Kirzner, I.M. (1992), *The Meaning of Market Process: Essays in the Development of Modern Austrian Economics*, London: Routledge.
Knaack, R. (1984), "Comparative economics: lessons from socialist planning", in *Comparative Economic Systems: Present Views*, ed. A. Zimbalist, Boston, MA: Kluwer-Nijhoff.
Knight, F.H. (1938), "Review of Ludwig von Mises' *Socialism*", *Journal of Political Economy*, **46** (April), 267–8.
Kornai, J. (1971), *Anti-Equilibrium: On Economic Systems Theory and the Task of Research*, Amsterdam: North-Holland.
Kornai, J. (1980), *Economics of Shortage*, Amsterdam: North-Holland.
Kornai, J. (1982), *Growth, Efficiency and Shortages*, Berkeley, CA: University of California Press.
Kornai, J. (1986), "The Hungarian reform process: visions, hopes and reality", *Journal of Economic Literature*, **24**, no. 4 (December), 1687–737. Reprinted as ch. 5 in Kornai, 1990, pp. 156–7.
Kornai, J. (1990), *Vision and Reality: Market and State*, New York: Harvester Wheatsheaf.

Kotarbinski, T. (1965), *Praxiology: An Introduction to the Sciences of Efficient Action*, Warsaw: Polish Scientific Publishers.

Kowalik, T. (1986), "Oskar Lange's lectures on the Economic Operation of a Socialist Society", *Contributions to Political Economy*, **6**: 1–24.

Kowalik, T. (1987a), "Lange–Lerner mechanism", in Eatwell et al. (eds), Vol. 3, pp. 129–31.

Kowalik, T. (1987b), "Oskar Ryszard Lange", in Eatwell et al. (eds), Vol. 3, pp. 123–9.

Kripke, S. (1982), *Wittgenstein, On Rules and Private Language*, Boston, MA: Harvard University Press.

Kukathas, C. (1989), *Hayek and Modern Liberalism*, Oxford: Clarendon Press.

Lachmann, L.M. (1977), "Methodological individualism and the market economy", in *Capital, Expectations and the Market Process: Essays on the Theory of the Market Economy*, Kansas City, KS: Sheed, Andrews & McMeel.

Landauer, C. (1931), *Planwirtschaft und Verkehrswirtschaft*, Munich: Duncker & Humblot. Spanish trans., Mexico: FCE, 1948.

Lange, O. (1936), "On the economic theory of socialism: Part I", *Review of Economic Studies*, **4**, no. 1 (October): 53–71.

Lange, O. (1937), "On the economic theory of socialism: Part II", *Review of Economic Studies*, **4**, no. 2 (February): 123–42.

Lange, O. (1938), "On the economic theory of socialism", in *On the Economic Theory of Socialism*, edited with an introduction by Benjamin M. Lippincott, Minneapolis, MN: University of Minnesota Press. 2nd edn, New York: McGraw-Hill, 1964, pp. 55–143. Spanish trans. Antonio Bosch Doménech and Alfredo Pastor Bodmer, *Sobre la Teoría Económica del Socialismo*, Barcelona: Ariel, 1971.

Lange, O. (1942), "The economic operation of a socialist society: I & II", Lectures delivered May 8 and 15, and edited and published by Tadeusz Kowalik in *Contributions to Political Economy*, **6** (1986): 1–24.

Lange, O. (1943), "Gospodarcze podstawy demokracji w Polsce" (Economic foundations of democracy in Poland), in *Ku gospodarcze planowej* (Toward a centrally planned economy), London.

Lange, O. (1949), "The practice of economic planning and the optimum allocation of resources", *Econometrica* (July): 166ff.

Lange, O. (1953), *Zagadnienia ekonomii politycmej w swietle pracy J. Stalina "Ekonomiczne problemy socjalizmu w ZSRR"* (Economic policy problems in light of J. Stalin's work, "Economic Problems of Socialism in the USSR"), Warsaw.

Lange, O. (ed.) (1962), *Problems of Political Economy of Socialism*, New Delhi: People's Publishing House.

Lange, O. (1963), *Political Economy*, Vol. 1, *General Problems*, London: Pergamon Press. Spanish trans. Silverio Ruiz Daimiel, *Economía Política, Problemas generales*, Mexico: Fondo de Cultura Económica, 1966.

Lange, O. (1967), "The computer and the market", in *Socialism, Capitalism and Economic Growth: Essays Presented to M. Dobb*, ed. C.H. Feinstein, Cambridge: Cambridge University Press. Reprinted in *Socialist Economics*, ed. Alec Nove and D.M. Nuti, Harmondsworth: Penguin Books, 1972.

Lange, O. (1968), *Ekonomia Polityezna*, Vol. 2, Warsaw: Panstwowe Wydawnictwo Naukowe. Spanish trans. Elzbieta G. de Kerlow, *Economía Política*, Vol. 2, *Teoría de la Reproducción*, Mexico: Fondo de Cultura Económica, 1980.

Lange, O. (1970), *Ensayos sobre Planificación Económica*, Barcelona: Ariel Quincenal.

Lange, O. (1973), *Dziela*, Vol. 2, Warsaw: Państwowe Wydawnicto Ekonomiczne.

Lange, O. and M. Breit (1934), "Droga do socjalistycznej gospodarki planowej" (The road to a socialist planned economy), in *Gospodarka-polityka-taktyka-organizacja socjalizmu* (Political economy and tactics for organization of socialism), Warsaw. Reprinted in *Dziela* (Works), Vol. 1, Warsaw: Polski Wydawnictwo Economiczne, 1973.

Langlois, R.N. (ed.) (1986), *Economics as a Process: Essays in the New Institutional Economics*, Cambridge and New York: Cambridge University Press.

Laski, K. (1974), "Condiciones para el Equilibrio General entre Producción y Consumo", in *Problemas de Economía Política del Socialismo*, ed. Oskar Lange, Mexico: F.C.E. English, *Problems of Political Economy of Socialism*, New Delhi: People's Publishing House, 1962.

Lavoie, D. (1981), "Introduction" and "A critique of the standard account of the socialist calculation debate", *Journal of Libertarian Studies: An Interdisciplinary Review*, **5**, no. 1 (winter): 41–87.

Lavoie, D. (1982), 'The Market as a Procedure for Discovery and Conveyance of Inarticulate Knowledge', Working Paper, Department of Economics, George Mason University, November. Reprinted in *Comparative Economic Studies*, **28**, no. 1 (1986): 1–19.

Lavoie, D. (1985a), *National Economic Planning: What is Left?*, Cambridge, MA: Ballinger.

Lavoie, D. (1985b), "Leontief and the critique of aggregative planning", in Lavoie, 1985a, pp. 93–124.

Lavoie, D. (1985c), *Rivalry and Central Planning: The Socialist Calculation Debate Reconsidered*, Cambridge: Cambridge University Press.

Lavoie, D., H. Baetjer and W. Tulloh (1990), "High-tech Hayekians: some

possible research topics in the economics of computation", *Market Process* (George Mason University), **8** (spring): 120–46.
Le Grand, J. and S. Estrin (eds) (1989), *Market Socialism*, Oxford: Clarendon Press.
Leichter, O. (1923), *Die Wirtschaftsrechnung in der Sozialistischen, Gesellschaft*, Vienna: Verlag der Wiener Volksbuchhandlung.
Lenin, V.I. (1918), *Die nächsten Aufgaben der Sowjetmacht*, Berlin.
Leoni, B. (1991), *Freedom and the Law*, enlarged 3rd edn, Indianapolis, IN: Liberty Press. (1st edn 1961, 2nd edn 1972); available at http://oll.libertyfund.org/Texts/LFBooks/Leoni0151/FreedomAndLaw/0124_Bk.html, September 23, 2004. Spanish trans., *La Libertad y la Ley*, Madrid: Unión Editorial, 1974; 2nd edn 1995.
Lépage, H. (1980), "Peut-on planifier une économie de marché?", in *Demain le Libéralisme*, Paris: Librairie Générale Française.
Lépage, H. (1983), *Planification et Économie de Marché*, Paris: Institut Économique.
Lerner, A.P. (1934a), "Economic theory and socialist economy", *Review of Economic Studies*, **2** (October): 51–61.
Lerner, A.P. (1934b), "The concept of monopoly and the measurement of monopoly power", *Review of Economic Studies*, **1**: 157–75.
Lerner, A.P. (1935), "A rejoinder", *Review of Economic Studies*, **2** (February): 152–4.
Lerner, A.P. (1936), "A note on socialist economics", *Review of Economic Studies*, **4** (October): 72–6.
Lerner, A.P. (1937), "Statics and dynamics in socialist economics", *Economic Journal*, **47** (June): 253–70.
Lerner, A.P. (1938), "Theory and practice of socialist economies", *Review of Economic Studies*, **6** (October): 71–5.
Lerner, A.P. (1944), *The Economics of Control*, New York: Macmillan. Spanish trans. Edmundo Flores, *Teoría Económica del Control: Principios de Economía del Bienestar*, Mexico: Fondo de Cultura Económica, 1951.
Levy, D.M. (1990), "The bias in centrally planned prices", *Public Choice*, **67**, no. 3 (December): 213–26.
Lindahl, E. (1939 [1970]), *Studies in the Theory of Money and Capital*, New York: Augustus M. Kelley.
Lindbeck, A. (1971), *The Political Economy of the New Left*. New York: Harper & Row. In Spanish, *La Economía Política de la Nueva Izquierda*, Madrid: Alianza Editorial, 1971.
Lippincott, B.M. (ed.) (1938), *On the Economic Theory of Socialism*, Minneapolis, MN: University of Minnesota Press. 2nd edn, New York: McGraw-Hill, 1964. Spanish trans. Antonio Bosch Doménech and

Alfredo Pastor Bodmer, *Sobre la Teoría Económica del Socialismo*, Barcelona: Ariel, 1971.
Littlechild, S. (1990), *Austrian Economics*, 3 vols, Aldershot, UK and Brookfield, VT, USA: Edward Elgar.
Lorenz, K. (1951), *Aspects of Form*, London: L.L. Whyte.
Lugo, J. de (1643), *Disputationes de Iustitia et Iure*, Lyon.
Lutz, V. (1969), *Central Planning for the Market Economy*, London: Longmans.
Machado, A. (1989), *Poesías Completas*, Oreste Macrí Critical Edition, Madrid: Espasa Calpe.
Machlup, F. (1976), "Closing remarks", in *The Economics of Ludwig von Mises: Toward a Critical Reappraisal*, ed. Laurence S. Moss, Kansas City, KS: Sheed & Ward.
Machlup, F. (1984), *Knowledge: Its Creation, Distribution and Economic Significance*, Vol. 3: *The Economics of Information and Human Capital*, Princeton, NJ: Princeton University Press.
Mackay, Th. (ed.) (1981), *A Plea for Liberty: An Argument against Socialism and Socialistic Legislation, Consisting of an Introduction by Herbert Spencer and Essays by Various Writers*, Indianapolis, IN: Liberty Classics.
Malinvaud, E. (1967), "Decentralized procedures for planning", in *Activity Analysis in the Theory of Growth and Planning*, London: Macmillan.
Malinvaud, E. (1971), "A planning approach to the public good problem", *Swedish Journal of Economics*, **73** (March): 96–112.
Mallock, W.H. (1908), *A Critical Examination of Socialism* (1908). Reprinted in 1990, Transaction Publishers, New Brunswick, NJ.
Marañón, G. (1971a), "Cajal: Su Tiempo y el Nuestro", in *Obras Completas*, Vol. 7, Madrid: Espasa Calpe.
Marañón, G. (1971b), "El Greco y Toledo", in *Obras Completas*, Vol. 7, Madrid: Espasa Calpe.
Marcos de la Fuente, J. (1983), *El empresario y su función social*, 3rd edn, Madrid: Fundación Cánovas del Castillo.
Martínez-Alier, J. (1990), *Ecological Economics: Energy, Environment and Society*, 2nd edn, Oxford: Basil Blackwell.
Marx, K. (1967), *Capital: A Critique of Political Economy*. Vol. 1, *The Process of Capitalist Production*, Vol. 2, *The Process of Circulation of Capital*, New York: International Publishers. (1st edn 1867.)
Marx, K. (1973), *Grundrisse: Foundations of the Critique of Political Economy*, New York: Random House.
Marx, K. (1974a), "The Civil War in France: Address of the General Council", in *The First International and After: Political Writings*, ed. D. Fernbach, Vol. 3, New York: Random House, pp. 187–268.

Marx, K. (1974b), "Critique of the Gotha Programme" (1891), in *The First International and After: Political Writings*, Vol. 3, New York: Random House, pp. 339–59. Also published in *Marx–Engels Selected Works*, Vol. 3, Moscow: Progress Publishers, 1970. Available at: http://www.marxists.org/archive/marx/works/1875/gotha/ch01.htm, October 26, 2004.

Matte Larrain, E. (ed.) (1988), *Cristianismo, Sociedad Libre y Opción por los Pobres*, Chile: Centro de Estudios Públicos.

Mayer, H. (1932), "Der Erkenntniswert der Funktionellen Preistheorien", in *Die Wirtschaftstheorie der Gegenwart*, Vol. 2, Vienna: Verlag von Julius Springer, pp. 147–239b. English version in *Classics in Austrian Economics*, Vol. II, ed. Israel M. Kirzner, London: W. Pickering, 1994, pp. 55–168.

Meade, J.E. (1948), *Planning and the Price Mechanism: The Liberal Socialist Solution*, London: George Allen & Unwin.

Meade, J.E. (1971), *The Controlled Economy*, London: George Allen & Unwin.

Meade, J.E. (1990), *The Theory of Indicative Planning*, Manchester: Manchester University Press.

Menger, C. (1883), *Untersuchungen über die Methode der Socialwissenschaften und der Politischen Ökonomie insbesondere*, Leipzig: Duncker & Humblot.

Menger, C. (1985), *Investigations into the Method of the Social Sciences with Special Reference to Economics*, New York: New York University Press. Foreword by Lawrence H. White and trans. Francis J. Nock.

Migué, J.L. and G. Bélanger (1974), "Toward a general theory of managerial discretion", *Public Choice*, **17**: 27–43.

Mill, S. (1976), *Principles of Political Economy*, reprint, Fairfield, NJ: Augustus M. Kelley.

Miller, D. (1989), *Market, State and Community: Theoretical Foundations of Market Socialism*, Oxford: Clarendon Press.

Miller, M.S. and K.E. Drexler (1988), "Market and computation: agoric open systems", in *The Ecology of Computation*, ed. B.A. Huberman, Amsterdam: North-Holland.

Mises, L. von (1912 [1924]), *Theorie des Geldes und der Umlaufsmittel*, Munich and Leipzig: Duncker & Humblot. English trans. H.E. Batson, with an introduction by Murray N. Rothbard, *The Theory of Money and Credit*, Liberty Classics, Indianapolis, IN: Liberty Press, 1980. Three Spanish translations: Antonio Riaño, *Teoría del Dinero y del Crédito*, Madrid: Aguilar, 1936; José María Clarmunda Bes, *Teoría del Dinero y del Crédito*, Barcelona: Ediciones Zeus, 1961; Juan Marcos de la Fuente, Madrid: Unión Editorial, 1997.

Mises, L. von (1920), "Die Wirtschaftsrechnung im sozialistischen Gemeinwesen", *Archiv für Sozialwissenschaft und Sozialpolitik*, **47**: 86–121. English trans. S. Adler, "Economic calculation in the socialist commonwealth", in *Collectivist Economic Planning*, ed. F.A. Hayek. Clifton, NJ: Augustus M. Kelley, 1975, pp. 87–130.

Mises, L. von (1922), *Die Gemeinwirtschaft: Untersuchungen über den Sozialismus*, Jena: Gustav Fischer; 2nd edn, Jena: Gustav Fischer, 1932; reprinted Munich: Philosophia Verlag, 1981. English trans. J. Kahane, *Socialism: An Economic and Sociological Analysis*, 3rd edn, Indianapolis, IN: Liberty Press, 1981: Spanish trans. Luis Montes de Oca, *Socialismo: Análisis Económico Sociológica*, Mexico: Editorial Hermes, 1931; 2nd edn, Buenos Aires: Instituto Nacional de Publicaciones de Buenos Aires, 1968; 3rd edn, New York: Western Books Foundation, 1989; 4th edn and 5th edn, Madrid: Unión Editorial, 2003 and 2007.

Mises, L. von (1924), "Neue Beiträge zum Problem der sozialistischen Wirtschaftsrechnung", *Archiv für Sozialwissenschaft und Sozialpolitik*, **51**: 488–500.

Mises, L. von (1928), "Neue Schriften zum Problem der sozialistischen Wirtschaftsrechnung", *Archiv für Sozialwissenschaft und Sozialpolitik*, **60**: 187–90.

Mises, L. von (1929 [1976]), *Kritik des Interventionismus*, Jena: Gustav Fischer Verlag. English trans., *A Critique of Interventionism*, New York: Arlington House, 1977. Spanish trans. Madrid: Unión Editorial, 2001.

Mises, L. von (1938), "Les équations de l'économie mathématique et le problème de calcul économique en régime socialiste", *Revue de Économie Politique*: 1055–62. Reprinted in the same journal, **6**, no. 97 (November–December 1987).

Mises, L. von (1940 [1980]), *Nationalökonomie: Theorie des Handelns und Wirtschaftens*, Geneva: Editions Union. 2nd edn, The International Carl Menger Library, Munich: Philosophia Verlag.

Mises, L. von (1957), *Theory and History*, New Haven, CT: Yale University Press. Spanish trans. Rigoberto Juárez Paz, *Teoría e Historia*, Madrid: Unión Editorial, 1975; 2nd edn 2003.

Mises, L. von (1966), *Human Action: A Treatise on Economics*, 3rd rev edn, Chicago, IL: Henry Regnery Company. Spanish trans. Joaquín Reig Albiol, *La Acción Humana: Tratado de Economía*, 9th edn, Madrid: Unión Editorial, 2009.

Mises, L. von (1969), *Bureaucracy*, New Rochelle, NY: Arlington House (first published 1944). Spanish trans. Dalmacio Negro Pavón, *Burocracia*, Madrid: Unión Editorial, 1974; 2nd edn 2005.

Mises, L. von (1978), *Notes and Recollections*, South Holland, IL: Libertarian Press.

Mises, L. von (1985), *Liberalism*. San Francisco, CA: Cobden Press. Spanish trans. Joaquín Reig Albiol, *Liberalismo*, Madrid: Unión Editorial, 1977, 1982 and 2005.

Mises, L. von (1990), *Economic Calculation in the Socialist Commonwealth*, reprint, with an introduction by Yuri N. Maltsev and Jacek Kochanowicz, and a postscript entitled "Why a Socialist Economy is Impossible", by Joseph T. Salerno, Auburn, AL: Ludwig von Mises Institute, Auburn University.

Mitchel, W. (1979), *The Anatomy of Government Failures*, Los Angeles, CA: International Institute of Economic Research.

Montesquieu (1843), *Oeuvres Complètes. Avec des notes de Dupin, Crevier, Voltaire, Mably, Servan, La Harpe, etc.*, Paris: Chez Firmin Didot Frères, Libraires.

Moreno, F. (1988), "El Trabajo según Juan Pablo II", in Matte Larrain (ed.), pp. 395–400.

Moss, L.S. (ed.) (1976), *The Economics of Ludwig von Mises: A Critical Reappraisal*, Kansas City, KS: Sheed & Ward.

Mulgen, G. (1988), "The power of the weak", *Marxism Today* (December).

Musgrave, R.A. (1977), "National Economic Planning: the U.S. case", *American Economic Review*, **67**, part one (February): 50–54.

Naishul, V.A. (1991), *The Supreme and Last Stage of Socialism*, London: Centre for Research into Communist Economies.

Negishi, T. (1987), "Tâtonnement and recontracting", in Eatwell et al. (eds), Vol. 4, pp. 589–95.

Nelson, R.R. (1981), "Assessing private enterprise: an exegesis of tangled doctrine", *Bell Journal of Economics*, **1**, no. 12 (spring).

Neuberger, E. (1966), "Libermanism, computopia and visible hand: the question of informational efficiency", *American Economic Review, Papers and Proceedings* (May).

Neurath, O. (1919), *Durch die Kriegswirtschaft zur Naturalwirtschaft*, Munich: G.D.W. Callwey. English trans., "Through war economy to economy in kind", in *Empiricism and Sociology*, Dordrecht: D. Reidel, 1973.

Neurath, O. (1925), *Wirtschaftsplan und Naturalrechnung von der sozialistischen Lebensordnung und vom kommenden Menschen*, Berlin: E. Laubsche.

Nishiyama, Ch. and K.R. Leube (eds) (1984), *The Essence of Hayek*, Standford, CA: Hoover Institution Press, Stanford University.

Niskanen, W. (1971), *Bureaucracy and Representative Government*, Chicago, IL: Aldine-Atherton Press.

Novak, M. (1993), *The Catholic Ethic and the Spirit of Capitalism*, New York: Free Press.
Nove, A. (1983), *The Economics of Feasible Socialism*, London: Allen & Unwin.
Nove, A. (1987a), "Planned economy", in Eatwell et al. (eds), Vol. 3, pp. 879–85.
Nove, A. (1987b), "Socialism", in Eatwell et al. (eds), Vol. 4, pp. 398–407.
Nove, A. (1990), *Studies in Economics and Russia*, London: Macmillan.
Nozick, R. (1974), *Anarchy, State and Utopia*, New York: Basic Books. Spanish trans. Rolando Tamayo, Mexico: Fondo de Cultura Económica, 1988.
Nozick, R. (1989), *The Examined Life*, New York: Simon & Schuster.
Nutter, G.W. (1983a), "Central economic planning: the visible hand", ch. 15 in *Political Economy and Freedom: A Collection of Essays*, Indianapolis, IN: Liberty Press.
Nutter, G.W. (1983b), "Markets without property: a grand illusion", in *Political Economy and Freedom: A Collection of Essays*, Indianapolis, IN: Liberty Press.
O'Driscoll, G.P. (1989), "A Tribute to F.A. Hayek", *Cato Journal*, **9**, no. 2 (autumn): 345–52.
O'Driscoll, G.P. and M.J. Rizzo (1985), *The Economics of Time and Ignorance*, Oxford: Basil Blackwell.
Oakeshott, M. (1962), *Rationalism in Politics*, London: Methuen.
Oakeshott, M. (1975), *On Human Conduct*, Oxford: Oxford University Press. Clarendon Paperbacks Reprint, Oxford: Clarendon Press, 1991.
Oakeshott, M. (1991), *Rationalism in Politics and Other Essays*, With a foreword by Timothy Fuller, Indianapolis, IN: Liberty Press.
Ortega y Gasset, J. (1947), *Mirabeau o el Político*. Vol. 3 of *Obras Completas*, Madrid: Revista de Occidente.
Pareto, V. (1966), *Manuel d'Économie Politique*, Geneva: Librairie Droz. English trans. Ann S. Schwier, *Manual of Political Economy*, New York: Augustus M. Kelley, 1971. Spanish trans. Guillermo Cabanellas, Buenos Aires, 1946.
Pejovich, S. (1987), "The case of self-management in Yugoslavia", in *Socialism: Institutional, Philosophical and Economic Issues*, Dordrecht: Kluwer Academic Publishers, pp. 239–49.
Penrose, R. (1989), *The Emperor's New Mind: Concerning Computers, Minds and the Laws of Physics*, Oxford: Oxford University Press. Spanish trans. by Javier García Sanz, *La Nueva Mente del Emperador*, Spain: Mondadori, 1991.

Pierson, N.G. (1902), "The problem of value in the socialist community", in *Collectivist Economic Planning*, London: Routledge, 1935, pp. 41–85, English trans. G. Gardiner of "Het waardeprobleem in een socialistische Maatschappij", *De Economist*, **1**: 423–56.

Pierson, N.G. (1912), *Principles of Economics*, trans. A. Wotzel, Vol. 2, London: Macmillan.

Pohle, L. and G. Halm (1931), *Kapitalismus und Sozialismus*, 4th edn, Berlin.

Polanyi, K. (1922), "Sozialistische Rechnungslegung", *Archiv für Sozialwissenschaft und Sozialpolitik*, **49**: 377–420.

Polanyi, K. (1924), "Die funktionelle Theorie der Gesellschaft und das Problem der sozialistischen Rechnungslegung. (Eine Erwiderung an Prof. Mises und Dr. Felix Weil)", *Archiv für Sozialwissenschaft und Sozialpolitik*, **52**: 218–28.

Polanyi, M. (1951), *The Logic of Liberty*, Chicago, IL: University of Chicago Press.

Polanyi, M. (1958), *Personal Knowledge*, Chicago, IL: University of Chicago Press.

Polanyi, M. (1959), *The Study of Man*, Chicago, IL: University of Chicago Press.

Polanyi, M. (1969a), *Knowing and Being*, ed. Marjorie Grene, Chicago, IL: University of Chicago Press.

Polanyi, M. (1969b), "The republic of science: its political and economic theory", in Polanyi (1969a).

Polanyi, M. (1988), "Ciencia, Fe y Sociedad", *Estudios Públicos* (journal of the Centro de Estudios Públicos de Santiago de Chile), **29** (summer): 271–330.

Pribram, K. (1983), *A History of Economic Reasoning*, Baltimore, MD: Johns Hopkins University Press.

Prybila, J.S. (1987), *Market and Plan under Socialism*, Stanford, CA: Hoover Institution Press.

Raga, J.T. (1982), "Proceso Económico y Acción Empresarial", in *Homenaje a Lucas Beltrán*, Madrid: Moneda y Crédito, pp. 597–619.

Real Academia Española (1984), *Diccionario de la Lengua Española*, 20th edn, Madrid: Espasa Calpe.

Revel, F. (1981), *El Estado Megalómano*, Madrid: Planeta.

Robbins, L. (1934), *The Great Depression*, New York: Macmillan.

Robbins, L. (1963), *Politics and Economics*, London: Macmillan.

Robbins, L. (1971), *Autobiography of an Economist*, London: Macmillan.

Robbins, L. (1972), *An Essay on the Nature and Significance of Economic Science*, London: Macmillan.

Robbins, L. (1976), *Political Economy, Past and Present*, New York: Columbia University Press.

Roberts, P.C. (1990), *Alienation and the Soviet Economy*, New York: Holmes & Meier. (1st edn 1971).
Robertson, E.S. (1891 [1981]), "The impracticability of socialism", in MacKay (ed.), pp. 35–79.
Rodríguez Braun, C. (1986), "Entrevista a F.A. Hayek", *Revista de Occidente*, **58** (March): 124–35.
Roper, W.C. (1931), *The Problem of Pricing in a Socialist State*, Cambridge, MA: Harvard University Press.
Rosenberg, W.G. (1977), "Observations on the Soviet incentive system", *ACES Bulletin*, **19**, nos 3, 4: 27–43.
Rothbard, M.N. (1970a), *Man, Economy, and State: A Treatise on Economic Principles*, Vol. 2, Los Angeles, CA: Nash.
Rothbard, M.N. (1970b), *Power and Market: Government and the Economy*. 2nd edn, Menlo Park, CA: Institute for Humane Studies.
Rothbard, M.N. (1971), "Lange, Mises and praxeology: the retreat from Marxism", in *Toward Liberty: Essays in Honor of L. von Mises on His 90th Birthday*, Berkeley, CA: Institute for Humane Studies, pp. 307–21.
Rothbard, M.N. (1973), *For a New Liberty*, New York: Macmillan.
Rothbard, M.N. (1976), "New light on the prehistory of the Austrian school", in *The Foundations of Modern Austrian Economics*, Kansas City, KS: Sheed & Ward, pp. 52–74.
Rothbard, M.N. (1980), *Individualism and the Philosophy of Social Sciences*, San Francisco, CA: Cato Institute.
Rothbard, M.N. (1982), *The Ethicks of Liberty*, Atlantic Highlands, NJ: Humanities Press.
Rothbard, M.N. (1986), "Lo Ilusorio del Precio de Monopolio", in *Lecturas de Economía Política*, Vol. 1, Compiled by Jesús Huerta de Soto, 2nd edn, Madrid: Unión Editorial, 2005. Spanish trans. Carmen Liaño Reig, *Man, Economy, and State*, Vol. 2, ch. 10, Los Angeles, CA: Nash, 1970, pp. 181–211.
Rothbard, M.N. (1988), *Ludwig von Mises: Scholar, Creator and Hero*, Auburn, AL: The Ludwig von Mises Institute, Auburn University.
Rothbard, M.N. (1991), "The end of socialism and the calculation debate revisited", *The Review of Austrian Economics*, **5**, no. 2: 51–76.
Rothschild, M. (1990), *"Bionomics": The Inevitability of Capitalism*, New York: Henry Holt.
Rudolf, Archduke (Crown Prince of Austria) (1876), Handwritten notes on *Politische Oekonomie*, January–August, Österreichisches Staatsarchiv.
Ryle, G. (1949), "Knowing how and knowing that", in *The Concept of Mind*, London: Hutchinson's University Library.
Salas, J. de (1617), *Commentarii in Secundam Secundae divi Thomae de Contractibus*, Lyon.

Salerno, J.T. (1990a), "Ludwig von Mises as social rationalist", *Review of Austrian Economics*, **4**: 36–48.
Salerno, J.T. (1990b), "Why a socialist economy is impossible: a postscript to Mises", in *Economic Calculation in the Socialist Economy*, Auburn, AL: Ludwig von Mises Institute, Auburn University.
Samuelson, P.A. (1989), *Economics*, 13th edn, New York: McGraw Hill.
Samuelson, P.A. and Nordhaus, W.D. (1985), *Economics*, 12th edn, New York: McGraw-Hill. Spanish edn *Economía*, Madrid: MacGraw-Hill, 1986.
Say, J.-B. (1803), *Traité d'Économie Politique*, Paris: Deterville; reprint, Geneva: Slatkine, 1982. English trans. 1821 C.R. Prinsep, *A Treatise on Political Economy*, New York: Augustus M. Kelley, 1971.
Scaramozzino, P. (1969), *Omaggio a Bruno Leoni*, Milan: A. Giuffrè.
Schäffle, A. (1874), *Die Quintessenz des Sozialismus*, 13th edn, Gotha: F.A. Perthes, 1891; 18th edn, Gotha: F.A. Perthes, 1919.
Schiff, W. (1932), *Die Planwirtschaft und ihre Ökonomischen Hauptprobleme*, Berlin.
Schumpeter, J.A. (1950), *Capitalism, Socialism and Democracy*, London: George Allen & Unwin. Spanish trans. José Díaz García, *Capitalismo, Socialismo y Democracia*, Madrid: Aguilar, 1971.
Schwartz, P. (1981), *Empresa y Libertad*, Madrid: Unión Editorial.
Scitovsky, T. (1984), "Lerner's contribution to economics", *Journal of Economic Literature*, **22**, no. 4 (December), 1547–71.
Seco, M. (1990), *Diccionario de Dudas y Dificultades de la Lengua Española*, 9th edn, Madrid: Espasa Calpe.
Seidl, Ch. (1982), "Allokationsmechanismus, asymmetrische Information und Wirtschaftssystem", *Jahrbücher für Nationalökonomie und Statistik*, **197**, no. 3: 193–220.
Seldon, A. (1984), "Recollections: before and after 'The Road to Serfdom.' Reflections on Hayek in 1935, 1944, 1960, 1982", in *Hayek's "Serfdom" Revisited: Essays by Economists, Philosophers and Political Scientists on "The Road to Serfdom" after 40 Years*, Hobart Paperback no. 18, London: Institute of Economic Affairs.
Seldon, A. (1990), *Capitalism*, Oxford: Basil Blackwell.
Sen, A. (1987), "Maurice Herbert Dobb", in Eatwell et al. (eds), Vol. 1, pp. 910–12.
Seurot, F. (1983), *Les Économies Socialistes*, Paris: Presses Universitaires de France.
Shackle, G.L. (1972), *Epistemics and Economics*, Cambridge: Cambridge University Press. Spanish trans. Francisco González Aramburo, *Epistémica y Economía*, Madrid: Fondo de Cultura Económica, 1976.

Shakespeare, W. (1974), *As You Like It*, in *The Riverside Shakespeare*, Boston, MA: Houghton Mifflin.
Sheanan, J. (1975), "Planning in France", *Challenge*, March–April.
Skidelsky, R. (1983), *John Maynard Keynes*. Vol. 1, *Hopes Betrayed 1883–1920*, London: Macmillan.
Skousen, M. (1991), "Conversation with Robert Heilbroner", *Liberty*, **4**, no. 6 (July): 45–50, 63, and in *Forbes* (27 May).
Smith, A. (1981), *An Inquiry into the Nature and Causes of the Wealth of Nations*, ed. R.K. Campbell and A.S. Skinner, textual editor W.B. Todd, in *The Glasgow Edition of the Works and Correspondence of Adam Smith*, Indianapolis, IN: Liberty Press.
Snavely, W.P. (ed.) (1969), *Theory of Economic Systems: Capitalism, Socialism, Corporation*, Columbus, OH: Merrill.
Snowberger, V. (1977), "Comment on the 'New Soviet Incentive Model'", *Bell Journal of Economics*, **8**, no. 2 (autumn).
Sorman, G. (1993), *Esperando a los bárbaros* (Waiting for the barbarians), Barcelona: Seix Barral.
Soto, H. de. (1987), *El Otro Sendero: La Revolución Informal*, Mexico: Diana.
Sowell, T. (1980), *Knowledge and Decisions*, New York: Basic Books.
Stankiewicz, T. (1989), "Investment under socialism", *Communist Economies*, **1**, no. 2: 123–39.
Steele, D.R. (1981a), "The failure of Bolshevism and its aftermath", *Journal of Libertarian Studies: An Interdisciplinary Review*, **5**, no. 1 (winter): 99–111.
Steele, D.R. (1981b), "Posing the problem: the impossibility of economic calculation under socialism", *Journal of Libertarian Studies: An Interdisciplinary Review*, **5**, no. 1 (winter): 7–22.
Stigler, G. (1975), *The Citizen and the State*, Chicago, IL: Chicago University Press.
Streissler, E.W. (1990a), "The influence of German economics on the work of Menger and Marshall", in *Carl Menger and His Legacy in Economics*, ed. Bruce J. Caldwell, Annual supplement to Vol. 22, *History of Political Economy*, Durham, NC: Duke University Press, pp. 31–68.
Streissler, E.W. (1990b), "Carl Menger on economic policy: the lectures to Crown Prince Rudolf", in *Carl Menger and His Legacy in Economics*, ed. Bruce J. Caldwell, Annual supplement to Vol. 22, *History of Political Economy*, Durham, NC: Duke University Press, pp. 107–30.
Strumilin, S. (1920), *Ekonomitscheskaja Shishni*, Nos 237, 284 and 290, October 23, December 17 and December 24.
Sulzer, G. (1899), *Die Zukunft des Sozialismus*, Dresden.

Sweezy, P.M. (1949), *Socialism*, New York: McGraw-Hill.
Tamedly, E.L. (1969), *Socialism and International Economic Order*, Caldwell, ID: Caxton Printers.
Taylor, F.M. (1929), "The guidance of production in a socialist state", *American Economic Review*, **19**, no. 1 (March). Reprinted in *On the Economic Theory of Socialism*, ed. Benjamin E. Lippincott, New York: McGraw-Hill, 1964. Spanish trans. Antonio Bosch Doménech and Alfredo Pastor Bodmer, "La Orientación de la Producción en un Estado Socialista", 4th edn, Barcelona: Ariel, December 1973.
Taylor, R. (1980), *Action and Purpose*, Atlantic Highlands, NJ: Humanities Press.
Temkin, G. (1989), "On economic reforms in socialist countries: the debate on economic calculation under socialism revisited", *Communist Economies*, **1**, no. 1: 31–59.
Thirlby, G.F. (1946), "The ruler", *South African Journal of Economics* (December). Reprinted as ch. 7 in Buchanan and Thirlby (eds) (1981), pp. 163–98.
Thomsen, E.F. (1992), *Prices and Knowledge: A Market Process Perspective*, London: Routledge.
Tipler, F.J. (1988–89), "A liberal utopia", in "A Special Symposium on 'The Fatal Conceit' by F.A. Hayek", *Humane Studies Review*, **6**, no. 2 (winter): 4–5.
Tisch, K. (1932), *Wirtschaftsrechnung und Verteilung im Zentralistich Organisierten Sozialistischen Gemeinwesen*, Wuppertal-Elberfeld: University of Bonn.
Trigo Portela, J. (1988), *Barreras a la Creación de Empresas y Economía Irregular*, Madrid: Instituto de Estudios Económicos.
Trigo Portela, J. and C. Vázquez Arango (1983), *La Economía Irregular*. "Textos i Documents" Collection, 2, Barcelona: Generalitat de Catalunya, Servei Central de Publicacions.
Tschayanoff, A. (1923), "Zur Frage einer Theorie der Nichtkapitalistischen Wirtschaftssysteme", *Archiv für Sozialwissenschaft und Sozialpolitik*, **57**: 577–613.
Tullock, G. (1965), *The Politics of Bureaucracy*, Washington, DC: Public Affairs Press.
Turgot, A.R.J. (1844), "Éloge de Gournay (1759)", in *Oeuvres*, Vol. 1, Paris: Guillaumin, pp. 262–91.
Van Maarseveen, J.G. (1981), *Nicolaas G. Pierson*, Rotterdam: Erasmus University.
Vaughn, K.I. (1976), "Critical discussion of the four papers", in *The Economics of Ludwig von Mises: A Critical Reappraisal*, Kansas City, KS: Sheed & Ward, pp. 107ff.

Vaughn, K.I. (1980), "Economic calculation under socialism: the Austrian contribution", *Economic Enquiry*, **18** (October). Reprinted in Vol. 3 of *Austrian Economics*, ed. Stephen Littlechild, Aldershot, UK and Brookfield, VT, USA: Edward Elgar, pp. 332–51.
Vaughn, K.I. (1981), "Introduction", in Hoff (1981).
Verrijn Stuart, C.A. (n.d.), "Winstbejag versus behoeftenbevrediging", *Overdruk Economist*, **76**, no. 1: 18ff.
Villapalos, G. (1992), "Serendipidad", *ABC* (Madrid), 3 January: 3.
Ward, B. (1967a), "Linear programming and soviet planning", in Hardt et al. (eds).
Ward, B. (1967b), *The Socialist Economy: A Study of Organizational Alternatives*, New York: Random House.
Weber, A. (1932), *Allgemeine volkswirtschaftslehre*, 4th edn, Munich and Leipzig.
Weber, M. (1922), "Wirtschaft und Gesellschaft", in *Grundriss der Sozialökonomie*, Vol. 3, Tübingen: Verlag von J.C.B. Mohr (Paul Siebeck), 1922, 45–59.
Weber, M. (1964), *The Theory of Social and Economic Organization*, New York: Free Press of Glencoe.
Weber, M. (1978), *Economy and Society*, Berkeley, CA: University of California Press. English trans., by several authors, of *Wirtschaft und Gesellschaft: Grundriss der Verstehenden Soziologie*, Tübingen, 1921.
Weil, F. (1924), "Gildensozialistische Rechnungslegung. Kritische Bemerkungen zu Karl Polanyi: 'Sozialistische Rechnungslegung' in diesem Archiv 49/2, s.377 ff", *Archiv für Sozialwissenschaft und Sozialpolitik*, **52**: 196–217.
Weitzman, M.L. (1977), "The new Soviet incentive model", *Bell Journal of Economics*, **8**, no. 2 (autumn), 251–7.
Wicksteed, P.H. (1933), *The Common Sense in Political Economy*, 2nd edn, London: Routledge. Reprinted New York: Augustus M. Kelley, 1967.
Wieser, F. von (1889), *Der Natürliche Wert*, Vienna: A. Hölder. English trans. C.A. Malloch, *Natural Value*, New York: Augustus M. Kelley, 1971.
Wieser, F. von (1914 [1967]), *Social Economics*, New York: Augustus M. Kelley. English trans. A. Ford Hinrichs of *Theorie der Gessellschaftlichen Wirtschaft*, Tübingen: J.C.B. Mohr, 1914.
Wilczynski, J. (1978), *The Economics of Socialism: Principles Governing the Operation of the Centrally Planned Economies in the USSR and Eastern Europe under the New System*, 3rd edn, London: George Allen & Unwin.
Williamson, O.E. and S.G. Winter (1991), *The Nature of the Firm: Origins, Evolution and Development*, Oxford: Oxford University Press.

Winiecki, J. (1987), *Economic Prospects – East and West: A View from the East*, London: Centre for Research into Communist Economies.
Winiecki, J. (1988 [1991]), *The Distorted World of Soviet-Type Economies*, London: Routledge.
Wiseman, J. (1953), "Uncertainty, costs, and collectivist economic planning", *Economica* (May): 234–35. Reprinted as ch. 9 in Buchanan and Thirlby (eds) 1981.
Wiseman, J. (1957), "The theory of public utility price: an empty box", in *Oxford Economic Papers*, no. 9: 56–74. Reprinted in Buchanan and Thirlby (eds) (1981).
Wood, J.C. and R.N. Woods (eds) (1991), *Friedrich A. Hayek: Critical Assessments*, London: Routledge.
Zassenhaus, H. (1934), "Über die ökonomische Theorie der Planwirtschaft", *Zeitschrift für Nationalökonomie*, **5** (September). English trans., "On the economic theory of planning", *International Economic Papers*, **6** (1956): 88–107.

# Index

accounting and business reform
   basic error in 163
   socialist foundation of 141, 238–9
Alchian, A.A. 45, 98
Allais, M. 168, 169
Allen, W.R. 98
Alvarez, V.A. 93
anarcho-capitalism 88
Antonelli, E. 261
Aquinas, St Thomas 38, 39, 42, 44
Aranson, P.H. 123
arbitration 27
Armentano, D.T. 271
Arnold, N.S. 125, 128
Arrow, K.J. 153, 157, 168, 170, 224, 262, 268, 269
Arruñada, B. 163
artificial intelligence 91
Austrian school
   content of the alternative paradigm of 249–50
   conversion of Mark Blaug 162
   increasing influence of 265–6
   the main contribution of, according to Mises 107
   young theorists 260
average cost rule: Lerner's criticism of Lange and Durbin 244

Baetjer, H. 91, 171
Bagehot, W. 100, 124
Bailey, S. 46
Ballesteros Beretta, A. 96
Ballod, K. 132
Barella, A. 95
Barone, E. 101, 124, 125, 137, 138, 139, 164, 165, 217, 224
Barrow, J.D. 47
Barry, N.P. 97, 231, 272
Bauer, O. 126, 129

Bayes's theorem 17
Becker, G. 14
Becker, J. 261
Bélanger, G. 93
Bennett, J. 168, 171
Bergson, A. 228
Bergson, H. 38, 41, 55
Bergun, D.F. 171
Bernholz, P. 159, 168, 171
Blaug, M. 162, 172, 223
Block, W. 13, 63, 97
Boettke, P.J. 125
Böhm-Bawerk, E. von 92, 107, 108, 111, 126, 129, 132, 135, 136, 137, 162, 261
bonus or incentives (system of) 182, 211–12, 221, 229, 241–2
Borrell Fontelles, J. 261
Bradley, R. 167, 226
Breit, M. 185, 186, 222
Brus, W. 169, 218, 224, 225, 232, 248, 265, 266
Brutzkus, B. 103, 125, 132, 133
Buchanan, J.M. 39, 204, 209, 226, 227, 229
Bukharin, N.I. 132
bureaucracy
   ignorance, in Lange's model, of the typical behavior of bureaucratic agencies 209–12
   Mises's theory of the pernicious and inevitable emergence of bureaucracy under socialism 210
   tendency toward overexpansion 69
business consolidation 117–19

Caffé, F. 125
Caldwell, B. 128, 272
Campos, J.G. 95

capital and interest
  criticism of the theory of capital productivity 10
  subjective theory 10
capital goods: definition 201–2
capitalism: as an entrepreneurial system, not a managerial system 243
capitalist, as an entrepreneur 30
capitalist system: entrepreneurial, rather than managerial, nature of 243
Cassel, G. 138, 143, 163
Cato 100
Cave, M. 168
Cela, C.J. 93
Cervantes, M. 37, 95
Chaloupek, G.K. 133
Chicago school
  criticism of 250, 265
  the positivist scientism of 271–2
Cicero, M.T. 100, 123
*ciencismo* 96
*cientificismo* 96
Coase, R.H. 45, 131
coercion
  definition 87–8
  effects of 50–51
  kinds, systematic and asystematic 49–50
  types 88
Collard, D. 163, 238, 261
competition
  artificial 178
  concept of 32
  and coordination 32
  and entrepreneurship 32–3
  etymological definition 46
  "peaceful" or "friendly" (*Freundlichen Wettbewerb*), Heimann's concept of 176–7
  *see also* pseudo-competition
"competitive" solution (to the problem of economic calculation)
  contradiction 247–9
  early criticism leveled by Mises and Hayek against 178–84
  historical precedents for (E. Heimann and K. Polanyi) 175–8
  implicit acknowledgement of the soundness of Mises's contribution 174
  *see also* market socialism
computational or algebraic argument in Hayek
  its secondary nature with respect to the main epistemological argument 144–6
  its unnecessary and irrelevant nature according to Mises 146
computer science
  criticism of Lange's theory on 218–19
  the development of and the impossibility of socialism 58–62
computers
  criticism of Lange's theory on 218–19
  and impossibility of socialism 58–62
*computopia see* planometrics
conservatism: "right-wing" socialism 79–80
  Hayek's criticism of 96
constructivist rationalism 99
  and social engineering *see* scientism
consumer: as entrepreneur 30
consumer market: a true one is lacking in Lange's model 203
coordination and adjustment 26–7
  competition 32
  core of the social process 27
corruption: inevitable result of socialism 67–9
cost: as subjective concept 17–18
counterspeculation: Lerner's concept of 263
creativity 17
  creativity versus maximization 34–5
  as defined by Saint Thomas Aquinas 42
  and entrepreneurship (theological digression) 42
  essence 24
Crozier, B. 265

de Jasay, A. 220, 248, 265, 267
de Marchi, N. 162
debate on socialist economic calculation
  background and prehistory 99–103

consequences for the future
  development of economics
  9–12
summary 5–7
del Vecchio, G. 125
demarchy 79
Dembinski, P.H. 228
destructionism 253
  inevitable result of socialism 269
Di Lorenzo, T.J. 93
Dickinson, H.D. 7, 141–2, 143, 146,
  163, 166, 173, 175, 178, 226,
  237–43
discoordination and social disorder:
  inevitable result of socialism
  62–5
division of knowledge 33–4
  population growth 33
division of labor *see* division of
  knowledge
Dobb, M.H. 7, 141, 231, 233, 244,
  250–53, 267, 268, 269
Drexler, K.E. 91
Durbin, E. 261
Durbin, E.F.M. 7, 173, 175, 233,
  234–7, 244, 245, 246, 261, 263
Durbin's rules 234–5

Eatwell, J. 261
economic analysis of law: criticism of
  its static model 11–12
economic calculation
  "bridge" between the internal
    (ordinal) and external (cardinal)
    realms 126
  calculation in labor hours 120–22
  calculation in units of utility 122–3
  etymological definition 43–4
  generic definition 22
  impossibility of calculation *in natura*
    114, 119–20
  impossibility of economic
    calculation under socialism
    50–58
  impossibility; the computational
    or algebraic argument and the
    epistemological argument 107–8
  Mises's definition 45
  money and economic calculation
    28–9

practical sufficiency of economic
  calculation 115–16
strict definition 29
economic equilibrium 101–2
  irrelevant nature of the theory of
    109
economic problem
  definition, distinction between
    economic and technical or
    technological problems 117
  non-technical nature of 35
economic welfare theory 11
  errors of 160–61
economics
  concerns spiritual realities (ideas and
    knowledge) and not objects 128,
    130
  objective nature of 39
  purpose of 48
  redundant definition 37
economics and technique, differences
  between 116–17
efficiency and ethics: false separation
  between 268
Elliott, J.H. 97
Ellman, M. 158, 168, 171
Endres, A.M. 130
Engels, F. 112, 119, 129
enterprise
  as a "firm" or unit of economic
    organization 45
  as synonym for "action" 16
entrepreneurial alertness 19
entrepreneurial error: Kirzner's
  conception of 42
entrepreneurial knowledge
  characteristics of 19–35
  creation and transmission of 25–6
  exclusive and dispersed nature of
    20–22
  relationship between practical and
    scientific knowledge 40
  subjective and practical nature of
    20
  tacit, inarticulable nature of 22–4
entrepreneurial loss 18
entrepreneurial profit
  definition 17–18
  and Pope John Paul II 39
  "pure" entrepreneurial profit 24–5

entrepreneurship
  alertness 19
  broad definition 15
  and competition 32–3
  and the concept of socialism 35–6
  essential principle 30–32
  etymology 15–16
  fundamentally creative nature of 24–5
  theological digression 42
  ubiquity of 29–30
Estrin, S. 220
ethics
  and efficiency 268
  and socialism 12–13
expectations 17
exploitation (theory of) *see* surplus value (theory of)

Fedorenko, N. 145, 164
Felipe, L. 46, 91
Ferguson, A. 44
Ferguson, C.E. 226
Feucht, M. 267
financial accounting 23
  cost accounting 23
formal similarity
  arguments of, between capitalism and socialism 134–8
  the arguments of Cassel and Lindahl 138, 162–3
  Barone's argument 137–8
  impossibility of eliminating the category of interest 136, 162
  impossibility of eliminating the category of value 135, 161
Friedman, D. 88
Friedman, M. 250, 264–5
functional theory of price determination 10
  criticism of and need for replacement with a praxeological or sequential theory 205–6, 236–7, 261
Furubotn, E. 97

Garcia Villarejo, A. 37
Gardner, R. 168
Garello, J. 94
Gillespie, S. 92, 164

Gödel, K. 41
Gödel's Theorem 41
González, F. 91
Gossen, H.H. 100, 124
Gould, J.P. 226
governing or coercive body: higher level in socialist system 57–8
Gray, J. 224

Hahn, F. 169
Halm, G. 163, 164, 176, 180, 220
Hardin, G. 92
Hardt, J.P. 168
Hayek
  his concept of "order" 63
  his critical reference to the farce of planometrics 157
  his criticism of conservatism 96
  his criticism of unlimited power in democracy 79
  his key distinction between dispersed and centralized knowledge 20–22, 40–41
  secondary importance he attaches to the algebraic or computational argument with respect to the epistemological one 143–6
Hayek, F.A. *passim*
Heertje, A. 125
Heilbroner, R. 194, 219, 220, 224
Heimann, E. 175–6, 177, 180, 184, 185, 186, 205
Hexham, I. 97
Hilferding, R. 126, 129
Hoff, T.J.B. 127, 130, 132, 164, 166, 167, 219, 221, 237, 252, 261, 263, 268, 271
Hoppe, H.H. 84–5, 92, 95, 97, 270, 271
Hoselitz, B.F. 37
Huberman, B.A. (Miller and Drexler 1988) 91
human action
  definition 16
  marginal utility and time preference 18–19
  and scarcity 16
  ultimate given 18
Hume, D. 44
Hurwicz, L. 154, 155, 156, 157, 168, 169, 170, 224

ignorance (inevitable): of the directing authorities in a socialist system 57–8
immorality as an absence of principles
   Keynes's self-description as an immoralist 73
   the three senses in which socialism is immoral 271
   typical in socialist systems 73
incentive
   definition 45–6
   the two different meanings of the term 241–2
industry or sector: impossibility of defining unequivocally 181
information *see* entrepreneurial knowledge
information transparency: obsession of socialists with 163, 238
Ingrao, B. 231
institutional aggression: theory of 3
   *see also* coercion
institutions
   definition 44
   Menger's theory on the emergence of 44
intellectual division of labor 104
interest rate: arbitrary fixing of in Lange's model 208–9
interpersonal exchange: "bridge" between the subjective (ordinal) and external (cardinal) realms 126
interventionism 11
   as a type of socialism 86
intrapreneurship 118
irregular economy 69
irresponsibility (typical consequence of socialism)
   concept of 66
   effects on the environment 67
isonomy 95
Israel, G. 231

Jaffé, W. 124
John Paul, II 39, 42, 43, 88–9, 90, 94–5
just price 90
justice: the inevitable corruption of under socialism 71–3

Kantorovich, I.V. 168
Kaser, M.C. 133
Kauder, E. 261
Kautsky, K. 103, 125, 126, 132, 133
Keizer, W. 128, 133
Keynes: his lack of principles and his immorality 73
Kirzner, I.M. 14, 19, 35, 36–7, 39, 41, 42, 44, 45, 46, 48, 68, 84, 92, 93, 97, 98, 169, 193, 196, 223, 224, 229, 241, 261, 262, 263, 270, 271
Knight, F.H. 265
Kornai, J. 92, 149, 210, 219, 225, 265, 266
*kosmos*: natural, spontaneous order 99
Kotarbinski, T. 37
Kowalik, T. 186, 216, 217, 230, 247, 263
Kukathas, C. 128

labor market: a true one is lacking in Lange's model 203
labor unions: exercise of systematic coercion and violence by 89
Lachmann, L.M. 209, 229
Landauer, C. 120, 132
Lange, O. 7, 98, 104, 113, 127, 137, 147, 155, 165, 167, 169, 170, 171, chaps. 6 and 7 (*passim*)
Lange–Breit model 185–6
Lange–Lerner rule 226
Lange's classic model
   criticism of 200–212
   description of 198–9
   two possible interpretations of 199–200
Lange's rules 198–9
   inanity of 203–6
Langlois, R.N. 223
Laski, K. 169, 218, 224, 225, 248
Lavoie, D. 14, 42, 91, 98, 128, 165, 168, 169, 170, 171, 190, 193, 222, 223, 228, 238, 242, 261, 262, 263
law 28
   criticism of Saint Thomas Aquinas's concept of 44–5
   substantive 71
law of association 47
Le Grand, J. 220

Leichter, O. 104, 132, 133
Lenin, V.I. 92, 132, 133, 272
Leoni, B. 123
Leontief, W. 14, 186
Lerner, A.P. 7, 141, 169, 173, 175, 178, 209, 226, 228, 243–7
Lerner's rule 244–5
Levy, D.M. 229
Lindahl, E. 138, 162, 163
Lindbeck, A. 171
Lippincott, B.M. 127, 163, 186, 222, 223, 224, 225
Littlechild, S. 261
Lorenz, K. 42
Lugo, J. de 90

Machado, A. 133
Machlup, F. 131, 171, 174, 219, 261, 272
Mackay, T. 124
Malinvaud, E. 171
Mallock, W.H. 127
Maltsev, Y.N. 127
Mandeville, B. 44
Marañón, G. 39, 41, 46, 96
Marcos de la Fuente, J. 37
marginal cost rule
 Lange's version and criticism thereof 203–6
 Lerner's version and criticism thereof 244–7
 Mises's and Hayek's early criticism of 178–84
market
 concept of 48
 Lange's view of as a mechanism of the pre-electronic age 217–18
 criticism of this position 231
market and common law: parallelism 123
market price: concept radically different from that of parametric price 115, 187–8
market socialism
 contradiction inherent in 247–9
 Maurice H. Dobb's criticism of 251–2
 pathos of 220
 see also competitive solution
Martínez-Alier, J. 126, 132

Marx
 dictatorship of the proletariat as the imposition of a normative equilibrium 109
 his dynamic criticism of capitalism, including his view of the role institutions play 109–10
 Marx's essential error 110–11
 Mises's refutation of Marx's analysis 112–14, 132
 socialism according to 108–12
Marx, K. 108–14, 119, 120, 128–30, 132, 228
Marxism
 as justification for a normative equilibrium 109
 as a utopian socialism 110–11
mathematical economists: errors of 160–61, 172, 238, 261
mathematical equilibrium analysis: errors and confusion it generates 168–9, 172
"mathematical" solution (to the problem of economic calculation) 139–46
 adverse consequences for the debate 143–6
 contribution of Fred M. Taylor 140–41
 contribution of H.D. Dickinson 141–2
 contribution of Kläre Tisch 143, 164
mathematics: criticism of the use of in economics 120, 160, 172, 238, 261
maximization: criticism 117
Mayer, H. 261
Meade, J.E. 261, 275
means: definition 16
mechanisms for resource allocation (theory of) see planometrics
Menger, C. 28, 44, 45, 107, 124, 127, 128, 130, 223, 261
mental images of the future see expectations
method of economic science 10
 criticism of positivism 258–9, 272
Migué, J.L. 93
Milgate, M. 261
Mill, J.S. 37

Miller, D. 266, 267
Miller, M.S. 91
Mises
  essential contribution of 103–8
  evolution and summary of his arguments on the impossibility of economic calculation 165–6
  his concept of competition 113
  his concept of market price 113
  his original argument against the trial and error method 150–51
  start of the debate on socialist economic calculation 99–103
Mises, L. von *passim*
Mitchel, W. 93
money 28–9
  definition 29
  disappearance of in the equilibrium model 130
  Menger's theory on the emergence of 45
  non-existence of real money in a socialist system 112–13
Montesquieu 44, 100, 123–4
Moreno, F. 43
Moss, L.S. 131
Mulgen, G. 266

Naishul, V.A. 94
Negishi, T. 225
Nelson, R.R. 172
Neuberger, E. 168
Neurath, O. 103, 104, 126, 132
Newman, P. 261
Niskanen, W. 93
Novak, M. 43
Nove, A. 98, 145, 164, 265–6
Nozick, R. 42, 88, 270

Oakeshott, M. 40
obligatory accounting information: superfluous nature of 163
O'Driscoll, G.P. 38, 140, 163, 261
"omniscience" and "omnipresence" of the government 240, 262
order
  concept of 63
  hierarchical and etymology 74–5
  spontaneous 74
Ortega y Gasset, J. 91

paradox of planning 38, 64, 90
parametric prices: definition of 187
Pareto, V. 100–101, 124, 125, 138, 141, 164, 217, 224
partial, Marshallian equilibrium 163, 237
Pejovich, S. 97
Penrose, R. 41, 91
Pierson, N.G. 102, 103, 125, 142, 164
plan: concept and types of 37–8
planning
  central 38
  indicative 8, 38
  paradox of 38, 64, 90
planometrics
  criticism of 153–61
  definition of 167–8
  frustration and disappointment caused by 168
  objective of 153
Pohle, L. 133
Polanyi, K. 41, 175, 177–8, 180, 184, 185, 205, 220, 221
Polanyi, M. 23, 40, 41, 90, 91, 170
polycentric and hierarchical structures (M. Polanyi's theory) 227
population
  impossibility that socialism could maintain increasing volumes of 102
  increase in as the cause and necessary condition of economic development 33–4
positive legislation and socialism: parallelism between 98
positivism: criticism of 258
praxeology 39, 48
Preobrazhensky, E. 132
Pribram, K. 169, 230
price
  criticism of the functional theory of 261
  dynamic theory of 10
probability
  of class 38
  of a unique event 38
production functions 191
propaganda: excessive use of in socialist systems 68
Prybila, J.S. 168

pseudo-competition 180, 181
  *see also* competition: artificial
public choice school 93, 209–10
public goods: criticism of the static
  nature of the theory of 11

rate of interest *see* interest rate
Reig Albiol, L. 91
responsibility
  absence of in socialist systems 66
  economic concept of 58, 92
Revel, F. 93
Rizzo, M.J. 38
Robbins, L. 35, 47, 48, 130, 134, 143,
  162, 165, 183–4, 217, 222, 259, 273
Roberts, P.C. 227, 228
Robertson, E.S. 124
Rodríguez Braun, C. 91
Roper, W.C. 146, 166, 175, 178, 221
Rosenberg, W.G. 229
Rothbard, M.N. 39, 45, 88, 90, 92, 126,
  128, 130, 222, 231, 263, 265
Rothschild, M. 92
Rudolf, Archduke (Crown Prince of
  Austria) 127, 128
Ryle, G. 41

Salas, J. de 90
Salerno, J.T. 45, 128
Salinas Sánchez, J. 37
Samuelson, P.A. 145, 164, 231, 250
Say, J.-B. 37
scarcity
  chronic, recurrent feature of the
    socialist system 149
  false automatic indicator in "trial
    and error" method 149–50
  prerequisite for human action 16
  as a typical effect of socialism 65
Schäffle, A. 100, 124
Schumpeter, J.A. 125, 137, 138, 143,
  164, 170, 186, 222, 273
Schwartz, P. 37
scientific knowledge: the tacit
  foundation of 40, 43
scientism 80–82
  definition 96
  positivist scientism of the Chicago
    school 271–2
Scitovsky, T. 262

Seco, M. 96
Seidl, C. 168
Seldon, A. 169, 222, 265
Sen, A. 268
serendipity
  definition of 39
  history of the term's formation 39
Seurot, F. 132
Shackle, G.L. 38
Shakespeare, W. 94
Skidelsky, R. 95
Skousen, M. 220
Smith, A. 41, 47
Snavely, W.P. 271
Snowberger, V. 229
social "Big Bang" 46–7, 48
social democracy 78–9
social disorder 62–5
social engineering 80–82
social ethics: most recent Austrian
  contributions 270–71
social justice: criticism of the concept
  of 72, 75, 95
socialism
  Christian or solidarity-based 82–3
  and computers 58–62
  conservative (or right-wing) 79–80
  definition of 3, 49–52
  effects of 62–77
  ethical inadmissibility of 12–13
  extensive and voluntaristic nature
    of 66
  guild (proposed by K. Polanyi)
    177–8
  historic failure of 1–2
  idyllic concepts of 86–7
  impossibility of from the standpoint
    of society 54–6
  impossibility of from the standpoint
    of the governing body 56–8
  as an intellectual error 52–3
  lag in economic, technological and
    cultural development 69–70
  moral perversion socialism creates
    73–6
  as the opium of the people 76
  prostitution of the traditional
    concepts of law and justice 71–3
  real 77–8
  self-management 8

theory on the prevention and
    dismantling of 13
  traditional concept of, criticism
    83–6
  types of 77–83
socialist megalomania 69
society
  concept of 35
  and market 48
solidarity: correct and spurious
  concepts of 94–5
Sorman, G. 94
Sowell, T. 41
speculation 27
Stalin, J. 216
Stalinism: Lange's praise of 216–18
Stankiewicz, T. 229
statistics: obsessive proliferation of
  under socialism 66
Steele, D.R. 126, 272
Stigler, G. 272
Streissler, E.W. 124, 127, 128
Strumilin, S. 133
subjectivism, definition of 3
Sulzer, G. 126
supply and demand functions
  criticism of the functional theory of
    prices 261
  non-existence of 207, 235–6
surplus value (theory of): criticism 111,
    129
surprise: definition of 38–9
Sweezy, P.M. 186, 267

Tamedly, E.L. 267
*tâtonnement* 198
Taylor, F.M. 8, 140–41, 143, 146, 163,
    166, 186, 199, 244
Taylor, R. 37
technique and economics, difference
  between 116–17
technique and social engineering
    80–83, 271
technological revolution 118
Temkin, G. 214, 225, 230, 248
temporal present: Mises's definition
    of 44
theoretical impossibility of socialism
  dynamic argument 54–6
  "static" argument 54

theory and praxis: false dichotomy
  between 109
Thirlby, G.F. 39, 226, 227
time: subjective concept of 16–17
time preference (law of) 19
Tipler, F.J. 46, 47
Tisch, K. 138, 143, 164
transactions costs: criticism of the
  theory of 131–2, 265
trial and error method 146–52
  additional errors committed by
    Lange 206–8
  criticism of 147–52
  description of 146–7
Trigo Portela, J. 94
Tschayanoff, A. 132
Tullock, G. 93
Tulloh, W. 91, 171
Turgot, A.R.J. 46, 99, 100, 124

uncertainty
  Arrow's mistake concerning 262, 269
  the permanent nature of 17
underground economy 69
unemployment (concealed): inevitable
  consequence of socialism 65
utility
  definition of 16
  marginal (law of) 18–19

value
  definition of 16
  economic category of socialism
    119–20
  unnecessary, according to Engels 112
Van Maarseveen, J.G. 125
Vaughn, K.I. 189, 222, 223, 263
Vázquez Arango, C. 94
Verrijn Stuart, C.A. 133
voluntarism: typical characteristic of
  socialism 66

Walras (model of): criticism of the
  static nature of 162
Walras, L. 124, 141, 143, 146, 162, 165,
    168, 169, 171, 191, 192, 198, 199,
    200, 219, 223, 225, 226, 237, 261
Walrasian paradigm: crisis of the 162
Ward, B. 157, 168, 171
"weasel words" 94

Weber, A. 133
Weber, M. 102, 103, 125, 133
Weil, F. 180, 221
Weitzman, M.L. 229
Wicksteed, P.H. 188, 189, 222
Wieser, F. von 102, 135–6, 137, 139, 161, 162
Wilczynski, J. 167, 168
Williamson, O.E. 131
Winiecki, J. 92

Winter, S.G. 131
Wiseman, J. 204, 227
Wood, J.C. 127
Woods, R.N. 127
worker (as entrepreneur) 29–30

x-inefficiency and entrepreneurial error 131–2

Zassenhaus, H. 143, 164, 270